AF653930

An Encyclopaedic Dictionary of Indian Geography

An Encyclopaedic Dictionary of Indian Geography

A. N. Kapoor
V. P. Gupta
Mohini Gupta

RADHA PUBLICATIONS
New Delhi - 110 002

© Reserved

Edition 2006

ISBN : 81-7487-291-4

RADHA PUBLICATIONS
4378/4B, Ansari Road, Daryaganj
New Delhi-110 002
Phone : 23261839, 23254306

Published by Nitin Garg for Radha Publications and printed by
Tarun Offset Printers, Mauzpur, Shahadra, Delhi.

Preface

Geography is the scientific study of the earth's surface, physical features, divisions, climate, products, population etc. It is usually divided in the following sections—physical geography, biogeography and human geography. While physical geography deals with landforms and climates, biogeography discusses conditions that affect the distribution of animals and plants. Human geography concentrates on the distribution and activities of people on earth.

Geography is a very broad subject and has led to a number of disciplines such as geology, geophysics and geopolitics. **Geology** happens to be the science of the earth, its origin, composition, structure and history. **Geophysics** is the branch of geology using physics to study the earth's surface, interior and atmosphere. Studies also include winds, weather, tides, earthquakes volcanoes and their effects. **Geopolitics** conceives geographical location as an important determinant of political identity, political thought and political action. It sees nations as organisations struggling with each other for the occupancy of space. The term **Lebensraum** (space for living) played an important role in the Nazi rhetoric of conquest. Geography has played an important role in the history of nations and has much to do with the stage of their development in terms of their economic growth, national temper and foreign affairs.

The scope of Indian geography is as wide as that of India itself. It is not possible to capsule the entire geographical information about India in one short volume. However, an humble attempt is being made in the present volume, *An Encyclopaedic Dictionary of Indian Geography* which constitutes the eighth title in the ongoing series "**Encyclopaedic Dictionary of Indian History and Culture**". The volume deals with certain vital aspects of India's geography and is divided into five sections: (1) Land and People; (2) Drainage System; (3) Land Forms; (4) States and Union Territories; and (5) Miscellaneous.

The *first section*, **Land and People,** discusses the physical background, demographic background and environmental issues. The various topics discussed in the section are: physical features, geological structure, rivers, climate, flora, fauna, census, population density, sex ratio, literacy, survey of natural resources, forests, wild life, pollution, environmental information system, environmental legislation.

Section Two, **Drainage System**, highlights the major rivers, seas, bays, gulfs, lakes, oceans and straits.

Section Three, concerns itself with various **Land Forms,** such as plains, peaks, hills, ranges, regions, passes, plateaus, capes, coasts, harbours, valleys, uplands, islands, doabs, ghats, ranns, peninsulas, deserts, steppes, glaciers and wet lands.

Section Four, attempts to present a comprehensive survey of **States and Union Territories** in India. There are now twenty-eight states and seven union territories. The editors have tried to provide the physical and human geography, economy, history and the latest data on area, population and headquarters of districts in respect of each state and union territories.

Section Five, has been titled **Miscellaneous** and details information about coastal community programmes, coastal research vessels, heavy water production, height of some important Indian mountain peaks, human settlement systems, coastal and marine management, length of some important Indian rivers, mineral exploration and mining, national animal, national bird, national flower, ocean observations and survey of India.

— *Editors*

Contents

Section : ONE

LAND AND THE PEOPLE

1

Physical Background

INDIA is one of the oldest civilisations with a kaleidoscopic variety and rich cultural heritage. It has achieved multifaceted socio-economic progress during the last 54 years of its Independence. India has become self-sufficient in agricultural production and is now the tenth industrialised country in the world and the sixth nation to have gone into outer space to conquer nature for the benefit of the people.

Lying entirely in the northern hemisphere, the mainland extends between latitudes 8°4' and 37°6' north, longitudes 68°7' and 97°25' east and measures about 3,214 km from north to south between the extreme latitudes and about 2,933 km from east to west between the extreme longitudes. It has a land frontier of about 15,200 km. The total length of the coastline of the mainland, Lakshadweep Islands and Andaman and Nicobar Islands, is 7,516.6 km.

It covers an area of 32,87,263* sq. km. extending from the snow-covered Himalayan heights to the tropical rain forests of the south. As the seventh largest country in the world, India stands apart from the rest of Asia, marked off as it is by mountains and the sea, which give the country a distinct geographical entity. Bounded by the Great Himalayas in the north, it stretches southwards and at the Tropic of Cancer, tapers off into the Indian Ocean between the Bay of Bengal on the east and the Arabian Sea on the west.

*Provisional as on 31 March, 1982.

PHYSICAL BACKGROUND

Countries having a common border with India are Afghanistan and Pakistan to the north-west, China, Bhutan and Nepal to the north, Myanmar to the east and Bangladesh to the east of West Bengal. Sri Lanka is separated from India by a narrow channel of sea formed by the Palk Strait and the Gulf of Mannar.

Physical Features

The mainland comprises four regions, namely, the great mountain zone, plains of the Ganga and the Indus, the desert region and the southern Peninsula.

The Himalayas comprise three almost parallel ranges interspersed with large plateaus and valleys, some of which, like the Kashmir and Kullu valleys, are fertile, extensive and of great scenic beauty. Some of the highest peaks in the world are found in these ranges. The high altitudes admit travel only to a few passes, notably the Jelep La and Nathu La on the main Indo-Tibet trade route through the Chumbi Valley, north-east of Darjiling and Shipki La in the Satluj Valley, north-east of Kalpa (Kinnaur). The mountain wall extends over a distance of about 2,400 km with a varying depth of 240 to 320 km. In the east, between India and Myanmar and India and Bangladesh, hill ranges are much lower. Garo, Khasi, Jaintia and Naga Hills, running almost east-west, join the chain to Mizo and Rkhine Hills running north-south.

The Peninsular Plateau is marked off from the plains of the Ganga and the Indus by a mass of mountain and hill ranges varying from 460 to 1,220 metres in height. Prominent among these are the Aravalli, Vindhya, Satpura, Maikala and Ajanta. The Peninsula is flanked on the one side by the Eastern Ghats where average elevation is about 610 metres and on the other by the Western Ghats where it is generally from 915 to 1,220 metres, rising in places to over 2,440 metres. Between the Western Ghats and the Arabian Sea lies a narrow coastal strip, while between Eastern Ghats and the Bay of Bengal there is a broader coastal area. The southern point of the plateau is formed by the Nilgiri Hills where the Eastern and the Western Ghats meet. The Cardamom Hills lying beyond may be regarded as a continuation of the Western Ghats.

The desert region can be divided into two parts—the great desert and the little desert. The great desert extends from the edge of the Rann of Kuchch beyond the Luni river northward. The whole of the Rajasthan-Sind frontier runs through this. The little desert extends from the Luni between Jaisalmer and Jodhpur up to the northern wastes. Between the great and the little deserts lies a zone of absolutely sterile country, consisting of rocky land cut up by limestone ridges.

The plains of the Ganga and the Indus, about 2,400 km long and 240 to 320 km broad, are formed by basins of three distinct river systems—the Indus, the Ganga and the Brahmaputra. They are one of the world's greatest stretches of flat alluvium and also one of the most densely populated areas on the earth. Between the Yamuna at Delhi and the Bay of Bengal, nearly, 1,600 km away, there is a drop of only 200 metres in elevation.

Geologial Structure

The geological regions broadly follow the physical features and may be grouped into three regions: the Himalayas and their associated group of mountains, the Indo-Ganga Plain and the Peninsular Shield.

The Himalayan mountain belt to the north and the Naga-Lushai mountain in the east, are the regions of mountain-building movement. Most of this area, now presenting some of the most magnificent mountain scenery in the world, was under marine conditions about 60 crore years ago. In a series of mountain-building movements commencing about seven crore years ago, the sediments and the basement rocks rose to great heights. The weathering and erosive agencies worked on these to produce the relief seen today. The Indo-Ganga plains are a great alluvial tract that separates the Himalayas in the north from the Peninsula in the south.

The Peninsula is a region of relative stability and rare seismic disturbances. Highly metamorphosed rocks of the earliest periods, dating back as far as 380 crore years, occur in the area; the rest being covered by the coastal-bearing Gondwana formations, lava flows belonging to the Deccan Trap formation and younger sediments.

Rivers

Rivers in India may be classified as : (i) Himalayan rivers; (ii) Peninsular rivers; (iii) Coastal rivers and (iv) rivers of the inland drainage basin.

The Himalayan rivers are perennial as they are generally snow-fed and have reasonable flow throughout the year. During the monsoon the Himalayas receive very heavy rainfall and the rivers discharge the maximum quantity of water causing frequent floods. The Peninsular rivers are generally rain-fed and, therefore, fluctuate in volume. A large number of the streams are non-perennial. The coastal streams, especially on the west coast, are short in length and have limited catchment areas. Most of them are flashy and non-perennial. The streams of the inland drainage basin of western Rajasthan are few and far between. Most of them are of an ephemeral character. They drain towards the individual basins or salt lakes like the Sambhar or are lost in the sands having no outlet to the pea. The Luni is the only river of this category that drains into the Rann of Kuchch.

The Ganga sub-basin which is a part of the larger Ganga-Brahmaputra-Meghana basin is the largest in India receiving waters from an area which comprises about one-quarter of the total area of the country. Its boundaries are well-defined by the Himalayas in the north and the Vindhyas in the south. The Ganga flows through Uttar Pradesh; Bihar and West Bengal in India and enters Bangladesh thereafter. It has two main headwaters in the Himalayas: the Bhagirathi and the Alaknanda, the former rising from the Gangotri glacier at Gomukh and the latter from a glacier short of the Alkapuri glacier. The Ganga is joined by a number of Himalayan rivers including the Yamuna, Ghagra, Gomti, Gandak and Kosi. The western-most river of the Ganga system is the Yamuna which rises from the Yamunotri glacier and joins the Ganga at Allahabad. Among important rivers flowing north from central India into the Yamuna/Ganga are the Chambal, Betwa and Sone.

The Brahmaputra and the Barak flowing from east to west in north-eastern region are international rivers and have immense water resources potential which is still in the initial stages of development.

The Godavari in the southern Peninsula has the second largest river basin covering 10 per cent of the area of India. Next to it is the Krishna basin in the region, while the Mahanadi has the third largest basin. The basin of the Narmada in the uplands of the Deccan flowing to the Arabian Sea and of the Kaveri in the south falling into the Bay of Bengal are about the same size, though with different character and shape.

Two other river systems, which are small but agriculturally important, are those of the Tapti in the north and the Pennar in the south. These west-coast rivers are of great importance as they contain as much as 11 per cent of the country's water resources while draining about 10 per cent of the land area.

Climate

The climate of India may be broadly described as tropical monsoon type. There are four seasons: (i) winter (January-February), (ii) hot weather summer (March-May); (iii) rainy south-western monsoon (June-September) and (iv) post-monsoon, also known as north-east monsoon in the southern Peninsula (October-December). India's climate is affected by two seasonal winds - the north-east monsoon and the south-west monsoon. The north-east monsoon commonly known as winter monsoon blows from land to sea whereas south-west monsoon known as summer monsoon blows from sea to land after crossing the Indian Ocean, the Arabian Sea and the Bay of Bengal. The south-west monsoon brings most of the rainfall during the year in the country. It is now possible to make forecast about the monsoon rains successfully with developed models and trained manpower.

Flora

With a wide range of climatic conditions from the torrid to the arctic, India has a rich and varied vegetation, which only a few countries of comparable size possess. India can be divided into eight distinct-floristic-regions, namely, the western Himalayas, the eastern Himalayas, Assam, the Indus plain, the Ganga plain, the Deccan, Malabar and the Andamans.

The *Western Himalayan* region extends from Kashmir to Kumaon. Its temperate zone is rich in forests of *chir*, pine, other conifers and broad-leaved temperate trees. Higher up, forests of *deodar*, blue pine, spruce and silver fir occur. The alpine zone extends from the upper limit of the temperate zone of about 4,750 metres or even higher. The characteristic trees of this zone are high-level silver fir, silver birch and junipers. The *Eastern Himalayan region* extends from Sikkim eastwards and embraces Darjiling, Kurseong and the adjacent tract. The temperate zone has forests of oaks, laurels, maples, rhododendrons, alder and birch. Many conifers, junipers and dwarf willows also occur here. The *Assam region* comprises the Brahmaputra and the Surma valleys with evergreen forests, occasional thick clumps of bamboos and tall grasses. The *Indus plain region* comprises the plains of Punjab, western Rajasthan and northern Gujarat. It is dry and hot and supports natural vegetation. The *Ganga plain region* covers the area which is alluvial plain and is under cultivation for wheat, sugarcane and rice. Only small areas support forests of widely differing types. The *Deccan region* comprises the entire table land of the Indian Peninsula and supports vegetation of various kinds from scrub jungles to mixed deciduous forests. The *Malabar region* covers the excessively humid belt of mountain country parallel to the west coast of the Peninsula. Besides being rich in forest vegetation, this region produces important commercial crops, such as coconut, betelnut, pepper, coffee and tea, rubber and cashewnut The *Andaman region* abounds in evergreen, mangrove, beach and diluvial forests. The Himalayan region extending from Kashmir to Arunachal Pradesh through Nepal, Sikkim, Bhutan, Meghalaya and Nagaland and the Deccan Peninsula is rich in endemic flora, with a large number of plants which are not found elsewhere.

India is rich in flora. Currently available data place India in the tenth position in the world and fourth in Asia in plant diversity. From about 70 per cent geographical area surveyed so far, 47,000 species of plants have been described by the Botanical Survey of India. The vascular flora, which forms the conspicuous vegetation cover comprises 15,000 species. Of these, more than 35 per cent is endemic and has so far not been reported anywhere in the world. The total plant wealth of the country includes not only the useful large flowered plants including flowering shrubs, but also a large number of non-flowering plants like ferns, liverworts, algae and fungi.

Owing to destruction of forests for agricultural, industrial and urban development, several Indian plants are facing extinction. About 1,336 plant species are considered vulnerable and endangered. About 20 species of higher plants are categorised as possibly extinct as these have not been sighted during the last 6-10 decades. BSI brings out an inventory of endangered plants in the form of a publication titled *Red Data Book*. Four volumes of the book have already been published and the fifth is being compiled. Samples of some of these plants are preserved in botanical gardens and national parks. Collections of dried samples of these plants are preserved in the Central National Herbarium, the regional herbaria of BSI and in research and training institutions of the country.

Fauna

Possessing a tremendous diversity of climate and physical conditions, India has great variety of fauna numbering 89,451 species. Of these, protista number 2,577, mollusca 5,070, anthropoda 68,389, amphibia 209, mammalia 390, reptilia 456, members of protochordata 119, pisces 2,546, aves 1,232 and other invertebrates 8,329.

The great Himalayan range has a very interesting variety of fauna that includes the wild sheep and goats, markhor, ibex, shrew and tapir. The panda and the snow leopard are found in the upper reaches of the mountains.

Depletion of vegetative cover due to expansion of agriculture, habitat destruction, over-exploitation, pollution, introduction of toxic imbalance in community structure, epidemics, floods, droughts and cyclones, contribute to the loss of flora and fauna. More than 39 species of mammals, 72 species of birds, 17 species of reptiles, three species of amphibians, two species of fish and a large number of butterflies, moth and beetles are considered vulnerable and endangered.

The mammals include the majestic elephant, the *gaur* or Indian bison- the largest of existing bovines, the great Indian rhinoceros, the gigantic wild sheep of the Himalayas, the swamp deer, the thamin spotted deer, *nilgai*, the four-horned antelope, the Indian antelope or black-buck —the only representatives of these genera. Among the cats, the tiger and lion are the most magnificent of all; other splendid creatures such as the clouded leopard, the snow leopard, the marbled cat, etc., are also found. Many other species of mammals are remarkable for their beauty, colouring, grace and uniqueness. The abundant and colourful life of this country is one of its treasures. Several birds, like pheasants, geese, ducks, *mynahs*, parakeets, pigeons, cranes, hornbills and sunbirds, inhabit forests and wet lands.

There are presently 88 national parks and 490 wildlife sanctuaries covering 1.53 lakh sq km area of the country.

Rivers and lakes harbour crocodiles and *gharials*, the latter being the only representative of crocodilian order in the world. The salt water crocodile is found along the eastern coast and in the Andaman and Nicobar Islands. A project for breeding crocodiles started in 1974, has been instrumental in saving the crocodile from extinction. Twelve schemes are in operation in different states for breeding crocodiles.

●●●

2

Demographic Background

Census

The population enumeration of 2001 census was undertaken during 9-28 February 2001 with a revisional round from 1-5 March 2001. The Census moment, the referral time at which the snapshot of the population is taken was 00.00 hours of the I March 2001. Until the 1991 Census, the sunrise of 1 March was taken to be the census moment. The houseless population, as has been the usual practice was enumerated on the night of 28 February 2001.

The Census of India 2001, is historic and epoch making being the first census of the twenty-first century and the third millennium. It will reveal benchmark data on the state of abundant human resources habitating our country, their demography, culture and economic structure at a juncture, which marks a centennial and millenial transition.

Population

The population of India, which at the turn of the twentieth century, was around 238.4 million increased to reach 1,027 million at the dawn of the twenty-first century. The population of India as recorded at each decennial census from 1901 has grown steadily except for a decrease during 1911-21. Decadal growth of population from 1901 is shown in *table* 2.1.

India's population as on 1 March 2001 stood at 1,027 million (531.3 million males and 495.7 million females). India accounts for a meagre 2.4 per cent of the world surface area of 135.79 million sq km yet it supports and sustains a whopping 16.7 per cent of the world population.

Table 2.1 : Population 1901–2001

Census years	Population	Decadal Growth		Change in decadal growth		Average annual exponential growth rate (per cent)	Progressive growth rate over 1901 (per cent)
		Absolute	Per cent	Absolute	Per cent		
1	2	3	4	5	6	7	8
1901	23,83,96,327	-	-	-	-	-	-
1911	25,20,93,390	1,36,97,063	5.75	-	-	0.56	5.75
1921	25,13,21,213	-7,72,177	-0.31	-1,44,69,240	-6.05	-0.03	5.42
1931	27,89,77,238	2,76,56,025	11.00	2,84,28,202	11.31	1.04	17.02
1941	31,86,60,580	3,96,83,342	14.22	1,20,27,317	3.22	1.33	33.67
1951[1]	36,10,88,090	4,24,27,510	13.31	27,44,168	-0.91	1.25	51.47
1961[1]	43,92,34,771	7,81,46,681	21.64	3,57,19,171	8.33	1.96	84.25
1971	54,81,59,652	10,89,24,881	24.80	3,07,78,200	3.16	2.20	129.94
1981[2]	68,33,29,097	13,51,69,445	24.66	2,62,44,564	-0.14	2.22	186.64

Continue......

1	2	3	4	5	6	7	8
1991[3]	84,33,87,888	16,30,58,791	23.86	2,78,89,346	-0.80	2.14	255.03
2001[4]	1,02,70,15,247	18,06,27,359	21.34	1,75,68,568	-2.52	1.93	330.80

Source : Provisional Population Totals, Paper - 1 of 2001, Series - 1, Census of India, 2001.

Notes :

1. In working out 'Decadal Growth' and 'Percentage Decadal Growth' for India 1941-51 and 1951-61 the population of Tuensang district for 1951 (7,025) and the population of Tuensang (83,501) and Mon (5,774) districts for 1961 Census of Nagaland state have not been taken into account as the areas were censused for the first time in 1951 and the same are not comparable.
2. The 1981 Census could not be held owing to disturbances in Assam. Hence the population figures for 1981 of Assam have been worked out by 'interpolation'.
3. The 1991 Census could not be held owing to disturbances in Jammu and Kashmir. Hence the population figures for 1991 of Jammu and Kashmir have been worked out by "interpolation.
4. The population of India includes the estimated population of Kachch district, Morvi, Maliya-Miyana and Wankaner *talukas* of Rajkot district, Jodiya *taluka* of Jamnagar district of Gujarat and entire Kinnaur district of Himachal Pradesh where population enumeration of Census of India, 2001 could not be conducted due to natural calamities.

In 1950, China with 22 per cent share of the world population led the scene followed by India, which had a share of 14.2 per cent.

Table 2.2 gives the selected indicators of population growth in different States and Union Territories. The per cent decadal growth of population in the inter-censal period 1991-2001 varies from a low of 9.42 in Kerala to a very high 64.41 in Nagaland. Delhi with 46.31 per cent, Chandigarh with 40.33 per cent and Sikkim with 32.98 per cent registered very high growth rates. In addition to Kerala, Tamil Nadu and Andhra Pradesh registered low growth rates during 1991-2001. The per cent decadal growth rate has declined during the census decade 1991-2001 as compared to the previous census decade in all the States/Union Territories except Haryana, Uttar Pradesh, Bihar, Sikkim, Nagaland, Manipur, Gujarat, Daman & Diu and Dadra & Nagar Haveli. The States and Union Territories that have shown increases in per cent decadal growth together constitute about 32 per cent of India's population.

Table 2.2 : States and Union Territories by Population Size

Rank in 2001	*State/ Union Territory**	*Population 2001*	*Per cent to total Population of India 2001*	*1991*	*Rank in 1991*
1	*2*	*3*	*4*	*5*	*6*
1.	Uttar Pradesh	16,60,52,859	16.17	15.60	1
2.	Maharashtra	9,67,52,247	9.42	9.33	2
3.	Bihar	8,28,78,796	8.07	7.62	5
4.	West Bengal	8,02,21,171	7.81	8.04	3
5.	Andhra Pradesh	7,57,27,541	7.37	7.86	4
6.	Tamil Nadu	6,21,10,839	6.05	6.59	6
7.	Madhya Pradesh	6,03,85,118	5.88	5.74	7
8.	Rajasthan	5,64,73,122	5.50	5.20	9
9.	Karnataka	5,27,33,958	5.14	5.31	8
10.	Gujarat	5,05,96,992	4.93	4.88	10
11.	Orissa	3,67,06,920	3.57	3.74	11
12.	Kerala	3,18,38,619	3.10	3.44	12
13.	Jharkhand	2,69,09,428	2.62	2.58	14
14.	Assam	2,66,38,407	2.59	2.64	13
15.	Punjab	2,42,89,296	2.37	2.40	15
16.	Haryana	2,10,82,989	2.05	1.95	17

1	2	3	4	5	6
17.	Chhattisgarh	2,07,95,956	2.03	2.08	16
18.	Delhi	1,37,82,976	1.34	1.11	18
19.	Jammu & Kashmir[2]	1,00,69,917	0.98	0.92	19
20.	Uttaranchal	84,79,562	0.83	0.84	20
21.	Himachal Pradesh	60,77,248	0.59	0.61	21
22.	Tripura	31,91,168	0.31	0.33	22
23.	Manipur	23,88,634	0.23	0.23	23
24.	Meghalaya	23,06,069	0.22	0.21	24
25.	Nagaland	19,88,636	0.19	0.14	25
26.	Goa	13,43,998	0.13	0.14	26
27.	Arunachal Pradesh	10,91,117	0.11	0.10	27
28.	Pondicherry	19,73,829	0.09	0.10	28
29.	Chandigarh	9,00,914	0.09	0.08	30
30.	Mizoram	8,91,058	0.09	0.08	29
31.	Sikkim	5,40,493	0.05	0.05	31
32.	Andaman & Nicobar Islands	3,56,265	0.03	0.03	32
33.	Dadra & Nagar Haveli	2,20,451	0.02	0.02	33
34.	Daman & Diu	1,58,059	0.02	0.01	34
35.	Lakshadweep	60,595	0.01	0.01	35

Source : Provisional Population Totals, Paper—1 of 2001, Series - 1, Census of India, 2001.

Notes :

1. The population of India includes the estimated population of Kachchh district, Morvi, Maliya-Miyana and Warikaner *talukas* of Rajkot district, Jodiya *taluka* nf Jamnagat district of Gujarat and entire Kinnaur district of Himachal Pradesh where population enumeration of Census of India, 2001 could not be conducte due to natural calamities.
2. The 1991 Census could not be held owing to disturbances in Jammu an Kashmir. Hence the population figures for 1991 of Jammu and Kashmir have been worked out by 'interpolation'.

Population Density

The population density of India in 2001 is 324 persons per square kilometre.

The density of population has increased in all States and Union Territories between 1991 and 2001. Among major states. West Bengal is still the most thickly populated state with a population density of 904 in 2001. Bihar is now the second highest densely populated state pushing Kerala to the third place. Ranking of the States and Union Territories by density is shown in *table* 2.3.

Table 2.3 : States and Union Territories by Density 1991 and 2001

Rank in 2001	*State/ Union Territory**	*Density 2001*	*Density 1991*	*Rank in 1991*
1.	Delhi*	9,294	6,352	1
2.	Chandigarh*	7,903	5,632	2
3.	Pondicherry*	2,029	1,683	3
4.	Lakshadweep*	1,894	1,616	4
5.	Daman and Diu*	1,411	907	5
6.	West Bengal	904	767	6
7.	Bihar	880	685	8
8.	Kerala	819	749	7
9.	Uttar Pradesh	689	548	9
10.	Punjab	482	403	11
11.	Tamil Nadu	478	429	10
12.	Haryana	477	372	12
13.	Dadra and Nagar Haveli*	449	282	15
14.	Goa	363	316	13
15.	Assam	340	286	14
16.	Jharkhand	338	274	16
17.	Maharashtra	314	257	18
18.	Tripura	304	263	17
19.	Andhra Pradesh	275	242	19
20.	Karnataka	275	235	20
21.	Gujarat	258	211	21
22.	Orissa	236	203	22
23.	Madhya Pradesh	196	158	23
24.	Rajasthan	165	129	26
25.	Uttaranchal	159	133	24
26.	Chhattisgarh	154	130	25
27.	Nagaland	120	73	31
28.	Himachal Pradesh	109	93	27
29.	Manipur	107	82	28
30.	Meghalaya	103	79	29
31.	Jammu & Kashmir	99	74	30
32.	Sikkim	76	57	32
33.	Andaman & Nicobar Islands*	43	34	33
34.	Mizoram	42	33	34
35.	Arunachal Pradesh	13	10	35

Source : Provisional Population Totals, Paper—1 of 2001, Series - 1, Census of India, 2001.

Notes :

* The 1991 Census could not be held owing to disturbances in Jammu and Kashmir. Hence the population figures for 1991 of Jammu and Kashmir have been worked out by 'interpolation'.

2. The population of India includes the estimated population of Kachchh district, Morvi, Maliya-Miyana and Wankaner *talukas* of Rajkot district, Jodiya taluka of Jamnagar district of Gujarat and entire Kinnaur district of Himachal Pradesh where population enumeration of Census of India, 2001 could not be conducted due to natural calamities.

Sex Ratio

An important social indicator to measure the extent of prevailing equality between males and females in a society at a given point of time, the sex ratio in the country had always remained unfavourable to females. The sex ratio at the beginning of the twentieth century was 972 and thereafter showed continuous decline until 1941. In 1951 there was a marginal increase of one point, but thereafter it again dropped for two consecutive decades to reach 930 in 1971. Thereafter, it has fluctuated marginally around 930 in successive censuses. Sex ratio (1901-2001) is given in *table* 2.4.

Table 2.4 : Sex Ratio : 1901-2001

Census Year	*Sex ratio (females per 1,000 males)*
1901	972
1911	964
1921	955
1931	950
1941	945
1951	946
1961	941
1971	930
1981	934
1991	927
2001	933

Source : Provisional Population Totals, Paper—1 of 2001, Series-1, Census of India, 2001.

Notes :

1. For 1991, the interpolated figures for Jammu & Kashmir have been used.
2. While working out the sex ratio for India for the year 2001, the estimated population of entire Kachchh district, Morvi, Maliya-Miyana and Wankaner *talukas* of Rajkot district, Jodiya *taluka* of Jamnagar district of Gujarat and entire Kinnaur district of Himachal Pradesh have been used as the population enumeration of Census of India, 2001 could not be conducted in these areas due to natural calamities.

Literacy

In the census prior to 1991, children below five years of age were necessarily treated as illiterates. The provisional results of 2001 reveal that there has been an increase in literacy in the country. The literacy rate in the country is 65.38 per cent (75.85 for males and 54.16 for females). The steady improvement in literacy is apparent from the *table* 2.5.

Table 2.5 : Literacy Rate : 1951-2001

Census Year	*Previous*	*Males*	*Females*
1951	18.33	27.16	8.86
1961	28.30	40.40	15.35
1971	34.45	45.96	21.97
1981	43.57	56.38	29.76
1991	52.21	64.13	39.29
2001	65.38	75.85	54.16

Source : Provisional Population Totals, Paper—1 of 2001, Series-1, Census of India, 2001.

Notes :

1. Literacy rates for 1951, 1961 and 1971 Census relate to population aged five years and above. The rates for the 1981, 1991 and 2001 Census relate to the population aged seven years and above.
2. The 1981 Literacy rates exclude Assam where the 1981 Census could not be conducted. The 1991 Census Literacy rates exclude Jammu & Kashmir where the 1991 Census could not be conducted due to disturbances.
3. The 2001 Census, literacy rates exclude entire Kachchh district, Morvi, Maliya-Miyana and Wankaner *talukas* of Rajkot district, Jodiya *taluka* of Jamnagar district of Gujarat and entire Kinnaur district of Himachal Pradesh where population enumeration of Census of India, 2001, could not be conducted due to natural calamities.

Kerala retained its position by being on top with a 90.92 per cent literacy rate, closely followed by Mizoram (85.99 per cent) and Lakshadweep (87.52 per cent). Bihar with a literacy rate of 47.53 per cent ranks last in the country preceded by Jharkhand (54.13 per cent) and Jammu & Kashmir (54.46 per cent). Kerala also occupies the top spot in the country both in male literacy with 94.20 per cent and female literacy with 87.86 per cent. On the contrary, Bihar has recorded the lowest literacy rates both in case of males (60.32 per cent) and females (33.57 per cent). *Table* 2.6 shows the literacy rate among persons, males and females in States and UTs, and their ranking.

Table 2.6 : Ranking of States/UTs by Literacy Rate among Persons, Males and Females, 2001

Rank	Persons		Males		Females	
	*State/ Union Territory**	*Literacy rate*	*State/ Union Territory**	*Literacy rate*	*State Union Territory**	*Literacy rate*
1	2	3	4	5	6	7
1.	Kerala	90.92	Kerala	94.20	Kerala	87.86
2.	Mizoram	88.49	Lakshadweep*	93.15	Mizoram	86.13
3.	Lakshadweep*	87.52	Mizoram	90.69	Lakshadweep*	81.56
4.	Goa	82.32	Pondicherry*	88.89	Chandigarh*	76.65
5.	Delhi*	81.82	Goa	88.88	Goa	75.51
6.	Chandigarh*	81.76	Daman & Diu*	88.40	A. & N. Islands*	75.29
7.	Pondicherry*	81.49	Delhi*	87.37	Delhi*	75.00
8.	A. & N. Islands*	81.18	Maharashtra	86.27	Pondicherry*	74.13
9.	Daman & Diu*	81.09	A. & N. Islands*	86.07	Daman & Diu*	70.37
10.	Maharashtra	77.27	Himachal Pradesh	86.02	Himachal Pradesh	68.08
11.	Himachal Pradesh[2]	77.13	Chandigarh*	85.65	Maharashtra	67.51
12.	Tripura	73.66	Uttaranchal	84.01	Tripura	65.41
13.	Tamil Nadu	73.47	Tamil Nadu	82.33	Tamil Nadu	64.55
14.	Uttaranchal[3]	72.28	Tripura	81.47	Punjab	63.55
15.	Gujarat	69.97	Gujarat	80.50	Nagaland	61.92
16.	Punjab	69.95	Haryana	79.25	Sikkim	61.46
17.	Sikkim	69.68	Manipur	77.87	Meghalaya	60.41
18.	West Bengal	69.22	Chhattisgarh	77.86	Uttaranchal	60.26
19.	Manipur	68.87	West Bengal	77.58	West Bengal	60.22
20.	Haryana	68.59	Madhya Pradesh	76.80	Manipur	59.70
21.	Nagaland	67.11	Sikkim	76.73	Gujarat	58.60

22.	Karnataka	67.04	Rajasthan	76.46	Karnataka	57.45
	INDIA	65.38	Karnataka	76.29	Haryana	56.31
23.	Chhattisgarh	65.18	Orissa	75.95	Assam	56.03
24.	Assam	64.28	INDIA	75.85	INDIA	54.16
25.	Madhya Pradesh	64.11	Punjab	75.63	Chhattisgarh	52.40
26.	Orissa	63.61	Dadra & Nagar Haveli*	73.32	Andhra Pradesh	51.17
27.	Meghalaya	63.31	Assam	71.93	Orissa	50.97
28.	Andhra Pradesh	61.11	Nagaland	71.77	Madhya Pradesh	50.28
29.	Rajasthan	61.03	Andhra Prdesh	70.85	Rajasthan	44.34
30.	Dadra & Nagar Haveli*	60.03	Uttar Pradesh	70.23	Arunachal Pradesh	44.24
31.	Uttar Pradesh	57.36	Jharkhand	67.94	Dadra & Nagar Haveli*	42.99
32.	Arunachal Pradesh	54.74	Meghalaya	66.14	Uttar Pradesh	42.98
33.	Jammu & Kashmir	54.46	Jammu & Kashmir	65.75	Jammu & Kashmir	41.82
34.	Jharkhand	54.13	Arunachal Pradesh	64.07	Jharkhand	39.38
35.	Bihar	47.53	Bihar	60.32	Bihar	33.57

Source : Provisional Population Totals, Paper-1 of 2001, Series-1, Census of India, 2001.

Notes :

1. The Literacy rates for India have been worked out by excluding entire Kachchh district, Morvi, Maliya-Miyana and Wankaner talukas of Rajkot district, Jodiya *taluka* of Jamnagar district of Gujarat and entire Kinnaur district of Himachal Pradesh where population enumeration of Census of India, 2001, could not be conducted due to natural calamites.
2. The Literacy rates for Himachal Pradesh have been worked out by excluding entire Kinnaur district as population emumeration of Census of India, 2001, could not be conducted there due to natural calamity.
3. The literacy rates for Gujarat have been worked out by excluding entire Kachchh district, Morvi, Maliya-Miyana and Wankaner *talukas* of Rajkot district, Jodiya *taluka* of Jamnagar district of Gujarat where population enumeration of Census of India, 2001, could not be conducted due to natural calamity.

Table 2.7 : Total population and percentage of Scheduled Caste and Scheduled Tribe 1991

Sl. No.	India/State or Union Territory	Total Population ('000)	Scheduled Caste Population ('000)	Scheduled Caste Percentage of total population	Scheduled Tribe Population ('000)	Scheduled Tribe Percentage of total population
1	2	3	4	5	6	7
	INDIA[1]	8,38,584	1,38,223	16.48	67,758	8.08
	STATES					
1.	Andhra Pradesh	66,508	10,592	15.93	4,199	6.31
2.	Arunachal Pradesh	865	4	0.47	550	63.66
3.	Assam	22,414	1,659	7.40	2,874	12.82
4.	Bihar	86,374	12,572	14.56	6,617	7.66
5.	Goa	1,170	24	2.08	-	0.03
6.	Gujarat	41,310	3,060	7.41	6,162	14.92
7.	Haryana	16,464	3,251	19.75	-	-
8.	Himachal Pradesh	5,171	1,310	25.34	218	4.22
9.	Karnataka	44,977	7,369	16.38	1,916	4.26
10.	Kerala	29,099	2,887	9.92	321	1.10
11.	Madhya Pradesh	66,181	9,627	14.54	15,399	23.27
12.	Maharashtra	78,937	8,758	11.10	7,318	9.27
13.	Manipur	1,837	37	2.02	632	34.41
14.	Meghalaya	1,775	9	0.51	1,518	85.53
15.	Mizoram	690	1	0.10	654	94.75
16.	Nagaland	1,210	-	-	1,061	87.70
17.	Orissa	31,660	5,129	16.20	7,032	22.21
18.	Punjab	20,282	5,743	28.31	-	-
19.	Rajasthan	44,006	7,608	17.29	5,475	12.44
20.	Sikkim	406	24	5.93	91	22.36
21.	Tamil Nadu	55,859	10,712	19.18	574	1.03
22.	Tripura	2,757	451	16.36	853	30.95
23.	Uttar Pradesh	1,39,112	29,276	21.05	288	0.21
24.	West Bengal	68,078	16,081	23.62	3,809	5.60
	UNION TERRITORIES					
1.	A&N Islands	281	-	-	27	9.54
2.	Chandigarh	642	106	16.51	-	-
3.	D&N Haveli	138	3	1.97	109	78.99
4.	Daman and Diu	102	4	3.83	12	11.54
5.	Delhi	9,421	1,795	19.05	-	-
6.	Lakshadweep	52	-	-	48	93.15
7.	Pondicherry	808	131	16.25	-	-

[1] Excludes figures of Jammu & Kashmir where 1991 census was not taken.

Source: Census of India 1991, Series 1. Paper 2 of 1992, Final Population totals.

Table 2.8 : Rural and Urban Population : 1901-1991

Census Year	*Population (Million)*		*Percentage of total population*	
	Rural	*Urban*	*Rural*	*Urban*
1901	213	26	89.2	10.8
1911	226	26	89.7	10.3
1921	223	28	88.8	11.2
1931	246	33	88.0	12.0
1941	275	44	86.1	13.9
1951	299	62	82.7	17.3
1961	360	79	82.0	18.0
1971	439	109	80.1	19.9
1981	524	159	76.7	23.3
1991	629	218	74.3	25.7

Source : Census of India 1991, Series I, India, Paper 2 of 1992. Final Population Totals.

1 The 1991 census could not be held in Assam. The figures for 1981 for Assam have been worked out by interpolation.

2 Includes projected population of Jammu and Kashmir.

Table 2.9 : Growth of Urbanisation by Class of Towns

Class of town		*Population in '000s*					
		1901	*1951*	*1961*	*1971*	*1981*	*1991*
I.	1,00,000 and above	5,570	23,483	34,736	52,808	82,227	1,122,291
II.	50,000 – 99,999	2,948	7,548	9,530	14,712	22,037	28,764
III.	20,000 – 49,999	4,346	11,115	15,728	19,865	26,719	35,273
IV.	10,000 – 19,999	5,847	9,331	11,241	13,929	17,588	21,079
V.	5,000 – 9,999	5,332	8,463	6,304	6,089	6,788	7,397
VI.	Less than 5,000	1,650	2,047	805	853	1,062	967
	All Classes	25,693	61,987	78,343	1,08,256	1,56,420	2,15,772
	Urban Population as percentage to total Population	10.84	17.29	19.97	19.91	23.34	25.72

Source : Part II-A(ii) - A-Series - Towns & Urban Agglomerations 1991 with their Populations 1901-1991 - Table A-4.

Notes :

Excludes figures for Jammu & Kashmir in 1991 where 1991 Census was not conducted owing to disturbances. For comparative purposes the figures of J&K have also been excluded for 1901 to 1981.

Excludes figures for Assam in 1981 where census of 1981 was not held.

[1]Data includes Jammu & Kashmir and Assam.

Table 2.10 : Distribution of villages according to population : 1991

Sl. No.	*Status/UTs*	*Less than 1,000*	*1,000 to 1,999*	*2,000 to 4,999*	*5,000 to 9,999*	*10,000 and over*	*Total*
1	*2*	*3*	*4*	*5*	*6*	*7*	*8*
	INDIA[1+2]	3,90,093	1,14,395	62,915	10,597	2,779	5,80,781[3]
1.	Andhra Pradesh	11,856	6,433	6,510	1,474	313	26,586
2.	Arunachal Pradesh	3,538	82	25	3	1	3,649
3.	Assam	17,784	4,988	1,793	111	9	24,685
4.	Bihar	45,164	12,768	7,647	1,604	330	67,513
5.	Goa	156	78	94	31	1	360
6.	Gujarat	8,528	5,432	3,418	575	75	18,,028
7.	Haryana	2,627	2,021	1,703	364	44	6,759
8.	Himachal Pradesh	16,361	495	136	5	-	16,997
9.	Karnataka	17,113	5,861	3,422	570	100	27,066
10.	Kerala	7	16	102	252	1,007	1,384
11.	Madhya Pradesh	56,568	11,426	3,264	261	7	71,526
12.	Maharashtra	24,111	10,632	4,715	762	192	40,412
13.	Manipur	1,834	192	135	16	3	2,182
14.	Meghalaya	5,316	129	38	1	-	5,484
15.	Mizoram	616	61	19	2	-	698
16.	Nagaland	929	170	108	8	1	1,216
17.	Orissa	39,309	5,761	1,812	103	4	46,989
18.	Punjab	7,447	3,130	1,628	209	14	12,428
19.	Rajasthan	27,123	7,060	3,255	420	31	37,889
20.	Sikkim	336	79	29	3	-	447
21.	Tamil Nadu	4,915	4,625	4,764	1,247	271	15,822
22.	Tripura	195	203	348	94	15	855
23.	Uttar Pradesh	74,866	24,523	11,949	1,336	129	1,12,803
24.	West Bengal	22,701	8,065	5,819	1,117	208	37,910
25.	A&N Islands	445	44	15	-	-	504
26.	Chandigarh	7	6	8	3	1	25
27.	D&N Haveli	27	17	25	1	1	71
28.	Daman and Diu	9	6	6	2	1	24
29.	Delhi	29	44	86	19	21	199
30.	Lakshadweep	2	-	4	1	-	7
31.	Pondicherry	174	48	38	3	-	263

1 Excludes the population of Jammu & Kashmir where the 1991 census could not be conducted due to disturbances.

2 The population figures exclude population of areas under China where census could not be taken.

3 As separate population figures of the following villages are not been excluded from the range classification. However, the villages enumerated are included in the range classification

Name of village	**Enumerated**	**Sub-division**
1. Phaijol	Soraland	Sadar Hills
2. Kamarangkha Kuki	Phaitol	Tamenglon

Table 2.11 : Population of Million Plus Cities

Sl. No.	City	Population in '000s			Growth ratio		Sex ratio		Literacy rate	
		1991	1981	1951	1991	1981	1991	1981	1991	1981
1.	Kolkata	11,022	9,194	4,670	2.36	1.97	830	781	77	65
2.	Greater Mumbai	12,596	8,243	2,967	4.25	2.78	828	772	82	68
3.	Delhi	8,419	5,729	1,437	5.86	3.99	830	808	76	63
4.	Chennai	5,422	4,289	1,542	3.52	2.78	933	930	81	67
5.	Bangalore	4,130	2,922	786	5.25	3.72	902	896	79	64
6.	Hyderabad	4,344	2,546	1,131	3.84	2.25	920	919	71	58
7.	Ahmedabad	3,312	2,548	877	3.78	2.91	889	869	80	63
8.	Kanpur	2,030	1,639	705	2.88	2.32	822	804	72	55
9.	Pune	2,494	1,686	609	4.09	2.77	903	880	81	67
10.	Nagpur	1,664	1,302	485	3.43	2.68	915	910	82	66
11.	Lucknow	1,669	1,008	497	3.36	2.03	871	832	71	58
12.	Jaipur	1,518	1,015	304	4.99	3.34	868	861	70	54
13.	Surat	1,519	924	237	6.41	3.90	828	840	76	60
14.	Kochi	1,141	825	212	5.38	3.89	977	989	94	79
15.	Vadodara	1,127	782	211	5.34	3.71	899	888	82	68
16.	Indore	1,109	829	311	3.57	2.67	900	855	77	61
17.	Coimbatore	1,101	920	287	3.84	3.21	930	924	80	67
18.	Patna	1,100	919	326	3.37	2.82	829	815	77	58
19.	Madurai	1,086	907	371	2.93	2.44	954	952	82	68
20.	Bhopal	1,063	671	102	10.42	6.58	894	870	72	57
21.	Visakhapatnam	1,057	604	108	9.79	5.59	937	933	72	56
22.	Ludhiana	1,043	607	154	6.77	3.94	795	815	72	62
23.	Varanasi	1,031	797	370	2.79	2.15	861	842	64	47

Source : Paper 2, 1991, Final Population Total.

Table 2.12 : Population By Religion

Religious group	1961[3] Number (million)	1961[3] Per cent to total	1971 Number (million)	1971 Per cent to toal	1981 Number (million)	1981 Per cent to total	1991 Number (million)	1991 Per cent to total
Hindus	366.5	83.5	453.4	82.7	549.7	82.6	672.6	82.41
Muslims	46.9	10.7	61.4	11.2	75.6	11.4	95.2	11.67
Christians	10.7	2.4	14.3	2.6	16.2	2.4	18.9	2.32
Sikhs	7.8	1.8	10.4	1.9	13.1	2.0	16.3	0.77
Buddhists	3.2	0.7	3.9	0.7	4.7	0.7	6.3	0.77
Jains	2.0	0.5	2.6	0.5	3.2	0.5	3.4	0.41
Other[1]	1.6	0.4	2.2	0.4	2.8	0.4	3.5	0.43
Total	439.2	100.0	548.2	100.0	665.3	100.0	816.2[2]	100.0

Source : (i) Census of India, Series 1, India, Part II c(i), (ii) Census of India 1981, Series I, Paper 3 of 1984 (Religion), (iii) Census of India, Series I, Paper I of 1995 (Religion)

1 Including unclassified persons

2 Excludes Assam and J & K

3 Excludes Mizo district, now constitued of U.T. of Mizoram

Notes : 1981 data do not include Assam.

Table 2.13 : Comparative Strengths of Scheduled Languages

	Language	*Persons who returned the language as their mother tongue*			*Percentage to total population*		
		1971	*1981*	*1991*	*1971*	*1981*[1]	*1991*
1.	Hindi	20,85,14,005	26,45,14,117	33,72,72,114	38.04	38.71	39.85
2.	Bengali	4,47,92,312	5,12,98,319	6,95,95,738	8.17	7.51	8.22
3.	Telugu	4,47,56,923	5.06,24,611	6,60,17,615	8.16	7.41	7.80
4.	Marathi	4,17,65,190	4,94,52,922	6,24,81,681	7.62	7.24	7.38
5.	Tamil	3,76,90,106	N.A.[2]	5,30,06,368	6.88	N.A.[2]	6.26
6.	Urdu	2,86,20,895	3,49,41,435	4,34,06,932	5.22	5.11	5.13
7.	Gujarati	2,58,65,012	3,30,63,267,	4,06,73,814	4.72	4.84	4.81
8.	Kannada	2,17,10,649	2,56,97,146	3,27,53,676	3.96	3.76	3.87
9.	Malyalam	2,19,38,760	2,57,00,705	3,03,77,176	4.00	3.76	3.59
10.	Oriya	1,98,63,198	2,30,21,528	2,80,61,313	3.62	3.37	3.32
11.	Punjabi	1,41,08,443	1,96,11,199	2,33,78,744	2.57	2.87	2.76
12.	Assamese	89,59,558	N.A.[3]	1,30,79,696	1.63	N.A.[3]	1.55
13.	Sindhi	16,76,875	20,44,389	21,22,848	0.31	0.30	0.25
14.	Nepali	14,19,835	13,60,636	20,76,645	0.26	0.20	0.25
15.	Konkani	15,08,432	15,70,108	17,60,607	0.28	0.23	0.21
16.	Manipuri	7,91,714	9,01,407	12,70,216	0.14	0.13	0.15
17.	Kashmiri	24,95,487	31,76,975	N.A.[4]	0.46	0.46	N.A.[4]
18.	Sanskrit	2,212	6,106	49,736	N	N	0.01

Notes : 1 The percentage of speakers of each language for 1981 have been worked out on the total population of India including the estimated population of Assam where the 1981 Census was not conducted due to disturbed conditions.

2 Full figures for Tamil and Assamese for 1981 are not available as the census records for Tamil Nadu were lost in floods and the 1981 Census could not be conducted in Assam due to disturbances then in the State. Therefore, percentage to total population for Tamil and Assamese is not given.

3 The percentage of speakers of each language for 1991 has been worked out on the total population of India including the projected population for Jammu & Kashmir where the 1991 Census could not be conducted due to disturbances..

4 Full figures for Kashmiri language for 1991 are not available as the 1991 Census was not conducted in Jammu & Kashmir for reasons explained above.

N.A. — Not available
N — Negligible

3

Environment

CONSERVATION and survey of flora, fauna, forests and wildlife, prevention and control of pollution, afforestation and regeneration of degraded areas and protection of environment, are the mandates of the Government. These objectives are well supported by legislative and regulatory measures, aimed at the preservation and protection of the environment.

Survey of Natural Resources

The Botanical Survey of India (BSI), established in 1890, is responsible for surveying and identifying the plant resources of the country. With its headquarters at Kolkata and nine circle offices located in different regions of the country, the BSI undertakes exploration tours of the country regularly and the results of such tours are published in the form of national, state and district flora.

The Zoological Survey of India (ZSI), established in 1916, is responsible for carrying out survey and inventorisation of the faunal resources of the country. While the headquarters of the Zoological Survey of India is at Kolkata, it has 16 regional stations located in different parts of the country. ZSI also undertakes regular faunistic survey tours of the entire country.

The Forest Survey of India (FSI) established in 1981, is entrusted with the task of surveying the forest resources of the country. Besides the headquarters at Dehra Dun, FSI has four regional offices located at Bangalore, Kolkata, Nagpur and Shimla. It prepares thematic maps on 1:50,000 scale and forest vegetation maps on 1:2,50,000 scale of the county. The maps are prepared for the entire country on a ten-year cycle. The vegetation maps are prepared on a two-year cycle for the entire country. As per the State of Forest Report 1999, the total forest cover of the country has been estimated to be 63.73 million hactares, i.e., 19.39 per cent of the geographic area of the country.

Biosphere Reserves

Biosphere Reserves are multi-purpose protected areas to preserve the genetic diversity in representative eco-systems. The major objectives of biosphere reserves are: (i) to conserve diversity and integrity of plants, animals and micro-organisms; (ii) to promote research on ecological conservation and other environmental aspects and; (iii) to provide facilities for education, awareness and training. So far twelve biosphere reserves have been set up. They are: Nilgiri; Nanda Devi; Nokrek; Great Nicobar; Gulf of Mannar; Manas; Sunderbans; Similipal; Dibru Daikhowa; Dehong Deband; Pachmarhi; and Kanchanjanga.

Mangroves, Wetlands and Coral Reefs

Mangroves are salt-tolerant forest ecosystems found mainly in the tropical and sub-tropical inter-tidal regions of the world. They are reservoirs of a large number of plant and animal species associated together over a long evolutionary period and exhibiting remarkable capacity for salt tolerance. They stabilize the shoreline and act as a bulwark against encroachments by the sea. India harbours some of the best mangroves in the world and these occur all along the Indian coastline in sheltered estuary, tidal creeks, backwaters, salt marshes and mud flats. As per the State of Forest Report, 1997 the total area covered by mangroves in India is estimated at about 6,000 sq km.

Under the scheme on Conservation and Management of Mangroves, 15 mangrove areas have been identified for intensive conservation and management purposes: North Andaman and Nicobar (Andaman and Nicobar Islands), Sunderbans (West Bengal), Bhitarkanika (Orissa), Coringa, Godavari Delta and Krishna Estuary (Andhra Pradesh), Mahanadi Delta (Orissa), Pitchavaram and Point Calimer (Tamil Nadu), Goa (Goa), Gulf of Kutch (Gujarat), Coondapur (Karnataka), Achra/ Ratnagiri (Maharashtra) and) \Vernbanad (Kerala),

India has a wealth of wetland eco-systems distributed in different geographical regions from the cold arid zone of Ladakh in the North to the wet humid climate of Imphal in the East, the warm arid zone of Rajasthan in the West to the tropical monosonic Central India and the wet and humid zone of Southern Peninsula. Most of the wetlands in India are directly or indirectly linked with major river systems such as Ganga, Brahmputra, Narmada, Tapti, Godavari, Krishna, Cauveri, etc.

A programme on conservation of wetlands is being implemented by the Government since 1987 and a total number of 20 wetlands in 13 States are covered under this programme. Several initiatives have been taken up with the main focus on biological methods of conservation rather than adopting engineering options. Steering Committees have been set up by the concerned State Governments and nodal research/academic institutions have been identified for the selected wetlands. Management Action Plans prepared for 18 wetlands are in operation and two Action Plans for wetlands from Kerala have been finalised. A directory on wetlands in India already published gives information on location, area and ecological categorisation of wetlands. India is a signatory to the Convention on Wetlands of international importance, especially as Waterfowl Habitat (Ramsar Convention)

Coral reefs are shallow-water tropical marine ecosystems, characterised by high biomass production and rich floral and faunal diversity. Four coral reefs, namely. Gulf of Mannar, Andaman and Nicubar Islands, Lakshadweep Islands and Gulf of Kutch have been identified for conservation and management. State-level steering committees have been constituted for the formulation and implementation of management action plans.

Biodiversity

Biological diversity has direct consumptive value in food, agriculture, medicine and industry. It also maintains ecological balance and continues evolutionary process. The indirect eco-system services provided through biodiversity are photosynthesis, pollination, transpiration, chemical cycling, nutrient cycling, soil maintenance, climate regulation, air, water, system management, waste treatment and pest control.

India is one of the twelve mega-biodiversity countries of the world and became a party to the International Convention on Biological Diversity in May 1994. The objectives of the Convention on Biological Diversity (CBD), to be pursued in accordance with its relevant provisions are: the conservation of Biological Diversity; the sustainable use of its component; and the fair and equitable sharing of the benefits arising out of the utilisation of genetic resources.

Following this a National Policy and Action Strategy on Biodiversity, which seeks to consolidate the on-going efforts of conservation and sustainable use of biological diversity and to establish a policy and programme regime for the purpose, was released by the Ministry on 6 January 2000. The Bio-Diversity Bill 2000 introduced in the Parliament in May 2000, has been referred to the department related Parliamentary Standing Committee for examination and report.

Forests

Forests are a renewable source and contribute substantially to economic development. They play a major role in enhancing the quality of environment. The total forest cover which includes dense forest, open forest and mangrove is estimated to be 63.73 million hactares. This constitutes 19.39 per cent of country's geographic area. Out of this, the dense forest accounts to 11.48 per cent, open forest represents 7.76 per cent while mangrove forest 0.15 per cent and scrub area 1.58 per cent. There has been an increase of 3,896 sq km of forest cover between 1997 and 1999 assessment.

Forest Policy and Law

India is one of the few countries, which has had a forest policy since 1894. It was revised in 1952 and again in 1988. The main plank of the forest policy is protection, conservation and development of forest. Its aims are : (i) maintenance of environmental stability through preservation and restoration of ecological balance; (ii) conservation of natural heritage; (iii) check on soil erosion and denudation in catchment area of rivers, lakes and reservoirs; (iv) check on extension of sand dunes in desert areas of Rajasthan and along coastal tracts; (v) substantial increase in forest tree cover through massive afforestation and social forestry programmes; (vi) steps to meet requirements of fuelwood, fodder, minor forest produce and soil timber of rural and tribal populations; (vii) increase in productivity of forest to meet the national needs; (viii) encouragement of efficient utilisation of forest produce and optimum substitution of wood and; (ix) steps to create massive people's movement with involvement of women to achieve the objectives and minimise pressure on existing forests.

Under the provisions of the Forest (Conservation) Act, 1980, prior approval of the Central Government is required for diversion of forest lands for non-forest purposes.

In 1990, the Ministry issued guidelines to involve the village communities in the development and protection of degraded forests on the basis of their taking a share of the usufruct from such areas. The concept of Joint Forest Management (JFM) was accordingly initiated. Twenty six States have so far issued resolutions for JFM. As on 1 September 2000, 10.25 million ha. of forest land in the country is being managed and protected by 36,165 village forest protection committees.

In pursuit of the National Forests Policy, 1998, the 100 per cent Centrally sponsored scheme, namely, Association of Scheduled Tribe and Rural Poor in Regeneration of Degraded Forests on Usufruct Sharing Basis" was continued to involve the local people in rehabilitation of degraded forests in tribal dominant areas. The scheme aiming at providing wage-employment and usufructs to the tribal people is being implemented in various States.

Forest Fire Control

The Centrallv-sponsored scheme, namely : *'Introduction of Modern Forest Fire Methods'* continued to be implemented with the objectives: (i) to control forest fires with a view to protecting and conserving both natural and man-made forests and to improve the productivity of forests by reducing the incidents and extent of forest fire; and (ii) to devise, test and demonstrate principles and techniques for prevention, detection and suppression of forest fires.

The scheme being implemented in eleven states is proposed to be extended to all the States. A National Master Plan has been prepared for the scheme for the Tenth Five Year Plan period and modified and renamed as "Forest Fire Control and Management".

Wildlife

Indian Board for Wildlife (IBWL) an apex advisory body in the field of wildlife conservation in the country is headed by the Prime Minister. As per the recommendation of IBWL, a committee is being set up to prepare a revised guideline for wildlife research.

The National Wildlife Action Plan provides the framework of strategy as well as programme for conservation of wildlife. The Indian Board of Wildlife, headed by the Prime Minister, is the apex advisory body overseeing and guiding the implementation of various schemes for wildlife conservation. At present, the protected area network comprises of 88 national parks and 490 sanctuaries covering an area of 1.53 lakh sq km. The Wildlife (Protection) Act, 1972 adopted by all states except Jammu and Kashmir (which has its own Act), governs wildlife conservation and protection of endangered species. The Act prohibits trade in rare and endangered species. An Inter-State Committee has been set up to review the Wildlife (Protection) Act, 1972 and other laws. India is a signatory to the Convention on International Trade in Endangered Species (CITES) of wild flora and fauna. Under this, export or import of endangered species and their products are governed by the conditions and stipulations laid down therein. India is also a signatory to the Memorandum of Understanding concerning the conservation of Siberian Cranes.

Under Project Tiger, launched on I April 1973, 27 Tiger Reserves have been set up in 14 states covering an area of about 37,761 sq km. Financial assistance is provided for voluntary relocation of tribal families from the Protected Areas.

Under the Project Elephant, states having free-ranging population of wild elephants are being given financial as well as technical and scientific assistance to ensure long-term survival of identified viable populations of elephants in their natural habitats. A Central Zoo Authority has been set up to look after the management of zoological parks in the country. It coordinates the activities of over 200 existing zoos and also supervises the exchange of animals on a scientific basis. A national policy on zoos prepared by the Authority provides appropriate directions to the Government and other zoo operators.

Environment Impact Assessment

The programme of Environment Impact Assessment (EIA) was introduced in India in 1978. A notification issued in January 1994 makes EIA statutary for 29 categories of developmental projects under various sectors such as industrial, mining, irrigation, power, transport, tourism, communication, etc. The EIA Notification was amended in 1997 in order to make public hearing an integral part of the assessment procedure. Environmental clearance is granted by the Impact Assessment Agency in the Ministry.

Special groups/committees and task forces are constituted as and when needed for expert inputs on major projects. After detailed scrutiny and assessment, the appraisal committee makes its recommendations for approval or rejection of the project. To ensure transparency, the position of forest and environmental clearance has been brought out on website: http://envfor.nic.in since February 1999. Depending on the nature of the project, certain safeguards are recommended. For monitoring and timely implementation of safeguards suggested, six regional offices of the Ministry have been set up at Shillong, Bhubaneswar, Chandigarh. Bangalore, Lucknow and Bhopal.

Prevention and Control of Pollution

The Policy Statement on Abatement of Pollution, adopted in 1992, provides instruments in the form of legislation and regulation, fiscal incentives, voluntary agreements, educational programmes and information campaigns to prevent and control pollution of water, air and land. Since the adoption of the policy statement, the focus of activities has been on issues such at promotion of clean and low waste technologies, waste water minimisation, reuse/recycling, improvement of water quality, environment audit, natural resource accounting development of mass-based standards, institutional and human resource development etc. The whole issue of pollution prevention and control is dealt with by a combination of command and control methods as well as voluntary regulations, fiscal measures, promotion of awareness and involvement of public.

An "Eco-mark" label has been introduced to label consumer products that are environment-friendly. So far, the Ministry has issued 18 notifications on different products criteria.

To facilitate industries in preparing environmental statements, sector-specific environmental audit manuals have been prepared.

Under the scheme for adoption of clean technology in small-scale industries and for extending necessary technical support, training and awareness programmes for personnel in Small Industry Development Organisation and for entrepreneurs are being organised. Waste Minimisation Circles (WMCs) are being established to promote group efforts in increasing productivity and improving the environmental conditions in small and medium scale industries through adoption of waste minimisation techniques. Forty-five WMCs have been established so far in different industrial clusters across the country.

Action Plans to control pollution for various major cities have been prepared and are being implemented by the concerned State Governments. A major programme for improvement of automotive fuels such as motor gasoline and diesel is being introduced in the country in a phased manner. Only unloaded petrol is supplied in all outlets of the entire country with effect from I February 2000 and 0.25 per cent sulphur in diesel with effect from 1 January 2000 respectively.

Compressed Natural Gas (CNG) as a cleaner auto fuel has been introduced in Mumbai, Delhi, Baroda and Surat. The Central Government has also provided indirect fiscal incentives in the form of concessional customs duty on the import of CNG kits and its parts.

Central Pollution Control Board

The Central Pollution Control Board (CPCB) is the national apex body for assessment, monitoring and control of water and air pollution. The executive responsibilities for enforcement of the Acts for Prevention and Control of Pollution of Water (1974) and Air (1981) and also of the Water (Cess) Act, 1977 are carried out through the Board. The CPCB advises the Central Government on all matters concerning the prevention and control of air, water and noise pollution and provides technical services to the Ministry for implementing the provisions of the Environment (Protection) Act, 1986. Under this Act, effluent and emission standards in respect of various categories of industries have been notified. During 2000-2001 standards for coal mines, standards for effluents from textile industries and primary water quality criteria for bathing waters have been finalised and notified in the gazette.

The Central Pollution Control Board (CPCB), in consultation with State Pollution Control Boards (SPCB), has identified 24 critically polluted areas in the country which need special attention for control of pollution. These are: Vapi (Gujarat), Singrauli (Uttar Pradesh), Korba (Chhattisgarh), Ratlam, Nagda (Madhya Pradesh), Digboi (Assam), Talcher (Orissa), Bhadravati (Kamataka), Howrah (West Bengal), Dhanbad (Jharkhand), Pali and Jodhpur (Rajasthan), Manali and North Arcot (Tamil Nadu), Visakhapatnam and Patancheru (Andhra Pradesh), Chembur (Maharashtra), Najafgarh (Delhi), Govindgarh (Punjab), Udyog Mandal (Kerala) and Parwanoo and Kala Amb (Himachal Pradesh). Actions Plans have been prepared and are being implemented in these areas.

Seventeen categories of heavily polluting industries have been identified. They are : cement, thermal power plant, distilleries, sugar, fertilizer, integrated iron and steel, oil refineries, pulp and paper, petrochemicals, pesticides, tanneries, basic drugs and pharmaceuticals, dye and dye intermediates, caustic soda, zinc smelter, copper smelter and aluminium smelter. Out of a total of 1,551 units identified so far under these categories, 1,326 units have installed adequate facilities for pollution control, 172 units have been closed down and remaining 53 units are defaulters.

Management of Hazardous Substances

The Ministry of Environment and Forests is the nodal agency for the mangement and control of hazardous substances, which include hazardous chemicals, waste and micro-organisms.

India is a signatory to the UNEP-sponsored Convention on Control of Transboundary Movement of Hazardous Wastes, which was adopted at Basel, Switzerland, by 126 governments of the world in 1989. The Convention aims at checking the reported illegal traffic in hazardous wastes from one country to another. India participated in the sixteenth technical and first legal Working Group meeting of the Fifth Conference of Parties (COP) of the Basel Convention held in Geneva in October 2000. India also participated in the fourth and fifth Inter-Governmental Negotiating Committee (INC) meetings on Persistent Organic Pollutants (POPs) in 2000.

Municipal Solid Wastes (Management and Handling) Rules, were finalized based on the comments and suggestions from the public and notified on 25 September 2000. A draft notification of 25 May 2000 entitled 'Lead Acid Batteries (Management & Handling) Rules, 1999" was issued seeking objections/suggestions from the public. The status of implementation of Hazardous Waste Rules is continuously monitored. As on 13 May 2000 there were 13,011 hazardous waste-generating units in 373 districts in the country. They generate over 4.40 million tonnes of waste, of which, 1.68 million tonnes are recyclable, 0.19 million tonnes are incinerable and 2.52 million tonnes are disposed on lands.

A central control room has been set up in the Ministry to deal with emergencies arising from hazardous chemicals and a Crisis Alert System has been established. Guidelines for preparation of crisis management plans have been issued to the State Governments and financial support is being provided to them to strengthen infrastructure for the purpose. Emergency Response centres have been set up at Bhopal, Baroda, Manali and Khapali. The Red Book entitled "Central Crisis Group Alert System" which includes names, addresses and telephone numbers of the Central and state authorities and experts to be contacted in case of emergency, has been published and circulated.

National River Conservation

The expanded National River Conservation Plan (NRCP) now cover 149 towns located along 27 inter-state rivers in 16 states. Under this Action Plan, pollution abatement works are being taken up in 29 towns. A total of 41 schemes of pollution abatement have been sanctioned. So far five schemes have been completed under this action plan. About 618 MLD of sewage is targeted to be intercepted, diverted and treated.

Under the National River Conservation Plan (NRCP) pollution abatement works are being taken up in 46 towns of Andhra Pradesh,

Jharkhand, Gujarat, Karnataka, Maharashtra, Uttar Pradesh, Orissa, Punjab, Rajasthan and Tamil Nadu. Under this plan, 60 schemes have been completed, out of 181 schemes. The National Lake Conservation Plan (NLCP) was posed to different external agencies for funding. Terms of Reference of the project with the World Bank have been finalised and three wetlands, namely, Ropar, Kanjli and Harike from Punjab and two wetlands, namely, Sambhar and Udaipur Lake Complex from Rajasthan have been specifically identified for undertaking conservation programme.

National Afforestation and Eco-development Board

The National Afforestation and Eco-Development Board (NAEB) constituted in 1992 looks after promoting afforestation, tree plantation, ecological restoration and eco-development activities in the country with Special attention to degraded forest areas and lands adjoining the forest areas, national parks, sanctuaries and other protected areas, as well as the ecologically fragile areas like the Western Himalayas, Aravallis, Western Ghats, etc. The NAEB seeks to carry out its responsibilities through several schemes such as the Integrated Afforestation and Eco-Development Projects, area-oriented fuelwood and fodder projects, non-timber forest produce (including medicinal plants) scheme, aerial seeding, seed development, technology extension, grants-in-aid to voluntary agencies, etc.

The NAEB has evolved specific schemes to promote afforestation and management strategies, which help the states in developing specific afforestation and eco-development packages for augmenting bio-mass production through a participatory planning process of Joint Forest Management (JFM). Two major programmes. namely. Coastal Shelterbelt Plantation Programme (CSPP) for afforesting coastal areas in the country with suitable tree species to form shelterbelts and bamboo and medicinal plantation project have been taken up by the NAEB as thrust areas.

The Ministry of Environment and Forests functions as a nodal agency for United Nations Environment Programme (UNEP), South Asia Cooperation Environment Programme (SACEP), International Centre for Integrated Mountain Development (ICIMOD), International Union for Conservation of Nature and Natural Resources (IUCN) and various international agencies, regional bodies and multilateral institutions. The Ministry and its agencies receive assistance from various countries such as Sweden, Netherlands, Norway, Denmark, Australia, U.K., U.S.A., Canada, Japan, FRG, etc., on bilateral basis and from several UN and other multilateral agencies such as UNDP; World Bank, Asian

Development Bank, OECF(Japan) and ODA(U.K.) for various environmental and forestry projects.

Ozone Cell

Global efforts to protect the ozone layer started in the early seventies leading to the adoption of the Vienna Convention on Ozone Depleting Substances (ODS) in 1985 and the Montreal Protocol in 1987. India acceded to the Montreal Protocol, along with its London Amendment in 1992. To meet the country's commitment on ODS phase-out under the protocol and to disseminate information on ozone and ODS, the Ministry has established an Ozone Cell. A bi-monthly newsletter on ozone issues is published by the Cell. Workshops and seminars are also conducted to create awareness about ozone among industries. The Ministry provides custom/excise duty exemption for ODS phase-out projects and detailed guidelines/procedures have been finalised to grant duty exemption for new investments with non-ODS technologies. A policy to issue licences for import of ODS has been implemented and the Reserve Bank of India has issued instructions to all commercial banks prohibiting finance or refinance of new investments with ODS technologies. A ban has also been imposed on trade of ODS with new parties.

●●●

Section : TWO

DRAINAGE SYSTEM

A

Andaman Sea—It is a part of the northeastern Indian Ocean, with an area of 798,000 sq km. Through such ports as Bassein, Moulmein, Tavoy, and Mergui — as well as Yangon (Rangoon) itself— it forms the most important sea link between Myanmar (Burma) and other nations; it also forms part of a shipping route between India and China, via the Strait of Malacca.

Neither the Andaman's surface waters nor its bottom are rich in marine life. Its waters along the Malay Peninsula, however, favour molluscan growth, and there are about 250 edible species of fish in those intensively fished coastal waters. The sea's mineral resources are similarly limited but include tin deposits off the coasts of Malaysia and Thailand. Trading vessels have plied the Andaman Sea since ancient times. It was part of the early coastal trade route between India and China and, from the 8th century, formed a link in a thriving trade between India and Sri Lanka (Ceylon) to the west and the Myanmar ports of Thaton, Martaban, and Tavoy to the east. The two largest modern ports on the sea are Pinang in Malaysia to the southeast and Yangon in Myanmar to the north.

Andaman Sea is 1,200 km long, from north to south, and 645 km wide. Less than 5 per cent of the sea is deeper than 3,000 m, but, in a system of submarine valleys east of the Andaman-Nicobar Ridge, depths exceed 4,400 m. The sea's northern and eastern third is less than 180 m deep, in part because of silt deposited by the Irrawaddy River at its delta. The western and central half of the sea is approximately 900 to 3,000 m deep.

The Andaman Sea is bounded to the north by the Irrawaddy River delta of Myanmar; to the east by peninsular Myanmar, Thailand, and

Malaysia; to the west by the Andaman and Nicobar Islands, which are under Indian administration; and to the south by the island of Sumatra (part of Indonesia) and by the Strait of Malacca. The sea takes its name from the Andaman Islands.

Arabian Sea—northwestern part of the Indian Ocean, covering a total area of about 3,862,000 sq km and forming part of the principal sea route between Europe and India, it is bounded to the west by the Horn of Africa and the Arabian Peninsula, to the north by Iran and Pakistan to the east by India, and to the south by the remainder of the Indian Ocean. Political units bordering the sea—in addition to India, Iran, and Pakistan—are the Sultanate of Oman, Yemen, and Somalia. Islands in the sea include Socotra (a part of Yemen) off the Horn of Africa, the Kuria Muria Islands off the coast of Oman, and Lakshadweep (a Union Territory of India consisting of the Laccadive, Minicoy, and Amindivi islands; the latter constitute a group of coral atolls lying between 160 and 400 km off the southwestern (Malabar) coast of India. The Indus River is the principal river draining into this sea.

To the north the Gulf of Oman connects the sea with the Persian Gulf via the Strait of Hormuz. To the west the Gulf of Aden connects it with the Red Sea via the Bab el-Mandeb Strait. It has a mean depth of 2,734 m. In Roman times its name was Mare Erythraeum (Erythraean Sea).

Physical features : Most of the Arabian Sea has depths that exceed 2,987 m, and there are no islands in the middle. Deep water reaches close to the bordering lands except in the northeast, off Pakistan and India. To the southeast the Lakshadweep atolls form part of the submarine Maldive Ridge, which extends farther south into the Indian Ocean where it rises above the surface to form the atolls of the Maldives. On the western side of the sea, the plateau island of Socotra, about 113 km long and with an area of about 3,626 sq km, is an insular extension of the Horn of Africa, lying 257 km east of Cape Gwardafuy (Guardafui).

Submarine morphology and geology : The Arabian Sea was formed within the past 150 million years (during the Mesozoic and Cenozoic eras) as the Indian subcontinent migrated north and collided with Asia. Stretching south-eastwards from Socotra is the submarine Carlsberg Ridge, which coincides with the belt of seismic activity in the Indian Ocean that divides the Arabian Sea into two major basins — the Arabian Basin to the east and the Somali Basin to the west. The maximum depth of the sea (5,803 m), occurs at Wheatley Deep. The Carlsberg Ridge is longitudinally split by a central valley that reaches depths of 3,597 m below the sea's surface. The coastal escarpments of the Gulf of Aden are formed by rift faults that converge toward the southwest to continue into Africa as the boundary scarps of the Eastern, or Great, Rift Valley, which forms part of the East African Rift System. The Arabian Basin is separated from the Gulf of Oman Basin by the Murray Ridge, a narrow, seismically active submarine ridge that extends northeast to southwest to meet the Carlsberg Ridge. West of Murray Ridge is the Malian subduction zone, an area where the ocean floor sinks below the adjacent continental crust.

A deep submarine canyon has been cut by the Indus River, which also has deposited an abyssal (deep-sea) cone of thick sediments 861 km wide and 1,496 km long. This cone and an associated abyssal plain in the Arabian Basin occupy much of the northeastern floor of the Arabian Sea. To the east of the Somali coast, the Somali Basin forms another large abyssal plain.

The continental shelf is narrow along the coast of the Arabian Peninsula and is even narrower along the Somali coast. No true coral reefs are found along the Arabian coast. Sediments near Cape al-Hadd (the easternmost headland of the Arabian Peninsula), where upwelling of deep water occurs in summer, consist of fine greenish mud with a high organic content containing hydrogen sulphide. The region, which contains many fish remains, is known as a fish cemetery. Terrigenous (land-derived) deposits cover the major part of the continental slope to a depth of about 2,743 m. Below this, deposits consist of the calcareous tests (shells) of *Globigerina* (a genus of protozoans belonging to the order Foraminiferida), while basins below 3,962 m are covered by red clay. Authigenic (that is, formed-in-place) ferromanganese nodules have been discovered in the Somali and Arabian basins, and polymetallic sulphides have been found along the Carlsberg Ridge. Sediment thickness decreases from 2,499 m in the north to about 489 m in the south of the Arabian Basin.

Climate and hydrology : The Arabian Sea has a monsoon climate. Minimum air temperatures of about 24 to 25 °C at the sea's surface occur in the central Arabian Sea in January and February, while temperatures higher than 28 °C occur in both June and November. During the rainy season, which occurs when the southwest monsoon winds blow (April to November), salinities of less than 35 parts per thousand have been recorded in the upper 46 m of the sea, while during the dry season (November to March), when the northeast monsoon winds blow, salinities of more than 36 parts per thousand have been recorded at the surface over the entire Arabian Sea north of latitude five degrees north, except off the Somali coast. Because evaporation exceeds the combined precipitation and riverine input, the sea exhibits a net water loss annually.

The complex Somali Current, which attains speeds of about seven knots off the coast of Socotra, becomes part of a clockwise circulation system that in summer continues to the northeast along the coast of Arabia and thence south along the coast of India to 10 degrees north. At that point it merges with the Southwestern Monsoon Current, flowing east between 5 and 10 degrees north. Pronounced upwelling of deeper waters occurs along the Somali and Arabian coasts in summer. The Somali Current weakens and reverses direction during the northeast (winter) monsoon. Of the five water masses that have been distinguished in the upper 914 m of the north Indian Ocean, three have been identified as originating in the Red Sea, the Persian Gulf, and the Arabian Sea, respectively. The paths of flow of these water masses are to the south and east.

Economic Resources : Pelagic fish (those living at or near the surface far from the land) in the Arabian Sea include tuna, sardine, billfish (a species having a long sharp bill or snout), wahoo (a large, swift game fish), sharks, lancet fish (a large species having daggerlike teeth), and moonfish (a species of silvery fish with thin, deep-chested bodies).

A periodic occurrence in the Arabian Sea, however, is mass mortality of fish. This phenomenon is attributed to a subsurface layer of water of tropical origin that is poor in oxygen but rich in phosphate; under certain circumstances this layer is brought to the surface by strong upwelling, resulting in the death of fish from lack of oxygen.

Extensive small-scale fishing is carried on in the Arabian Sea, particularly off the east coasts of Africa and the Arabian Peninsula. These operations employ dugout and outrigger canoes, *dhows*, and a variety of other small craft. Commercial fishing also is undertaken by larger vessels. India, Pakistan, Sri Lanka, Iran, .Oman, Yemen, France, the United Arab Emirates, South Korea, and the Maldives are the principal fishing nations.

Transportation : The Arabian Sea, with its strategic location vis-a-vis the Red Sea (including the Suez Canal) and the Persian Gulf, contains some of the world's busiest shipping lanes; and the chief routes originate in those two extensions. Persian Gulf shipping largely consists of tankers, some of immense capacity, that transit the Arabian Sea en route to destinations in East Asia, Europe, and North and South America. The

Suez Canal-Red Sea route is used mainly by general-cargo vessels on their way to ports in South, Southeast, and East Asia. There are a number of ports serving the countries bordering the sea. Among the largest are Muhammad Bin Qasim and Karachi in Pakistan, and Mumbai (general cargo) and Marmagao (iron ore) in India.

B

Baghmati River—Rising in several headstreams in the lowland area of Nepal, it flows southward through the Shiwaliks. The southernmost range of the Himalaya. It continues across the plains of Tarai into Bihar and then flows south-eastward to enter the Burhi Gandak River after a course of 360 Km.

Banas River—It rises near Kumbhalgarh Rajasthan State, northwestern India and cuts its way tortuously through the Aravali Range. It then flows in a northeasterly course onto the plains and joins the Chambal River, just north of Sheopur, after a course of 500 km. The Banas is a seasonal river that is often dry in the hot months, but it is still a source of irrigation. Its main tributaries are the Berach and Kotari rivers.

Beas River—also spelt Bias, it flows through the States of Himachal Pradesh and Punjab, northwestern India. It was called Hyphasis in ancient Greek, and Vipasha in Sanskrit. The Beas is one of the five bodies of water that give Punjab ("Five Rivers") its name. The river originates in the Rohtang Pass at an elevation of 4,361 m in the Zanskar Range of the Greater Himalaya, in central Himachal Pradesh. From there it flows south through the Kullu Valley where it receives tributaries, and then turns west to flow past Mandi town into the Kangra Valley. After crossing the valley, the Beas enters Punjab State and veers south and then southwest, where it joins with the Sutlej River at Harike after a course of about 470 km. The Beas River was the approximate eastern limit of Alexander the Great's invasion of India in 326 BC.

Bay of Bengal—large but relatively shallow embayment of the northeastern Indian Ocean, occupying an area of 2,173,000 sq km, it lies roughly between latitudes 5 and 22 degrees north and longitudes 80 and 90 degrees east. It is bordered by Sri Lanka and India to the west, Bangladesh to the north, and Myanmar (Burma) and the northern part of the Malay Peninsula to the east. Its southern boundary extends from

Dondra Head at the southern end of Sri Lanka in the west to the northern tip of the Indonesian island of Sumatra in the east. The bay is about 1,600 km wide, with an average depth of more than 2,600 m. The maximum depth is 4,694 m. A number of large rivers—the Mahanadi, Godavari, Krishna, and Kaveri (Cauvery) on the west and the Ganga and Brahmaputra on the north — flow into the Bay of Bengal. The Andaman and Nicobar groups, which are the only islands, separate the bay from the Andaman Sea.

Physiography : The Bay of Bengal is bordered to the north by a wide continental shelf that narrows to the south and by slopes of varying gradient on the northwest, north, and northeast, all cut by canyons from the rivers. Most important are the Ganga-Brahmaputra, Andhra, Mahadevan, Krishna, and Godavari canyons. These were former estuaries, when the shoreline was at the margin of the continental shelf during the Pleistocene Epoch (1,600,000 to 10,000 years ago). The deep floor of the bay is occupied by a vast abyssal (deep-sea) plain that slopes to the south. The main submarine features include the beginning of the long, seismically active Java Trench near the Nicobar-Sumatra mainland and of the aseismic Ninetyeast Ridge. The fan of sediments of the Ganga River is the widest (8-11 km) and thickest in the world. The bay itself was formed as the Indian subcontinent collided with Asia within the past 150 million years.

Climate : The climate of the Bay of Bengal is dominated by the monsoons. From November through April a continental high-pressure system north of the bay produces northeast winds (the northeast monsoon) characteristic of the winter season. During the northern summer (June through September) the rain-bearing southwest monsoon prevails, as intense heat produces a low-pressure system over the continent and a subsequent air flow from the ocean.

Cyclones : intense tropical storms of high winds and torrential rains—occur in spring (April and May) and fall (October and November); these are the weeks proceeding the onset of monsoon rains and the weeks following their retreat. A cyclone in November 1970 in the Ganga River delta resulted in the deaths of an enormous number of people and livestock, and a storm of comparable magnitude in April 1991 devastated the eastern shore of Bangladesh. Waterspouts occur frequently in the bay during the summer months.

Hydrology : A unique feature of the bay is the extreme variability of its physical properties. Temperature in the offshore areas, however, is warm and markedly uniform at all seasons, decreasing somewhat toward the north. Surface densities are considerably greater in spring than in fall, when river discharge is highest. Surface salinity, normally measuring 33 to 34 parts per thousand, can fall to nearly half that level and can extend well south of the bay during the fall. Below the surface layer is an oxygen-poor intermediate layer that has high salinity and undergoes only weak circulation. Weak upwelling occurs in the northeast during the northeast monsoon. The sea presents alternately slick and ruffled surfaces over shallow internal waves all along the east-coast shelf. Surface movements of the waters change direction with the season, the northeast monsoon giving them a clockwise circulation, the southeast monsoon a counterclockwise circulation. Severe storms occur at the change of monsoon, particularly to the south in October.

In addition to water-level changes resulting from waves and tide, the average sea level varies throughout the year. Because rainfall and riverine input exceed evaporation, the bay exhibits a net water gain annually.

Bottom deposits : Sediments in the Bay of Bengal are dominated by terrigenous deposits from the rivers, derived mainly from the Indian subcontinent and from the Himalaya. Calcareous clays and oozes are found near the Andaman and Nicobar Islands and atop the Ninetyeast Ridge. The amount of organic matter present in the continental-shelf sediment of the northern part of the east coast is poor compared with the world's average for nearshore sediments.

Economic Resource Exploitation : The Bay of Bengal has a distinct tropical marine ecosystem; copious river drainage into the northern part of the bay and the profusion of wetlands, marshes, and mangroves increase productivity of nearshore fish species. The exploitation of these resources, however, has been hampered by the small scale of operations and the lack of mechanized gear. Fishing typically is carried out by hand from outrigger canoes. The annual catch of prawns, the major export crop, has remained stable despite intensified harvesting. Several species of tuna found in the bay also are important. The tuna fishery is confined to the true oceanic sector of the bay, south of 15 degrees north, since freshwater runoff from the large rivers greatly influences the nearshore waters.

Petroleum discoveries have been made in the Bay of Bengal, but there has been no commercial exploitation. However, the bay has a geologic setting similar to that of the Indus River basin and the western margin of the Indian Peninsula, areas that have produced exploitable quantities of hydrocarbons. There are placer deposits of titanium off northeastern

Sri Lanka and rare earths off northeastern India. Heavy mineral sands occur around Thanjavur (in Tamil Nadu State) on the southeastern Indian coast, near Chennai, and in coastal areas around Visakhapatnam. They consist of ilmenite, garnet, sillimanite, zircon, rutile, and manganite.

Transportation : The principal trade routes for large tankers en route from the Persian Gulf to the Strait of Malacca pass south of the Bay of Bengal. Hence, oceanic transportation is limited to carriage of cargoes to and from Sri Lanka, Bangladesh, and the east coast of India. Principal ports in India are Calcutta, Haldia, Visakhapatnam, Chennai, Cuddalore, and Paradwip. Sri Lankan ports of importance are Colombo and Trincomalee. Dhaka and Chittagong are noteworthy in Bangladesh, and Akyab (Sittwe) is Myanmar's chief port on the Bay of Bengal. Haldia, Visakhapatnam, and Paradwip are well developed as iron ore terminals, reflecting India's profitable exportation of raw materials.

Betwa River—Sanskrit Vetravati or Betrawati ("Containing Reeds"), river, it rises in the Vindhya Range just north of Hoshangabad. The source of the river is just 30 km from the course of the sacred Narmada River. It flows generally north-east through Madhya Pradesh and Uttar Pradesh States and empties into the Yamuna just east of Hamirpur after a 610-km course. It appears as a consequent stream on the Mesozoic surface, superimposed on scarps. It is the third largest river of the Malwa-Bundelkhand Plateau. Its length is over 805 km. Nearly one-half of its course, which is not navigable, runs over the Malwa Plateau before it breaks into the upland of Bundelkhand. The Jamni and Dhasan rivers are the main right bank tributaries. The main left bank tributaries are the Nareu, Bes, and Orr. The Betwa is dammed at Dukwan and Deogarh. The Matatila Dam is a joint venture of Madhya Pradesh and Uttar Pradesh in Jhansi. Bilsa and Kurwai are towns on its banks.

Bhagirathi River—Flowing through West Bengal State, northeastern India, it forms the western boundary of the Ganga Delta. A distributary of the Ganga, it leaves that river just northeast of Jangipur, flows south, and joins the Jalangi at Nabaḍwip to form the Hugli (Hoogly) River after a total course of 190 km. Until the sixteenth century, when the main flow of the Ganga shifted eastward to the Padma, the Bhagirathi contained the original flow of the Ganga. Its banks sheltered important medieval towns of Bengal, including Murshidabad, once Bengal's capital. The Farakka Barrage was constructed in India on the Ganga to divert some water of the Ganga-Padma River into the decaying Bhagirathi-Hugli River, on which are located the Calcutta and the Haldia ports of the

Calcutta Port Commissioners. The Bhagirathi is spanned by a bridge at Baharampur.

Bhima River—major tributary of the Krishna River, its flows through Maharashtra and Karnataka States, western India. It rises in the Bhimaihankar heights of the Western Ghats and flows southeastward for 725 km in Maharashtra to join the Krishna in Karnataka. Its major tributaries are the Sina and Nira rivers. The Bhima drainage area is defined by the Western Ghats (west), the Balaghat Range (north), and the Mahadeo Range (south).

The Bhima runs in a well-entrenched valley, and its banks are heavily populated. Its water level is marked by monsoonal changes; receding flood-waters leave rich alluvial belts. The recently constructed dam at Ujani provides relief to agriculture by irrigation and has lessened threats of floods to down-stream settlements. Local irrigation works augment the scant supply of rainfall; major crops are *jowar* (sorghum), *bajra* (pearl millet), and oilseeds. Sugarcane is an important irrigated cash crop.

Brahmani River—an important river of northeastern Orissa State in eastern India, it is formed by the confluence of the Sankha and South Koel river that orginated from the southern slopes of Chota Nagpur Plateau in Bihar State. The Brahmani enters Orissa in Sundargarh district, and its total length from source to mouth is 701 km. It flows winding generally south-southeast, past Bonaigarh and Talcher, and then turns east to join the northern branches of the Mahanadi River and finally emptying into the Bay of Bengal at Palmyras Point. It is one of the few rivers that has cut across the Eastern Ghats, and it has formed a minor gorge at Rengali, where an important multipurpose river dam project has been established.

Brahmaputra River—known in Bengali Jamuna, Chinese Ya-Lu-Tsang-Pu Chiang, or Yarlung Zangbo Jiang, Tibetan Tsang-Po, it is a major river of Central and South Asia. It flows some 2,900 km from its source in the Himalaya to its confluence with the Ganga River, after which the mingled waters of the two rivers empty into the Bay of Bengal. Along its course it passes through the Tibet Autonomous Region of China, the Indian States of Arunachal Pradesh and Assam, and Bangladesh. For most of its length, the river serves as an important inland waterway; it is not, however, navigable between the mountains of Tibet and the plains of India. In its lower course, the river is both a creator and a destroyer — depositing huge quantities of fertile alluvial soil but also causing disastrous and frequent floods.

Physiography : The Brahmaputra's source lies in the Chemayungdung Glacier, which covers the slopes of the Himalaya about 97 km southeast of Mapang Yongcuo (Mapam) Lake in southwestern Tibet. The three headstreams that arise there are the Kubi, the Angsi, and the Chemayungdung. From its source the river runs for nearly 1,126 km in a generally easterly direction between the main range of the Himalaya to the south and the Nianqing tanggula (Nyenchen) Mountains to the north. Throughout its upper course the river is generally known as the Tsangpo ("the Purifier"); it is also known by its Chinese name and by other local Tibetan names at various points along its course.

In Tibet the Tsangpo receives a number of tributaries. The most important left-bank tributaries are the Laka zangbo (Raga Tsangpo), which joins the river west of Rikaze (Xigeze), and the Lhasa He (Kyi), which flows past the Tibetan capital of Lhasa and joins the Tsangpo at Qushui. The Niyang (Gyamda) River joins the river from the north at Tse-la (Tsela Dzong). On the right bank the Nianchu (Nyang Chu) River meets the river at Rikaze. After passing P'i (Pe) in Tibet, the river turns suddenly to the north and north-east and cuts a course through a succession of great, narrow gorges between the mountainous complex of Gyala Peri and Namcha Barwa (Mount Namjabrawa Feng) in a series of rapids and cascades. Thereafter, the river turns south and southwest and forces its way through the eastern extremity of the Himalaya to enter the Assam Valley of northeastern India as the Dihang River.

Just west of the town of Sadiya, India, the Dihang turns to the south-west and is joined by two mountain streams, the Lohit and the Dibang. After the confluence, about 1,448 km from the Bay of Bengal, the river is known as the Brahmaputra ("Son of Brahma"). In Assam the river is mighty, even in the dry season, and during the rains its banks are more than 8 km apart. As the river follows its braided, 724 km course through the valley, it receives several rapidly rushing Himalayan streams, including the Subansiri, Kameng, Bhareli, Dhansiri, Manas, Champamati, Saralbhanga, and Sankosh rivers. The main tributaries from the hills and from the plateau to the south are the Burhi Dihing, the Disang, the Dikhu, and the Kopili.

The Brahmaputra enters the plains of Bangladesh after turning south around the Garo Hills below Dhubri, India. After flowing past Chilmari, Bangladesh, it is joined on its right bank by the Tista River and then follows a 241 km course due south as the Yamuna River. (South of Gaibanda, the Old Brahmaputra leaves the left bank of the mainstream and flows past Jamalpur and Mymensingh to join the Meghna River at Bhairab Bazar). Before its confluence with the Ganga, the Yamuna receives the combined waters of the Baral, Atrai, and Hurasagar rivers on its right bank and becomes the point of departure of the large Dhaleswari River on its left bank. A tributary of the Dhaleswari, the Burhi Ganga ("Old Ganga"), flows past Dhaka and joins the Meghna River above Munshiganj.

The Yamuna joins with the Ganga north of Goalundo Ghat, after which, as the Padma, their combined waters flow to the southeast for a distance of about 121 km. The Padma reaches its confluence with the Meghna River near Chandpur and then enters the Bay of Bengal through the Meghna estuary and lesser channels.

Climate : The climate of the Brahmaputra valley varies from the harsh, cold, and dry conditions found in Tibet to the generally hot and humid conditions prevailing in the Assam Valley and Bangladesh. Tibetan winters are severely cold, with minimum temperatures below 0 °C, while summers are mild and sunny. The river valley lies in the rain shadow of the Himalaya, and precipitation there is relatively light: Lhasa receives about 400 mm annually.

In the Indian and Bangladeshi part of the valley, the monsoon climate is somewhat modified; the hot season is shorter than usual, and the average temperature ranges from 26 °C in Dhubri, Assam, to 29 °C at Dhaka. Precipitation is relatively heavy, and humidity is high throughout the year. The annual rainfall of between 1,778 and 3,810 mm falls mostly between June and early October; light rains also fall from March to May.

Hydrology : Constant changes in the river's course constitute a significant factor in the hydrology of the Brahmaputra. The most spectacular of these changes was the eastward diversion of the Tista River and the ensuing development of the new channel of the Yamuna, which occurred in 1787 with an exceptionally high flood in the Tista. The waters of the Tista were suddenly diverted eastward into an old abandoned course, causing the river to join the Brahmaputra opposite Bahadurabad Ghat in Mymensingh district. Until the late eighteenth century the Brahmaputra flowed past the town of Mymensingh and joined the Meghna River near Bhairab Bazar (the path of the present-day Old Brahmaputra channel). At that time, the course of the Yamuna River (now the main Brahmaputra channel) was a minor stream called the Konai-Jenai, which was probably a spill channel of the Old Brahmaputra. After being reinforced by the Tista flood of 1787, the Brahmaputra began to cut a new channel along the Konai-Jenai and gradually converted it after 1810 into the main stream, now known as the Yamuna.

Along the lower courses of the Ganga and Brahmaputra and along the Meghna, the land is subjected to constant erosion and deposition of silt because of the shifts and changes in these active river courses. Vast areas are subject to large-scale inundation during the monsoon months from June to September. The oscillations of the Yamuna since 1787 have been considerable, and the river is never in exactly the same place for two successive years. Islands and sizable newly deposited lands (chars) in the river appear and disappear seasonally. The chars are valuable to the economy of Bangladesh as additional cultivable areas.

In Tibet the waters of the Brahmaputra are clear because little silt is carried downstream. As soon as the river enters the Assam Valley, however, the silt load becomes heavy. Because of the speed and volume of water in the northern tributaries that flow down from the rain-soaked Himalayan slopes, their silt load is much heavier than that carried by the tributaries crossing the hard rocks of the old plateau to the south. In Assam the deep channel of the Brahmaputra follows the southern bank closer than the northern. This tendency is reinforced by the silt-laden northern tributaries pushing the channel south.

Another important hydrographic feature of the river is its tendency to flood. The quantity of water carried by the Brahmaputra in India and Bangladesh is enormous, discharge during the rainy season being estimated at 14,200 cu m per second. The Assam Valley is enclosed by hill ranges on the north, east, and south and receives more than 2,540 mm of rainfall annually, while in the Bengal Plain heavy rainfall 1,778 to 2,540 mm is reinforced by the huge discharge of the Tista, Torsa, and Jaldhaka rivers. Extensive flooding, aggravated by landslides associated with the Assam earthquake of 1950, is virtually an annual occurrence in the Brahmaputra valley. In addition, tidal surges accompanying tropical cyclones sweeping inland from the Bay of Bengal periodically bring great destruction to the delta region.

Plant and animal life : Large areas in Assam are covered with forests of sal (valuable timber trees that yield resin), and tall reed jungle grows in the swamps and depressed, water-filled areas (*jhils*) of the immense floodplains. Around the settlements in the Assam Valley, the many fruit trees yield plantains, papayas, mangoes and jack-fruit. Bamboo thickets abound everywhere.

The most notable animal of the swamps in Assam is the one-horned rhinoceros, which has become extinct in other parts of the world; Kaziranga National Park provides a refuge for the rhinoceros and for other wildlife in the valley, including elephants, tigers, leopards, wild buffalo, and deer. Numerous varieties of fish include the betki, pabda, ruhi, chital, and mrigal. Manas Sanctuary and Tiger Reserve, established in 1928 and spread over a 360 sq km area, has come under Project Tiger. This sanctuary is considered to be the most attractive of any Indian parks. In addition to wildlife, rich bird life is distinctive and abundant. Similarly, in Barnadi Wildlife Sanctuary (established in 1980) and Garampan Sanctuary (established in 1952), one can see leopards, tigers, elephants, hispid hares, and pigmy hogs.

The people : People living in the different sections of the Brahmaputra valley are of diverse origin and culture. North of the Himalayan rampart, the Tibetans practise Buddhism and speak the Tibetan language. They engage in animal husbandry and cultivate the valley with irrigation water taken from the river.

The Assamese represent a mixture of Mongolian-Tibetan, Aryan, and Burman ethnic origins. Their language is akin to Bengali, which is spoken in West Bengal State in India and in Bangladesh. Since the late nineteenth century a vast number of immigrants from the Bengal Plain of Bangladesh have entered the valley, where they have settled to cultivate the almost empty lands, particularly the low floodplains. In the Bengal Plain itself the river flaws through an area that is densely populated by the Bengali people, who cultivate the fertile valley. The hilly margins of the plain are inhabited by the hill tribes of the Garo, Khasi, and Hajong.

Irrigation and flood control : Flood-control schemes and the building of embankments were initiated after 1954. In Bangladesh the Brahmaputra embankment running west of the Yamuna River from north to south helps to control floods. The Tista Barrage Project is both an irrigation and a flood-protection scheme.

Little power has been harnessed along the Brahmaputra or the Assam Valley, although the estimated potential is great — some 12,000 MW in India alone. Some hydroelectric stations have been completed in Assam, most notably the Kopili Hydel Project, and others are under construction.

Navigation and transport : Near Lazi (Lhatse Dzong) in Tibet, the river opens into a navigable channel for about 644 km. Coracles (boats made of hides and bamboo) and large ferries ply its waters at 3,962 m above sea level. The Tsangpo is spanned in several places by suspension bridges.

Because it flows through a region of heavy rainfall in Assam and Bangladesh, the Brahmaputra is more important for inland navigation than for irrigation. The river has long formed a waterway between West Bengal and Assam, although, on occasion, political conflicts have disrupted the movement of traffic through Bangladesh. The Brahmaputra is navigable throughout the Bengal Plain and Assam upstream to Dibrugarh, 1,126 km from the sea. In addition to all types of local craft, powered launches and steamers can easily ply up and down the river, carrying bulky raw materials, timber, and crude oil.

The Brahmaputra remained unbridged throughout its course in the plains until the Saraighat Bridge — carrying both road and rail traffic — was opened in 1962 near Guwahati, Assam. A second crossing, the Kalia Bhomora road bridge near Tezpur, was opened in 1987. Ferries, however, have continued as the most important — and in Bangladesh the only — means of crossing the Brahmaputra. Sadiya, Dibrugarh, Jorhat, Tezpur, Guwahati, Goalpara, and Dhubri are important towns and crossing points in Assam, while Kurigram, Rahumari, Chilmari, Bahadurabad Ghat, Phulchari, Sarishabari, Jagannathganj Ghat, Nagarbari, Sirajganj, and Goalundo Ghat are important crossing points in Bangladesh. The railheads are located at Bahadurabad Ghat, Phulchari, Jagannathganj Ghat, Sirajganj, and Goalundo Ghat.

C

Cambay, Gulf of—Trumpet-shaped gulf of the Arabian Sea, also called *Gulf of Khambhat*, it indents northward the coast of Gujarat State, western India, between Mumbai and the Kathiawar Peninsula. It is 190 km wide at its mouth between Diu and Daman, but it rapidly narrows to 24 km. The Gulf receives many rivers, including the Sabarmati, Mahi, Narmada (Narbada), and Tapri. Its shape and its orientation in relation to the southwest monsoon winds account for its high tidal range (12 m) and the high velocity of the entering tides (6-7 knots). Shoals and sandbanks are treacherous for navigation, and all the gulf ports have suffered from silting caused by tides and flood torrents from the rivers.

On the eastern side of the gulf are Bharuch, one of the oldest Indian ports, and Surat, identified with early European commercial contacts with

India. Cambay is at the head of the gulf. Although the importance of the gulf ports has been only local, the discovery and exploration of oil, particularly near Bharuch, around the head of the gulf, and in the offshore Bombay High field, has caused a commercial revival in the region.

Cauvery River—also spelt Kaveri, a sacred river of southern India, it rises in the Brahmagiri hill in the Western Ghats in Coorg district of Karnataka State. It follows a south-easterly direction for 765 km through Karnataka and Tamil Nadu States and descends in the Eastern Ghats in a series of great falls before emptying into the Bay of Bengal south of Cuddalore, Tamil Nadu. It breaks into a large number of distributaries, including a wide delta called the "garden of southern India". Known to devout Hindus as Dakshina Ganga ("Ganga of the South"), it is celebrated for its scenery and sanctity in Tamil literature, and its entire course is considered to be holy ground. The river is also important for its irrigation-canal projects.

Its uppermost course is tortuous with a rocky bed and high banks with luxuriant vegetation. After passing through a narrow gorge and tumbling 18-24 m in the rapids of Chunchankatte, the river widens to 274-366 m across the Karnataka Plateau. There, its flow is interrupted by a number of anicuts or weirs. At the Krishnaraja Sagara, the Cauvery is joined by two tributaries, the Hemavati and the Lakshmantirtha, and has been dammed for irrigation, forming a 31 sq km reservoir.

In Karnataka, the river bifurcates twice, forming the sacred islands of Shrirangapattana and Sivasamudram, 80 km apart. Around Sivasamudram are the scenic Sivasamudram Falls, comprising two series of rapids, Bhar Chukki and Gagana Chukki, plunging down 98 km and reaching a width of 305 m during the rainy season. The falls generate and supply hydroelectric power to Mysore, Bangalore, and the Kolar Gold Fields, more than 160 km away.

Upon entering Tamil Nadu, the Cauvery continues through a series of twisted wild gorges until it reaches the Hogenakal Falls and flows through a straight, narrow gorge near Salem. There, the Mettur Dam, 1,615 m long and 54 m high, impounds a lake (Stanley Reservoir) of 155 sq km. The Mettur Project, completed in 1934, created an important agricultural and industrial area by improving irrigation and providing hydropower.

After sweeping past the historic rock of Tiruchirappalli (Trichinopoly), the Cauvery breaks at Srirangam Island, a major pilprimage centre. In Thanjavur (Tanjore) district of Tamil Nadu State begins braided and extensively irrigated deltaic region of about 10,360 sq km. The Grand Anicut was built in the second century at the point where the river divides. A second anicut (1836-38) across the Coleroon, the northern and larger channel, saved the old system from silting and extended irrigation. The open roadsteads of Nagappattinam and Karikal are on the seaward side of the delta. The only navigation on any part of the Cauvery course is in basketwork boats. Its main tributaries are the Kabbani, Amaravati, Noyil, and Bhavani rivers. The entire area irrigated by Cauvery water has contributed to its pollution owing to the use of chemicals, fertilizers, and pesticides.

Chambal River—A river of northern India, Chambal is the chief tributary of the Yamuna and rises in the Vindhva Range just south of Mhow, western Madhya Pradesh State. From its source it flows north into southeastern Rajasthan State. Turning northeast, it flows past Kota and along the Rajasthan-Madhya Pradesh border; shifting east-southeast, it forms a portion of the Uttar Pradesh Madhya Pradesh border and flows through Uttar Pradesh to empty into the Yamuna after a 900-km course. The Banas, Kali Sindh, Sipra, and Parbati are its chief tributaries. The Chambal's lower course is lined by a 16 km belt of badland gullies resulting from accelerated soil erosion and is the site of a major project in soil conservation.

Chenab River—an important river of northwestern India and eastern Pakistan it is formed by the confluence of two streams (Chandra and Bhaga) in the Himachal Himalaya in India's Himachal Pradesh State. It flows west through Jammu and Kashmir, between the steep cliffs of the Shiwalik Hills and the Lesser Himalaya, then south-west into Pakistan to its junction with the Sutlej River, a tributary of the Indus. It is about 974 km long and feeds several irrigation canals.

Chilka Lake—a lagoon lake, also spelt Chilika it is situated in eastern Orissa State, eastern India. It is separated from the Bay of Bengal by a narrow spit. It is the most magnificent and largest saltwater lake in India. It is 72 km long, 8-21 km wide, and about 2 m deep, spreading for about 1,100 sq km area. The Daya and Bhargavi rivers feed the lake except during the dry months from December to June, when saline ocean water enters through a small passage. Chilka was once a bay of the ocean until silted up by strong monsoon tides. Dotted with many emerald-green islands, with enchanting names such as Honeymoon Island and Breakfast Island, it is the home to a rich variety of aquatic fauna. It is known as a sanctuary and winter resort for migratory bilds from as far as Siberia. The famous temple of the goddess Kalijai is on Kalijai Island at a distance of about 16 km from the Rambha railway station on the southeastern railway. Chilka offeis good hunting, boating, and fishing. There are fisheries and salt pans around its shores. Hundreds of boats sail out daily on the lake's expanse in search of crabs, mackerel, and prawns.

Coleroon River—flowing through in Tiruchirappalli and Thanjavur districts, Tamil Nadu State, south-eastern India, it is formed by the northern bifurcation of the Cauvery (Kaveri) River at Sriangam. The river flows between South Arcot and Thanjavur districts for 58 km and empties through several mouths into the Bay of Bengal, about 5 km south of Porto Novo. The Coleroon is part of the Cauvery Delta, the most fertile and densely populated region of southern India, noted for its rice production. The town Chidambaram lies on its banks in Thanjavur district.

D

Damodar River—an important river of northeastern India, it rises with in many tributaries, notably the Bokaro and Konar, in the Chota Nagpur plateau, south-central Bihar State. It follows a generally eastward course for 592 km through West Bengal to join the Hugli (Hooghly) River southwest of Calcutta. The Damodar valley along the Bihar-West Bengal border includes India's most important coaland mica-mining fields and has long been an area of active industrial development. The major coalfields (Jharia, Raniganj, and Giridih) are mostly open-pit and are easily mined. The Damodar Valley Corporation, which began work in 1948, constructed four multipurpose dams to form a scries of reservoirs — Tilaiya, Maithon, Konar, and Panchet Hill. Also included is the Durgapur diversionary barrage (dam) and a 130 km navigation canal linking the coalfields with the Hugli-Calcutta industrial complex. The project provides for flood control, hydroelectricity, coal-fed power plants, irrigation of about 385,000 hectares chiefly in West Bengal, afforestation, fish breeding, recreation, and the general development of agriculture and industry throughout the valley, which experienced a great influx of people during the twentieth century. Numerous towns along the river, including Dhanbad, Jharia, and Sindri, are connected by a dense rail and road network.

Dhebar Lake—a large reservoir lake, in the southeastern Aravali Range, south-central Rajasthan State, northwestern India, it is approximately

50 sq km in area when full it was originally named Jai Samand and was formed by a marble dam built across the Gomati River in the late seventeenth century. Canals carry water from the lake to villages in the western area. Small wooded islands dot the northern end of the lake, where fishing hamlets fringe the shore. Two palaces stand on the hills to the south.

G

Gandak River—also called Narayani River it flows through central Nepal and northern India. It is formed by the union of the Kali and Trisuli rivers, which rise in the Great Himalaya range in Nepal. From this junction to the Indian border the river is called the Narayani. It flows southwest into India and then turns southeast along the Uttar Pradesh-Bihar State border and across the Gangetic Plain. It enters the Ganga River opposite Patna after a winding course of 765 km. The Burhi ("Old") Gandak flows parallel to and east of the Gandak River in an old channel. It Joins the Ganga northeast of Monghyr (now Munger).

Ganga River—also called Ganges, is a great river of the plains of northern India. Although officially as well as popularly called the Ganga, both in Hindi and in other Indian languages, internationally it is known by its Anglicized name, the Ganges. For several millennia it has been the holy river of the Hindus. For most of its course it is a wide and sluggish stream, flowing through one of the most fertile and densely populated tracts of territory in the world. Despite its importance, its length of 2,510 km makes it relatively short by both world and Asian standards.

Rising in the Himalaya and emptying into the Bay of Bengal, it drains a quarter of the territory of India, while its basin supports an immense concentration of people. The Gangetic Plain, across which it flows, is the heartland of the region known as Hindustan and has been the cradle of successive civilizations from the kingdom of Ashoka in the third century BC, down to the Mughal Empire, founded in the sixteenth century.

For most of its course the Ganga flows through Indian territory, although its large delta in the Bengal area lies mostly in Bangladesh. The general direction of the river's flow is from north-northwest to southeast. At its delta, the flow is generally southward.

Physiography : The Ganga rises in the southern Himalaya on the Indian side of the Tibet border. Its five headstreams—the Bhagirathi, Alaknanda, Mandakini, Dhauliganga, and Pindar—all rise in the Uttarakhand region (the northern mountainous districts), a division of the State of Uttar Pradesh. Of these, the two main headstreams are the Alaknanda (the longer of the two), which rises about 48 km north of the Himalayan peak of Nanda Devi, and the Bhagirathi, which originates about 3,050 m above sea level in an ice cave at the foot of the Himalayan glacier known as Gangotri. Gangotri itself is a sacred place for Hindu pilgrimage. The true source of the Ganga, however, is considered to be at Gaumukh, about 21 km southeast of Gangotri.

Although there is a seasonal variation in the river's flow, its volume increases markedly as it receives more tributaries and enters a region of heavier rainfall. From April to June the melting Himalayan snows feed the river, while in the rainy season from July to September the rain-bearing monsoon winds cause floods.

After the Alaknanda and Bhagirathi unite at Devaprayag, they form a main stream known as the Ganga which cuts through the outer (southern) Himalaya to emerge from the mountains at Rishikesh. It then flows onto the plain at Haridwar (Hardwar), another place held sacred by the Hindus.

Within the State of Uttar Pradesh, the principal right bank tributaries are the Yamuna River, which flows past Delhi, the capital of India, to join the Ganga near Allahabad, and the Tons, which flows north from the Vindhya Range in the State of Madhya Pradesh and joins it soon after. The main left-bank tributaries in Uttar Pradesh are the Ramganga, the Gomati, and the Ghaghara.

The Ganga next enters the State of Bihar, where its main tributaries from the Himalayan region to the north are the Gandak, the Burhi Gandak, the Ghugri, and the Kosi, and its most important southern tributary is the Son. The river then skirts the Rajmahal Hills to the south and flows southeast to Farakka, at the apex of the delta. In West Bengal, the last Indian State that the Ganga enters, the Mahananda joins it from the north. (Throughout West Bengal in India, as well as in Bangladesh, the Ganga is locally called the Padma.) The westernmost distributary of the delta is the Hugli (Hooghly), on the east bank of which stands the city of Calcutta. The Hugli itself is joined by two tributaries flowing in from the west, the Damodar and the Rupnarayan. In Bangladesh the Ganga is joined by the mighty Brahmaputra (which for about 241 km before the junction is called the Yamuna) near Goalundo Ghat. The combined stream, now called the Padma, joins with the Meghna River above Chandpur. The waters then flow to the Bay of Bengal through innumerable channels, the largest of which is known as the Meghna estuary.

Dhaka (Dacca), the capital of Bangladesh, stands on the Buriganga ("Old Ganga"), a tributary of the Dhaleswari. Apart from the Hugli and the Meghna, the other distributary streams that form the Ganga delta arc, in West Bengal, the Jalangi and, in Bangladesh, the Matabhanga, the Bhairab, the Kabadak, the Garai-Madhumati, and the Arial Khan.

The Ganga, as well as its tributaries and distributaries, is constantly vulnerable to changes in its course in the delta region. Such changes have occurred in comparatively recent times, especially since 1750. In 1785 the Brahmaputra flowed past the city of Mymensingh; it now flows more than 64 km west of it before joining the Ganga.

The rivers in the West Bengal area are sluggish; little water passes down them to the sea. In the Bangladeshi delta region, the rivers are broad and active, carrying plentiful water and connected by innumerable creeks. During the rains (from June to October) the greater part of the region is flooded to a depth of several feet, leaving the villages and homesteads, which are built on artificially raised land, isolated above the floodwaters. Communication between settlements during this season can be accomplished only by boat.

The delta, the seaward prolongation of salt deposits from the Ganga and Brahmaputra river valleys, covers an area of about 60,000 sq km and is composed of repeated alternations of clays, sands, and marls, with recurring layers of peat, lignite, and beds of what were once forests. The new deposits of the delta, known in Hindi and Urdu as the *khadar*, naturally occur in the vicinity of the present channels.

The southern surface of the Ganga delta has been formed by the rapid and comparatively recent deposition of enormous loads of silt. To the east the seaward side of the delta is being changed at a rapid rate by the formation of new lands, known as *chars*, and new islands. The western coastline of the delta, however, has remained practically unchanged since the eighteenth century.

To the seaward side of the delta 35 a whole there is a vast stretch of tidal forests and swampland. The forests, called Sundarbans, are protected by India and Bangladesh for conservation purposes.

In certain parts of the delta there occur layers of peat, composed of forest vegetation and rice plants. In many natural depressions, known as *bil*, peat, still in the process of formation, has been used as a fertilizer by local farmers, and it has also been dried and used as a domestic and industrial fuel.

Climate and hydrology : The Ganga basin contains the largest river system on the subcontinent. The water supply is dependent partly on the rains brought by the southwesterly monsoon winds from July to October, as well as on the flow from melting Himalayan snows, in the hot season from April to June. Precipitation in the river basin accompanies the southwest monsoon winds, but it also comes with tropical cyclones that originate in the Bay of Bengal between June and October. Only a small amount of rainfall occurs in December and January. The average annual rainfall varies from 760 mm at the western end of the basin to more than 2,286 mm at the eastern end. (In the upper Gangetic Plain in Uttar Pradesh rainfall averages about 762 to 1,016 mm, in the Middle Plain of Bihar from 1,016 to 1,524 mm, and in the delta region between 1,524 and 2,540 mm). The delta region experiences strong cyclonic storms both before the commencement of the monsoon season, from March to May, and at the end of it, from September to October. Some of these storms result in much loss of life and the destruction of homes, crops, and livestock. One such storm, which occurred in November 1970, was of catastrophic proportions, resulting in the deaths of at least 200,000 and possibly as many as 500,000 people.

Since there is little variation in relief over the entire surface of the Gangeric Plain, the rivers rate of flow is slow. Between the Yamuna River at Delhi and the Bay of Bengal, a distance of nearly 1,609 km, the elevation drops only some 213 m. Altogether the Ganga-Brahmaputra plains extend over an area of 777,000 sq km. The alluvial mantle of the plain, which in some places is more than 1,829 m thick, is possibly not more than 10,000 years old.

Plant and animal life : The Ganga-Yamuna area was once densely forested. Historical writings indicate that in the sixteenth and seventeenth centuries wild elephants, buffalo, bison, rhinoceroses, lions, and tigers were hunted there. Most of the original natural vegetation has disappeared from the Ganga basin as a whole, and the land is now intensely cultivated to meet the needs of an ever-growing population. Wild animals are few, except for deer, boars, and wildcats, and some wolves, jackals, and foxes. Only in the Sundarbans area of the delta are some Bengal tigers, crocodiles, and marsh deer still found. Fish abound in all the rivets, especially in the delta area, where they form an important part of the inhabitants' diet. Many varieties of birds are found, such as mynah, parrots, crows, kites, partridges, and fowls. In winter, duck and snipe migrate south across the high Himalaya, settling in large numbers in water-covered areas. In the Bengal area common fish include featherbacks (Notopteridae), barbs (Cyprinidae), walking catfish, gouramis (Anabantidae), and milkfish (Chanidae).

The people : Historically the Gangetic Plain has constituted the heartland of Hindustan and has cradled its successive civilizations. The centre of the pre-Christian empire of Ashoka was Patna (Pataliputra), standing on the banks of the Ganga in Bihar. The centres of the great Mughal Empire were at Delhi and Agra, on the western peripheries of the Ganga basin. Kannauj on the Ganga, north of Kanpur, was the centre of the feudatory empire of Harsa, which covered most of northern India in the middle of the seventh century. During the Muslim era, which began in the twelfth century; Muslim rule extended not only over the plain, but over all Bengal as well. Dhaka (Dacca) and Murshidabad in the delta region were centres of Muslim power.

Ethnically, the people of the Ganga basin are of mixed origin. In the west and centre of the basin they were originally descended from Aryan ancestors. Later, Turks, Mongols, Afghans, Persians, and Arabs came from the west and intermingled with them. To the east and south, largely in the Bengal area, an admixture of Tibetan, Burman, and miscellaneous hill people has also occurred. The Europeans, arriving still later, did not settle or intermarry to any extent.

The British, having founded Calcutta on the banks of the Hugli in the late seventeenth century, gradually advanced up the valley of the Ganga, reaching Delhi in the mid-nineteenth century.

A great number of cities have been built on the Gangetic Plain. Among the most notable are Roorkee, Saharanpur, Meerut, Agra (the city of the famous Taj Mahal mausoleum), Mathura (esteemed as the birthplace of the Lord Krishna), Aligarh, Kanpur, Bareilly, Lucknow, Allahabad, Varanasi (Banaras; the holy city), Patna, Bhagalpur, Rajshahi, Murshidabad, Burdwan, Calcutta, Howrah (Haora), Dhaka, Khulna, and Barisal.

In the delta, Calcutta and its satellite towns stretch for about 80 km along both banks of the Hugli, forming one of India's most important concentrations of population, commerce, and industry.

The holy river, rituals, the legends : The religious importance of the Ganga may exceed that of any other river in the world. It has been revered from the earliest times and today is still regarded as the holiest of rivers by the Hindus. She is personified as a goddess. The legend is that Lord

Vishnu yielded to the prayers of a great sage and sent the goddess Ganga to earth. But the force with which she descended threatened to flood all that came in her path. So Lord Shiva entwined her in his long hair, to control her force, and make her tranquil. Those who sought salvation could then bathe in her waters. While places of Hindu pilgrimage, called *tirthas*, are located throughout the subcontinent, those that are situated on the Ganga have particular significance. Among thee are the confluence of the Ganga and the Yamuna near Allahabad, where a bathing festival, or the Kumbh *mela* (fair), is held in January and February. During this ceremony, hundreds of thousands of pilgrims immerse themselves in the river. Other holy places for immersion are at Varanasi (Banaras), or Kashi, and at Haridwar. The Hugli River at Calcutta also is regarded as holy. The places of pilgrimage on the Ganga also include Gangotri and the junction of the Alaknanda and Bhagirathi headstreams. The Hindus cast the ashes of their dead upon the river, believing that they thus will go straight to heaven, and cremation *ghats* (temples at the summit of riverside steps) for burning the dead have been built in many places on the banks of the Ganga.

Hydroelectric power : The Gangetic Plain is one of the most fertile and densely populated regions in the world. Because there is little relief across the surface of the plain the Ganga for most of its course is a wide and sluggish stream. Its total drainage basin covers an area of about 975,900 sq km, or roughly a quarter of the territory of India, and supports nearly half a billion people. The land of the basin is intensely cultivated. The water supply of the Ganga system is dependent partly on the rains brought by the monsoon winds from July to October, as well as on the flow from melting Himalayan snows in the hot season from April to June.

Also called North Indian Plain, extensive north-central section of the Indian subcontinent, stretching westward from (and including) the Brahmaputra River valley and the Ganga Delta to the Indus River valley. The region contains the subcontinent's richest and most densely populated areas. The greater part of the plain is made up of alluvial soil, deposited by the Ganga and Brahmaputra rivers in the east and the Indus River in the west The eastern part of the plain has light rains or drought in the winter, but in summer rainfall is so heavy that vast areas become swamps or shallow lakes The plain becomes progressively drier toward the west where it incorporates the Thar (Great Indian) Desert.

The Hydroelectric potential of the Ganga has been estimated at 13 million/kilowatts, of which about two-fifths lie within India and the rest in Nepal Some of this potential has been exploited in India with such hydroelectric developments as those along the Chambal and Rihand rivers.

Irrigation : Use of the Ganga water for irrigation, either when the river is in flood or by means of gravity canals, has been common since ancient times. Such irrigation is described in scriptures and mythological books written more than 2,000 years ago. Megasthenes, a Greek ambassador who was in India, recorded the use of irrigation in the fourth century BC. Irrigation was highly developed during the period of Muslim rule from the twelfth century onward, and the Mughal kings later constructed several canals. The canal system was further extended by the British.

The cultivated area of the Ganga valley in Uttar Pradesh and Bihar benefits from a system of irrigation canals that has increased the production of such cash crops as sugar cane, cotton, and oilseeds. The older canals are mainly in the Ganga-Yamuna Doab (doab meaning 'land between two rivers'). The Upper Ganga Canal, with its distributaries, is 9,574 km long; it begins at Haridwar. The Lower Ganga Canal, which is 8238 fan with distributaries, begins at Naraura. The Sarda Canal irrigates land in Ayodhya, in Uttar Pradesh. The land north of the Ganga, being higher, is difficult to irrigate by canal, and ground-water must be pumped to the surface. Large areas in Uttar Pradesh and in Bihar are also irrigated by channels running from hand-dug wells.

The Ganga-Kabadak scheme in Bangladesh, largely an irrigation plan, covers parts of the districts of Khulna, Jessore, and Kushtia that lie within the moribund part of the delta where silt and overgrowth choke the rivers.

Total annual rainfall in this region is generally below 1,524 mm, and winters are comparatively dry. The system of irrigation is based on both gravity canals and electrically powered lifting devices.

Navigation : In ancient times the Ganga and some of its tributaries, especially in the east, were navigable. According to Megasthenes, the Ganga and its main tributaries were being navigated in the fourth century BC. In the fourteenth century, inland-river navigation in the Ganga basin was still flourishing. By the nineteenth century, irrigation-cum-navigation canals formed the main arteries of the water-transport system. The advent of paddle steamers revolutionized inland transport, stimulating the growth of the indigo industry in Bihar and Bengal. Regular steamer services ran from Calcutta up the Ganga to Allahabad and far beyond, as well as to Agra on the Yamuna and up the Brahmaputra River.

The decline of large-scale water transport began with the construction of railways during the mid-nineteenth century. The increasing withdrawal of water for irrigation also has affected navigation. River traffic now is insignificant beyond the middle Ganga basin around Allahabad, much of what there is consisting of various types of rural rivercraft.

West Bengal and Bangladesh, however, continue to rely on the waterways to transport jute, tea, grain, and other agricultural and rural products. Principal river ports are Chalna, Khulna, Barisal, Chandpur, Narayanganj, Goalundo Ghat, Sirajganj, Bhairab Bazar, and Fenchuganj in Bangladesh, and Calcutta, Goalpara, Dhubri, and Dibrugarh in India. The partition of India and Pakistan in 1947 produced far-reaching changes, virtually halting the large trade in tea and jute formerly carried to Calcutta from Assam by inland waterway.

In Bangladesh, inland water transport is the responsibility of the Inland Water Transport Authority. In India, the Central Inland Water Transport Board formulates policy for inland waterways, while the Inland Waterways Authority develops and maintains an extensive system of national waterways. Approximately 1,609 km of waterways in the Ganga basin from Allahabad to Haldia are included in the system.

The construction of the Farakka Barrage at the head of the delta, just inside Indian territory in West Bengal, has been a source of contention between India and Bangladesh.

According to the Indian view, the port of Calcutta had deteriorated because of the deposit of silt and the intrusion of saline seawater. In order to ameliorate the condition of Calcutta by flushing away the seawater and raising the water level, India sought to have quantities of fresh water diverted from the Ganga at the site of the Farakka Barrage. The water there is now carried by means of a large canal into the Bhagirathi River, which joins the Hugli River above Calcutta.

Ghaggar River—The Ghaggar River rises in the Shiwalik Range, northwestern Himachal Pradesh State, and flows about 320 km southwest through Haryana State, where it receives the Saraswati River. Beyond die Otu Barrage, the Ghaggar River is known as the Hakia River which loses itself in the Thar Desert. Just southwest of Sirsa it feeds two irrigation canals that extend into Rajasthan. The Ghaggar was probably an affluent of the Indus River. Its seasonal flow is determined by monsoon rainfall.

Ghaghara River—also spelt Gogra, Ghaghra, or Ghagra, Nepali Kauriala, this major left-bank tributary of the Ganga River, rising as the Karnali River (Chinese: K'ung-ch'iao Ho) in the Tibetan Himalaya, flows southeast into Nepal. Cutting southwards across the Shiwalik Hills, it splits into two branches that rejoin south of the Indian border and form the Ghaghara proper. It flows southeast through Uttar Pradesh and Bihar States to enter the Ganga below Chhapra after a 970 km course. The major tributaries—the Kuwana, the Rapti, and the Little Gandak rivers—ail flow into the Ghaghara from the mountains to the north. Together with the Ganga and its tributaries, it has helped form the vast alluvial plain of northern Bihar. Along its lower couise it is also called the Sarju River (the Sarabos of the second-century-AD Greek geographer Ptolemy) and the Deoha.

Godavari River—sacred river of central India, it rises in the Western Ghats 80 km from the Arabian Sea and flows generally eastwards across the Deccan Plateau, along the Maharashtra-Andhra Pradesh border and across Andhra Pradesh State, turning southeastwards for the last 320 km of its course before reaching the Bay of Bengal. There it empties via its two mouths: the Gautami Godavari to the north and the Vasishta Godavari to the south. Its total length is approximately 1,465 km, and it has a drainage basin of 313,000 sq km.

From its source to the Eastern Ghats, the Godavari River flows through gentle, somewhat monotonous terrain, along the way receiving the Darna, Purna, Manjra, Pranhita, and Indravati rivers. Upon entering the Eastern Ghats region, however, the river flows between steep and precipitous banks, its width contracting until it flows through a deep cleft only 180 m wide, known as the Gorge. On either side wooded hills rise almost vertically from the waters. Having passed through the Eastern Ghats, the river widens again, traversing wide plains, the low islands in its stream being used for tobacco growing. At this point the Godavari flows placidly. Just above the town of Rajahmundry, a dam was constructed on the river in 1948 to provide irrigation and hydroelectric power.

The upper reaches of the Godavari are dry in winter and spring, making it virtually useless for irrigation. At its mouths, however, the development of a navigable irrigation-canal system, linking its delta with that of the Krishna River to the southwest, has made the land one of the richest rice-growing areas of India. The Godavari, throughout its entire length, is sacred to the Hindus.

Gomati River—Also called Gumti, this tributary of the Ganga River, which flows through central Uttar Pradesh, northern India, rises in northern Uttar Pradesh about 51 km cast of Pilibhit and is intermittent for the first 56 km of its course, becoming perennial after its junction with the Joknai. Below this point it flows generally southeastwards for some 800 km, receiving its only major tributary, the right-bank Sai River, near Jaunpur and emptying into the Ganga near Saidpur. It drains a basin of approximately 18,750 sq km.

Gundlakamma River—The Gundlakamma river of east-central Andhra Pradesh State, southern India rises in the Nallamala Range of the Eastern Ghats. Alter crossing the mountains, it enters the plains and flows in a northeasterly direction past Markapur to the Coromandel Coast of the Bay of Bengal, into which it empties 19 km east of Ongole, after a course of 225 km.

H

Hugli River—also spelt Hooghly, this river flowing through West Bengal State, northeastern India is an arm of the Ganga River, providing access to Calcutta from the Bay of Bengal. It is formed by the confluence of the Bhagirathi and Jalangi rivers at Nabadwip. From there the Hugli flows generally south for about 260 km to the Bay of Bengal, through a heavily industrialized area with more than half of West Bengal's population. The rivers lower reaches are fed by the Damodar, Rupnarayan, and Haldi (Kasai) rivers, which rise to the northwest on the Chota Nagpur plateau. Although above Calcutta the river is silted up, it is navigable to the city by ocean liners. Navigation is facilitated by constant dredging and the scour of a tidal bore that rushes inland at high tide. Negotiations with Bangladesh have resulted in the diversion of some waters from the Ganga River at Farakka in a way as to reduce silting at Calcutta. From Calcutta the Hugli flows west and south to the Rupnarayan estuary, then twists south and south-west, entering the Bay of Bengal through an estuary 5 to 32 km wide. The new port of Haldia is located a few kilometres downstream at the confluence with the Haldi River. The Hugli River is spanned by six bridges between Nabadwip and Calcutta, of which only one is a road-cum-railway bridge.

I

Indian Ocean—covering approximately one-fifth of the total ocean area of the world, it is the smallest, youngest, and physically most complex of the world's three major oceans. It stretches for more than 10,000 km between the southern tips of Africa and Australia and, without its marginal seas, has an area of about 73,440,000 sq km. The Indian Oceans average depth is 3 890 m, and, its deepest point, in the Sunda Deep of the Java Trench off the southern coast of Java, is 7,450 m.

The Indian Ocean is bounded by Iran, Pakistan, India, and Bangladesh to the north; the Malay Peninsula, the Sunda Islands of Indonesia, and Australia to the east; Antarctica to the south; and Africa and the Arabian Peninsula to the west. In the southwest it joins the Atlantic Ocean south of the southern tip of Africa, and to the east and southeast, its waters mingle with those of the Pacific.

The Indian Ocean has the fewest seas of the major oceans. To the north are the inland Red Sea and Persian Gulf. The Arabian Sea is to the northwest, and the Andaman Sea to the northeast. The large gulfs of Aden and Oman are to the northwest, the Bay of Bengal is to the northeast, and the Great Australian Bight is off the southern coast of Australia. The Indian Ocean differs from the Atlantic and Pacific Oceans in several other respects. In the Northern Hemisphere it is landlocked, does not extend to Arctic waters, or have a temperate-to-cold zone. It has fewer islands and narrower continental shelves. It is the only ocean with an asymmetric and, in the north, semi-annually reversing surface circulation. It has no separate, source of bottom water (the Indian Ocean's bottom water originates outside its boundaries) and has two sources of highly saline water (the Persian Gulf and the Red Sea). Below the surface layers, especially in the north, the ocean's water is extremely low in oxygen.

Physiography and geology : *Origin :* Its formation is a consequence of the break-up, about 150 million years ago, of the southern supercontinent Gondwana, or Gondwanaland; by the movement to the northeast of the Indian subcontinent (beginning about 125 million years ago), which began colliding with Eurasia about 50 million years ago; and by the western movement of Africa and separation of Australia from Antarctica some 53 million years ago.

By 36 million years ago, the Indian Ocean had taken on its present configuration. Although it first opened some 125 million years ago, almost the entire Indian Ocean basin is less than 80 million years old.

Submarine features : *Oceanic ridges and fracture zones* : The oceanic ridges consist of a rugged, seismically active mountain chain that is part of the worldwide oceanic ridge system and still contains centres of seafloor spreading in several places. The ridges form an inverted Y on the ocean floor, starting in the upper northwest with the Carlsberg

Ridge in the Arabian Sea, turning due south past the Chagos-Lakshadweep Plateau, and becoming the Mid-Indian (or Central Indian) Ridge. Southeast of Madagascar the ridge branches: the Southwest Indian Ridge continues to the southwest until it merges into the Atlantic-Indian Ridge south of Africa, and the Southeast Indian Ridge trends to the east until it joins the Pacific-Antarctic Ridge south of Tasmania. Most striking is the aseismic (virtually earthquake-free) Ninetyeast Ridge, which is the longest and straightest in the worlds oceans. First discovered in 1962, it runs northward along the 90 degrees east meridian (hence its name) for 4,505 km from the zonal Broken Ridge at 31 degrees south to 9 degrees north and can be traced farther under the sediments of the Bay of Bengal.

Seamounts : These are extinct submarine volcanoes that are conically shaped and often flat-topped. They rise abruptly from the abyssal plain to heights at least 1,006 m above the ocean floor. In the Indian Ocean, seamounts are particularly abundant between Reunion and Seychelles in the Central Indian Basin and the Vening Meinesz group near Wharton Basin. Bardin, Kohler, Nikitin, and Williams seamounts are some examples.

Ocean basins : Ocean basins are characterized by smooth, flat plains of thick sediment with abyssal hills (less than 1,006 m high) at the bottom flanks of the oceanic ridges. The Indian Ocean's complex ridge topography led to the formation of many basins that range in width from 322 km to 9,010 km. From roughly north to south they include the Arabian, Somali, Mascarene, Madagascar, Mozambique, Agulhas, and Crozet basins in the west and the Central Indian (the largest), Wharton, and South Australia basins in the east.

Continental rise, slope, and shelf : The continental shelf extends to an average width of about 121 km in the Indian Ocean, with its widest points (306 km) off Mumbai and northwestern Australia. The island shelves are only about 305 m wide. The shelf break is at a depth of about 140 m. Submarine canyons indent the steep slope below the break. The Ganga, Indus, and Zambezi rivers have all carved particularly large canyons. Their sediment loads extend far beyond the shelf, form the rises at the foot of the slope, and contribute to the abyssal plains of their respective basins. The Ganga sediment cone is the world's widest and thickest.

Trenches : The Indian Ocean has the fewest trenches of any of the world's oceans. The narrow (80 km), volcanic, and seismically active Java

Trench is the world's second longest, stretching more than 2,574 km from southwest of Java and continuing northward as the Sunda Trench past Sumatra, with an extension along the Andaman and Nicobar Islands.

Bottom deposits : The immense load of suspended sediments from the rivers emptying into the Indian Ocean is the highest of the three oceans, and nearly half of it comes from the Indian subcontinent alone. These terrigenous sediments occur mostly on the continental shelves, slopes, and rises, and they merge into abyssal plains. Cones of thicknesses of over one km are found in the Bay of Bengal, the Arabian Sea, and the Somali and Mozambique basins. Wharton Basin off northern Australia has the oldest sediments. In the Ganga-Brahmaputra cone, sediments exceed 11 km in thickness and extend to 10 degrees south. Brown and red clay sediments dominate in the deep sea between 10 degrees north and 40 degrees south away from islands and continents and are 305 m thick In the equatorial zone, an area of high oceanic productivity, calcareous and siliceous oozes are abundant.

Coasts : Several well-defined coastal configurations are found in the Indian Ocean: estuaries, deltas, salt marshes, mangrove swamps, cliffs, coral reels, and complexes of barrier islands, lagoons, beaches, and dunes. A particularly important estuarine system is the Hugli (Hooghly) complex, formed by three branches of the Hugli River on the Bay of Bengal near Calcutta. Pakistan combines one of the most tectonically active coasts in the world with the 193 km-wide Indus River delta, the mud flats and salty wastes of which are often flooded. The Indian subcontinent has the most extensive beach area (more than half of its coastline). Mangroves are found in most estuaries and deltas. The Sundarbans, the lower part of the Ganga River delta, contain the largest mangrove forests in the world. Coral reefs — in either fringing, barrier, or atoll form — are abundant around all the islands in the tropics and are also found along the southern coasts of Bangladesh, Myanmar (Burma), and India, and along the eastern coast of Africa.

Islands : The Indian Ocean has few islands. Madagascar — the fourth largest island in the world — the Maldives, Seychelles, Socotra, and Sri Lanka are continental. fragments. The other islands — including Amirante, Andaman-Nicobar, Chagos, Lakshadweep (Laccadive, Minicoy, and Amindivi islands), Christmas, Cocos, Comoros, Crozet, Farquhar, Kerguelen, Mauritius, Prince Edward, Reunion, St. Paul and Amsterdam, and the Sunda Islands — are of volcanic origin. The

Andamans and Sundas are island arc-trench subduction systems, with the trench on the oceanic side of the arc.

The Indian Ocean can be subdivided into four general latitudinal climatic zones based on atmospheric circulation.

Monsoon zone : The first zone, extending north from 10 degrees south, has a monsoon climate (characterized by semi-annual reversing winds). In the Northern Hemisphere "summer" (May to October), low atmospheric pressure over Asia and high pressure over Australia result in the southwest monsoon, with wind speeds up to 45 km per hour and a wet season in South Asia. During the northern "winter" (November to April), high pressure over Asia and low pressure from 10 degrees south to northern Australia bring the northeast monsoon winds and a wet season for southern Indonesia and northern Australia. The region is subject to destructive cyclones that form over the open ocean and head for shore in a generally westward direction. These Storms typically occur just before and after the southwest monsoon rains, with west-facing coasts generally being the most severely affected. The northwestern part of the region has the driest climate, with some areas receiving less than 250 mm of rain per year; conversely, the equatorial regions are the wettest, with an average of more than 2,032 mm.

Trade-winds zone : The second zone, that of the trade winds, lies between 10 and 30 degrees south. There, steady southeasterly trade winds prevail throughout the year and are strongest between June and September. Cyclones also occur east of Madagascar between December and March. In the northern part of the zone the air temperature averages 25 °C during the southern winter (May to October) and slightly higher the rest of the time.

Subtropical and temperate zone : The third zone lies in the subtropical and temperate latitudes of the Southern Hemisphere, between 30 and 45 degrees south. In the northern part of the zone the prevailing winds are light and variable, while in the southern area moderate to strong westerly winds prevail. The average air temperature decreases with increasing southern latitude: from 20 to 22 °C down to 10 °C in the Austral summer (December through February) and from 16 to 17 °C to 6 to 7 °C in winter. Rainfall is moderate and uniformly distributed.

Subantarctic and Antarctic zone : Finally, the fourth, or subantarctic and Antarctic, zone occupies the wide belt between 45 degrees south and the continent of Antarctica. Steady westerly winds prevail, reaching gale force at times with their passage through deep Antarctic low-pressure zones. The average winter air temperature varies from 6 to 7 °C in the north to -16 °C near the continent. The corresponding summer temperatures vary within the limits of 10 to -4 °C.

Hydrology : The hydrological characteristics of the Indian Ocean are derived from the interaction of atmospheric conditions (rain, wind, and solar energy) with the surface, the sources of its water, and the deep (thermohaline) circulation, all of which combine to form generally horizontal layers of water. Each layer has different temperature and salinity combinations that form discrete water masses of different densities, with lighter water overlying denser water. Surface-water temperature varies with season, latitude, and surface circulation; surface salinity is the balance between precipitation, evaporation, and river runoff.

Surface temperatures : A zonal asymmetry is rioted in the surface-water temperature distribution in summer north of 20 degrees south. Summer surface temperatures are higher in the eastern part of this region than in the west. In the Bay of Bengal the maximum temperature is around 28 °C. The minimum temperature is about 22 °C in the area of Cape Gwardafuy (Guardafui), on the Horn of Africa, and is associated with the upwelling off the African coast.

Ice : Ice is formed in the extreme south during the Antarctic winter. Between January and February the melting ice along the Antarctic coast is broken up by severe storms and, in the form of large blocks and broad floes, is carried away by wind and currents to the open ocean. In some coastal areas the tongues of ice-shelf glaciers break off to form icebergs. West of the 90 degrees east meridian the northern limit for floating ice lies close to 65 degrees south. To the east of that meridian, however, floating ice is commonly encountered to 60 degrees south; icebergs are sometimes found as far north as 40 degrees south.

Tides : Examples of all three tidal types — diurnal, semidiurnal, and mixed — can be found in the Indian Ocean, although semidiurnal (twice daily) are the most widespread. Semidiurnal tides prevail on the coast of eastern Africa as far north as the Equator and in the Bay of Bengal. The tides are mixed in the Arabian Sea and the inner part of the Persian Gulf. The southwestern coast of Australia has a small area of diurnal (daily) tides, as do the coast of Thailand in the Andaman Sea and the south shore of the central Persian Gulf.

Mineral resources : By far the most valuable mineral resource is oil, and the Persian Gulf is the largest oil-producing region in the world. Exploration for offshore oil and natural gas also has been under way in the Arabian Sea and the Bay of Bengal, both of which are believed to have large reserves. Other sites of exploration activity are off the northwestern coast of Australia, in the Andaman Sea, off the coast of Africa south of the Equator, and off the southwestern coast of Madagascar. Other than the countries of the Persian Gulf, only India produces commercial quantities of oil from offshore areas, with a large proportion of its total production coming from fields off the coast of Mumbai (formerly Bombay). Some natural gas also is produced from fields off the northwestern coast of Australia.

Another potentially valuable mineral resource is contained in manganese nodules, which abound in the Indian Ocean. Sampling sites throughout the central part of the ocean, as far south as South Africa, and east in the South Australian Basin have yielded nodules; the manganese content has been highest in the east and lowest towards the northwest. The difficulty in mining and processing these minerals, despite advances in technology, has precluded their commercial extraction. Other minerals of potential commercial value are ilmenite (a mixture of iron and titanium oxide), tin, monazite (a rare earth), zircon, and chromite, all of which are found in nearshore sand bodies.

Biological resources : The greater part of the water area of the Indian Ocean lies within the tropical and temperate zones. The shallow waters of the tropical zone are characterized by numerous corals and other organisms capable of building, together with calcareous red algae and coral islands. These coralline structures shelter a thriving marine fauna consisting of sponges, worms, crabs, molluscs, sea urchins, brittle stars, starfish, and small but exceedingly brightly coloured reef fish.

The major portion of the tropical coasts is covered with mangrove thickets with an animal life specific to that environment. Mangroves act to stabilize the land along the coastal margin and are important breeding and nursery grounds for offshore species.

The small crustaceans, including more than 100 species of minute copepods, form the bulk of the animal life, followed by small molluscs, jellyfish, and polyps, and other invertebrate animals ranging from single-celled radiolaria to large Portuguese man-of-war jellyfish, which attain a size of several feet. The squid form large schools. Of the fishes, the most abundant are several species of flying fish, luminous anchovies, lantern fish, large and small tunnies, sailfish, and various types of sharks. Here and there are found sea turtles and large marine mammals, such as dugongs (or sea cows), toothed and baleen whales, dolphins, and seals.

Among the birds, the most common are the albatross and frigate birds; several species of penguins populate the islands lying in the ocean's temperate zone and the Antarctic coast.

Fisheries : The upwellings that occur in several coastal regions of the Indian Ocean — particularly in the northern Arabian Sea and on the South African coast — cause nutrients to concentrate in surface waters. This, in turn, produces immense quantities of phytoplankton that are the basis for large populations of commercially valuable marine animals. Despite great fishery potentials, however, most commercial fishing is conducted on a small scale, and large areas remain undeveloped.

Shrimp is the most important commercial species for coastal countries, with India accounting for the largest catch. Lesser quantities of sardines, mackerel, and anchovies also are exploited by the littoral States. Since coastal nations can now claim sovereignty over resources within an exclusive economic zone that extends 370 km from their coasts, it has become possible for small States such as the Maldives to increase their national income by selling fishing rights in their zones to the major fishing nations that have the capital and technology to exploit pelagic resources.

Trade and transport : Despite the growth in the economic development of the countries bordering the Indian Ocean since 1950, most trade continues to be between the former colonial powers of the region and the littoral States that have emerged. Intra-regional trade has remained small because of uncertain political relationships among the coastal States — particularly between India and Pakistan and between India and Sri Lanka — and because of a lack of compatibility between the products that the various countries need and what is produced. Thus, Indian Ocean States export raw materials and import manufactured goods that are produced elsewhere. Petroleum dominates commerce, as the Indian Ocean has come to be an important throughway for transport of crude oil to Europe, North America, and East Asia. Other major commodities include iron, coal, rubber, and tea. Iron ore from Western Australia and from India and South Africa is shipped to Japan, while coal is exported to the United Kingdom from Australia via the Indian Ocean.

Shipping in the Indian Ocean can be divided into three components: dhows, dry-cargo carriers, and tankers. For more than two millennia the small, lateen-rigged sailing vessels called dhows were predominant. The dhow trade was particularly important in the western Indian Ocean, where these vessels could lake advantage of the monsoon winds; a great variety of products were transported between ports on the coast of East Africa and ports on the Arabian Peninsula and even Mumbai and Mangalore on the west coast of India. Most dhow traffic has been supplanted by larger, powered ships and by land transport, and the remaining dhows have been equipped with auxiliary engines.

Environmental impact of human activity : European colonial exploitation of Indian Ocean resources resulted in the first clear evidence of the degradation of both the terrestrial and oceanic environments. Deforestation, cultivation, and guano mining have had undesirable effects on terrestrial ecosystems. Guano mining, which removed vegetation and scraped the land surface, has caused the destruction of much native flora and fauna, and hunting and the introduction of exotic species have altered the ecological balance that previously existed. Man-made threats to the oceanic environment are of more recent origin. One is the quantity of domestic and industrial waste that has accumulated in nearshore waters as a result of increased urbanization and industrialization along the coast. This has been most evident in India, which is the most populous country of the region. Another is the concern caused by the transport of large quantities of crude oil across the ocean and its adjacent semi-enclosed seas. Oil spills from normal tanker operations and occasional large-scale tanker catastrophes have had deleterious effects on phytoplankton and zooplankton, both necessary parts of the food-chain of commercial fisheries,

Early exploration : There is evidence that the Egyptians explored the Indian Ocean as early as about 2300 BC, when they sent maritime expeditions to the "land of Punt", which was somewhere on the Somali coast. The expeditions, which may have begun even earlier — perhaps about 2900 BC, were numerous until about 2200 BC. Egyptian annals make no mention of journeys to Punt during the period 2200-2100 BC, but they began again in the eleventh dynasty (2081-1938 BC), and records mention them continuously until the twentieth dynasty (1190-1075 BC).

Early trade in the northwestern Indian Ocean was aided by an irrigation canal (navigable in high water) through the Isthmus of Suez that was built by the Egyptians during the twelfth dynasty (1938-C.1756 BC) and operated almost continuously until it was filled in AD 775. It was on an Indian trading vessel that the Russian voyager Afanasy Nikitin sailed to India in 1469. Vasco da Gama, sailing around Africa in 1497, signed on an Arabian pilot at Malindi before he crossed the Indian Ocean to reach the western shores of India.

The Dutch, English, and French followed the Portuguese to the Indian Ocean. In 1521 the Spanish navigator Juan Sebastian de Elcano crossed the central part of the ocean, continuing the first voyage of circumnavigation of the globe after the death of the original commander, Ferdinand Magellan, in the Philippine Islands.

The southern waters of the Indian Ocean were explored by James Cook in 1772. Beginning in 1806 the Indian Ocean was crossed repeatedly by Russian ships commanded by Adam Johann Krusenstern, Otto von Kotzebue, and others.

Between 1819 and 1821 the expedition of the Russian explorer Fabian Gottlieb von Bellingshausen that circumnavigated Antarctica penetrated the Indian Ocean south of the 60th parallel. A number of important voyages to Antarctica followed in the nineteenth and early twentieth centuries, led by the explorers Charles Wilkes (American), Jules-Sebastien-Cesar Dumont d'Urville and Jean-Baptiste-Etienne-Auguste Charcot (French), James dark Ross (Scottish), and others.

Later Expeditions : The famous round-the-world expedition of the British naval vessel *Challenger*, which began in 1872, marked the beginning of systematic investigation of the oceans, including the Indian Ocean. Thereafter, there were numerous expeditions.

Other circumnavigational voyages were made following World War II by the Danish Galathea, the Swedish *Albatross*, and the English *Challenger* II, which explored the northern portion of the Indian Ocean. During the preparation and execution of the International Geophysical Year (1957-1958) and in subsequent years, scientific explorations of the southern Indian Ocean were carried out by Australia, New Zealand, Soviet Russia, France, and Japan. The International Indian Ocean Expedition (1960-1965) was a cooperative effort by some three dozen research ships of many countries.

Research activity since then has built on the work of that expedition, with studies on the nature of monsoons. Several ships have crossed the Indian Ocean to collect information on mineral resources of the continental shelves and the deep ocean floor. Several legs of the Deep Sea Drilling Project (1968-1983) were in the Indian Ocean. These more recent and technologically advanced scientific explorations have provided insights into the marine geology, geophysics, and resource potentials of the Indian Ocean.

Indus River—great trans-Himalayan river of South Asia and one of the longest rivers in the world, with a length of 2,900 km. it has a total drainage area of about 1,165,500 sq km, of which 453,250 sq km lie in the Himalayan mountains and foothills and the rest in the semi-arid plains of Pakistan. The river's annual flow is about 207 billion cu m — twice that of the Nile and three times that of the Tigris and the Euphrates combined. The name of the river has been derived from the Sanskrit word *sindhu* ("river" or "stream"). It is mentioned in the Rigveda,.the earliest (c. 1500-1200 BC) chronicles and hymns of the Aryan peoples of ancient India, and is the source of the country's name.

Physical features : The river rises in southwestern Tibet at an altitude of about 5,500 m. For about 322 km it flows northwest, crossing the southeastern boundary of Jammu and Kashmir at about 4,572 m. A short way beyond Leh, in Ladakh, it is joined on its left by its first tributary, the Zaskar. Continuing for 241 km in the same direction, the Indus is joined by its notable tributary the Shyok on the right bank. After its confluence with the Shyok and up to the Kohistan region, it is fed by mighty glaciers on the slopes of the Karakoram Range, the Nanga Parbat massif, and the Kohistan highlands. The Shyok, Shigar, Gilgit, and other streams carry the glacial waters into the Indus. Since the present-day precipitation of snow in this region is not sufficient to feed these great rivers of ice, it is fairly certain that the giant ice streams of the Karakoram are survivors of the last ice age of the Himalaya.

The Shigar joins the Indus on the right bank near Skardu in Baltistan. The Gilgit, farther down, is another right-bank tributary, joining it at Bunji. Some kilometres farther downstream, the Astor River joins as a left-bank tributary. The Indus then flows west, crosses the Kashmir border, and turns south and southwest to enter Pakistan. There it skirts around the Nanga Parbat massif (8,126 m) in gorges as deep as 4,572 m to 5,182 m and 19 km to 26 km wide. Trails cling grimly to precipitous slopes overlooking the river from elevations of 1,219 m to 1,524 m.

After emerging from this region of high altitude, the Indus flows as a rapid mountain stream between the Swat and Hazara areas in Pakistan until it reaches the reservoir of Tarbela Dam. The Kabul River joins the Indus just above Attock, where the Indus flows at an elevation of 610 m and is crossed by the first p rail and road bridge. Finally, it cuts across the Salt Range near Kalabagh co enter the Punjab plain.

The Indus receives its most notable tributaries from the eastern Punjab plain. These five rivers — the Jhelum, the Chenab, the Ravi, the Beas, and the Sutlej — give the name Punjab ("Land of Five Rivers") to the land shared between Pakistan and India.

After receiving the waters of the Punjab rivers, the Indus becomes much larger and, during the flood season (July to September), is several kilometres wide. It flows there at an elevation of about 79 m. Its slow speed at this stage results in its accumulated silt being deposited on its bed, which is thus raised above the level of the sandy plain; indeed, most of the plain in Sind has been built up by alluvium laid down by the Indus. Embankments have been built to prevent flooding, but occasionally these give way, and large areas are destroyed by inundation. Such floods occurred in 1947 and 1958. During heavy flooding the river sometimes changes its course.

Near Thatta (Tatta) the Indus begins its deltaic stage and breaks into distributaries that join the sea at various points south-southeast of Karachi. The delta covers an area of 7,770 sq km or more and extends along the coast for about 209 km. The uneven surface of the delta area is marked by a network of existing and abandoned channels. The coastal strip, from about 8 to 32 km inland, is flooded by high tides.

Hydrology : The principal rivers of the Indus River system are snow-fed. Their flow varies greatly at different times of the year: the discharge is at a minimum during the winter months (December to February), there is a rise of water in spring and early summer (March to June), floods occur during the rainy season (July to September), and occasionally there are devastating flash floods. The Indus and its tributaries receive all their waters in the upper hilly parts of their catchment areas. Therefore, their flow is at a maximum where they emerge out of the foothills, and little surface flow is added in the plains, where much loss of water occurs because of evaporation and seepage. On the other hand, some water is added by seepage in the period after the monsoon months. In the main stream of the Indus, the water level is at its lowest from mid-December to mid-February. After this the river starts rising, slowly at first and then more rapidly at the end of March. The high-water level usually occurs between mid-July and mid-August. The river then falls rapidly until the beginning of October, when the water level subsides more gradually. Annually, the Indus carries slightly more than half of the total supply of water in the Indus River system. The Jhelum and Chenab combined carry roughly one-fourth, and the Ravi, Beas, and the Sutlej combined constitute the remainder of the total supply of the system.

There is considerable physiographic and historical evidence to prove that since the dawn of civilization — at least since the days of

Mohenjodaro culture, 4,000 years ago — the Indus, from the southern Punjab to the sea, has been shifting its course. It was confined between limestone ridges at Rohri-Sukkur, but thereafter it has wandered, shifting generally to the west, particularly in its deltaic sector, so that about 200 years ago it began to flow into the Rann of Kachchh (Kutch). In upper Sind the Indus has shifted westward a distance of about 16 km to 32 km in the last seven centuries. The river is now held back to some extent by higher ground from Sehwan to Thatta at the head of the delta, but the possibility of future shifting cannot be ruled out. There is also evidence of the shifting of the Chenab, Ravi, Beas, and Sutlej rivers during the historical period.

Climate : From its source to its mouth, the annual rainfall in the Indus region varies between 125 to 500 mm. Except for the mountainous section of Pakistan, the Indus valley lies in the driest part of the subcontinent. Northwestern winds sweep the upper Indus valley in winter and bring 102 to 203 mm of rainfall — vital to the successful growing of wheat and barley. The mountainous region of the valley receives precipitation largely in the form of snow. A large amount of the Indus' water is provided by melting snows and glaciers of the Karakoram, Hindu Kush, and Himalayan mountains. The monsoon rains (July to September) provide the rest of the flow. The climate of the Indus valley ranges from that of the dry semi-desert areas of Sind and lower Punjab to the severe high mountain climate of Kohistan, Hunza, Gilgit, Ladakh, and western Tibet. January temperatures there are below freezing point in the north, while July temperatures reach a maximum of 38 °C in Sind and Punjab. Jacobabad, one of the hottest spots on earth, is situated west of the Indus River in upper Sind and often records summer maximums of 49°C.

Plant and animal life : The Indus is moderately rich in fish. The best-known variety is called hilsa and is the most important edible fish found in the river. Thatta, Kotri, and Sukkur, all in Sind, are important fishing centres. Between the Swat and Hazara areas the river is noted for trout fishing. Fish farming has become important in the reservoirs of dams and barrages. Near the mouth of the Indus — for about 241 km along the coast — there are numerous creeks and a shallow sea beyond. The area is rich in marine fish, the most important catches include pomfrets and prawns, which are obtained from November to March. A modern fish harbour has been built near the port of Karachi, providing cold storage and marketing. An export trade in prawns has developed, and salt-water fish are marketed in different parts of Pakistan.

There is a close relationship between climate and vegetation in the Indus valley. In the lower Indus region of Sind, desert conditions prevail 16 km to 40 km away from the river, and the area is dominated by sand and poor grass cover. Irrigation by floods or canals permits some cultivation. In upper Sind and Punjab, overgrazing and felling timber for fuel has led to destruction of much of the natural vegetation. Further, prolonged human interference with natural drainage and deforestation on the Shiwaliks has led to marked deterioration in groundwater conditions and so in vegetation. It appears that in prehistoric and earlier historic times the middle Indus region was more wooded than it is at present: accounts of Alexander the Great's Indian campaigns (c. 325 BC) and records of Mughal hunts in the sixteenth century and after suggest considerable forest growth. Even today, in the Indus plain not far from the river, there are thorn forests of open acacia and bush and undergrowth of poppies, vetch, thistles, and chickweed. Near the river are stretches of tall pampalike grass, and streams and canals are often lined with tamarisk trees and some dense scrub, but there is nowhere a natural forest. Efforts at reforestation in some parts of the Thal area in the Punjab, east of the Indus, have been successful. Cultivated areas close to the river have many trees, and the strip below the mountains has something of the appearance of parkland. Coniferous trees abound in the northern areas of the Indus region.

The people : Peoples living along the upper reaches of the Indus (for example, Tibetans, Ladakhi, and Balti) show affinities with Central rather than South Asia. They are of Asiatic stock, speak Tibetan languages, and practise Buddhism (although the Balti have adopted Islam). Pastoralism is important to the local economy. In the main Himalayan ranges, areas drained by the headwaters of the major Indus tributaries form a transitional zone where Tibetan influences mingle with those of the Indian *pahari* (hill) region,

The well-watered northern Indus plains are settled by agricultural groups who speak Punjabi and related dialects and who form the most numerous of the Indus valley peoples. Language, race, and tribal organization play a less important role in differentiating groups there. The major distinguishing feature among Punjabi peoples is caste, although without the religious and ritual connotations of the Hindu system. Muslim Jats and Rajputs are important Punjabi communities.

The lower Indus valley is inhabited by agricultural people who speak Sindhi and related dialects. Many cultural traits in the region appear to be of considerable antiquity, and the Sindhi pride themselves on their regional distinctiveness. Karachi, though in Sind, is predominantly an Urdu-speaking city, where Punjabis and muhajirs, immigrants from India who arrived in Pakistan after the partition of the subcontinent in 1947, have settled down.

West of the Indus River, the lands stretching from Quetta to the Makran coast form the territory of the Balochi tribes. Speaking a language derived from Old Persian, the Balochi are a nomadic people, herding camels, cattle, sheep, and goats, although some have adopted settled agriculture. Nomadic Brahui tribes around Kalat appear to be remnants of an earlier immigrant group from the Mediterranean region, who have since been supplanted by more recent migrants into the Indus valley. Brahui is a Dravidian-based language related to those of southern India.

Pathans, speaking Pashto and closely related to the tribes of Afghanistan. are found in northwestern Pakistan. The Yusufzai are the largest of the Pathan tribes, others being the Afridi, Muhmand, Khattak, and Wazir. In the mountainous tribal areas of Pakistan's North-West Frontier Province, the fiercely, independent Pathans retain their traditional tribal structure and political organization.

Elsewhere in the Indus Valley the inhabitants are of Indo-European descent and are Muslims, reflecting repeated incursions of peoples entering the Indian subcontinent from the west over several millennia. The rugged mountains of western Kashmir are inhabited by Dardic-speaking groups (Kafir, Kohistani, Shina, and Kashmiri Gujar), whose languages, like most in the region, are Indo-European in origin. In the Hunza River valley, the long-lived Burusho speak a language (Burushaski) that has no known ties to other languages in the area. These groups combine herding with irrigation-based cultivation.

K

Kachchh, Gulf of—also spelt Kutch, Cutch, or Kachh, northeastern arm of the Arabian Sea, it extends, between the Rann of Kachchh (a salt waste) and the Kathiawar Peninsula of west-central India, located to the south of the district of Kachchh, Gujarat State. Reaching eastwards for some 180 km the gulf varies in width between 16 and 65 km. It is rimmed with mudflats and many small islands rise from its waters. The port at the entrance of the gulf is Okha; other ports include Mandvi, Bedi. and Kandia.

Kaveri River—It rises in Coorg and flows east across peninsular India to empty in the Bay of Bengal. It is known as Dakshina Ganga or the Ganges of the south, and numerous centers of pilgrimage are found along its banks, notably at Seringapatam, Sivasamudram, and Seringam. Though not navigable, the Kaveri has always been an important source of water for irrigation and a barrage dating to the second century is still in use. The river has also been harnessed for hydroelectric power in recent times. Proportionate use of its waters if disputed between the riparian states Karnataka and Tamil Nadu both within the Indian Union.

The large Kaveri delta is one of the most fertile rice-growing areas of the Indian subcontinent. The heartland of Tamil country and Chola culture it features many historic towns, such as Tanjore and an abundance of temples and learned persons.

Kolleru Lake—also called Colair Lake it is situated in northeastern Andhra Pradesh State, southeastern India. It lies between the Godavari and Krishna river deltas near the town of Eluru (Ellore). At the height of the monsoon season the lake often expands to 260 sq km. Carp and prawns are fished commercially in the lake, and prawns are processed in the village of Akid.

Kommamur Canal—also called Buckingham Canal, it runs through in eastern Andhra Pradesh State and northeastern Tamil Nadu State, southeastern India. It was constructed, section by section, between 1806 and 1882 along the backwaters of the Coromandel Coast, which extends for a distance of 1,100 km from Cape Comorin northwards to the Krishna and Godavari deltas.

Although the canal was extensively rebuilt after 1880, it is of poor workmanship, and the expense of repairs is always high. It cannot be used by craft drawing more than I m. Even so, it is the only main route by which bulky commodities, such as fuel, salt, and dried fish, can be profitably brought to the city of Chennai in Tamil Nadu.

Kosi River—This river of Nepal flows through northern India. With its tributaries, the Kosi drains the eastern third of Nepal and part of Tibet, including the country around Mount Everest. Some of its headstreams rise beyond the Nepalese border in Tibet. About 48 km north of the Indian-Nepalese frontier, the Kosi is joined by several major tributaries and breaks southwards through the Shiwalik Hills at the narrow Chatra gorge. The river then emerges on the great plain of northern India in Bihar State on its way to the Ganga River, which it enters south of Purnea after a course of about 724 km. Because of its great outflushing of debris, the Kosi has no permanent channel in its course through the great plain of northern India. It has long been notorious for its devastating floods, when the waters may rise as much as 9 m in 24 hours and which long made vast tracts of northern Bihar unsafe for habitation or cultivation. Now a dam across the Chatra gorge at Barakakshetra controls floods, permits irrigation of the floodplain, provides hydropower, and supports fish hatcheries. Maize is extensively cultivated on the sandy soils of the Kosi basin.

Krishna River—formerly Kistna, an important river in southern India, it rises in Maharashtra State in the Western Ghats range near the old town of Mahabaleshwar close to India's west coast. It flows cast to Wai and then in a generally southeasterly direction past Sangli to the border of Karnataka State. There the river turns east and then flows in an irregular course across Karnataka, and into Andhra Pradesh State. It veers southeast and then northeast, and then flows east to its delta head at Vijayawada, and (from there flows into the Bay of Bengal after a course of about 1,290 km. The Krishna has a large and very fertile delta continuous with that of the Godavari River to the northeast. Although it is not navigable, the Krishna provides water for irrigation; a weir at Vijayawada controls the flow of water into a system of canals in the delta. Because it is fed by seasonal monsoon rains, the river's flow undergoes great fluctuation during the year, limiting its usefulness for irrigation. However, the Krishna valley project (in Maharashtra) is expected to augment irrigation waters in the State. The two largest tributaries are the Bhima (north) and the Tungabhadra (south). The Ujani dam on the Bhima (Maharashtra) and another at Hospet, on the Tungabhadra augment irrigation, and the latter supplies electric power.

L

Luni River—Rising on the western slopes of the Aravali Range near Ajmer town, where it is known as the Sagarmati, the river flows generally southwestwards through the hills and across the plains of the region. It then enters a patch of desert before it finally dissipates into the wastes of the northeastern part of the Rann of Kachchh in Gujarat State. A seasonal river, it receives much of the drainage of the southwest slopes of the Aravali Range; the Jowai, Sukri, and Jojari rivers are its main tributaries. The Luni derives its name from the Sanskrit Lavanavari ("Salt River") and is so called because of its excessive salinity. With a course of some 530 km, the Luni is the only major river of the area, and it serves as an essential source of irrigation waters.

M

Madhumati River—a tributary of the Padma (Ganga) River, flowing through southwestern Bangladesh, it leaves the Padma just north of Kushtia and flows 306 km southeast before turning south across the Sundarbans to empty into the Bay of Bengal. In its upper course, it is called the Garai; in its lower course, it is know as the Baleswar; and its 14-km-wide estuary mouth is called the Haringhata. The Madhumati is one of the largest of the Padma distributaries in the southern part of the Gangetic Plain, and it offers the best navigation conditions of any river at the head of the Bay of Bengal.

Mahanadi River—rising in the hills of southeastern Madhya Pradesh State, its upper course runs north as an insignificant stream, draining the eastern Chhattisgarh plain. After receiving the Seonath River, below Baloda bazar, it turns east and enters Orissa State, its flow is augmented by the drainage of hills to the north and south. At Sambalpur the Hirakud Dam on the river has formed a man-made lake 55 km long. The dam has several hydroelectric plants. Below the dam, the Mahanadi turns south along a tortuous course, piercing the Eastern Ghats through a forest-clad gorge. Bending east, it enters the Orissa plains near Cuttack and enters the Bay of Bengal at False Point by several channels.

The Mahanadi ("Great River") follows a total course of 900 km and has an estimated drainage area of 132,100 sq km. It is one of the most active silt-depositing streams in the Indian subcontinent. The river supplies several irrigation canals, mainly near Cuttack. Puri, at one of its mouths, is a famous pilgrimage site.

Mahananda River—This river of northern India and Bangladesh rises in the Darjeeling hills in extreme northern west Bengal State. The river flows south through a rich agricultural area in Bihar State, enters

West Bengal State, flows past Angrezabad, and then continues southeastwards into Bangladesh to join the Ganga River after a 360 km course. The Mahananda forms, in its upper course, an important eastward linguistic boundary between the Bengali- and Hindi-speaking areas.

Mahi River—This stream of western India rises in the western Vindhya Range, just south of Sardarpur, and flows northwards through Madhya Pradesh State. Turning northwest, it enters Rajasthan State and then turns southwest to flow through Gujarat State and enters the sea by a wide estuary past Cambay after about a 580-km course. The silt brought down by the Mahi has contributed to the shallowing of the Gulf of Cambay and the abandonment of its once-prosperous ports. The riverbed lies considerably lower than the land level and is of little use for irrigation.

Mannar, Gulf of—inlet of the Indian Ocean, between southeastern India and western Sri Lanka, it is bounded on the northeast by Rameswaram (island), Adam's (Rama's) Bridge (a chain of shoals), and Mannar Island. The gulf is 130-275 km wide and 160 km long. It receives several rivers, including theTambraparni (India) and the Aruvi (Sri Lanka). The port of Tuticorin is on the Indian coast. The gulf is noted for the pearl banks off Sri Lanka.

Mapam Lake—also called Manasarowar this lake lies in western Tibet, to the south of the Kailash Range. Lying nearly 4,570 m above sea level, it is generally recognized as the highest body of freshwater in the world. The lake is prominent in Hindu mythology, and it has traditionally been one of the most important Hindu pilgrimage centres.

N

Narmada River—also called Narbada, or Nerbudda this important river of central India, rises in the Maikala Range, east-central Madhya Pradesh State, central India. Rising on the summit of the plateau of Amarkantak, at the northeastern apex of the Satpura Range in Rewa, it enters the sea below Bharuch, after a total course of 1,289 km. It rises in a small tank, 1,067 m above the mean sea level, surrounded by a group of temples, guarded by an isolated family of priests. It is identified with Namados of Ptolemy, Namnadios of the Periplus, and the Reva of the Puranas. Hindus believe it sprang from the body of the god Shiva, and the Narmada ranks only after the Ganga in sanctity. The *pradakahina* pilgrimage takes pilgrims from Bharuch to Amarkantak, up one bank of the river and down the other.

Following a tortuous course through the hills of Mandla, it enters the structural trough between the Vindhya and Satpura ranges at the Marble Rocks gorge and then flows westwards across Madhya Pradesh and Gujarat States, entering the Gulf of Cambay through an estuary 21 km wide, just below Bharuch. Along its course, the Narmada drains the northern slopes of the Satpura Range and flows through the Hoshangabad plains, the Dhar upland, the Mahishmati plains, and the gorges at Mandhata and Murakta. It has numerous waterfalls in its course, like the Dhuadhar or "fall of the mist".

The river has always been an important route between the Arabian Sea and the Ganga River valley.

It has numerous tributaries that cause floods in the valley occasionally. The banks of the Narmada also contain microliths, small flakes, and implements. Some important towns on its banks indude Hoshangabad, Jabalpur, Handia, and Mandhata.

P

Palar River—a river of southern India, it rises near the Ponnaiyar River, southwest of Chintamani, in Karnataka State, and flows 295 km southeastwards through Tamil Nadu State to the Bay of Bengal, south of Chennai. Its major tributaries are the Ponnai and Cheyyar rivers.

The flow of the Palar is irregular, with considerable variations from year to year. Although it generally does not flood, heavy rains have caused the river to remain in flood for as long as six months. The river has been dammed for irrigation, especially along its course in Tamil Nadu. The largest communities along its banks are Vellore, Arcot, and Chingleput.

Palk Strait—inlet of the Bay of Bengal, between southeastern India and northern Sri Lanka, it is bounded on the south by Pamban Island (India), Adam's (Rama's) Bridge (a chain of shoals), and Mannar Island (Sri Lanka). The strait is 64-137 km wide and 137 km long. It receives several rivers, including the Vaigai (India), and it contains many islands of Sri Lanka. The port of Jaffna, the commercial centre for northern Sri Lanka, has trade with the State of Tamil Nadu, India. The southwestern portion of the strait is also called Palk Bay.

Penneru River—also spelt Penner River, also called northern Penner River, it rises on the Deccan Plateau 11 km west-southwest of Chik Ballapur, in Karnataka State of southwestern India. It flows north into Andhra Pradesh State and turns east-southeast towards the Coromandel Coast, emptying into the Bay of Bengal near Nellore, about 560 km from its source. The river is seasonal, becoming a torrent after the rains and a thin stream during dry periods.

Periyar—It is the name of a river and a lake in southern Kerala State, southern India. The river, 225 km long, rises in the Western Ghats range near the border with Tamil Nadu State and flows north to Periyar Lake in Kottayam district. The lake, 31 sq km in area, is an artificial reservoir created by damming the river. It lies at an altitude of 850 m, is ringed by mountain peaks, and is surrounded by a wildlife sanctuary. A tunnel carries water from the lake eastwards through the mountains to the Vaigai River in Tamil Nadu, where it is used for irrigation.

From the lake the Periyar River flows in a generally northwest direction through the mountains and onto the coastal plain, past Alwaye, emptying into the Arabian Sea at Parur. Further development of the river during the late twentieth century included construction of a hydroelectric project and another irrigation dam.

Ponnaiyar River—river in southern India, rising as the southern Pinakim on the eastern slope of Nandidrug mountain, in the Chennakaseva Hills of Karnataka State it flows southwards for 80 km through Karnataka to Tamil Nadu State, where it turns southeastwards and flows 320 km to enter the Bay of Bengal at Cuddalore. Major tributaries are the Chinnar, Markanda, Vaniar, and Pamban.

Heavy rains at the river's source cause sudden, but short-lived floods. The river is extensively dammed for irrigation, especially in Tamil Nadu. There are also reservoirs at Krishnagiri and Sathanur. The Ponnaiyar is considered sacred by Hindus, and festivals are held during the Tamil month of Tai (January-February).

Ponnani River—a river in central Kerala State, southern India, the Ponnani rises in the Western Ghats range northeast of Palakkad (formerly Palghat) town. Flowing first southwest and then west across the coastal plain, the river empties into the Arabian Sea at Ponnani after a course of about 160 km.

R

Ravi River—a river in northwestern India and northeastern Pakistan it is one of the rivers that give the Punjab (meaning "Land of Five Rivers") its name. It rises in the Greater Himalaya in Himachal Pradesh, India, and flows west-northwest past Chamba town, turning southwest at the boundary of Jammu and Kashmir. The river then flows to the Pakistani border and along it for more than 80 km before entering Pakistani Punjab. It flows past Lahore and turns west near Kamalia, emptying into the Chenab River south of Ahmadpur Sial after a course of about 725 km.

The Ravi's waters are used for irrigating large tracts along its course. The upper Bari (Ba-Beas Ri-Rayi) Doab canal, with the headworks at Madhopur at the northern tip of the Indian Punjab was completed in 1878-1879; it irrigates a large area east of the Ravi and its distributary canals extend into Pakistan. The two nations had frequent disputes over the water before reaching an agreement in 1960. The lower Bari Doab Canal, completed in 1917, lies entirely in Pakistan.

Rupnarayan River—river of south-central West Bengal State in northeastern India, it rises as the Dhaleshwari (Dhalkisor) in the Chota Nagpur plateau foothills northeast of Puruliya town and follows a tortuous southeasterly course past the town of Bankura, where it is known as the Dwarkeswar. It is joined by the Silai near the town of Ghatal, where it takes the name Rupnarayan. The river then joins the Hugli (Hooghly) after completing a 240-km course. The Rupnarayan originally formed a western exit of the Ganga River and is important for its irrigation potential. It is tidal through its entire course and constitutes a principal danger to navigation of the Hugli because it forces that river to deposit silt upon dangerous shoals.

S

Sambhar Salt Lake—the largest lake in India, west of Jaipur in east-central Rajasthan State northwestern India it is an ephemera salt lake about 230 sq km in area, it represents a depression of the Aravali Range. The soluble sodium compounds stored in the lake's underlying silt have accumulated by the evaporation of water brought down by annual river flooding. Salt sheets, which from a distance resemble snow, often cover the lake's bed, which is usually dry in the hot months.

The lake is traditionally said to have been created in the sixth century by Shakambari, a form of Durga and the consort of Shiva (one of the three supreme gods of Hinduism). Its salt supply was worked by the Mughal dynasty (1526-1858). Its salt supply was worked by the Mughal dynasty (1526-1858); it was later owned jointly by the Jaipur and Jodhpur Princely States. Salt evaporation pans and refineries are located on the lake's eastèrn shore.

Sarda River—rising in the Himalaya and flowing south-southeast along the India-Nepal border, it joins the Ghaghara River after a course of about 480 km. In its upper course, where the stream is known as the Kali River, it enters the Gangetic Plain at Parmdeo Mandi, widening there above the Sarda Barrage; below this point it is known as the Sarda River. Its major tributaries are the Dhauliganga, Goriganga, and Sarju. The Sarda Barrage, near Banbasa, is the source of the Sarda Canal (completed 1930), one of the longest irrigation canals in northern India.

Shyok River—a river in Jammu and Kashmir State, northern India, it rises in the Karakoram Range. The Shyok, which flows generally northwestwards, is fed by numerous glacers on its journey through the range. At rimes the Chong Kumdan in the dams the river, causing serious floods in nearby areas. Near Khapalu, Pakistani-held sector, the river joins the Indus. Its total length is 550 km, and its main right-bank tributary is the Nubra.

Sileru River—also called Machkund in Andhra Pradesh State, of southeastern India, the river rises as the Machkund in the Eastern Ghats in northeastern Andhra Pradesh. Leaving the Machkund reservoir, it flows (as the Sileru) parallel to the mountain ranges at an elevation of 600 m to 900 m in a northeast-to-southwest direction to empty into the Sabari River, opposite Konta, in Madhya Pradesh State, 100 km north-northwest of Rajahmundry. The river is 305 km long. There is a small hydroelectric project and dam on the river at Jalaput.

Sirhind Canal—a canal in Punjab State, northwestern India, it opened in 1882 and consists of an extensive canal system irrigating more than 5200 sq km of farm land, much of it in western Malwa. The system's headworks are on the Sutlej River at Ropar where it takes a sharp turn to flow in a westerly direction. From Ropar the canal runs west-southwest to Doraha where it splits into three branches: Abohar Branch, Bathinda Branch, and Patiala Branch. These three branches along with their numerous distributories make an extensive network, irrigating a large part of western Malwa.

Son River—also spelt Sone the principal southern tributary of the Ganga River, rising in Madhya Pradesh State, central India, it flows north past Manpur and then turns northeast. The river cuts through the Kaimur Range and joins the Ganga River above Pama, after a 784-km course. The Son valley is geologically almost a continuation of that of the Narmada River to the southwest, Largely forested, it is sparsely populated. The valley is bordered by the Kaimur Range (north) and the Chota Nagpur plateau (south). The river's flow is seasonal, and the Son is unimportant for navigation. Dams have been constructed on some of its tributaries, and at Dehri, Uttar Pradesh State, are the headworks of the Son canal system.

Subarnarekha River—rising in southern Bihar State, in northeastern India, the Subarnarekha (meaning "Streak of Gold") flows east through a copper-mining region and leaves the Chota Nagpur plateau by the Hundrugbagh waterfall. Continuing eastwards, it flows across West Bengal State to enter the Bay of Bengal after a 470-km course. The Kanchi and Karkari rivers are its chief tributaries.

Surma River—also called Barak, it flows through northeastern India and eastern Bangladesh and is 900 km in length. It rises in the Manipur Hills in northern Manipur State, India, where it is called the Barak, and flows west and then southwest into Mizoram State. There it veers north into Assam State and flows west past the town of Silchar. The river next splits into two branches, the Surma (north) and the Kusiyara (south), which enter Bangladesh and turn southwest. The Surma flows past Sylhet in a rich tea-growing valley, while the Kusiyara subdivides into two more branches, both of which rejoin the Surma. At Bhairab Bazar, in east-central Bangladesh, the river enters an old channel of the Brahmaputra and becomes the Meghna River, which flows south past Dhaka (formerly Dacca) and merges with the Ganga. Steamers can navigate the river as far upstream as Silchar in the rainy season.

Sutlej River—ancient Greek Zaradros, Vedic Shatadru, it is the longest of the rivers that give the Punjab ("Land of Five Rivers") its name, rising in La'nga Co (lake) in south-western Tibet at an elevation of more than 4,600 m above sea level. It is an antecedent stream. From the lake of its origin the river takes a westerly course along the slopes of the Mount Kailash before entering the Indian State of Himachal Pradesh. Hereafter it flows through deep gorges. Successive uplifts of the mountain ranges have resulted in the formation of terraces along the Sutlej valley. After making its way through the mountainous topography of Himachal Pradesh, the river enters the Punjab near Nangal. A few kilometres above Nangal, the river has been dammed at Bhakra (Himachal Pradesh). Behind the dam a huge reservoir of water (called Gobind Sagar) has been formed. The hydroelectric power produced from the Bhakra-Nangal project supplies power not only to the Punjab but also to the adjoining States. On entering the Punjab, the river flows to the southeast through the Jaswan *dun* between two ranges of the Shiwalik Hills in Ropar district. At Ropar, it pierces through the hills and enters the plain proper. Here it takes a sharp westward turn to pursue its course through the middle of the Punjab, separating the Bist doab in the north from the Malwa in the south. At Harike the Beas River joins it. Then it adopts a southwesterly course, marking the boundary between India and Pakistan. Later it leaves India for Pakistan at some distance to the west of Fazilka. Subsequently it joins the Chenab River at some distance west of Bahawalpur. The combined rivers then form the Panjnad, the link between the "Five Rivers" and the Indus.

The Punjab owes a part of its prosperity to the Sutlej. The Bhakra dam on the Sutlej not only provides hydroelectric power but also saves large parts of the State from floods. The Nangal Barrage canal originating at Nangal, the Sirhind and the Bist doab canals starting from Ropar, the Sirhind feeder and Rajasthan canal with their source at Harike, and Bikaner canal with its headworks at Husainiwala, all derive their water from this river.

T

Tapti River—also spelt Tapi, it flows through central India, after rising in the Gawilgarh Hills of the central Deccan Plateau in south-central Madhya Pradesh State. It flows westwards between two spurs of the

Satpura Range, across the Jalgaon plateau in Maharashtra State, and through the plain of Surat in Gujarat State to the Gulf of Cambay (an inlet of the Arabian Sea). It has a total length of about 700 km and drains an area of 65,300 sq km. For the last 51 km it is tidal but is navigable by small vessels. The port of Swally, at the river's mouth, well known in Anglo-Portuguese colonial history, is now deserted, having become silted up. The Tapti flows roughly parallel to the longer Narmada River to the north, from which it is separated by the main part of the Satpura Range. The two river valleys and the intervening range form the natural barrier between northern and peninsular India. Its three major tributaries — the Purna, Girna, and Panjhra — flow from the south in Maharashtra.

Tista River—a tributary of the Brahmaputra River it flows through Sikkim (India) and Bangladesh. It rises in the Himalaya near Chunthang, Sikkim, flows south cutting a deep gorge through the Darjeeling (Darjiling) Himalaya, and turns southeast to run through Sivok Gota Pass onto the plains of West Bengal. It then crosses the Rangpur region of Bangladesh rejoin the Brahmaputra River downstream from Chilmari after a total course of 400 km. Its lower reaches are marked by frequent, violent course changes; navigation is made difficult by the shoals and quicksand near the junction with the Brahmaputra River, The Tista Barrage project is part of a programme of river projects in the Barind region to provide irrigation for the plain between the Ganga and Brahmaputra rivers,

V

Vaigai River—flows 240 km generally southeast in Tamil Nadu State of southern India. Rising in the Varushanad Hills of western Tamil Nadu, it initially flows north-east through the Kambam and Varushanad valleys. In its central reaches the Vaigai flows eastwards into the Vaigai reservoir at Narasingapuram. Near Sholavandan it bends to the southeast, passing Madurai city on its course to its mouth on Palk Strait, which separates the southeast coast of India from Sri Lanka (formerly Ceylon), The Vaigai River rarely floods. Its chief tributaries are the Similar, Theniar, Varaha Nadi, and Mangalar.

W

Wainganga River—It is a tributary of the Godavari River in western India. It means "the arrow of water". The name seems ro be derived from Ganga and Vena or Ben, a ling who ruled in Damoh during Puranic times. It rises in the Mahadeo Hills in south-central Madhya Pradesh State, from a hill near the village of Partabpur or Mundara about 28 sq km from Seoni township, on the Satpura plateau. It flows 580 km south to join the Wardha River (a headwater of the Godavari) northeast of Kagaznagar in Maharashtra State, The river makes a wide half-circle, bending and winding among the spurs of the Mahadeo Hills, in a west-to-east direction. The bed of the river is a wide stretch of sand in the plains, but rocks come up at places. After joining the Wardha and the Penganga, the river is known as Pranhita, before it finally enters the Godavari. Along this final 229 km of its course, the river known as the Pranhita forms the boundary between the States of Maharashtra and Andhra Pradesh. The Wainganga receives the waters of numerous affluents, namely Bagh in Balaghat; the Bawanthadi, Kanhan, and Chulband in Bhandara; Garhvi in Chanda; and the Thanwar in Mandla. The river flows through the districts of Seoni, Balaghat, Bhandara, and Chanda. The Wainganga River valley is forested and relatively sparsely populated, except in the northern industrial area around Nagpur city in Maharashtra State. Most of the population is concentrated along the river, where rice is extensively irrigated. Major river towns include Kamptee, Bhandara, Tumsar, Balaghat, and Pauni.

In the hot weather, the stream is normal everywhere. In the rainy season, it becomes a swollen rapid which is navigable from the confluence of the Bagh as far as Garhchiroli in Chanda. Timber is floated down it and grain and vegetables are carried short distances by boat. The drainage area of the Wainganga includes the eastern Nagpur plain comprising bulk of the districts of Seoni and Chhindwara.

Wular Lake—the largest in the Jammu and Kashmir territory, northern part of the Indian subcontinent, the lake is 16 km long and 10 km wide. It lies at the north end of the Vale of Kashmir, 32 km north-northwest of Srinagar. Its area varies from 30 sq km to 260 sq km according to the season. The lake controls the flow of the Jhelum River, which traverses it. The town of Sopur is on the southwest shore of the lake, and an island to the northeast contains fifteenth-century ruins.

Y

Yamuna River—also called Jumna in Uttar Pradesh State of north-central India, it rises in the Himalaya near Jamnotri. It flows in a southerly direction through the Himalayan foothills and onto the northern Indian plain, along the Uttar Pradesh-Haryana State border. The Eastern and Western Yamuna canals are fed from the river at that point.

The Yamuna then passes Delhi, where it feeds the Agra canal. Near Mathura it turns southeastwards and passes Agra, Firozabad, and Etawah. Below Etawah it receives a number of southern tributaries, the largest of which are the Chambal, the Sind, the Betwa, and the Ken. Near Allahabad, after a course of about 1,376 km, the Yamuna joins the Ganga River; their confluence is a sacred place for Hindus.

Traffic on the Yamuna is light. Above Agra it shrinks to a small stream in summer, partly because of the amount of water removed by the canals.

Section : THREE

LAND FORMS

A

Aksai Chin—also spelt (Pinyin) Akesaiqin, it is an isolated, inhospitable, and mostly uninhabitable plain on the northern tip of the Indian subcontinent, in the Hindu Kush and Karakoram mountain ranges. It is considered a part of Ladakh and is geographically an extension of the plateau of Tibet. It is called the White Stone Desert by the Chinese. Aksai Chin figured in the boundary discussions between India and China in 1960, and severe fighting took place in Ladakh during the 1962 Indo-China conflict.

Anai Peak—also called Anaimudi Peak in Western Ghats, southwestern India, it is the highest peak in India (2,695 m) outside the Himalayan mountain range. From this point radiate three ranges — the Anaimalai to the north, the Palni to the northeast, and the Cardamom Hills to the south. The Ghats contain a succession of hills of varying altitude. Several rivers, including the Periyar and the Amaravathi, rise in the surrounding ranges. Anai Peak is an ideal spot for trekking.

Anaimalai Hills—also called Elephant Mountains they are in Western Ghats of Tamil Nadu State in southeastern India. The Anaimalai Hills are a junction of the Eastern Ghats and Western Ghats and have a general northwest-southeast trend. Anai Peak, at 2,695 m, lies at the extreme southwestern end of the range and is the highest peak in southern India. Formed by fault-block movements in the Holocene Epoch, the Anaimalai Hills descend to form a series of terraces about 1,000 m high. Dense monsoon forests including rosewood, sandalwood, teak, and sago palm cover most of the region. The soils are mottled red and brown containing oxides of aluminium and iron and are used as building material mixed with mortar and in road construction. The Kadar, Maravar, and Pooliyar peoples inhabit the sparsely populated hills; their economy is based on hunting and gathering and on shifting cultivation. There are tea, coffee, and rubber plantations where the hills have been cleared of forests. Industries are mainly household varieties and comprise basket weaving and the making of coir and coir mat, metal articles, and *bidi* (cigarettes). Srivilliputtur, Uttamapalaiyam, and Manur are the important towns.

Annapurna—a massif of the Himalayan Range in north-central Nepal, it forms a ridge 48 km long between the basins of the Kali Gandak and Marsyandi rivers. It contains four main summits, two of which, Annapurna 1 (8,091 m) and Annapurna II (7,937 m), stand at the western and eastern ends of the range, respectively; Annapurna III (7,555 m) and Annapuma IV (7,525 m) lie between them. Annapuma I is one of the world's highest peaks. Although climbers had reached 8,580 m on Mount Everest in 1924, Annapurna I became famous in 1950 as the first peak more than 8,000 m high that was ascended to the summit. The feat was achieved by a French expedition led by Maurice Herzog, who with Louis Lachenal, reached the top on June 3. Annapurna IV was climbed on May 30, 1955, by H. Biller, H. Steinmetz, and J. Wellenkamp, and Annapurna II on May 17, 1960, by R.H. Grant and C.J. Bonington in an expedition led by James O.M. Roberts. In 1970 an all-woman Japanese climbing team scaled Annapurna III.

Aravali Range—also called Aravali Range it runs northeasterly for 560 km through Rajasthan State. Isolated rocky offshoots continue to just south of Delhi. The series of peaks and ridges, with breadths varying from 10 to 100 km are generally between 300 and 900 m in elevation. The system is divided into two sections — the Sambhar-Sirohi ranges, taller and including Guru Peak on Mount Abu (the highest peak in the Aravali Range at 1,722 m), and the Sambhar-Khetri ranges, consisting of three ridges that are discontinuous. The Aravali Range is rich in natural resources (including minerals) and serves as a check to the growth of the western desert. It gives rise to several rivers, including the Banas, Luni, Sakhi, and Sabarmati. Though heavily forested in the south, it is generally bare and thinly populated, consisting of large areas of sand and stone and of masses of rose-coloured quartzite.

Avanti—This kingdom of ancient India is within the territory of present Madhya Pradesh State. For some time it was part of the historical province of Malwa. In 600 BC the capital of Avanti was Mahismati (probably modern Godarpura on the Narmada River), but it was soon moved to Ujjayini (near modern Ujjain). The kingdom was on the overland trade routes between northern and southern India and also to those on the port of Bharukaccha (modern Bharuch) on the Arabian Sea.

By Gautama Buddha's time (c. sixth-fourth century BC) Avanti was one of the four powers of northern India. It was strong enough at that time, under King Pradyota the Fierce, to threaten the empire of Magadha. During the same period there was an Avanti-dakshinapatha (Sanskrit: "vanti of the South"), of which Mahismati may have been the capital.

In the fourth century BC, Chandra Gupta Maurya of Magadha conquered and annexed Avanti to his dominions. Ujjayini, one of the seven holy cities of the Hindus, renowned for its beauty and wealth, became a centre of early Buddhism and Jainism.

After 50 BC, with the Magadha Empire's decline, the Shungas, Andhrabhrtyas, and Shakas fought over Avanti. In the second century AD Ujjayini, under Rudradaman I, was the prosperous capital of the western Shaka satrapy. In about AD 390 Chandra Gupta II (who was also called Vikramaditya, patron of the poet Kalidasa) expelled the Shakas and held court at Ujjayini. The name of the Malava tribe (which had moved to Avanti at an uncertain date) gradually replaced that of the Avantis as the designation of this land.

Awadh—also called Oudh, it is a fertile region in the middle-Ganga valley, around Ayodhya, west of Banaras [now Varanasi]. In ancient times Awadh was known as Kosali and was an administrative unit of the Mughal Empire, ruled by the Nawabs. Lucknow was the main city and was known for its refined culture and way of life. The administration, however, was weak, and the Nawab was pressurized by the East India Company, and finally the region was annexed by Lord Dalhousie in 1856. This was perhaps the event that set off the uprising of 1857 known as the Indian Mutiny, or Sepoy Mutiny.

B

Baghelkhand—A historico-cultural region in eastern Madhya Pradesh State, central India, this plateau complex lies to the east of Bundelkhand and has a northeast-to-southeast orientation. The area is divided into two natural regions by the Kaimur Range. The entire area is drained by the Tons, and Son rivers and their tributaries. Lying in the northeast of the region, these river valleys are the only truly open and accessible part. To the west lie elevated plains; to the east is a rough, hilly tract intersected by a succession of parallel forested ridges of the Vindhya Range. Within the region, the more prominent relief features are the Vindhyan scarplands (consisting of the Bhanrer range, Rcwa plateau, Sonapur hill ranges, and the Son trough). The rest of Baghelkhand is a plateau terrain underlain by granite in the south and the east. Gondawanas and Deccan trap lies in the central part and the Vindhyans in the northeast. An alluvial cover is found in the narrow Son trough. The population of the region consists chiefly of tribal Gonds and Kols.

Known as Dahala before the Muslims, Baghelkhand was held by the warlike Kalachuri dynasty (sixth-twelfth century), whose stronghold was at Kalinjar. With the advent of the Baghela Rajputs (warrior caste) in the fourteenth century, after whom the tract is named, it was absorbed into Rewa State. Baghelkhand Agency, a subdivision of the British Central India Agency, was created in 1871 and included Rewa and several other States, with headquarters at Satna. It merged with Bundelkhand Agency in 1931 and formed the eastern half of Vindhya Pradesh, created at Indian independence in 1947.

The urban element is low, with Rewa, Rajgarh, Satna, and Shahdol as administrative and commercial centres. Other centres include Umaria, Burhar, and Gaurela, in the Sohagpur basin, with rich coal deposits and mining activities; Ambikapur, Manendragarh, and Baikunthpur, the rice bowl of the region; and Singrauli, Renukut, Pipri, and Dudhi, known for coal mining; and Obra, Dala, Sidhi, and Agori, characterized by the development of a rail and road link and thermal power generation.

Agricultural development in the region is low, with rice as the principal crop; some wheat, maize, and gram are also grown. The region has undeveloped, but rich, mineral deposits of coal, bauxite clay, and quartzite. Baghelkhand region stands neglected because of its location, economic isolation, poor peasantry that is largely tribal, and mineral resources that have not yet attracted exploitative commercial enterprise.

Balaghat Range—It is a series of hills in western Maharashtra State, western India. Originating in the Western Ghats at the Harishchandra Range, the range extends south-eastward for about 320 km to the border of Maharashtra and Karnataka States. Its width varies from 5 to 9 km. Higher in the west, the Balaghat hills have elevations of 550-825 m, gradually diminishing eastward until they end at the Bhima River. The flat-topped hills are separated by saddles, which become progressively wider towards the east. The Balaghat Range forms the watershed between the Godavari River to the north and the Bhima to the south. In the rainier west the hills bear vegetation, but they are barren and stony in the east. Shepherds occupy the entire range, and sheep trails connect the small villages and occasional hilltop temples. Traversing the Balaghat are a highway from Pune to Nasik and the railway from Dhond to Manmad.

Banihal Pass—It is a pass in the Pir Panjal Range, Jammu and Kashmir State, northern India. Banihal — a name that in Kashmiri means "blizzard" — lies at an altitude of 2,832 m in the Doda district. It forms the main gateway to the Vale of Kashmir from the Indian plains. The Jammu-Srinagar road enters the pass through the Jawahar Tunnel, which is occasionally blocked by snow in winter. Goods formerly crossed the pass on the backs of porters, who made the journev in a day.

Bhander Plateau—A plateau in Madhya Pradesh State of central India, it lies in the south central highlands. It has an area of about 10,000 sq km and constitutes a transitional zone between the North Deccan Plateau to the south, the Eastern Plateau to the east, and the alluvial stretch of the Ganga River plains to the north. The plateau is part of the Vindhya Range and is composed of fluvio-marine deposits of Cambrian age that have been uplifted and peneplained several times and are overlain by dissected sandstone. It has an average elevation of 500 m and slopes from west to east. The swift-flowing Tons and Sonar rivers have numerous falls and rapids along their courses and have cut deep gorges in the scarplands of the Vindhya.

Forests of teak and catechu trees are characteristic of the plateau. Agriculture is the basis of the economy; rice, wheat, *jowar* (sorghum), gram (chick-pea), barley, maize, peas, sesame seed, and mustard seed are grown. Although the region is rich in coal and other mineral and forest resources, the only major industrial plant is a large cement factory at Kymore (Katni town); local limestone and coal are utilized. Cottage industries produce brick and tile, stoneware, cement, glass, and shellac; flour, *dal* (pulses), and oilseeds are milled.

The plateau is a region of low population density; the only major road is the National Highway through Katni. The other important towns are Damoh, Maihar, and Hatta.

Barind—A geographic region, also called Barind Tract, it is situated in parts of northwestern Bangladesh and north-central West Bengal State of India. It lies northwest of the confluence of the Ganga (Padma) and

Brahmaputra (Jamuna) rivers and is bordered by the floodplains of the Mahananda River (west) and the Karatoya River (east), tributaries of the Ganga and of the Brahmaputra, respectively. Barind is a comparatively high, undulating region, belonging to an older alluvial formation, usually composed of massive argillaceous beds of pale reddish brown hue, often weathering into yellowish clay soils. It is cut by ravines and is divided into separate sections by the Atrai River and one of its tributaries, the Jamuna, or Little Jamuna (not to be confused with the Brahmaputra River to the east). Agricultural plots are commonly irrigated and stand between stretches of wasteland and scrub. Rice is the predominant crop, but wheat, mustard, pulses, and palmyra (*tal*) palms also are cultivated.

To the east and southeast of the Barind is the lower Atrai Basin (Bhar Basin), a vast area of lowland marshes that floods completely during the rainy season; settlements there must be raised on stilts or built on earthen mounds. The fertile soils of this region are especially suited to rice cultivation, provided water is available.

Berar—A cotton-growing region, also spelt Birar it stands in east-central Maharashtra State, western India. The region extends for approximately 320 km east-west along the Purna River basin and lies 200 to 500 m above sea level. Berar is bounded on the north by the Gawilgarh Hills (Melghat) and on the south by the Ajanta Range. Historically the name Berar was given to a province of varying extent, but it no longer has any administrative meaning, having been superseded by the term Vidarbha, though this name refers to a larger area including the Nagpur Plain and other areas of the easternmost part of Maharashtra.

Berar emerged as a distinct political entity after the incursions of Muslim armies in the thirteenth century. It formed part of several Muslim kingdoms, until on the breakup of the Mughal Empire it fell to the *nizam* of Hyderabad. It came under British control in 1853 and was administratively abolished as a province in 1948.

The southernmost reaches of Berar on the Buldhana-Yeotmal plateau are generally less developed than the rich cotton area of the Purna River basin. The region is predominantly agricultural, with half of the land under cash crops (cotton and oilseeds). Almost all industry is based on the processing of these crops. The principal cities are Amravari and Akola.

C

Cardamom Hills—A mountainous area in southeastern Kerala State, southern India it forms part of the Western Ghats range. Some of their eastern peaks are more than 1,370 m high. The Cardamom Hills region produces tea, coffee, teak, and bamboo as well as the cardamom for which it is named. Most of its produce is shipped eastward through Tamil Nadu State down the Kambam River valley. The name Cardamom Hills is sometimes used for the entire Western Ghats range south of the Palghat (Palakkad) Gap.

Chhattisgarh Plain—forming the upper Mahanadi River Basin, it is at an elevation of between 300 and 250 m above sea level. It is a structural plain with topographic variations resulting from long denudation. Knolls, undulating inierfluves, and valley courses flanked by belts of clayey soils are characteristic there. About 160 km wide, it is bounded by the Chota Nagpur plateau (north), the Maikala Range (west), the Raigarh hills (northeast), the Raipur Upland (southeast), and the Bastar plateau (south). The highlands comprise mostly erosional plateau forms reaching a height of more than 700 m in the Maikala Range and the Dandakaranya hills. The region remained isolated almost till the close of the British rule in India. It lies between the two important routes connecting the southern plateau to the northern plains, in a wild, tribal country under the control of local feudal princes (whose capital forts have given the region its name). The name Chhattisgarh ("thirty-six forts") was formerly applied to the territory of the Haihaya dynasty of Ratanpur, founded about AD 750. Under British rule, the Chhattisgarh States consisted of a subagency of 14 feudatory princely kingdoms under the Eastern States Agency. Raipur was the agency headquarters

The rich mineral resources of the region opened the way for its development, mainly after independence. Extensive coal and good deposits of iron ore, bauxite, manganese, and commercial clays aided its development. A vast, undulating tract, it consists of rich rice fields and grainfields, though it is a weak agricultural region otherwise. Rice dominates the lowlands, while maize and millet dominate the highlands. Cotton and oilseeds are the important commercial crops of the region. Modern farming techniques are slow to catch on in the basin. As one moves from the eastern and southeastern margin to the interior, the vegetation changes from dry moist deciduous to dry deciduous, often degenerating locally into scrub.

With an industrial belt and several developing industrial townships, its economic surface is modern. Bhilai, Bilaspur, Raipur, Raigarh, and Durg are the chief towns. Urban expansion has occurred along the railway line east and west of Bhilai. Korba, Nandgaon, and Rajgarh are other developing urban centres. There are belts of canal command areas. The region has a weak rural base, and the interior remains rural and undeveloped. The urban nodes hardly influence the regional tribal economy. The distance, isolation, difficult terrain, and local sentiment have led to a demand for administrative decentralization, with Raipur as the regional node.

Chota Nagpur—A plateau in Bihar State (now Jharkhand State) of eastern India, it is composed of Precambrian rocks (more than 540,000,000 years old). Chota Nagpur is the collective name for the Ranchi, Hazaribag, and Kodarma plateaus, which have an area of 65,509 sq km. Its largest division is the Ranchi Plateau, which has an average elevation of 700 m. The Chota Nagpur plateau in its entirety lies between the basins of the Ganges and Son rivers to the north and the Mahanadi River to the south. Through its centre, from west to east, runs the coal-bearing, faulted Damodar Valley. Numerous streams have dissected the uplands into a peneplain (an area reduced almost to a plain by erosion) with isolated hills.

Centuries of heavy cultivation have depleted the plateau of much of its natural vegetation, though some valuable forests still remain. Forest products, such as tussar silk and lac, are economically important. The Chota Nagpur area has the most valuable concentration of mineral resources in India. The Damodar Valley has vast coal reserves, and Hazaribagh district is one of the main sources of mica in the world. Other minerals are copper, limestone, bauxite, iron ore, asbestos, and apatite (useful in the manufacture of phosphate fertilizers). A huge thermal plant for generating electricity and a large steel mill are located at Bokaro. Railroads cross the plateau, connecting Calcutta to the southeast with Parna to the north, and also link other cities in the south and west.

Comorin, Cape—Rocky headland on the Indian Ocean in Tamil Nadu State of southeastern India, it forms the southernmost point of the subcontinent. It is the southern tip of the Cardamom Hills, an extension of the Western Ghats range along the west coast of India. The town of Kanniyakumari on the headland contains an ancient temple dedicated to Shiva, which is a much-frequented Hindu pilgrimage site. The main temple here is also dedicated to "Kanniyakumari", the virgin goddess. It is said that in this place the goddess Parvati, incarnated as Devi Kanya, did penance to woo Shiva. Unsuccessful, she vowed to remain a virgin (kanya; hence Kanniyakumari).

Coromandel Coast—This broad coastal plain in eastern Tamil Nadu State, southern India, extends over an area of about 22,800 sq km. It is bounded by the Bay of Bengal on the east, the Eastern Ghats on the west the Cauvery delta on the south, and the Utkal Plains on the north, the region derives its name from the Tamil Chola Mandalam ("Land of the Chola", an ancient dynasty that ruled the region from the middle of the ninth century AD to 1279). The coast has an average elevation of 80 m and is backed by the Eastern Ghats, a chain of low, flat-topped hills. The shoreline Is relatively straight, with several sandbars and an offshore chain of coral islands. The lower courses of the Palar, Ponnaiyar, and Cheyyar rivers and their tributaries, the Pamban and Ponnai, which rise in the Ghats, remain dry during most of the year. There is little forest cover, but marshes, swamps, scrub woodlands, and thorny thickets are common. Agriculture is the mainstay of the coastal economy; rice, pulse (legumes), sugar cane, cotton, and peanuts (groundnuts) are grown. Bananas and betel nuts are grown together with rice in the low-rainfall region of the interior. There are casuarina and coconut plantations along the coast. Large-scale industries produce fertilizers, chemicals, film projectors, amplifiers, trucks, and automobiles. There is a heavy-vehicle and armoured-car factory at Avadi and a nuclear power station at Kalapakkam. Roads and railways linking Chennai, Cuddalore, Chidambaram, Chingleput, and Pondicherry run parallel to the coast. The region has been known since ancient times as the "land of the temples" for the many temples that are located at such places as Mahabalipuram and Mamallapuram.

D

Dandakaranya—A physical region, in east-central India it extends over an area of about 92,300 sq km, and includes the Abujhmar Hills in the west and borders the Eastern Ghats in the east. The Dandakaranya includes parts of Madhya Pradesh, Orissa, and Andhra Pradesh States. It extends about 320 km from north to south and about 480 km from east to west. The region derives its name from the Dandak Forest, the abode of the demon Dandak in the Hindu epic the Ramayana. It was successively ruled by the Nalas, Vakatakas, and Chalukyas in ancient times and is the home of the Adivasi (Gond) people.

Most of the region is a sanded-over peneplain with a gradual slope from north to southwest. The Dandakaranya consists of wide, forested plateaus and hills that rise abruptly on the eastern side and gradually decrease in elevation towards the west. There are also several relatively extensive plains. It is drained by the Mahanadi River (with its tributaries, including the Tel, Jonk, Udanti, Hatiti, and Sandul) and the Godavari River (with its tributaries, including the Indiavati and Sabari). The plateaus and hillsides have a thin veneer of loamy soils; the plains and valleys have fertile, alluvial soils. The region has economically valuable moist forests of sal (*Shorea*) that occupy almost half of its total area. The economy is based on subsistence agriculture; crops include rice, pulse (legumes), and oilseeds. Industries consist of rice and dal (pigeon-pea) milling, sawmilling, bonemeal manufacturing, *bidi* (indigenous cigarette) making, beekeeping, and furniture making. There are deposits of bauxite, iron ore, and manganese. The Dandakaranya Development Authority was created by the Union (central) government in 1958 to assist the refugees from Pakistan. It constructed the Bhaskel Dam and Pakhanjore reservoir; woodworking centres at Jagdalpur, Boregaon, and Umerkote; and roads and railways in the refugee resettlement areas, including the Bolangir-Kozilum railway project. The Aero-Engine Factory, mainly producing aircraft engines, is located at Sunabeda. The National Mineral Development Corporation works iron ore at Bailadila. Important towns are Jagdalpur, Bhawanipatna, and Koraput.

Deccan—The name derives from the Sanskrit dakshina (South), and refers to the entire southern peninsula of India, south of the Narmada River. Marked centrally by a high triangular tableland, the plateau is bounded on the east and west by the Ghats. escarpments that meet at the plateau's southern tip. Its northern extremity is the Satpura mountain range. The Deccan's average elevation is about 600 m, sloping generally eastward; its principal rivers, the Godavari, Krishna, and Cauvery, flow from the Western Ghats eastward to the Bay of Bengal. The plateau's climate is drier than that on the coasts and is arid in places.

The Deccan's early history is obscure. There is evidence of prehistoric human habitation; low rainfall must have made farming difficult until the introduction of irrigation. The plateau's mineral wealth led many lowland rulers, including those of the Mauryan (fourth-second century BC) and Gupta (fourth-sixth century AD) dynasties, to fight over it. From the sixth to the thirteenth century, the Chalukya, Rashtrakuta, Later Chalukya, Hoysala, and Yadava families successively established regional kingdoms in the Deccan, but they were continually in conflict with neighbouring

States and recalcitrant feudatories. The later kingdoms also were subject to looting raids by the Muslim Delhi sultanate, which eventually gained control of the area.

In 1347, the Muslim Bahmani dynasty established an independent kingdom in the Deccan. The five Muslim States that succeeded the Bahmani and divided its territory joined forces in 1565 at the Battle of Talikota to defeat Vijayanagar, the Hindu empire to the south. For most of their reigns, however, the five successor States formed shifting patterns of alliances in an effort to keep any one State from dominating the area and, from 1656, to fend off incursions by the Mughal empire to the north. During the Mughal decline in the eighteenth century, the Marathas, the *nizam* of Hyderabad, and the Arcot *nawab* vied for control of the Deccan. Their rivalries, as well as conflicts over succession, led to the gradual absorption of the Deccan by the British. When India became independent in 1947, the Princely State of Hyderabad resisted initially but joined the Indian Union in 1948.

Deosai Mountains—part of a range in the Himalayan mountain system in the northern part of the Indian sub-continent, there mountains are located in the Pakistani-held sector of the west-central part of the State of Jammu and Kashmir. The range extends for 190 km from the Indus River bend at Bunji to the Suru (Karcha) River, which separates the range from the Zaskar Range. The main body of the Deosai massif (mountainous mass) is composed of sedimentary rock of the Precambrian Era (which occurred from 3.96 billion to 540 million years ago) combined with granite bodies of younger age. Several peaks reach elevations of more than 5,500 m. The Deosai Basin lies between mountain ranges at an elevation of 4,000 m; it possesses steep sides and a level floor and appears to be an ancient cirque (deep, steep-walled recess in a mountain, caused by glacial erosion). The terrain of the Deosai Mountains is nugged and almost devoid of human population. Sparse vegetation vies for existence with a few hardy alpine mammals such as the marmot. The Burji Pass is situated southwest of Skardu, which is one of several villages lying at the foot of the mountains.

Dhulagiri—The name of the peak is derived from two Sanskrit words meaning "white mountain". This mountain of the Himalaya stands in north-central Nepal, on the western side of the deep Kali Gandak River gorge. Many of its snow and glacier-covered peaks exceed 7,620 m, including Dhaulagiri I, II, III, and IV. At 8,167 m, Dhaulagiri I is one of the world's highest mountains. With a south wall 4,600 m high, the peaks steep sides and bitter climate prevented an ascent to the top until May 13, 1960, when a Swiss expedition led by Max Eiselin reached the summit.

Dibang Valley—Part of northeastern Arunachal Pradesh State, eastern India, the region is located in the Great Himalayan Mountain Range, with its northern and eastern reaches fronting Tibet. The Mishmi Hills, a southward extension of the Himalaya, compose most of the northern part of the region. They have an average elevation of 4,500 m and are dotted with passes such as Yonggyap at 3,950 m and Kaya at 4,750 m. The region derives its name from the Dibang River. The Dibang, together with the Ahui, Emra, Adzon, and Dri streams, flows southward to join the Brahmaputra River. Subtropical ever-green forests of oak, maple, juniper, and pine cover the hilly parts of the region. The Mishmi, Miju, ldu (Chulikatta), Khampti, and Singpho ethnic groups inhabit the region and speak dialects of the Tibeto-Burman linguistic family. Rice, maize, millet, potatoes, and cotton are grown on the terraced hill slopes and in the more level patches bordering the rivers. Barter markets are important to the regional economy; the Mishmi trade musk, beeswax, ginger, and chillies with the people of the Assam Plains to the south. Deposits of clay, graphite, limestone, and copper are worked. Cottage industries include caneworking, cloth weaving, silverworking, and blacksmithing. The system of roads in the Dibang Valley region is largely undeveloped. Most distances are travelled over simple tracks, though there are a few all-weather roads. Anini is the chief settlement in the region. The lgu, a sombre dance performed by the ldu Mishmi priests, is closely associated with the region.

Doda Betta—It is a mountain peak, highest point in Tamil Nadu State, southeastern India which rises to an elevation of 2,637 m near Uthagamandalam (Ootacamund). Doda Betta is a glass-covered hill that is frequently climbed by slimmer visitors, and the summit is accessible by automobile. It is the second highest peak in the Western Ghats.

Duars—also spelt Dwars, or Dooars, is a region of northeastern India, at the foot of the western Assam Himalaya. Its 8,800 sq km area is divided by the Sankosh River into the Western and Eastern Duars. Both were ceded by Bhutan to the British at the end of the Bhutan War (1864-1865). The Eastern Duars, in western Assam State, comprises a level plain intersected by numerous rivers and only slightly populated. The Western Duars lies in northern West Bengal State and is a portion of the Tarai, a lowland belt linking the Himalaya and the plains region. The Western Duars is an important centre of the tea industry. The name Duars (literally "doors") is derived from the several passes that lead from the region into the Lesser Himalaya.

E

East Rajasthan Uplands—Situated in southeastern Rajasthan State, northwestern India, with the Aravali Range, the uplands range in height from 250 m in the northeast to 495 m in the (southwest and form tne northern part of the Central Highlands. The east Rajasthan uplands, formed by past fluvial erosion and by geologically recent desert erosion, are bounded by the Indo-Gangetic Plain on the north, the Malwa region on the south, the Madhya Bharat plateau on the east, and the Aravali Range on the west. The uplands are wide and stony, with a sandy central region. The valleys between the hill ranges are wide and stretch for many miles; flattened hilltops form small plateaus. Teak, sal (Shorea *robusta*), and acacia trees and bamboo grow on the lower slopes of hills, and grasslands and pastures are found on the hilltops. The Banas River, rising in the eastern flank of the Aravali, is the main waterway in the highlands; the Kari, Kathari, and Banganga rivers flow eastward.

Agriculture provides the main occupation of the uplands population. Cereals, pulses (legumes), oilseeds, cotton, peanuts (groundnuts), sugar cane, and tobacco are grown. Most industries in the region are cottage industries.

Elephanta Island—about 8 km east of Mumbai (Bombay) city and island, and 3 km west of the mainland coast of Maharashtra State, western India, Elephanta Island has an area of 10-16 sq km varying with the tide. Its Hindi name, Gharapuri ("Fortress City"), derives from a small village in the south of the island. The Portuguese name refers to a large stone elephant that was later removed from the island and placed in Victoria Gardens (now called Jijamata Udyan). Elephanta is famous for its sixth-century cave temples. When it was ceded to the Portuguese by the Ikings of Ahmedabad, however, it ceased to be a place of worship, and the caves and sculptures were damaged by Portuguese soldiers. In the 1970s they were restored and preserved, and the island became a popular tourist resort. The most-celebrated of the sculptures is the Trimurti, a three-headed bust of Shiva some 6 m high.

Erramala Range—are the hills in western Andhra Pradesh State of southern India. These are situated on the Deccan plateau and are composed of quartzites and slates of the Cambrian Period (540 million to 505 million years ago) with interbedded lavas of a younger age. The range trends northeast to southwest, and tributaries of the Kunderu River have divided it into longitudinal hills and valleys.

Everest, Mount—Tibetan Chomolungma, Chinese (Wade-Giles) Chu-mu-lang-ma Feng, (Pinyin) Qomolangma Feng, Nepali Sagarmatha this peak on the crest of the Great Himalaya Range in Asia lies on the border between Nepal and China (Tibet). It is the highest point on Earth.

Physical features : Three barren ridges — the Southeast, Northeast, and West — culminate in two summits at 8,848 m (Everest) and 8,748 m (South Peak). The mountain can be seen directly from its northeastern side, where it rises about 3,600 m above the Plateau of Tibet. The lesser peaks of Changtse (north; 7,560 m), Khumbutse (northwest; 6,665 m), Nuptse (southwest; 7,861 m), and Lhotse (south; 8,501 m), which rise around its base, hide the summit from Nepal.

The mountain's drainage pattern radiates to the south-west, north, and east. The Khumbu Glacier melts into the Lobujya (Lobuche) River of Nepal, which flows southward as the lmja River to its confluence with the Dudh Kosi River In Tibet the Rong Chu River originates from the Pumori and Rongbuk glaciers, and the Karma Chu River from the Kangshung Glacier. The Rong Chu and Dudh Kosi river valleys form, respectively, the northern and southern access routes to the summit.

Individual glaciers around Mount Everest are the Kangshung Glacier (east); the East, Main, and West Rongbuk glaciers (north and northwest); the Pumori Glacier (north-west); the Khumbu Glacier (west and south); and the West Cwm, an enclosed valley of ice between Everest and the Lhotse-Nuptse Ridge.

The summit of Everest reaches up two-thirds of the way through the air of the Earth's atmosphere to where oxygen levels are low. Lack of oxygen, powerful winds, and extremely cold temperatures preclude the development of any plant or animal life on the upper slopes. Precipitation falls as snow during the summer monsoon (May-September). The flanks of the mountain are separated from each other by the main ridges; ice sheets on them cover the slopes to the mountain's base. The summit itself consists of rock-hard snow surmounted by a layer of snow that fluctuates annually by some 1.5-2 m; it is highest in September and lowest in May after depletion by the strong northwesterly winter winds.

Exploration : Attempts to climb Everest began with the opening of the Tibetan route in 1920. Seven successive attempts on the Northeast Ridge (1921-38) and three missions up the Southeast Ridge (1951-52) failed because of the combined difficulties caused by cold arid air, high winds, difficult terrain, and high altitude.

Everest was finally surmounted in 1953, as the result of efforts by an expedition sponsored by the Royal Geographical Society and the Joint Himalayan Committee of the Alpine Club. Open- and closed-circuit oxygen systems, specially insulated boots and clothing, and portable radio equipment were used by the climbers. Eight camps were established on the route that was taken up the Khumbu Icefall and Glacier, the West Cwm, and the face of Lhotse to the South Col, a rocky ridge at 8,000 m. From there, on May 29, 1953, Edmund (later Sir Edmund) Hillary of New Zealand and Tenzing Norgay of Nepal ascended the Southeast Ridge, past South Peak, to the summit.

The first successful American expedition was in 1963. James W. Whittaker and Nawang Gombu of Nepal were the First to the top (May 1). Four climbers readied the summit on May 22; one pair, Thomas F. Hornbein and William F. Unsoeld, climbed the mountain by the previously unscaled West Ridge and returned by the South Col, completing the first transverse crossing. Since then, numerous expeditions sponsored by different countries have been undertaken. Tabei Junko of Japan, accompanied by Ang Tsering of Nepal, became the first woman to reach the summit (May 16, 1975). Two British climbers first surmounted the southwest face (September 25, 1975), and two Japanese made the first ascent by the North Wall on the Tibetan side (May 11,1980).

Mount Everest is revered by local people. Its Tibetan and Nepali names mean "goddess mother of the world". Its identity as the highest point on the Earth's surface was not recognized, however, until 1852, when the governmental Survey of India established that fact. In 1865 the mountain — previously referred to as Peak XV — was renamed for Sir George Everest, British surveyor general of India from 1830 to 1843. Controversy over the exact elevation of the summit developed because of variations in snow level, gravity deviation, and light refraction. The figure currently accepted — 8,848 m (plus or minus a fraction) — was established by the Survey of India between 1952 and 1954.

G

Gandhara—a historical region, now northwestern Pakistan, it corresponds to the Vale of Peshawar having extensions into the lower valleys of the Kabul and Swat Rivers. In ancient times Gandhara was a trade crossroad and cultural meeting place between India, Central Asia, and the Middle East. The region was subject to Achaemenian Persia in the sixth and fifth centuries BC and was conquered by Alexander the Great in the fourth century BC. Thereafter it was ruled by the Maurya dynasty of India, under whom it became a centre for the spread of Buddhism to Afghanistan and Central Asia. Gandhara was then successively ruled by Indo-Greeks, Shakas, Pasthians, and Kushanas. After its conquest by Mahmud of Ghazni in the eleventh century AD, the region was held by various Muslim dynasties.

Gandhara's capital was the famous city of Taxila, which along with the city of Peshawar, was an important cultural and educational centre. From the first century BC to the sixth-seventh century AD, Gandhara was the home of a distinctive art style that was a mixture of Indian Buddhist and Greco-Roman influences.

Ganga-Yamuna Doab—A segment of the Indo-Gangetic Plain in western and southwestern Uttar Pradesh State of northeastern India, it has an area of about 60,500 sq km. It lies between the Ganga and Yamuna rivers, west of the Upper Gangetic Plain. The doab is about 800 km in length and 100 km in width and consists of a wide trough between the Great Himalaya to the north and the Deccan plateau to the south. It was formed by sediment deposited by rivers flowing southward from the Himalaya.

The doab can be divided into three sections: Upper, Middle, and Lower. The Upper Doab extends from Haridwar town on the north to Aligarh town on the south. It has a gentle slope and is crisscrossed by a number of streams. Secondary transverse slopes on older floodplains have developed in the Middle Doab. The topography flattens out in the Lower Doab, where the Sind, Betwa, and Ken streams run parallel to each other. Geologically, the whole region forms part of the alluvial Indo-Gangetic trough. Forests, occurring in patches, are composed of acacia and teak. The regional economy is dominated by agriculture based on intensive cultivation and crop rotation; crops include cereals, pulses (legumes), sugar cane, fruits, and vegetables. Livestock raising and dairy (farming is also important. The region is highly industrialized and produces refined sugar, printed calico, fans, automobile radiators, insulated wire, textile machinery, textiles, brass and copper utensils, and railroad equipment. Roads and railways link the regional centres, and there are airports at Kanpur and Allahabad. Meerut, Aligarh, Saharanpur, and Ghaziabad are other important towns. The doab is one of the most fertile and densely populated regions in India.

Garo Hills—a region in western Meghalaya State, northeastern India, it comprises the western margin of the Shillong Plateau and rises to an elevation of 1,400 m. Drained by various tributaries of the Brahmaputra River, it has extremely high rainfall and is heavily forested. The region has an agricultural economy, with rice, cotton, sal, bamboo, and lac as the principal products. Large quantities of coal and limestone have been found, as has some petroleum. The region's clans practise a complex matrilineal social system. The population is mainly Garo.

Ghats—are the two mountain ranges which form the eastern and western edges, respectively, of the Deccan plateau of peninsular India. In Hindi ghat means "river landing stairs", or "mountain pass", and has been extended in its anglicized plural form (formerly "ghauts") to include the mountains themselves. The word refers as well to river-banks that have been artificially terraced for bathing, for religious purposes, and also to ferry landings.

The two mountain ranges, respectively, run roughly parallel to the Bay of Bengal and Arabian Sea coasts, from which they are separated by strips of fairly level coastal land. The Eastern Ghats include several unconnected and dissimilar hill masses, with an average height of about 600 m and peaks reaching 1,200 m and higher. There is a gap in the chain, 160 km wide, through which the Krishna and Godavari rivers reach the coast. The mountains' slopes have sparse forests containing valuable timber.

The *Western Ghats*, which are possibly a fault scarp, are the crest of the western edge of the Deccan plateau. Their steep seaward slopes are deeply dissected by streams and canyonlike valleys, but on the landward side their slopes are gentle and give way to wide, mature valleys. The range extends northwards to the Tapti River and southwards almost to Cape Comorin at India's southern tip. The mountains reach elevations of between 914 and 1,524 m in the north, less than 914 m in the area south of Goa, and are higher again in the far south, reaching 2,637 m at Doda Betta mountain. The Palghat (Palakkad) Gap separates the Western Ghats proper from their southward extension, known as the Southern

Ghais. The Western Ghats, because they receive extremely heavy rainfall from the southwest monsoon, comprise peninsular India's principal watershed; rainfall is much lighter inland on the plateau. The high rainfall has produced dense forests on the seaward slopes, with bamboo, teak, and other valuable trees. Some rivers among the Western Ghats have been dammed to produce electric power. A number of hill resorts are also located in the mountains.

The *Eastern Ghats* are a series of discontinuous low ranges running generally northeast-southwest and parallel to the coast of the Bay of Bengal. The largest single sector — the remnant of an old mountain range that eroded and subsequently rejuvenated — 'is found in the Dandakaranya region between the Mahanadi and Godavari rivers. This narrow range has a central ridge, the highest peak of which is Arma Konda (1,680 m) in Andhra Pradesh. The hills become subdued farther southwest, where they are traversed by the Godavari River through a goige 64 km long. Still farther southwest, beyond the Krishna River, the Eastern Ghats appear as a series of low ranges, including the Erramala, Nallamala, Velikonda, and Palkonda. Southwest of the city of Chennai, the Eastern Ghats continue as the Javadi and Shevaroy hills, beyond which they merge with the Western Ghats.

Gir Range—a low mountain range in western Gujarat Stare, west-central India, on the southern Kathiawar peninsula, it is extremely rugged with a steep slope seawards to the south and a gradual slope inland to the north. From it (to) the north runs a low, narrow, dissected range rising to Gorakhnath (1,117 m), believed to be an extinct volcano, in the broad mass of the Girnar Hills. The Gir Range is considered to be sacred because of the ancient Jain temple of Girnar (historically called Raivata, or Ujjayanta) situated on one of the hills; the temple is a major place of pilgrimage. The range is covered by forests, including sal (Shorea) and dhak (*Butea frondosa*) trees.

The Bhadar, Rohza, Shatarant, and Ghelo rivers flow west and east from the Girnar Hills. The hills are inhabited mainly by the Bhil and Dubla peoples. The economy of this sparsely populated region is dominated by subsistence agriculture; crops include cereals, peanuts (groundnuts), and cotton. A few large-scale industries manufacture textiles and iron and steel furniture. Cottage industries include carpentry, wood carving, lacquer ware, embroidery (particularly the widely known Kathiawari pattern), and wool weaving. The Gir Forest National Park, noted for its Asiatic lion, is located in the region. Khambalia, Dhari, Visvadar, Mendarda, and Adityana are the important towns.

Girnar Hills—a region of the Kathiawar peninsula in Gujarat State of west-central India, the hills are composed of gabbros and allied basic intrusive locks. Hills rise abruptly from the trap-built plateau of Saurashtra. At the foot of one of the hills is a cock bearing one of the edicts of the Maurya emperor, Ashoka (third century Br. The same rock bears an inscription referring to the construction of a lake, called Sudarshana, by the Maurya emperor Chandra Gupta (late fourth century BC). In the hills surrounding these two important historical records are numerous Jain temples built by kings of the Solanki dynasty (c. 961-1242).

H

Harishchandra Range—eastward-extending spur of the Western Ghats, west-central India, the range lies between the Godavari and the Bhima rivers in the northwestern Deccan plateau. With an average elevation of about 600 m, its peaks decrease in height gradually to the southeast and comprise parts of Maharashtra State. The range is flat-topped, consisting of basaltic lava, and the slopes of the hills have weathered to form terraces corresponding to the direction of the lava flow. The range attains higher elevations in the west until it merges into the Western Ghats. The range is named for the Harishchandragarh, its highest peak. Forests of hardwood including teak (covered with climbing vines) are found on its slopes. The undergrowth consists of tangled masses of cane, bamboo, climbing vines, and ferns. Ahamadnagar is the chief town in the area.

Himalaya—(Sanskrit: *hima*, "snow"; *alaya*, "abode"), also spelt Himalayas, it is the great mountain system of Asia, forming a barrier between the Tibetan Plateau to the north and the alluvial plains of the Indian subcontinent to the south. The Himalayan range includes the highest mountains in the world, above the line of perpetual snow, with more than 110 peaks rising to elevations of 7,300 m or more above sea level. One of these peaks, the world's highest, is Mount Everest (Tibetan: Chomolungma; Chinese [Wade-Giles romanization]: Chu-mu-lang-ma Feng; Pinyin: Zhumulangma; Nepali: Sagarmatha), reaching height of 8,848 m.

Forming the northern border of the Indian subcontinent and an almost impassable barrier to the lands to the north, the range is part of a great mountain belt that stretches halfway around the world from North Africa to the Pacific coast of Southeast Asia. The Himalayan range stretches uninterruptedly for about 2,500 km from west to east between Nanga Parbat (8,126 m), in the region of Jammu and Kashmir, and Namcha Barwa (7,756 m), in Tibet. Between these eastern and western extremities lie the two Himalayan kingdoms of Nepal and Bhutan. The Himalaya are bordered to the northwest by the mountain ranges of the Hindu Kush and Karakoram and to the north by the high Plateau of Tibet. The width of the Himalaya from south to north varies between 201 and 402 km. Its total area is approximately 594,400 sq km.

For thousands of years the Himalaya have exerted a personal and profound effect on the peoples of South Asia, as reflected in their literature, politics, economies, as well as their mythologies and religions. The vast glacial heights long attracted the attention of the pilgrim mountaineers of ancient India, who coined the Sanskrit name for this great mountain system. In modern times the Himalaya have constituted the greatest attraction and the greatest challenge to mountaineers throughout the world.

Physical features : The Himalayan ranges can be grouped into four parallel, longitudinal mountain belts of varying width, each having distinct physiographic features and its own geologic history. They are designated, from south to north, as the Outer, or Sub, Himalaya; the Lesser, or Lower, Himalaya; the Great, or Higher, Himalaya; and the Tethys, or Tibetan, Himalaya. Farther north lie the Trans-Himalaya in Tibet proper, eastward continuations of some of the most northerly Himalayan ranges. From west to east the Himalaya is divided broadly into three mountainous regions: western, central, and eastern.

The most characteristic features of the Himalaya are its soaring heights, steep sided jagged peaks, valleys, and Alpine glaciers, often of stupendous size, topography deeply cut by erosion, seemingly unfathomable river gorges, complex geologic structure, and a series of elevational belts (or zones) that display different ecological associations of flora, fauna, and climate. Viewed from the south, the Himalaya appears as a gigantic crescent with the main axis rising above the snow line, where snowfields. Alpine glaciers, and avalanches all feed lower-valley glaciers that, in turn, constitute the sources of most of the Himalayan rivers. The greater part of the Himalaya, however, lies below the snow line. The mountain-building process that created the range is still active and is accompanied by considerable stream erosion and by massive landslides.

Geological history : The Himalayan range is part of the string of Eurasian mountain ranges from the Alps to the mountains of Southeast Asia that were formed within the past 65 million years by global plate-tectonic forces that produced tremendous upheavals in the earth's crust.

Some 180 million years ago, during the Jurassic Period, when a deep geosynclinal trench — the Tethys Ocean — bordered the entire southern fringe of .Eurasia, the old supercontinent of Gondwana (or Gondwanaland) began to break up. One of Gondwana's fragments, the lithospheric plate that formed the Indian subcontinent, pursued a northward collision course with the Eurasian Plate during the ensuing 130 million years; this Indian-Australian Plate gradually confined the Tethys trench within a giant pincer between itself and the Eurasian Plate. As the Tethys trench narrowed, increasing compressive forces triggered many tectonic swells, depressions, and interlacing faults in its marine sediments, and masses of granites and basalts intruded from the depth of the mantle into this weakened sedimentary crust. Early in the Ternary Period (about 50 million years ago), India finally collided with Eurasia. India was sheared downward, or subducted, beneath the Tethys tertiary at an ever-increasing pitch.

During the next 30 million years, shallow parts of the Tethys sea gradually drained as its sea bottom was pushed up by the plunging Indian Australian Plate; this formed the Plateau of Tibet. On the plateau's southern edge, marginal mountains — the Trans-Himalayan ranges of today — became the region's first major watershed and rose high enough to become a climatic barrier. As heavier rains fell on the steepening southern slopes, the major southern rivers eroded northwards toward the headwaters with increasing force along old transverse faults and captured the streams flowing onto the plateau, thus laying the foundation for today's drainage patterns. To the south, old estuaries of the Arabian Sea and the Bay of Bengal rapidly filled with debris carried down by the ancient Indus, Ganga, and Brahmaputra rivers. The extensive erosion and deposition continue even now as these rivers carry immense quantities of material every day.

Finally, some 30 million years ago, during the Miocene Epoch, the tempo of the crunching union between the two plates increased sharply, and Himalayan mountain building began in earnest. As the Indian sub-continental plate continued to plunge beneath the Tethys trench, the topmost layers of old Gondwana metamorphic rocks peeled back over themselves for a long horizontal distance to the south, forming nappes. Wave after wave of nappes was thrust southward over the Indian landmass for as far as 97 km. Each new nappe consisted of Gondwana rocks older than the last. In time these nappes became folded, contracting the former trench by some 402 horizontal km (some authorities suggest 805 km). All the while, downcutting rivers matched the rate of uplift, carrying vast amounts of eroded material from the rising Himalaya to the plains where it was dumped by the Indus, Ganga, and Brahmaputra rivers. The weight of this sediment created depressions, which in turn could hold more sediment. In some places the alluvium beneath the Gangetic plain now exceeds 7,620 m.

Only within the past 600,000 years, during the Pleistocene Epoch (1.6 million to 10,000 years ago), did the Himalaya become the highest mountain range on earth. If strong horizontal thrusting characterized the Miocene and Pliocene epochs (23.7 to 1.6 million years ago), intense uplift epitomized the Pleistocene. Along the core zone of the northernmost nappes — and just beyond — crystalline rocks containing new gneiss and granite intrusions emerged to produce the staggering crests seen today. On a few peaks, like Mount Everest, old fossil-bearing Tethys sediments from the north were carried piggyback to the summits by the crystalline rocks.

Once the Great Himalaya became the climatic barrier, the marginal mountains to the north were deprived of rain and became as parched as the plateau of Tibet. In contrast, on the wet southern flanks the rivers surged with such erosive energy that they forced the crest line to slowly migrate northwards. Simultaneously, the great transverse rivers breaching the Himalaya continued their downcutting in pace with the uplift. Changes in the landscape, however, compelled all but these major rivers to reroute their lower courses because, as the northern crests rose, so also did the southern edge of the great nappes. The formations of the Shiwalik Series were overthrust and folded, and in between the Lesser Himalaya downwarped to shape the midlands. Now barred from flowing due south, most minor rivers ran east or west through structural weaknesses in the midlands until they could break through the new southern barrier or join a major torrent.

In some valleys, like the Vale of Kashmir and the Kathmandu valley of Nepal, lakes formed temporarily and then filled with Pleistocene deposits. After drying up some 200,000 years ago, the Kathmandu valley rose at least 198m, an indication of localized uplift within the Lesser Himalaya.

Physiography : The Outer Himalaya comprise flat-floored structural valleys and the Shiwalik hills, which border the Himalayan mountain system to the south. Except for small gaps in the east, the Shiwalik run for the entire length of the Himalaya with a maximum width of 100 km in the Indian State of Himachal Pradesh. In general, the 274 m contour line marks their southern boundary; they rise to another 762 m to the north. The main Shiwalik range has steeper southern slopes facing the Indian plains and descends gently northwards to flat-floored basins, called *duns*. The best known of these is the Dehra Dun, in Uttarakhand, which is in the mountainous part of Uttar Pradesh.

To the north, the Shiwalik range abuts an 80-km-wide massive mountainous tract, the Lesser Himalayas, where mountains rising to 4,572 m and valleys with altitudes of 914 m run in different directions. There is a general conformity of altitude among neighbouring summits, which creates the appearance of a highly dissected plateau. The three principal ranges of the Lesser Himalaya — the Nag Tibba, the Dhaola Dhar, and the Pir Panjal — have branched off from the Great Himalayan Range lying farther north. The Nag Tibba, the most easterly of the three ranges, is some 8,169 m high near its eastern end, in Nepal, and forms the watershed between the Ganga and Yamuna rivers, in Uttarakhand.

To the west the picturesque Vale of Kashmir, a structural basin (an elliptical basin in which the rock strata are inclined towards a central point), forms an important section of the Lesser Himalaya.

It extends from southeast to northwest for over 160 km, with a width of 80 km, and has an average elevation of 1,554 m; the basin is traversed by the meandering Jhelum River, which runs through Wular Lake, a large freshwater lake in the State of Jammu and Kashmir.

The backbone of the entire mountain system is the Great Himalayan Range, rising above the line of perpetual snow. The range reaches its maximum height in Nepal; among the peaks are 9 of the 14 highest in the world, each of which exceeds 7,925 m in elevation. From west to east they are: Dhaulagiri I, Annapurna I, Manaslu I, Cho Oyu, Gyachung Kang I, Mount Everest, Lhotse, Makalu I, and Kanchenjunga 1.

Farther east, the range changes from a southeasterly to an easterly direction as it enters Sikkim, an old Himalayan kingdom now a part of India. After this, it runs eastward for another 418 km through Bhutan and the eastern part of Arunachal Pradesh State as far as the peak of Kangto (7,090 m) and finally turns northeast, terminating in Namcha Barwa.

There is no sharp boundary between the Great Himalaya and the ranges, plateaus, and basins lying to the north generally grouped together under the name of the Tethys Himalaya and extending far northwards into Tibet. In Kashmir and in Himachal Pradesh, the Tethys are at their widest, forming the Spiti Basin and the Zaskar Mountains, the highest peaks of which, to the southeast, are Leo Pargial (6,791 m), rising north of the Sutlej River opposite Shipki Pass, and Shilla (7,026 m).

Drainage : The Great Himalayas, which normally would form the main water divide throughout their entire length, function as such only in limited areas. This situation exists because the major Himalayan rivers, such as the Indus, Brahmaputra, Sutlej, and at least two headwaters of the Ganga — the Alaknanda and Bhagirathi — are older than the mountains they traverse. It is believed that the Himalaya were uplifted so slowly that the old rivers had no difficulty in continuing to flow through their channels and, with the rise of the Himalaya, even acquired a greater momentum, which enabled them to cut their valleys more rapidly. The elevation of the Himalaya and the deepening of the valleys thus proceeded simultaneously, with the result that the mountain ranges emerged with a completely developed river system cut into deep transverse gorges that range in depth from 1,524 to 4,877 m and in width from 10 to 48 km. The earlier origin of the drainage system explains the peculiarity that the major rivers drain not only the southern slopes of the Great Himalaya but, to a large extent, its northern slopes as well, the water divide being north of the crest line.

The Himalayas are drained by 19 major rivers, of which the Indus and the Brahmaputra are the largest, each having catchment basins of about 259,000 sq km in extent, in the mountains. Of the other rivers, five belong to the Indus system—Jhelum, Chenab, Ravi, Beas, and Sutlej—with a total catchment area of about 132,090 sq km; nine belong to the Ganga system — the Ganga, Yamuna, Ramganga, Kali (Sarda), Karnali, Rapti, Gandak, Baghmati, and Kosi — draining another 217,560 sq km; and three belong to the Brahmaputra system — the Tista, Raidak, and Manas — draining another 183,890 sq km.

The major Himalayan rivers rise north of the mountain ranges and flow through deep gorges that generally reflect some geologic structural control. The rivers of the Indus system as a rule follow northwesterly courses, whereas most of those of the Ganga-Brahmaputra systems take easterly courses while flowing through the mountain region.

To the north of India, the Karakoram Range, with the Hindu Kush range on the west and the Ladakh Range on the east, forms the great water divide, shutting off the Indus system from the rivers of Central Asia. The counterpart of this divide on the east is formed by the Kailash Range and its eastward continuation, the Nianqing Tanggula Mountains, which prevent the Brahmaputra from flowing northward. South of this divide, the Brahmaputra flows to the east for about 1,448 km before cutting across the Great Himalayan Range in a transverse gorge, although many of its Tibetan tributaries flow in the opposite direction, as the Brahmaputra may once have done.

The role of the Great Himalayan Range as a watershed, nevertheless, can be seen between the Sutlej and Indus valleys for 579 km; the drainage of the northern slopes is carried by the north-flowing Zaskar and Dras rivers, which drain into the Indus. Glaciers also play an important role in draining the higher altitudes and in feeding the Himalayan rivers. Several glaciers occur in Uttarakhand, of which the largest, Gangotri, is 32 km long and is one of the sources of the Ganga River. The Khumbu Glacier drains the Everest region in Nepal and is one of the most popular routes for the ascent of the mountain. The rate of movement of the Himalayan region glaciers varies considerably, in the Karakoram Range, for example, the Baltoro Glacier moves about 2 m per day, while others, such as the Khumbu, move only about 30 cm daily. Most of the Himalayan glaciers are in retreat.

Soils : Not much is known about the Himalayan soils. The north-facing slopes generally have a fairly thick soil cover, supporting dense forests at lower altitudes and grasses higher up. The forest soils are dark brown in colour and silt loam in texture and occur mainly in Uttarakhand; they are ideally suited for growing fruit trees. The mountain meadow soils are well developed but vary in thickness and in their chemical properties. Some of the wet, deep, upland soils of this type in the eastern Himalaya— for example, in the Darjeeling hills and in the Assam valley — have a high humus content that is good for growing tea. Podzolic soils (infertile, acidic forest soils) occur in a belt some 644 km long in the valleys of the Indus River and its tributary the Shyok River, to the north of the Great Himalayan Range, and in patches in Himachal Pradesh State. Farther east, saline soils occur in the dry high plains of the Ladakh region. Of the soils that are not restricted to any particular area, alluvial soils (deposited by running water) are the most productive, though they occur in limited areas, such as the Vale of Kashmir, Dehra Dun, and the high terraces flanking the Himalayan valleys. Lithosols, consisting of imperfectly weathered rock fragments that are deficient in humus content, cover many large areas at high altitudes and are the least productive soils.

Climate : The Himalaya, as a great climatic divide affecting large systems of air and water circulation, exercise a dominating influence upon meteorological conditions in the Indian subcontinent to the south and in the Central Asian highlands to the north. By virtue of its location and stupendous height, the Great Himalayan Range obstructs the passage of cold continental air from the north into India in winter and also forces the southwestern monsoonal (rain-bearing) winds to give up most of their moisture before crossing the range northwards, thus causing heavy amounts of precipitation (both rain and snow) on the Indian side but arid conditions in Tibet. The average annual rainfall on the south slopes varies between 1,530 mm at Shimla and Mussoorie in the western Himalaya and 3,048 mm at Darjeeling in the eastern Himalaya. North of the Great Himalaya, at places such as Skardu, Gilgit, and Leh in the Kashmir portion of the Indus valley, only 76 to 152 mm of rainfall occurs.

Local relief and location determine the meteorological variations experienced not only in different parts of the Himalaya but even on different slopes of the same range. Because of its favourable location on top of the Mussoorie range facing Dehra Dun, the town of Mussoorie, for example, at an altitude of about 1,859 m, receives 2,337 mm of rainfall annually as against 1,575 mm recorded in the town of Shimla, which lies some 145 km to the northwest behind a series of ridges reaching 2,012 m elevation. The eastern Himalaya, which is at a lower latitude than the western Himalaya, is relatively warmer; the lowest minimum temperature recorded was at Shimla, -25°C. The average minimum temperature for the month of May, recorded in Darjeeling at an elevation of 1,945 m, is 11 °C. In the same month, at an altitude of 5,029 m in the neighbourhood of Mount Everest, the minimum temperature is about -8°C; at 5,944 m it falls to - 22°C, the lowest minimum being -29°C; during the day, in areas sheltered from strong winds that often blow at more than 161 km an hour, the sun is often pleasantly warm, even at such high altitudes.

There are two periods of wet weather: the winter rains and the rains brought by the southwestern monsoon winds. Winter precipitation results from low-pressure weather systems advancing into India from the west, which cause heavy snowfall. Within the regions where western disturbances are felt, condensation occurs in upper air levels at a height of 3,048 m from the surface; as a result, precipitation is much greater over the high mountains. It is during this season that snow accumulates on the high peaks of the Himalaya, and the western Himalaya receives more precipitation than the eastern Himalaya. In January, for example, Mussoorie in the west receives almost 76 mm of precipitation, while Darjeeling to the east receives less than 25 mm. By the end of May the meteorological conditions are reversed. Southwestern monsoon currents passing over the eastern Himalaya drop precipitation to elevations of 5,486 m; in June, therefore, Darjeeling receives about 610 mm and Mussoorie less than 203 mm. The rains cease in September, after which the finest weather in the Himalaya prevails until the beginning of winter in December.

Plant life : Himalayan vegetation can be broadly classified into four zones — tropical, subtropical, temperate, and Alpine — based mainly on altitude and rainfall. Local differences in relief and climate, as well as exposure to sunlight and wind, cause considerable variation in the composition of the vegetation within each zone.

Tropical evergreen rainforest is confined to the humid foothills of the eastern and central Himalaya. The evergreen dipterocarps — a group of timber- and resin-producing trees — are common; their different species grow on different soils and on hill slopes of varying steepness. Ironwood (*Mesua ferrea*) is found on porous soils at altitudes between 183 and 732 m; bamboos grow on steep slopes; oaks and chestnuts grow on the lithosol covering sandstones from Arunachal Pradesh State westward to central Nepal at altitudes from 1,097 to 1,737 m. Alder trees are found along the watercourses on the steeper slopes. At higher elevations they are succeeded by mountain forests in which the typical evergreen is *Pandanus furcatus*, a type of screw pine. Besides these trees, some 4,000 species of flowering plants, of which 20 are palm, are estimated to occur in the eastern Himalaya.

With decreasing rainfall and increasing altitude westward, the rainforests give way to tropical deciduous forests, where the valuable timber tree sal (Shorea robusta) is the dominant species; sal thrives best on high plateaus at elevations of 914 m (wet sal), as well as higher up, at 1,372 m (dry sal). Farther to the west, steppe forest (forest on an extensive plain), steppe, subtropical thorn steppe, and subtropical semi-desert vegetation occur successively.

Temperate forests extend from about 1,372 to roughly 3,353 m and contain conifers and broad-leaved temperate trees. Evergreen forests of oaks and conifers have their westernmost outpost on the hills above

Murree, some 48 km northwest of Rawalpindi, in Pakistan. These forests are typical of the Lesser Himalaya, being conspicuous on the outer slopes of the Pir Panjal, in Kashmir, in India. Chir pine (Pinus roxburghü) is the dominant species at altitudes from 823 to 1,646 m. In the inner valleys this species may occur even up to 1,920 m. Deodar cedar, a highly valued endemic species, grows mainly in the western part of the range. Stands of this species occur between 1,920 and 2,743 m and also tend to grow at still higher altitudes in the upper valleys of the Sutlej and the Ganga rivers. Of the other conifers, blue pine and spruce first appear between about 2,225 and 3,048 m.

The Alpine zone begins above the tree line, between altitudes of 3,200 and 3,566 m, and extends up to about 4,176 m in the western Himalaya and 4,450 m in the eastern Himalaya. In this zone can be found all the wet and moist Alpine vegetation. Juniper is widely distributed, preferring sunny sites, Steep and rocky slopes, and drier areas; on Nanga Parbat it is found even at an altitude of 3,886 m. Rhododendron occurs everywhere but more abundantly in the wetter parts of the eastern Himalaya, where it grows in all sizes from trees to low scrubs. Mosses and lichens grow in shaded areas at lower levels where the humidity is high; flowering plants are found at high altitudes, especially on Nanga Parbat and Mount Everest.

Animal life : The animal life of the eastern Himalaya is derived mainly from that of the southern Chinese and Indo-Chinese region: primarily the type of fauna found in tropical forests and only secondarily adapted to the subtropical, mountain, and temperate conditions prevailing at higher altitudes and in the drier western areas. The animal life of the western Himalaya, however, has more affinities with that of the Mediterranean, Ethiopian, and Turkmenian regions. The past presence in the region of some African animals, such as the giraffe and the hippopotamus, can be inferred from fossil remains in the Shiwalik deposits of the Outer Himalaya. The animal life at altitudes above the tree line consists almost exclusively of endemic species, adapted to the cold, that evolved from the wildlife of the steppes after the uplift of the Himalaya.

Elephants, bison, and rhinoceroses are restricted to certain areas of the forested Tarai region — moist or marshy areas, now largely drained— at the base of the low hills in southern Nepal. The Indian rhinoceros was once abundant throughout the foothill zone of the Himalaya but is now near extinction; the musk deer and the Kashmir stag, or *hangul*, are also on the point of extinction. The Himalayan black bear, the clouded leopard, the langur monkey (a long-tailed Asian monkey), and species of the cat family are some of the other denizens of the Himalayan forests. Himalayan goats, and antelopes such as the tahr, also are found.

Fish of the genus Glyptothorax live in most of the Himalayan streams, on the banks of which is found the Himalayan water shrew. Lizards of the genus Japalura are widely distributed. Typhlops, a genus of blind snake, is common in the eastern Himalaya. The butterflies of the Himalaya are extremely varied and beautiful, especially of the genus Troides.

At higher altitudes above the tree line, the snow leopard, the brown bear, the red panda, and the Tibetan yak can be seen occasionally. The yak has been domesticated and is used as a beast of burden in Ladakh The typical inhabitants above the tree line, however, are diverse typ of insects, spiders, and mites, which are the only animal forms that can live as high up as 6,309 m.

The birdlife is equally rich but is more in evidence in the east than in the west. In Nepal alone almost 800 species have been observed. Among some of the common Himalayan birds are different species of magpie (including the black-rumped, the blue, and the racket-tailed), titmouse, chough (related to the jackdaw), whistling thrush, and redstart. A few strong fliers, such as the lammergeicr (bearded vulture), the black-cared kite, and the Himalayan griffon (an Old World vulture), also can be seen. The snow partridge and the Cornish chough are found at elevations of 5,669 m.

The people : For some 200 years Sikkim and Bhutan have been the safety valves for the absorption of the excess population of eastern Nepal. More Sherpa (mountain-dwelling people of Nepal and Sikkim) now live in the Darjeeling area than in the Mount Everest homeland. The Pahari ("people of the hills") come in from Nepal to the Sikkim region of India and to the kingdom of Bhutan. Thus, the people of Sikkim belong to three distinct ethnic groups — the Lepcha, the Bhutia, and the Pahari. Generally, the Nepalese and the Lepchas live in western Bhutan, and the Bhutia, of Tibetan origin, in eastern Bhutan.

Arunachal Pradesh is the homeland of several groups — the Abor or Adi, Aka, Apa Tani, Dafla, Khampti, Khowa, Mishmi, Momba, Miri, and Singpho Ethnically, these groups are all Indo-Asiatic; linguistically, they are Tibeto-Burman. Each group lives in a distinct river valley, practising shifting cultivation (constantly changing the land on which they rise crops).

The Champa, Ladakhi, Balti, and Dard peoples live to the north of the Great Himalayan Range in the Kashmir Himalaya. The Dard are Indo-

European, while the others are Tibeto-Burman. The Champa lead a nomadic pastoral life in the upper Indus valley. The Ladakhi have settled on terraces and alluvial fans flanking the Indus in Kashmir. The Balti have spread farther down the Indus valley and have adopted Islam.

Of the four principal ethnic groups in the Indian subcontinent —Indo European, Tibeto-Burman, Austro-Asiatic, and Dravidian — the first two are well represented in the Himalaya, although they are mixed in varying proportions in different areas. Their distribution is the result of a long history of penetrations by European groups from the west, Indian peoples from the south, and Asiatic tribes from the east and the north. In Nepal, which constitutes the middle third of the Himalaya, these groups overlapped and intermingled. The penetrations of the lower Himalaya were instrumental to the migrations into and through the river-plain passageways of South Asia. Generally speaking, the Great Himalaya and the Tethys Himalaya are inhabited by Tibetans and other Tibeto-Burman peoples, while the Lesser Himalaya are the home of the tall, fair Indo-Europeans. In the Outer Himalayan region of Jammu and Kashmir, the Indo-Europeans are called the Dogri dynasty. In the Vale of Kashmir the same group is represented by the Kashmiri people. The Gaddi and Gujari, who live in the hilly areas of the Lesser Himalaya, also belong to the European group. The Gaddi are essentially a hill people; they possess large flocks of sheep and herds of goats and come down with the animals from their snowy abode in the Outer Himalaya only in winter, returning again to the highest pastures in June. The Gujari are a migrating, pastoral people who live off their herds of sheep, goats, and a few cattle, for which they seek pasture at various altitudes.

Economic Resources : Economic conditions in the Himalaya are fitted to the limited resources available in this expansive and heterogeneous region of varied ecological zones. The principal activity is animal husbandry, but the exploitation of the wild biota and trade are also important. The Himalaya abound in economic resources. These include rich arable land, extensive grassland and forest, workable mineral deposits, and easily harnessable hydropower. The most productive arable lands in the western Himalaya are in the Vale of Kashmir, the Kangra Valley, the Sudej River basin, and the terraces flanking the Ganga and Yamuna rivers in Uttarakhand; these areas produce rice, maize, wheat, and millet. In the central Himalaya in Nepal two-thirds of the arable land is in the foothills and on the adjacent plains; this land yields most of the total rice production of the country. The region also produces large crops of corn, wheat, potatoes, and sugarcane.

Most of the fruit orchards of the Himalaya lie in the Vale of Kashmir and in the Kullu Valley of Himachal Pradesh. Fruits such as apples, peaches, pears, and cherries — for which there is a great demand in the cities of India - are grown extensively. There are rich vineyards on the shores of the Dal Lake in Kashmir, which produce good-quality grapes from which wine and brandy are made. On the hills surrounding the Vale of Kashmir grow walnut and almond trees, the nuts of which are used to extract oil. Bhutan also has fruit orchards and exports oranges to India.

Of the plantation crops, tea is grown mainly on the hills and on the plains at the foot of the mountains in the Darjeeling district. Tea in limited quantity is also grown in the Kangra Valley. Plantations of cardamom are to be found in Sikkim, Bhutan, and the Darjeeling Hills. Medicinal herbs are grown in plantations in the Uttarkashi and Pithoragarh districts of Uttarakhand.

Transhumance (the seasonal migration of livestock) is practised widely during the summer months in the Himalayan pastures, called *margs*, in Kashmir. Sheep, goats, and yaks are raised on the rough grazing lands available.

The Himalaya is rich in minerals, although exploitation is restricted to the more accessible areas. Jammu and Kashmir is the region with the greatest concentration of minerals. Sapphires are found in the Zanskar Mountains, and alluvial gold is recovered in the nearby bed of the Indus River. There are deposits of copper ore in Baltistan, and iron ores are found in the Vale of Kashmir. Ladakh contains borax and sulphur deposits. Coal seams are found in the Jammu hills. Bauxite also occurs in Jammu and Kashmir. Nepal, Bhutan, and Sikkim have extensive deposits of coal, mica, gypsum, and graphite and ores of iron, copper, lead, and zinc.

The Himalayan rivers have a tremendous potential for hydroelectric generation, which has been harnessed intensively in India since the 1950s. A giant multi-purpose project is located at Bhakra-Nangal on the Sutlej River in the Outer Himalaya. Completed in 1963, its reservoir has a storage capacity of some 10 billion cubic m of water and a total installed generating capacity of 1,050 MW. Three other Himalayan rivers, the Kosi, Gandak (Narayani), and Jaldhaka, have been harnessed by India, which then supplies electric power to Nepal and Bhutan.

The explosive population growth that has occurred in the Himalaya since the 1940s has placed great strain on the forests in many areas. The resulting deforestation to make room for agriculture and for firewood has progressed up the steeper and higher slopes of the Lesser Himalaya, triggering environmental degradation. Only in Sikkim and Bhutan are large areas still heavily forested.

Transportation : Road transport has become well-established in the region, making the Himalaya accessible from both north and south. In Nepal an east-west highway stretches through the Tarai lowlands, connecting roads that penetrate into many of the country's catchment basins. The capital of Kathmandu is connected to Pokhara by a low Himalayan highway, and another highway through Kodari Pass gives Nepal access to Lhasa in Tibet. To the northwest in Pakistan, a highway links that country with China. The Hindustan-Tibet road, which passes through Himachal Pradesh, has been considerably improved; this 483-km highway runs through Shimla, once the summer capital of India, and connects the Punjab plains with the Indo-Tibetan border near Shipki Pass. From Manali in the Kullu Valley a highway now crosses not only the Great Himalaya but also the Zaskar Range and reaches Leh in the upper Indus valley. Leh is also connected to India via Srinagar in the Vale of Kashmir; the road from Srinagar to Leh passes over the 5,404-m-high Khardungla Pass — the first of the high passes on the historic caravan trail to Central Asia from India. Many other new roads have been built in recent years.

From the Punjab plains the only direct approach to the Vale of Kashmir is by the highway from Jalandhar in Punjab State, India, to Uri through Jammu, Banihal, Srinagar, and Baramula. It crosses the Pir Panjal Range through a tunnel at Banihal. The old road from Rawalpindi to Srinagar through Pakistan has lost much of its former importance.

The Sikkim Himalaya command the historic Kalimpong-to-Lhasa caravan trade route, which passes through Gangtok. Before the mid-1950s, there was only one (48 km) motorable highway running between Gangtok and Rongphu, on the Tista River, which then continued southwards to Siliguri for another 113 km. Since then, several roads passable by jeep have been built in the southern part of Sikkim, and a highway in northern Sikkim connects Gangtok with Lachen (Lachung).

Arunachal Pradesh is connected with the Brahmaputra River valley by roads running from Namsai to Chowkham, Sadiya to Roing, Pasighat to Dibrugarh, along to Sonarighat, North Lakhimpur to Hapoli, and Tezpur to Bomdila.

Only two main railroads, both of narrow gauge, penetrate into the Lesser Himalaya from the plains of India: one in the western Himalaya, between Kalka and Shimla, and the other in the eastern Himalaya, between Siliguri and Darjeeling. Another narrow-gauge line in Nepal, running some 48 km from Raxaul in Bihar State, India, to Amlekhganj and connected with Kathmandu by an electrically operated aerial cableway, transports goods to the capital in baskets. Two other short railroads run to the Outer Himalaya — one, the railroad of the Kullu Valley, from Pathankot to Jogindarnagar; the other from Haridwar to Dehradun. A short railway, formerly running between Wazirabad and Jammu through Sialkot, is now permanently closed.

There are two major airstrips in the Himalaya, one at Kathmandu and the other at Srinagar, capital of Kashmir, the airport at Kathmandu is served by international, as well as regional, flights. Besides these, there is also an increasing number of airstrips of local importance in the hills and in the Tarai region of Nepal that can accommodate STOL (short takeoff and landing) aircraft.

Improvements in both air and ground transportation have made tourism increasingly important to the economy of the Himalaya. Tourism has been recognized as a means of promoting economic development of the vast and varied Himalaya and at the same time conserving their environment and cultural assets.

Study and exploration : The first Himalayan sketch map of some accuracy was drawn up in 1590 by Antonio Monserrate, a Spanish missionary to the court of the Mughal emperor Akbar. In 1733 a French geographer, Jean-Baptiste Bourguignon d'Arville, compiled the first map of Tibet and the Himalayan range based on systematic exploration. In the mid-nineteenth century the Survey of India organized a systematic programme to measure correctly the heights of the Himalayan peaks. The Nepal and Uttarakhand peaks were observed and mapped between 1849 and 1855. Nanga Parbat, as well as the peaks of the Karakoram Range to the north, were surveyed between 1855 and 1859. The surveyors did not assign individual names to the innumerable peaks observed but designated them by figures and Roman numerals. Thus, at first. Mount Everest was simply labelled as "H"; this was later changed to Peak XV in 1849-1850. In 1865 Peak XV was renamed for Sir George Everest, surveyor-general of India from 1830 to 1843. Not until 1852 were the computations sufficiently advanced for it to be realized that Peak XV was higher than any other peak in the world. By 1862 more than 40 peaks with elevations exceeding 5,486 m had been climbed for surveying purposes.

In addition to the surveying expeditions, various scientific studies of the Himalaya were conducted in the nineteenth century. Between 1848 and 1849 the English botanist Joseph Dalton Hooker made a pioneering study of the plant life of the Sikkim Himalaya. He was followed by numerous others, including (in the early twentieth century) the British naturalist Richard W.G. Hingston, who wrote valuable accounts of the natural history of animals living at great altitudes in the Himalaya.

Since World War II the Survey of India has prepared some large-scale maps of the Himalaya from aerial photographs. Parts of the Himalaya also have been mapped by German geographers and cartographers with the help of ground photogrammetry. In addition, satellite reconnaissance has been employed to produce even more accurate and detailed maps.

Himalayan mountaineering began in the 1880s with the Briton W.W. Graham, who claimed to have climbed several peaks in 1883. Though his reports were received with scepticism, they did spark interest in the Himalaya among other European climbers. In the early twentieth century the number of mountaineering expeditions to the Karakoram Range and to the Kumaun and Sikkim Himalaya had increased markedly. Between World Wars I and II a certain national preference developed for the various peaks: the Germans concentrated on Nanga Parbat and Kanchenjunga, the Americans on K2 (also called Mount Godwin Austen), and the British on Mount Everest. Since 1921 there have been several dozen attempts at scaling Everest — about a dozen of them were undertaken before it was first successfully scaled in May 1953 by the New Zealand mountaineer Edmund Hillary and his Sherpa partner Tenzing Norgay. That same year an Austro-German team led by Karl Maria Herrligkoffer reached the summit of Nanga Parbat. As the great peaks were conquered one by one, climbers began to look for greater challenges to test their skills and equipment, attempting to reach the summits by increasingly difficult routes. By the end of the twentieth century the number of annual mountaineering expeditions and tourist excursions to the Himalaya had increased to such a degree that in some areas the participants were threatening the delicate environmental balance of the mountains by destroying plant and animal life and by leaving behind a growing quantity of refuse.

The earliest journeys through the Himalaya were undertaken by traders, shepherds, and pilgrims. The pilgrims believed that the harder the journey, the nearer it brought them to salvation or enlightenment; while the traders and shepherds accepted crossing passes as high as 5,486 to 5,791 m as a way of life. For all others, however, the Himalaya constituted a formidable and fearsome barrier.

Hindu Kush—(Arabic: "Mountains of India") a great mountain system of Central Asia, it is some 800 km long and 241 km wide. The Hindu Kush is one of the great watersheds of Central Asia, forming part of the vast Alpine zone that stretches across the continent from east to west. It runs northeast to southwest and divides the valley of the Amu Darya (the ancient Oxus River) to the north from the Indus River valley to the south. To the east the Hindu Kush buttresses the Pamirs range near the point where the borders of China, Pakistan, and Afghanistan meet, after which it runs south-west through Pakistan and into Afghanistan, finally merging into minor ranges in western Afghanistan. The highest peak is Mount Tirich Mir, which rises to 7,690 m on the Pakistan-Afghanistan border.

The eastern limit of the Hindu Kush is difficult to determine because of a locally complex topography, although the Karambar Pass (4,343 m) between the valleys of the Konar (called the Kunar, or Chitral, in Pakistan) and Gilgit rivers may be tentatively accepted as marking the boundary. The western limit also is uncertain, as the mountains lose height and fan out into minor ranges in Afghanistan. Geologists, however, consider the Hindu Kush range to extend much farther west to the Iranian border.

It was through the high passes of the Hindu Kush that invaders from Central Asia brought their Indo-European language into South Asia about 1500 BC. Historically, the passes have been of great military significance, providing access to the northern plains of India to such conquerors as Alexander the Great, king of Macedonia and the Mongols — Genghis Khan, Timur (Tamerlane), and their descendant Babur, the first Mughal emperor. During the period of British rule in India, the Indian government was keenly concerned with the security both of these passes and of an associated physical feature to the south, the Khyber Pass. The Hindu Kush range has rarely constituted the frontier between major powers; it has usually formed part of an intermediate bufler zone.

Physiography : The Hindu Kush may be divided into three main sections. In its extreme eastern section, between the passes of Karambar and Baroghil (Barowghil; 3,804 m), the eastern Hindu Kush region is not very high and has mountains that often take the form of rounded domes. Farther to the west the main ridge rises rapidly to Baba Tangi (6,513 m) and becomes rugged, after which, within the space of about 160 km, are concentrated the highest mountains of the entire region —

about two dozen summits more than 7,010 m in elevation. A first cluster of high peaks around Urgand in Afghanistan (7,039 m), is followed farther south by the massif (principal mountain mass) of Saraghrara (7,349 m). Another line of imposing mountains, which includes Mounts Langar (7,060 m), Shachaur (7,116 m), Udrem Zom (7,125 m), and Nadir Shah Zhara (7,125 m), leads to the three giant mountains of the Hindu Kush, which are Mounts Noshaq (Nowshak; 7,485 m), Istoro Nal (7,389 m), and Tirich Mir. Most major glaciers of the Hindu Kush — among them Kotgaz, Niroghi, Atrak, and Tirich — are in the valleys of this section.

The central section from the Dorah Pass to the Shebar Pass separates the traditional Afghan regions of Badakhshan to the north and Nurestan and Kulhestan (Kohistan) around the upper Kabul River to the south. The concentration of high summits in this region creates, from some vantage points, the appearance of an unbroken horizon, a phenomenon known as Gipfelflur (German: "summit plain"). Maximum heights, which are lower than those in the eastern section; indude Koh-i-Bandakor (6,843 m), Koh-i-Mondi (6,248 m), and Mir Samir (6,059 m). These peaks are surrounded by a host of lesser mountains. Glaciers are poorly developed, but the mountain passes — which include Putsigram (5,000 m), Veran (4,694 m). Ram Gol (4,694 m), and Anjoman (4,221 m) — are high, thus making transmontane communications difficult. The mountains of the western region fan out gradually towards the Afghan town of Herat, near the Iranian border, declining into hills of lesser importance. Communication is easier in this region, as the passes, such as the Shebar Pass (2,987 m), have long since been crossed by roads.

A wider definition of the Hindu Kush would include a fourth region known as Hindu Raj in Pakistan. This is formed by a long, winding chain of mountains — with some lofty peaks, such as Mounts Darkot (6,842 m) and Buni Zom (6,553 m) — which strikes southwards from the Lupsuk Peak (5,749 m) in the eastern region, then continues to the Lawarai Pass (3,688 m) and beyond to the Kabul River. If this chain were to be considered as part of the Hindu Kush, then the outlying mountains of the Swat Kohistan region of Pakistan to the south would also form part of the complex.

Geology : In many of its features, the Hindu Kush resembles its eastern neighbour, the Karakoram Range, that extends westwards, from Tibet into Pakistan. The Hindu Kush, which some authorities consider to be a continuation of the Karakoram, has the same core of igneous metamorphic rock (rock formed by heat and pressure that has solidified from a molten state) flanked, especially towards the north, by sedimentary material. In the Hindu Kush, however, there appears to be a greater prevalence of sedimentary rocks — a fact that may explain the softer and more rounded forms of many of the mountains. In the central and western sections the core of the chain is formed by a complex sequence of metamorphic rocks containing marble, together with intrusions of granodiorites (rocks formed deep down by heat and pressure and containing a certain admixture of both dark-coloured and light-coloured minerals).

Drainage : The eastern Hindu Kush appears to be formed of two parallel chains, consisting of a lower one to the north, which acts as a watershed, and a higher southern one that carries the main peaks. Drainage is comparatively simple on the northern side but highly complex on the southern one, where valleys follow two contrasting directions — northeast to southwest and roughly east to west. Most of the rivers, such as the Panjsher (Panjshir), the Alingar, the Konar, and the Panjkora, follow the northeast-to-southwest direction and are then suddenly deflected towards the east-west axis by the Kabul River, into which they flow. The Yarkhun and Ghizar river valleys also take the same east-to-west direction. The Indus River, however, swerves in its course from one direction to another as it makes its roundabout descent toward the lower plains. Summer runoff at peak level in the Konar River can be 60 times the amount of the lowest winter level.

Climate : A graphic image of climatic conditions is presented by the glaciers. The mantle of snow and ice is heaviest at the extreme eastern end of the Hindu Kush in Pakistan, where the Chiantar Glacier is situated, and is also heavy in the higher section around Tirich Mir and Saraghrara and in parts of the Hindu Raj mountains. Towards the west, however, glaciation is more sporadic. In the central Hindu Kush, mountains 3,658 m high are often bare almost to the summit. Some of the glaciers of the Hindu Kush appear to be retreating, while others are advancing. A striking feature of some glacial regions is ablated snow hummocks — called *nieves penitents*, or *Busserschnee* (literally, "snow penitents") — that give the illusion of kneeling human figures, sometimes less than a metre high; especially noticeable in the early morning, they are formed by the alternation of strong sunlight and rapid evaporation during the day and severe cold at night.

Since the Hindu Kush separates one major climate zone of Asia from another, the range's climate shows great variations. The mountains of Swat Kohistan are virtually within the area of the rain-bearing monsoon winds, and most of the eastern Hindu Kush, as well as the Hindu Raj, rises up at the extreme western limit of monsoonal Asia. The central and western Hindu Kush, however, border the Mediterranean climatic zone. Thus, moving from the southeast to the northwest and west, the climate changes from one of rainy or snowy summers (from July to September) and dry winters to one of hot dry summers and cold and rainy or snowy winters (from December to early March). Climatic variations between these opposites also occur, often producing striking local contrasts.

Plant life : Undulating grassland, called *pamir*, occurs above the tree line in the eastern Hindu Kush, while in the deep valleys barren rock walls are punctuated by brilliant emerald-green oases irrigated by glacial and snowfield meltwater. In the inaccessible reaches of Nurestan, the deodar forest is still substantial, but in the western portion of the range, where precipitation is less abundant, the higher slopes support grazing. On the northern slopes vegetation generally is sparse and limited to summer grazing by valley-dwelling inhabitants.

Forests cover many southern slopes of the eastern and central Hindu Kush, where there is abundant snowfall in the winter and intermittent precipitation from the summer monsoon. In the northernmost mountains in the Gilgit and Chitral districts in Pakistan, precipitation on lower slopes is sparse; hence forest vegetation is limited to occasional juniper and birch. Large stands of deodar cedar and blue pine cloak the eastern and central spurs of the Hindu Kush in Pakistan and Afghanistan. In the western Hindu Kush, forest is almost absent, and cultivated fodder trees such as poplar, willow, and Russian olive predominate. Other planted trees in irrigated mountain oases include plane trees and economically valuable species such as mulberry, jujube, and walnut. Meadowland is intermittent, depending on sunny and shady exposure, with substantial pastures found on slopes where snow accumulates; these pastures are occasionally cultivated in the summer by local and seasonally migrating populations. The valleys of the Swat and Dir districts, as well as parts of Chitral, support rice cultivation.

Animal life : Human depredation has reduced the variety and distribution of wildlife throughout the Hindu Kush, although efforts to create wildlife preserves in unpopulated areas have met with some success.

Well-adapted species of wildlife are found throughout the mountains. The Siberian ibex and the markhor, both wild goats, negotiate the high crags, while Marco Polo sheep and urial (another wild sheep) occasionally are found in the high *pamir*. Black and brown bears still exist in isolated valleys, and the Chitral valley wildlife preserve is a domain of the rare snow leopard. The rich birdlife of the mountains includes vultures and eagles. The streams of the northern slope contain brown trout in abundance.

Inner Himalaya—also called Lesser Himalaya, spurs from the Great Himalaya which radiate southward. The north-south ranges of the Lesser Himalaya comprise water-sheds between the principal rivers of Bhutan. Differences in elevation and the degree of exposure to moist southwest monsoon winds determine the prevailing vegetation, which ranges from dense forest on the rainswept windward slopes to Alpine vegetation at higher elevations. Several fertile valleys of central Bhutan are in the Lesser Himalaya at elevations varying from 1,524 m to 2,743 m. These valleys, notably the Paro, Punakha, Thimphu, and Ha, are relatively broad and flat, receive moderate rainfall (from about 1,000 to 1,270 mm or less a year), and are fairly well populated and cultivated.

J

Jaintia Hills—situated in eastern Meghalaya State, northeastern India, the sparsely populated mountainous region (part of the Meghalaya plateau) has an average elevation of more than 900 m. It receives generally heavy rainfall and is densely forested. Fine woods are produced, but there is little industry. The Kopili River, which is the largest stream in the region, is rocky and swift and has many spectacular waterfalls. There are several species of rare wildlife.

While the region remains isolated and less developed than much of India, British hegemony and its aftermath brought about a remarkable degree of unity among the peoples of the hill districts of Meghalaya.

The inhabitants of the Jaintia Hills are primarily tribal Jaintia, who like the Khasi to the west, are thought to be descendants of the first Mongolian migration to India. Until the nineteenth century, these people had a three-tiered system of administration. Under British rule, however this system was broken down, and after independence it was replaced by district council for tribal affairs and an Indian officer who administered other matters.

Partly because of their isolation, the Jaintia have largely maintained their matriarchal culture. They Still practise shifting cultivation, potatoes being the main crop, though the Indian government attempted — with some success — to promote settled farming. Jaintia, more than other tribal groups of the region, have been influenced by Hinduism and Aryan ways and thus settled farming was more readily accepted in the Jaintia Hills.

Jashpur Pats—extending over Jashpur Tahsil (northeastern Raigarh district) in eastern Madhya Pradesh State, central India and forming part of the Chota Nagpur plateau, it differs from the surrounding regions because of its geological composition, tectonic history, and the influence of a wetter climate. The plateau rises from the northern outer fringe, and the highest peneplained surface lies on the western fringe. It is a complex of small, flat-topped plateaus and hills, separated from each other by fault scarps and river valleys. The principal drainage is by the North and the South Koel rivers and the Damodar. To the north, the Upper Pats (known locally as Uparghat) have an elevation of about 750 m to 1,006 m. To the south, the Lower Pats (known locally as Nichghat) have an elevation of about 274 to 503 m. The Jashpur Pats form a divide between the Ganga and the Mahanadi drainage systems. The tops of the pats are generally barren or covered with grasslands, and the slopes are forested. Gash Pahar (988 m) and Laki Hill (1,013 m) are two of the higher peaks in the Jashpur Pats. The Maini, lb, Mand, and Kuskal rivers have cut narrow, rock-strewn valleys.

The hot moist monsoon climate is to some extent modified by the plateau heights. Dry deciduous forests fringe the graded plateau slopes with *palas, khair, harda*, ebony, and teak as the typical species. These are interspersed with bamboo and *sabai* grass (a valuable Indian fibre grass known as *bhabar*). Sal (*Shorea*) is found on dry areas. These forests provide the habitat for tribal communities of Santhals, Oraon, Ho, and Kharia.

Towards the mid-eighteenth century the three ruling local principalities were Ramgarh, Kharadigha, and Kandy. The British rule extended to the region from Bengal. The exploration for coal and Other minerals led to the construction of roads and railways, in the area. The region is rich in minerals like coal, iron ore, and mica and also has limestone, clay, and manganese. Bauxite, sandstone, building materials, clay, limestone, and dolomite are worked.

Most of this part of the Chota Nagpur plateau still retains its rurality. Cotton, rice, maize, sugar cane, peanuts (groundnuts), rapeseed and mustard, millet, and fruits are grown here. Industries centre on the milling of flour and oilseeds; sawmills and timber seasoning"; manufacture of iron, brass, and aluminium tools and utensils; and tussar silk production. There is growing activity in lac and shellac collection, agro-based industries such as rice-milling, and processing of forest products, particularly from *sabai* grass. Economic activity adheres to the main rail and road routes, and much of the interior has little communication facility. The Oraon, Kawar, Gond, Korwa, and other tribals comprise most of the population in the uplands, clustered in the few forest clearings. Jashpurnagar is the only important town. Population (1991) Town 14,788.

Javadi Hills—About 80 km wide and 32 km long, this range of hills is one of the larger of the Eastern Ghats, northern Tamil Nadu State, southern India. This is bisected into eastern and western sections by the Cheyyar and Agaram rivers, tributaries of the Palar. They consist of bluish-grey granites, with peaks averaging 1,100-1,150 m. The steep southeastern flanks of the hills are forested with sandalwood. They are sparsely populated. Grains, legumes, and oilseeds are the chief crops.

K

Kachchh, Rann of—also spelt Kutch, Cutch, or Kachh these are saline mudflats in west-central India and southern Pakistan. The Great Rann covers an area of about 18,000 sq km and lies almost entirely within Gujarat State, India, along the border with Pakistan. The Litde Rann of Kachchh extends northeast from the Gulf of Kachchh and occupies about 5,100 sq km in Gujarat State. Originally an extension of the Arabian Sea, the Rann of Kachchh has been closed off by centuries of silting. During the time of Alexander the Great it was a navigable lake, but it is now an extensive mudflat, inundated during monsoon seasons. Settlement is limited to low, isolated hills. In 1965 a dispute arose over the India-Pakistan boundary line toward the western end of the Great Rann. Fighting broke out in April and ended only when Great Britain intervened to secure a cease-fire. On the report of the United Nations secretary-general to the Security Council, the dispute was referred to an international tribunal, which in 1968 awarded about 10 per cent of the border area to Pakistan and about 90 per cent to India; the partition was effected in 1969.

Kailash Range—also known as Kang-Ti-Ssu Shan, Pinyin Gangdisi Shan this is one of the highest and most rugged parts of the Himalayan mountain system located in the southwestern part of the Tibet Autonomous Qu (region), China. The range has a roughly northwest-to-southeast axis and lies to the north of a trough drained in the western section by the Langzhu River — the name by which the Sutlej River is known in China — and drained in the east by the Machuan River, an extreme headwater of the Brahmaputra (known in Chinese as the Yaluzuangbu River, or Tsangpo). In the middle of this depression lies Mapam Lake (Mansarovar), reputed to be the highest freshwater lake in the world at 4,557 m above sea level. To the north of this lake lies Mount Kailash, which reaches an elevation of 6,714 m; it is known as Gangdisi to the Tibetans and is the highest peak in the range.

Mount Kailash is an important holy site, both to the Hindus, who identify it with the paradise of Shiva (one of the three supreme gods of Hinduism), and to the Tibetan Buddhists, who identify it with Mount Sumeru, cosmic centre of the universe. Although access to both Mount Kailash and Mapam Lake as places of religious pilgrimage was permitted after the Chinese occupation of Tibet in 1951 and guaranteed in the Sino-Indian Treaty of 1954, access was restricted after the suppression of the subsequent Tibetan rising, and the frontier was closed in 1962. Access to the area from the south is via the high Lipuliege Pass, south of Pulan. The Indus River rises on the north flank of the Kailash Range.

Kaimur Hills—the eastern portion of the Vindhya Range of hills, commencing near Katangi in the Jabalpur district of Madhya Pradesh, it runs a little north of east for a distance of over 483 km to Sasaram in Bihar.

After traversing the northern part of Jabalpur and southeast Maihar, the range turns to the east and runs through Rewa, There, it separates the valley of the Son and the Tons rivers and continues into the Mirzapur district of Uttar Pradesh, and the Shahabad district of West Bengal. Its maximum width is 80 km. The range has a distinctive appearance in Madhya Pradesh, with metamorphic rock-formations and a rock stratum that has experienced upheaval. The stratum is almost vertical, giving it a knife-edged and sharp ridge appearance. It almost disappears at places, being marked by a low rock-chain. The range never rises more than a few hundred metres above the plain. The ruined fort of Rohtas is situated in these hills. The rocks consist of sandstones and shales throughout. Interesting relics of prehistoric man have been found in the caves and rock shelters of the hills in the form of rough drawings and stone implements, near Bijaigarh.

Kanchenjunga—also spelt Kangchenjunga, or Kinchinjunga, Nepali Kumbhkaran Lungur, the world's third highest mountain (8,586 m) is part of the Himalayan range on the Nepalese border with Sikkim, India, 74 km north-northwest of Darjeeling.

The name Kanchenjunga is derived from four words of Tibetan origin, usually rendered Kang-chen-dzo-nga, or Yang-chhen-dzo-nga, and interpreted in Sikkim as the "Five Treasuries of the Great Snow".

The Kanchenjunga massif is in the form of a gigantic cross, the arms of which lie north, south, east, and west. The individual summits connect to neighbouring peaks by four main ridges, from which flow four glaciers: the Zemu (northeast), Talung (southeast), Yalung (southwest), and Kanchenjunga (northwest). The mountain holds an important place in the mythology and religious ritual of the local inhabitants, and its slopes were, no doubt, familiar to herdsmen and traders for centuries before a rough survey of it was made.

The first map of Kanchenjunga was made by Rinzin Namgyal, one of the *pandit* ("learned") explorers of the mid-nineteenth century, who made a circuital sketch. In 1848 and 1849 Sir Joseph Hooker, a botanist, was the first European to visit and describe the region, and, in 1899, Douglas Freshfield, the explorer-mountaineer, travelled around the mountain. In 1905 the suggested Yalung valley route was attempted by an Anglo-Swiss party, a venture during which four members perished in an avalanche.

Mountaineers later explored other faces of the massif. A Bavarian expedition led by Paul Bauer in 1929 and 1931 vainly attempted it from the Zemu side, and Gunter O. Dyhrenfurth, in 1930, attempted it from the Kanchenjunga glacier. The greatest height reached during these explorations was 7,700 m in 1931. Fatal accidents during two of these expeditions gave the mountain a reputation for unusual danger and difficulty. No more efforts were made to climb it until 1954, when attention was again turned to the Yalung face, which is in Nepal. Gilmour Lewis' visits to the Yalung in 1951, 1953, and 1954 led to a 1955 British expedition led by Charles Evans, under the auspices of the Royal Geographical Society and the Alpine Club (London), which stopped within a few yards of the actual summit in deference to the religious beliefs and wishes of the Sikkimese.

Karnataka Coast—coastal lowlands in westen Karnataka State, southwestern India, with an area of about 10,000 sq km, it is bounded by the Arabian Sea on the west, the Western Ghats on the east, Konkan on the north, and the Kerala plains on the south. Stretching from north to south for about 225 km, it has a maximum width of about 64 km in the south. Historically the coast was a contact zone between Indian merchants and European and African traders. It was successively ruled by the Kadambas, Rattas, Chalukyas, Yadavas, and Hoysalas until it passed to the Muslims (sixteenth century), with short interludes of Maratha supremacy. The British annexed the coast in 1789. The coastline is sandy and in places rocky cliffs overhang the sea. Sloping from east to west, it comprises a narrow belt of coastal sand dunes, marshes, and valley plains backed by a higher erosional platform, in turn succeeded by isolated hills that are 90 m to 305 m higher farther inland. Coconuts and casuarinas grow on the saline sandy beaches, mangroves in the marshes and estuaries, and bamboo and scrub are found on the hills. The coast is drained by the Kali Nadi, Gangavali Bedti, Tadri, Sharavari, and Netravari rivers, which have carved out narrow valleys with steep gradients and generally flow in a westerly direction. Alluvial soils occur in the south; the rest of the coast has infertile red soils that are often gravelly and sandy. The region forms a transitional zone between Maharashtra and Kerala States. The southern, or Mangalore, region has plantations of coconut and casuarina; the northern, or Udipi, region produces rice and pulses (legumes). Industries are mostly located at Mangalore, an important regional centre and major coffee port of India, and at Udipi. The ports of Karwar, Kumta, Honavar, and Malpe have lost their importance with the development of railways in the interior. Mangalore and Karwar have been developed as deepwater ports for the export of mineral ores.

Karnataka Plateau—Situated in Karnataka State, southwestern India, the name of the plateau is derived from Karnad (Land of Black Soil). The plateau has an area of about 189,000 sq km and an average elevation of about 800 m. It consists of the Dharwad system of volcanic rocks, crystalline schists, and granites. The major rivers include the Godavari, Krishna, Cauvery (Kaveri), Tungabhadra, Sharavati, and Bhima. The Sharavati has the highest (253 m) waterfall in India, known as the Jog Falls. These falls are the largest single source of hydroelectric power in the country and are also a major tourist attraction. The plateau merges with the Nilgiri Hills in the south. Rainfall varies from 2,030 mm in the southern hills to 711 mm in the northern region. Sandalwood is exported, and teak and eucalyptus are used chiefly to make furniture and paper. Manganese, chromium, copper, and bauxite are mined. There are large reserves of iron ore in the Baba Budan Hills and gold in the Kolar Gold

Fields. *Jowar* (sorghum), cotton, rice, sugar cane, sesame seeds, peanuts (groundnuts), tobacco, fruits, coconuts, and coffee are the major crops. Textile manufacturing, food- and tobacco-processing, and printing are the principal industries. Bangalore, capital of Karnataka State, is the site of most of the industrial development. Important towns include Mysore, Belgaum, Gulbarga, Bellary, and Bijapur.

Kashmir, Vale of—scenic intermontane valley between the main Himalayan ranges (northeast) and the Pir Panjal Range (southwest), northwestern India, the valley is an ancient lake basin 140 km long, 32km wide and 1,620 m high. Drained by the upper Jhelum River, the Valley is lined by 3,600 m to 4,800 m high mountains .that help shelter it from the wet southwest monsoon. It is the centre of population for the Kashmir area; Srinagar is the Capital of the Indian State of Jammu and Kashmir. The fertile alluvial soil yields rice, maize, fruit, and vegetables, and the scenic mountains and lakes (notably Wular and Dal) attract many tourists. The valley was the resort of Mughal emperors, notably Jahangir, the early seventeenth-century emperor of Hindustan (northern India) who constructed picturesque gardens and buildings for his empress, Noor Jahan. The vale is sometimes referred to as the "happy valley", perhaps because it gives a feeling of isolation from the rest of the world.

Kashmir is a high-altitude natural region of lakes and valleys surrounded by mountains in the northernmost section of the Indian subcontinent. It was known to the composers of the Vedas and formed part of the territories ruled by the Maurya and Kushan Dynasties in early times. It was an abode of Sanskrit learning and played an important part in the spread of Buddhism to adjoining Tibet and Chinese Turkestan. Many pilgrimage sites, including the ice-lingam cave at Amarnath sacred to Shiva are located in Kashmir, and the Martand temple dedicated to the Sun-god in the twelfth century is famous.

Kathiawar Peninsula—peninsula in southwestern Gujarat State, western India, it is bounded by the Little Rann (marsh) of Kachchh (Kutch; north), the Gulf of Cambay (east), the Arabian Sea (southwest), and the Gulf of Kachchh (northwest). From the northeast an ancient sandstone formation extends into the peninsula, which has an area of 60,000 sq km. Most of the sandstone, however, is masked by lavas. The coastal regions are flanked in the west and east by clays and lime-stones and in the south by alluvium and miliolite, a wind-deposited sand concretion known as Porbandar stone and widely used as building material. The area flanking the Gulf of Cambay is largely alluvial,

Much of the peninsula is less than 180 m above sea level, but the Girnar Hills and the isolated Gir Range reach heights of 1,117 m and 647 m, respectively. The natural vegetation of the dry, hot region is mainly thorn forest, but mangrove stands are common in low-lying areas near the sea. The Gir forests, site of a national park, contain the last wild Indian lions, and other wildlife. Agriculture is the chief occupation on the peninsula; the principal crops raised include wheat, millet, peanuts (groundnuts), and cotton. Bhavnagar is the principal port and city.

Kerala Plains—narrow strip of coastland, in southwestern India, in front of the Arabian Sea to the West it constitutes almost all of Kerala State and most of the Malabar Coast. With an area of approximately 28,000 sq km, the plains are indented by numerous shallow lagoons, known locally as *kayes*, that are formed by sand dunes (known locally as *teris*). The sandy beaches are covered with coconut palms. According to the Puranas, the region, also known as Parashurama-Khetram, was reclaimed from the sea by the sage Parashurama. The Kerala plains lie below 10 m, with hills of the Western Ghats, the Nilgiri and the Southern Ghats to the east. Narrow in the north and wide in the south, the plains are about 530 km long and from 19 to 96 km wide.

Many streams crisscross the plains and serve as inland waterways, constituting about one-fifth of India's total length of waterways. The Periyar River is the most important river that crosses the plains. About half the land is under cultivation mainly planted with rice and cassava. Sugarcane, ginger, *ragi* (cereal grass), peanuts (groundnuts), and sesame seeds are also grown. Cash crops include coconut, pepper, betelnut, cardamom, rubber, coffee, and tea. Cashew, tea, and fish are processed; cement, aluminium, rayon, and electrical goods are manufactured; and coir, plywood, and paper are made. The plains are densely populated, and Malayalam an offshoot of the westcoast dialect of Tamil, is the local language. The chief towns include Kochi (formerly Cochin), Thiruvananthapuram (formerly Trivandrum), Kozhikode (formerly Calicut), Alappuzha (formerly Alleppey), Thrissur (formerly Trichur), and Kollam (formerly Quilon).

Khasi Hills—These spread in central Meghalaya State, northeastern India. The area consists mostly of hilly regions and includes the Shillong plateau. It is drained by the tributaries of the Brahmaputra and Surma rivers. The Cherrapunji scarp in the south has one of the highest average annual rainfalls in the world. The Khasi Hills region is sometimes called the "Scotland of the East" because of its scenic beauty.

The vast majority of the population outside of Shillong, the capital of Meghalaya State, are engaged in agriculture, with wet rice, the largest crop, being cultivated in the valleys and on hillside terraces. Other farmers in the region practise shifting cultivation, burning the trees and farming the land for one or two years before moving on. The government has discouraged this wasteful method, urging instead settlement on conventional farms. The distinctive culture of the Khasi people includes a traditional matrilineal social system that has been modified by outside religious and modern legal influences. Many of the hill peoples have become Christians.

Khyber Pass—Khyber also spelt Khaybar, or Khaibar it is the most northerly and important of the passes between Afghanistan and Pakistan. It connects Kabul with Peshawar. The pass has historically been the gateway for invasions of the Indian subcontinent from the north-west. The name Khyber is also applied to the range of arid, broken hills through which the pass runs and which form the last spurs of the Spin Ghar (Safid Kuh) Range. On either side of the connecting ridge are the sources of two small streams, the beds of which form the Khyber gorge. This narrow gorge forms the Khyber Pass; it winds between cliffs of shale and limestone, 180-300 m high, and enters the Khyber Hills from the Shadi Bagiar opening, a few kilometres beyond Jamrud, Pakistan, and continues northwestwards for about 53 km. Just beyond the old Afghan fort of Haft Chah, it opens onto the barren Lowyah Dakkah plain, which stretches to the Kabul River.

The Khyber Pass is threaded by a caravan track and by a good hard-surface road. The railway (opened 1925) through the pass connects Jamrud with Landi Khana, near the Afghan frontier; the line, with its 34 tunnels and 94 bridges and culverts, revolutionized transportation in the area. The pass may be skirted by a road fork that enters the hills about 14 km north of Jamrud and emerges at Lowyah Dakkah.

After a steep accent at its southern entrance, the pass rises gradually to Fort Ali Masjid (967 m), where the Khyber River (Khyber Khwar) leaves the pass to the south. For 8 km from Ali Masjid the pass becomes a defile not more than 183 m wide, flanked by imposing and precipitous walls. From Zintara village on northwards, the pass becomes a valley a kilometre or more wide, with forts, villages, and scattered cultivation plots. About 16 km west of Ali Masjid lies Landi Kotal fort and cantonment (1,072 m); this is the highest point in the pass and is also an important market centre with an alternate route back to Peshawar. There the summit widens out northwards for 3 km. The main pass, however, descends from Landi Kotal through Shinwari territory to Landi Khana, where it runs through another gorge and enters Afghanistan territory at Towr Kham (Torkham; 701 m), winding another 16 km down the valley to Lowyah Dakkah.

Few passes have had such continuing Strategic importance or so many historic associations as the Khyber Pass. Through it have passed Persians, Greeks, Mughals, Afghans, and the British, for whom it was the key point in control of the Afghan border. In the fifth century BC Darius I the Great of Persia conquered the country around Kabul and marched through the Khyber Pass to the Indus River. Two centuries later Hephaestion and Perdiccas, generals of Alexander the Great, probably used the pass. Buddhism flourished in and around the Khyber when it was part of Ashoka's kingdom (third century BC); Buddhist remains include Kafir Kot (Citadel of the Kafirs), Shopla *stupa* (also called the Khyber Top), and the *stupa* near Ali Masjid. The pass was used by Mahmud of Ghazna, Babur, Nadir Shah, and Ahmad Shah Durrani and his grandson Shah Zaman in their invasions of India. Ranjit Singh, the Sikh ruler of the Punjabi extended his kingdom as far as Jamrud in the early nineteenth century.

The Pashtun Afridi people of the Khyber area always resisted foreign control, and numerous punitive expeditions were undertaken against them by the Mughals and the British. The first British advance northwards into the Khyber took place in 1839, and during the First Anglo-Afghan War the pass was the scene of many skirmishes with the Afridis, The Treaty of Gandamak, which was signed during the Second Anglo-Afghan War in 1879, left the Khyber tribes under British control. In 1897 the Afridis seized the pass and held it for several months but were defeated in the Tirah expedition of 1897. The British became responsible for the safety of the pass, which is now controlled by the Pakistani Khyber Agency.

L

Ladakh—region of eastern Kashmir it is part of Jammu and Kashmir State, northern India. It contains the western Himalayan Ladakh Range. Ladakh covers about 117,000 sq km and includes the Karakoram Range and the upper Indus River valley. Ladakh is one of the most elevated regions of the world. Its natural features consist mainly of high plains and deep valleys. The high plain predominates in the east, diminishing gradually westwards. In the southeast of Ladakh lies Rupshu, an area that has a uniform height of about 4,100 m and has large, brackish lakes. To the northwest of Rupshu lies Zaskar, a bleak, inaccessible region where the people and the cattle remain indoors for much of the year because of the cold. Zaskar is drained by the Zaskar River, which, flowing northwards, joins the Indus River below Leh. In Ladakh proper, farther to the north, cultivation by means of manuring and irrigation is done at heights ranging from 2,750 to 4,550 m. The people are divided into shepherds, who populate the upland valleys too high for cultivation, and the Ladakhis, who till the land around the valley villages. Leh, the most accessible town of Ladakh proper, is an important trade centre and lies 260 km east of Srinagar.

The climate of Ladakh is cold and dry. Average annual precipitation is 84 mm; fine, dry, flaked snow is frequent; sometimes the fall is heavy. Vegetation is confined to valleys and sheltered spots, where a stunted growth of tamarisk, furze, and other plants supply much-needed firewood. The principal products are wheat, barley, millet, buckwheat, peas, beans, and turnips. The only manufacture is woollen cloth.

Post-1947 Ladakh was contested by both India and Pakistan; after the cease-fire agreement of 1949, its southern portion went to India and the remainder to Pakistan. In the early 1960s Chinese forces gained control of the northeastern part of Ladakh.

Ladakh Range—It is a segment of the Karakoram Range, extending southeastwards for 370 km from the mouth of the Shyok River in northern Pakistan across northern India to the Tibetan (China) border. With a crest line of about 6,100 m, the range parallels the northeast bank of the Indus River. The Deosai Mountains, located southeast of the Indus River in northern Pakistan, are sometimes considered part of the range.

Lesser Himalaya—also called Inner Himalaya, Lower Himalayas, or Middle Himalaya this middle section of the Himalayan mountain ranges, extends southeastwards across north Pakistan, North India, Nepal, Sikidm (India), and into Bhutan. The range lies between Grey (north) and Shiwalik, or Outer (south), Himalayan ranges and has an average height of 3,700 to 4,500 m. It includes portions of the Punjab, Kumaun, Nepal, and Assam Himalaya.

M

Madhya Bharat Plateau—Known in Hindi as Madhya Bharat pathar, this plateau complex in the heart of the Indian subcontinent, comprises the northern part of the Central Highlands, central India. Extending over approximately 57,000 sq km and including most of northwestern Madhya Pradesh State and central Rajasthan State, it is bounded by the East Rajasthan Uplands on the west, the Upper Gangetic Plain on the north, the Bundelkhand upland on the east, and the Malwa plateau on the south. Its major tilt is towards the Yamuna plains in the north. The northern and central parts are drained by the rivers Chambal, Betwa, Ken, Tons, and Son. In the southwest, the Sabarmati, Mahi, Narmada, and Tapti systems dominate. The Godavari system drains the southeastern part. The landforms show regional variations, with characteristics of erosional topography on lithological variation, all modified by uplift and faulting. The underlying rock types materially influence the landscape. The bedrock of the Madhya Bharat plateau consists of a uniform formation of basalt; weathering has produced rounded boulders in some places.

The plateau has an average elevation of about 500 m and slopes from 602 m in the south to 301 m in the north. Erosion has created an almost level surface frequently punctuated by sandstone scarps. The Chambal River, rising in the northern flanks of the Vindhya Range, winds through a wide, bowl-like basin from southwest to northeast and enters a long, narrow gorge, site of the Gandhi Sagar Dam of the Chambal Valley Project (irrigation and hydroelectric power). The Chambal valley has areas of severe gullying and erosion aggravated by deforestation and overgrazing of the land; its ravines were said to be used as hideouts by bandits. The soils are black and alluvial. The Banganga, Kunwari, Sind, Parbati, and Kali Sindh are other major rivers. Savannas on the plateau, dense moist deciduous forests in the south, and drier deciduous forests in the north (with some teak) tending to poorly wooded scrublands in the west are common.

The economy is dominated by agriculture; cereals, pulses (legumes), oilseeds, cotton, sugar cane, and tobacco are produced. Industries include saw milling, oilseed crushing, the production of machine tools and implements, textile weaving, and the manufacture of pottery, bricks, and cement. Deposits of iron ore, copper, lead, beryl, steatite, and limestone are worked. The transport system consists of roads and narrow-gauge railways linking Gwalior (the main industrial centre) with Kota, Morena, Bhind, Shivpuri, and Bundi. Gwalior and Kota have airstrips.

The intensity of cultivation varies with the nature of soils, availability of irrigation, and the extent of surrounding hilly belts of low forest and scrublands, largely inhabited by tribals.

One in seven persons in the region is a tribal, the tribes have retained their identity because the land is hilly, forested and difficult to access. Regional language and culture helps to strengthen diverse identities as seen in the case of Chhattisgarh, Bundelkhanti, Dandkaranya, and other districts

Since historical times, the region has been home to aboriginals. The plateau lands acted as a barrier to the well-occupied northern plains and the more open south. It could be penetrated through the western route, skirting Rajasthan, the two gap routes in the centre, and through the route along the Orissa coast. This area also offered a political refuge to clans of Rajputs fleeing from Islamic powers. This affected not only the political organization of the region, but also its existing economic, social, and political development.

Initial political organization was that of tribal chiefs and kingships. The Rajput clans migrated to this area in the mediaeval period and built forts on habitable lowlands of the region. Their feudal outlook was either accepted by the tribals or they shifted farther to the forested hills. The sway of the Guptas, Mauryas, and King Harsha seems mostly to be along route ways, as seen from the location of Sanchi, Vidisha, and Ujjain. The *nawabs* of Bhopal, Tonk, Palanpur, as well as the Marathas and the Mughals preferred to consolidate their main strategic lanes and established their capitals at Indore and Gwalior. The British conquest of India hardly made any impact on Madhya Bharat, resulting in political immaturity and poor social and economic development, with much of the land inaccessible even today.

While old, established towns have acquired commercial and some industrial functions after independence, several new, planned industrial cities have also come up. Gwalior, Indore, Bhopal, and Jabalpur belong to the former category, while Bhilai, Durg, Nepanagar, Korba, and Katni belong to the latter. These cities have locational advantages because of the availability of local mineral and forest resources and improved accessibility provided by new rail and road links.

Although the rate of urbanization in the region is low, it is more marked in the case of towns with industrial functions. Thirty per cent of the total area of the region has forested hills with tribal habitat, patches of shifting cultivation, and overgrazed and overexploited forest scrubs.

Mahadeo Hills—sandstone hills located on the northern border of the Satpura Range in southern Madhya Pradesh State, central India, the hills have small plateaus and a gentle northern slope but are steep to the south, where they drop abruptly from 1,100 m to less than 275 m. The general trend of the hills is east-northeast. The bedrock is extensively overlain by tracts of brown soil on which flourish deciduous forests. Lumbering and charcoal burning are economically important on the Mahadeo slopes. The economy of the area, however, is generally poor. To the north, between the Satpura and Mahadeo scarps and the Vindhya Range, the valley floor is 32-64 km wide, and within this valley flows the Narmada River.

Maikala Range—is a mountain range of Madhya Pradesh State in central India. It runs in a north-south direction forming the eastern base of the triangular Satpura Range. The Maikala Range consists of laterite-capped, flat-topped plateaus (*pats*) with an elevation ranging from 600 m to 900 m. The Satpura-Maikala watershed is the second largest in India. The Narmada, Son, Pandu, Kanhar, Riband, Bijul, Gopad, and Banas rivers run almost parallel from south to north and have carved extensive basins in the relatively soft rock formations of the Maikala Range. Vegetation varies from grass and thorny trees to deciduous trees such as teak and sal (*Shorea*).

Agriculture, the principal economic activity, is practised mostly in the alluvial basins; crops include rice, wheat, gram (chickpea), *jowar* (sorghum), barley, maize, pulses (legumes), sesame seeds, and mustard seeds. Industries produce cement, ceramics, bricks, tiles, glass, dressed stone, lumber, and shellac; flour, *dal* (pigeonpea), and oil are milled. Mineral deposits include coal, limestone, bauxite, corundum, dolomite, marble, slate, and sandstone. The principal ethnic groups are the Gond (numerically and historically the most important), Halba, Bharai, Baiga, and Korku. The chief towns are Balaghat, Mandla, Nainpur, and Dindori. A fort at Mandla (the capital of the Gond kings), a palace at Ramnagar, and the Kanha National Park are places of interest.

Makalu—one of the world's highest mountains (8,463 m), in the Himalaya on the Nepalese-Tibetan (Chinese) border, it lies 23 km east-southeast of Mount Everest. Makalu had been observed by climbers of Mount Everest, but attempts to ascend its steep, glacier-covered sides did not begin until 1954. On May 15, 1955, two members, Jean Couzy and Lionel Terray, of a French party reached the summit, and seven more arrived within two days.

Malabar Coast—a name long applied to the southern part of India's western coast, which is bordered on the east by the Western Ghats range, it has sometimes encompassed the entire western coast of peninsular India. It now includes most of Kerala State and the coastal of Karnataka State. The coast consists of a continuous belt of sand dunes. Behind this are many lagoons paralleling the coast and linked by canals to form inland waterways, much used by small boats. Inland is level alluvial land, well watered by streams flowing down from the Western Ghats, Rice and spices are the principal crops, with coconut palms on the coastal sand dunes. Fishing is also important. Kochi (formerly Cochin) is the main port.

A large part of the Malabar Coast fell within the ancient kingdom of Keralaputra (Chera dynasty). The Portuguese established several trading posts there and were followed by the Dutch in the seventeenth century and the French in the eighteenth. The British gained control of the region in the late eighteenth century.

Malwa Plains—These alluvial plains in the central Punjab State, between the Sutlej and Ghaggar rivers, south of the Bist doab (plain), Malwa plain is named after the Malloi people (Malavas) who ruled the Punjab in the fourth century BC and offered resistance to Alexander the Great. The region came under Muslim rule in the tenth century and, except for a short period of Rajput ascendency (c. 1032-1192), remained under Muslim rule until the decline of Mughal power. Malwa plain includes the flood plains of the Sutlej, and the Ghaggar, and an upland plain between the two. The plain is bordered on the northeast by the Shiwalik hills. It ranges in elevation from about 300 m above sea level in the northeast to less than 200 m in the southwest.

Although the plain surface is the result of alluviation by water action, wind action has been important in western and southwestern Malwa, giving rise to sand-dune topography. But during the post-independence period, with the extension of irrigation, both by canals and tube wells, the land has been levelled and brought under effective cultivation. Presently the Ghaggar is a seasonal stream. It has a wide bed but contains only a narrow channel of water. The river is said to have lost a number of tributaries in its upper course through the process of river capture. It is thought that the Sutlej and Yamuna rivers at one stage were tributaries of the Ghaggar River. A slight tectonic uplift of the Yamuna-Sutlej divide caused a shift of the Sutlej to the west and of the Yamuna to the east, leaving the Ghaggar a truncated stream. Seasonal streams like Patiala nadi, Dangri, and Markanda join the Ghaggar which ultimately loses itself in the sands of the Thar Desert near Hanumangarh.

Along the roads, rail lines, canals and in the wastelands eucalyptus/ poplar trees are being planted in increasing numbers. Over 80 per cent of the region's land is under cultivation. Wheat and rice are the most dominant crops. Other crops include maize (in eastern Malwa), sugarcane, cotton (in western Malwa), pulses, and oilseeds. Malwa contributes substantially to wheat and rice stocks of the Central Pool. Small- and medium-scale industries producing machine tools, sewing machines and parts, cycles, water pipes and fittings, hosiery, plastic goods, and automobile parts, are important. Agro-based industries are well distributed. The whole tract has a dense network of roads and railways.

Malwa Plateau—plateau, north-central India, it is bounded by the Gujarat plains on the west, the Vindhya Range on the south, the Madhya Bharat plateau and Bundelkhand upland on the north, and the Vindhya Range on the east. Of volcanic origin, the plateau comprises central Madhya Pradesh State and southeastern Rajasthan State. The name Malwa is derived from the Sanskrit term *Malav* and means "part of the abode of Lakshmi (goddess of wealth)". The plateau was ruled successively by the Maurya, Gupta, and Paramara dynasties; many Buddhist temples and monuments (for example, the Sanchi *stupas*), noted for their architecture and sculpture, were built. The plateau was conquered by the Muslims in AD 1390 and became part of the Maratha Empire; then in 1817 it passed to the British.

The Malwa plateau has an elevation ranging from 500 m to 610 m; erosion has carved the lavas into isolated mesas found throughout the plateau, together with an occasional sandstone hill. The western part of the region is drained by the Mahi River, the middle section by the Chambal River, and the eastern part by the Betwa River and the headwaters of the Dhasan and Ken rivers. Other rivers include the Parbati, Sipra, Chaipbal, Gambhir, and Choti Kali Sindh, their valleys flanked by terraced slopes. Vegetation is of the savanna type with scattered teak and sal (*Shorea*) forests.

The regional economy is mostly agricultural; cereals, pulses (legumes), oilseeds and cotton are the main crops. Industries produce cotton textiles, ginned cotton, sugar, vegetable oil, lumber, and paper. The Chambal Valley Development Scheme provides water for irrigation and hydroelectric power. Ratlam has ceramic factories, Bhopal and Ujjain have engineering industries, and Indore has a foundry. Many trunk roads pass through the region; there are airports at Indore and Bhopal.

Manaslu I—also called Kutang I, one of the world's highest mountains (8,163 m), it lies in the Himalaya of north Nepal, 61 km north of the town of Gurkha. The summit of this snow- and glacier-covered peak was first reached on May 9 and II, 1956, by two separate Japanese parties.

Mizo Hills—formerly Lushai Hills, they are a mountain range in southeastern Mizoram State, northeastern India, forming part of the north Arakan Yoma system. They rise to about 2,125 m, and their slopes are covered with thick evergreen forest containing valuable timber and bamboo. In the inter-montane valleys, *jhum* (slash-and-burn) agriculture and some terrace cultivation are practised.

N

Naga Hills—are a part of the complex mountain barrier on the border of India and Myanmar (Burma). A northern extension of the Arakan Yoma system, the Naga Hills reach a height of 3,826 m in Mount Saramati on the India-Myanmar frontier. The part of the range within India constituted the Naga Hills district of Assam until 1961 and since 1963 has been part of Nagaland. The hills receive a heavy monsoon rainfall and are naturally covered with dense forest. Placed throughout the hills are villages of Naga tribes.

Nallamala Range—range of parallel hills and valleys of the Eastern Ghats in eastern Anahra Pradesh State, southeastern India, it is located south of the Krishna River. The hills run north to south, parallel to the Coromandel Coast on the Bay of Bengal. Their total length is about 430 km; the northern boundary is in the Palnad basin, and the southern boundary is in the Tirupati Hills.

Approximately 31 km wide, the Nallamala Range rises to an average elevation of 900 to 1,100 m. The rugged, sparsely populated hills are composed for the most part of jumbled quartzites and slates and exemplify the mountain scenery of the Eastern Ghats.

Nanga Parbat—also called **Diamir**, it is one of the world's highest mountains (8,126 m), situated in the western Himalaya. The mountain's steep south wall rises nearly 4,600 m above the valley immediately below and the north side drops about 7,000 m to the Indus River.

The British Alpine climber Albert F. Mummery led the first attempt to ascend the glacier- and snow-covered mountain in 1895, but he died in the attempt. At least 30 more climbers (mostly German-led) also perished on Nanga Parbat because of the severe weather conditions and frequent avalanches before the Austrian climber Hermann Buhl reached the top in 1953. The Kashmir; name Nanga Parbat is derived from the Sanskrit words *nagna parvata*, meaning "naked mountain". Diamir is a local name for the peak and means "King of the Mountains"

Nilgiri Hills—a mountainous region of Tamil Nadu State, southern India the peaks of the Nilgiri rise abruptly from the surrounding plains to an elevation of 1,800 to 2,400 m. One of them, Doda Betta (2,637 m), is the highest point in Tamil Nadu. Part of the Western Ghats, the hills are separated from the Karnataka plateau (north) by the Noyar River and from the Anaimalai and Palni hills (south) by the Palghat Gap. They are considerably cooler and wetter than the surrounding plains, the upper hills forming undulating grassy downs. Tea, cinchona (trees and shrubs whose bark yields quinine), coffee, and vegetables are grown extensively.

P

Pachaimalai Hills—the range of hills in Tamil Nadu State of southern India, these are an eastward extension of the Eastern Ghats in the north-eastern Tamilnad uplands. The Pachaimalai Hills, together with the Javadi, Shevaroy, and Kalrayan hills separate the Cauvery (Kaveri) River basin in the south from the Palar River basin in the north. Extending over approximately 13,500 sq km, they form a discontinuous line of highlands with a general elevation between 540 m and 1,408 m. The region consists of rounded hills composed of granitic gneiss. The hills have scrub jungles on broken ground and sal (*Shorea*) forests on the flat hilltops. Loamy and clayey soils are found in the valleys. The Vellar, Palar, and Ponnaiyar rivers are dry for much of the year. The economy of the region is based on agriculture; rice, *jowar* (sorghum), sugarcane, gram (chickpea), peanuts (groundnuts), and *bajra* (pearl millet) are subsistence crops. Coffee, cashew, and pepper are important plantation crops raised for export. Large scale industries produce textiles, foodstuffs, and chemicals; engineering is also important. Cottage industries include mat and basket weaving, carpentry, blacksmithing, and the manufacture of bidi (cigarettes). Iron ore, manganese, beryl, and zinc are mined. About three-fifths of the area's population live in the Coimbatore-Madurai uplands.

Roads from the northern upland region to the eastern seaboard run along the valleys or other gaps between the hill ranges. Tiruvannamalai, Attur, Ranipet, and Chengam are important towns. The hills are named after the Pachaimalaiyali peoples who live in the region.

Palghat Gap—a major break in the Western Ghats mountain range, southwestern India, it is located between the Nilgiri Hills (north) and the Anaimalai Hills (south). It is about 32 km wide and straddles the Kerala-Tamil Nadu border, serving as a major communication route between these two States. Highways and rail lines through the gap connect Palakkad in Kerala with Coimbatore and Pollachi in Tamil Nadu. Palghat Gap also influences southern India's climate; the southwest monsoons as well as storms from the Bay of Bengal cross the mountains through the opening.

Palkonda Hills—series of ranges in southern Andhra Pradesh State, southeastern India, the hills trend northwest to southeast and form the central part of the Eastern Ghats. Geologically they are relics of ancient mountains formed during the Cambrian period (570 to 505 million years ago) that were subsequently eroded by the Penner River and its tributaries. The Punchu and Cheyyeru rivers join in a spectacular confluence in a gorge in the corridor between the Velikonda and the Palkonda hills. Formed of quartzites, slates, and lavas, the Palkonda reach an elevation of 900 m in the south. The valleys between the mountains are drained by streams, many of which, having been dammed for storage tanks, provide irrigation for cultivation. The main crops are *jowar* (sorghum) and peanuts (groundnuts).

Palni Hills—a range of hills, an eastward extension of the Western Ghats, southwestern Tamil Nadu State, southern India, it is a continuation of the Anaimalai Hills in Kerala State. The Palni are about 70 km wide and 23 km long. In the south the hills terminate abruptly in steep slopes.

The upper Palni, in the west, consist of rolling hills covered with coarse grasses. Dense forests grow in the valleys. Peaks include Vandaravu, 2,553 m; Vembadi Shola, 2,505 m; and Karunmakadu, 2,451 m. The town of Kodaikanal is located in a high basin averaging 2,150 m above sea level. Hill villages cultivate vegetables and fruits such as potatoes, beans, root crops, pears, and peaches. There are also bauxite mines.

The lower Palni hills, in the east, form a confused jumble of peaks averaging 900-1,500 m above sea level and separated by steep wooded valleys. Teak trees have been extensively planted. Important cash crops include coffee, bananas, cardamom, citrus fruit, and turmeric.

Pir Panjal Range—It is a part of the western Punjab Himalaya, lying in northwestern India and northern Pakistan and extending southeastwards for more than 320 km from the Kishanganga River to the upper Beas River. Rising sharply to an average elevation of more than 4,000 m, it separates the hills to the south from the Vale of Kashmir, beyond which lie the Himalaya. The major passes through the range include the Pir Panjal (3,494 m) and Banihal (2,739 m); a highway tunnel near Banihal Pass makes the Vale of Kashmir accessible to traffic from the south, even in winter. The mountains extending to the north of the Kishanganga River in Pakistan are sometimes considered part of the range.

Punjab Plain—an extensive alluvial plain, extending over 99,200 sq km of area and covering most parts of the States of the Punjab and Haryana, and the Union Territories of Chandigarh and Delhi, northwestern India, it is bounded by the Yamuna River on the east, Shiwalik Hills on the north and northeast, Rajasthan desert on the south and southwest and the Ravi and Sutlej rivers on the northwest and southwest respectively. The southwestern margins of the plain in Haryana are strewn with sand dunes. On the southeastern tip of the plain in Haryana, south-to-north lying remnants of the Aravali mountains break its monotony. The plain is gently sloping from about 650 m above sea level in the northeast to about 200 m in the southeast. The plain, an area of early Aryan settlement, was, according to the epic the Mahabharata, the site of the war fought between the Pandavas and Kauravas. The Punjab plain was ruled by ancient northern Hindu dynasties until the Muslims established firm control after the defeat of Prithviraj Chauhan by Muhammad Ghuri in AD 1192. The death of Aurangzeb in 1707 and the weakening of the Mughal rule in Delhi enabled the Sikh dynasty to seize power in the region. In view of its western border with Pakistan, the region has great strategic importance.

The plain is the product of the process of alluviation. Bush and scrub vegetation is common in the arid and semi-arid southwest and south, while dry deciduous trees (like *shisham; Dalbergia sissoo*) are characteristic of the sub-humid northern and northeastern submontane zone. Along roads, canals, and in wastelands eucalyptus and/or poplar trees have emerged in dense groves in most parts of the region. Agriculture is the mainstay of the regions economy. Wheat and rice are dominant. Other crops include maize (in the north), bajra (in the south-and southwest), oilseeds, sugarcane, and cotton (in southwestern Punjab)

The whole region is effectively under irrigation both from canals and tube wells. Consolidation of landholdings has accelerated the development of tubewell irrigation. Major highways are becoming corridors of development both in the Punjab and Haryana States. Small- and medium-scale industries have developed in places like Ludhiana, Arnritsar, Jalandhar, Batala, Phagwara, Rajpura, Ambala, Panipat, Sonepat, and Chandigarh, producing textiles, bicycles, machine tools, agricultural implements, and sports goods. Around Delhi and along the highways converging on it, industrial growth is conspicuous.

Purvachal—also called Eastern Highlands, are mountain ranges in eastern India, extending over about 98,000 sq km in Arunachal Pradesh, Nagaland, Manipur Mizoram, Tripura, and eastern Assam States. The Patkai and other associated mountain ranges (including the Mishmi, Naga, Manipur, Tripura, and Mizo hills) that run through this region are referred to collectively as Purvachai (*purva*, "east," and *achal*, "mountain"). The area is bounded by Bangladesh in the southwest, Myanmar (Burma) in the southeast, and China in the northeast. The Indian epic the Mahabharata has several references to the region. The Purvachal was ruled by the Ahom from the beginning of the thirteenth century. It was occupied by the British in the last quarter of the nineteenth century.

Geologically, the region is unstable; it is criss-crossed with several faults. Its north-south-aligned hill ranges are defined by narrow parallel valleys tending towards the west. The highest peak in the region is Mount Dapha (in Lohit district ofArunachal Pradesh), with an elevation of (4,578 m. The major rivers are the Lohit, Burhi Dihang, Diyung, Kusiyara, Gumti, Kaladan, Manipur, Tixu, Namaleik, and Naurya. The vegetation is diverse, ranging from tropical evergreen to temperate evergreen and coniferous, and includes oak, chestnut, birch, magnolia, cherry, maple, laurel, and fig; there are also extensive bamboo thickets.

Rice, millet, maize, pulse (legumes), sesame, rapeseed, mustard, sugar cane, potato, barley, wheat, and cassava are grown by means of shifting cultivation with traditional implements. Poultry farming and livestock raising are also important. Industry, mainly cottage and small-scale, produces woven textiles, baskets, wooden utensils, bows and arrows, traps, sleeping benches, sugar, paper, metalware, traditional embroidered costumes, bricks, tiles, soap, hosiery, and preserved fruit. Mineral resources include lime, lignite, coal, iron ore, copper ore, rock salt, clay, and ochre.

The Nocte, Wancho, Tangsa, Naga, Kuki, Lushai, Lakher, Chakma, and Panei ethnic groups constitute most of the population. The North East Frontier Railway passes through only a part of the region, but the national highway has been extended to reach several towns in the region, including Agartala, Imphal, and Kohima. The administrative headquarters of most of the districts in the region are linked by air.

R

Rahr Plains—geographic region comprising part of the lower Gangetic Plains of southwestern West Bengal State in eastern India, it lies to the south of the Ganga and west of the Bhagirathi River. It consists of two sub-regions: northern Rahr and southern Rahr divided by the Damodar River covering parts of Murshidabad, Burdwan, Birbhum (northern Rahr), Midnapur, and Bankura (southern Rahr) districts. The region is covered with materials degraded from western tableland and older alluvium through rivers in inundation just outside the present deltaic region of West Bengal. The alluvial plains are essentially flat. Moist deciduous forests of sal (*Sharea*), champak, and acacia are frequently found, together with bamboo. Damodar, Ajay, and Mayurakshi rivers meander across the plains.

The economy is mostly agricultural (cereals, pulse [legumes], oilseeds, fruits, vegetables, betel nut, and date palm). The Raniganj coalfields, some of the country's largest, and adjacent deposits of iron ore, copper, lead, and zinc are used by the major iron and steel industrial complexes near Asansol and Durgapur. Other industries produce cotton and silk textiles, jute, paper, chemicals, fertilizers, gauges, bicycles, locomotives, and motorboats. Durgapur, Asansol, Burdwan, Bankura, Midnapore, Kharagpur, and Suri are the chief towns and are linked by roads and railways.

Rajasthan Steppe—desert in west-central Rajasthan State in northwestern India, it has an area of about 142,000 sq km.

Near Jodhpur the bedrock similar to that of the Vindhya Range; farther south there are Malani volcanic and Jalore Siwana granitic rocks. The region slopes from the Aravali Range in the northeast to the Luni River basin in the southeast; where rocks above the sandy surface bear evidence of wind erosion. Rajasthan Steppe has also been subject to extensive gullying. Large areas are covered with thorny scrub, acacia, and palm trees. The Luni is the only major river; the inland drainage pattern has created a number of salt lakes, such as the Didwana, Kuchman, Degna, and Sambhar. The desert soils contain a high percentage of soluble salts. Livestock (cattle, sheep, goats, and camels) raising and agriculture are economically important; cereals, pulses (legumes), oilseeds, cotton, and sugarcane are grown. The region suffers occasionally from severe droughts and attacks by swarms of locusts. It is rich in mineral resources (especially marble and salt), and gypsum, silver ore, and feldspar are mined; there is a sulphur plant at Sambhar Salt Lake. Rugs and woollen textiles, sugar, cement, pesticides, and dyes are produced. Jodhpur, Ganganagar, Churu, and Jhunjhunu are the important towns.

Rajgir Hill—388 m. high in central Bihar, it breaks the monotony of the south Gangetic Plain and appears as islands in the sea of alluvium. The hill, composed of massive quartizites, opens out to the southwest like the mouth of a crocodile with Aliani valley as its tongue. It is forest-clad too and presents a panoramic view to the tourists who enjoy its scenic beauty, hot springs, and healthy surroundings. It is a historical and religious centre also for the Hindus, Buddhists, and Jains.

The hill has parallel ridges. The valley between the ridges, south of the village of Rajgir, contains the site of Rajagriha ("Royal Residence"), said to have been the residence of the legendary Magadha emperor Jarasandha. The outer fortifications can be traced on the crests of the hills for more than 40 km; they are about 5 m thick, built of massive undressed stones without mortar. These ruined walls are generally dated to the sixth century BC. The remains of New Rajagriha, the reputed capital of Bimbisara (c. 520-490 BC), lie north of the valley.

An important Buddhist and Jain pilgrimage site, the Rajgir Hills are associated with the life of Gautama Buddha who often taught there. Chhatagiri is the former Gridhrakuta, or Vulture's Peak, which was one of his favourite resorts. One of the towers on Baibhar Hill (Vaibharagiri) has been identified as the Pippala stone house in which the Buddha lived. Sattapanni cave, which has been identified with a number of sites on Baibhar Hill and with the Sonbhandar cave at its foot, was the site of the first Buddhist synod (543 BC) to record the tenets of the faith. The Sonbhandar cave is now believed to have been excavated by the Jains in the third or fourth century AD. In the valley's centre, excavations at the

Maniyar Math revealed a circular shrine adorned with superb fifth-century stucco images of deities including Vishnu and a dancing Shiva. Several modern Jain temples lie on the hills around the valley. There are also hot springs in the valleys, surrounded by Hindu shrines.

Rohilkhand—low-lying, alluvial region in northwestern Uttar Pradesh State of north-central India, the Rohilkhand is part of upper Ganga Plain and has an area of about 25,000 sq km. It is bounded by the Ganga River on the south and the west and by the frontiers of China and Nepal on the north.

Part of the asymmetrical, alluvium-filled Indo-Ganga trough, the plain is broken by the Tarai-Bhabar submontane belt extending eastwards from the foot of the Shiwalik Hills. The Ramganga, Sukhata, Deona, Sarda, Pilkhara, and Garra rivers follow a northwest-to-southeast course through Rohilkhand. The region was once densely forested, but only a few small patches of forest remain. Agriculture, especially cereals, dominates the regional economy. Large-scale industries (producing textiles, sugar, general-engineering products, and chemicals) are located in urban centres such as Moradabad, Bareilly, Shahjahanpur, and Pilibhit. The region is one of the most densely populated in India and is well served by a network of roads.

The region is referred to as the Madhyadesh in the Hindu epics, Mahabharata and Ramayana. It was later called Hindustan by Muslim historians. The Rohilkhand was settled by the early Aryans and was successively ruled by various Hindu kings before it became part of the territory of the Muslim rulers of Delhi. With the eclipse of Mughal rule, the region was divided by Jat, Rohilla, and Maratha annexations until it passed to the British following the Indian Mutiny of 1857.

S

Sagar Island—westernmost island of the Ganga delta in West Bengal State of northeastern India, it lies at the mouth of the Hugli (Hooghly) River. An arm of the river separates it from the mainland to the east. Situated at a point where the Ganga once met the Bay of Bengal, it is held particularly sacred and is a noted Hindu pilgrimage centre. A three-day bathing festival and large fair are held annually. The island subject to severe cyclones, has a lighthouse on the southwestern shore to guide traffic up the Hugli River.

Satpura Range—range of hills, part of the Deccan Plateau in western India, it stretches for 900 km across the widest part of peninsular India, through.Maharashtra and Madhya Pradesh States. The range, the name of which means "seven folds", forms the watershed between the Narmada (north) and Tapti (south) rivers. With peaks more than 1,200 m high, the Satpura Range includes the Rajpipia Hills to the west, the Mahadeo Hills to the north, and the Maikala Range to the east.

Although it is economically poor, the Satpura Range contains some worked manganese and coal deposits in its southeastern flanks. It is largely forested, dissected plateau country, and it contains valuable teak forests in the west. In the upper Wainganga and Pench valleys of the Mahadeo Hills, there is some agriculture, and on the higher hills, Gond hill tribes practise *jhum* (slash-and-burn) cultivation. In Madhya Pradesh, Pachmarhi is a resort town and Chhindwara is a minor administrative centre.

Seshachalam Hills—These are hill ranges of the Eastern Ghats in southern Andhra Pradesh State of southeastern India. Formed during Precambrian time (about 3.8 billion to 540 million years ago), the ranges, containing sandstone and shale interbedded with limestone. They are highly dissected and have many longitudinal valleys. They are bounded by the Rayalaseema uplands in the west and northwest and the Nandyal valley (formed by the Kunderu River) in the northeast. The Seshachalam Hills extend over some 8,000 sq km, and their general trend is east-southeast. The Seshachalam Hills, together with the Erramala Range to the north, vary in elevation from 400 to 1,370 m. The hillslopes have only a thin forest cover because of scanty rainfall. Tributaries of the Penneru River drain the region. The ruggedness of the topography, the infertility of the soils, and the semi-arid climate restrict agriculture.

Jowar (sorghum) and peanuts (groundnuts) are the major crops. Asbestos, barite, and limestone are worked; handloom weaving, bamboo working, and brickmaking are the only other economically significant activities. Pulivendla is the only important town.

Shillong Plateau—in eastern Meghalaya State of northeastern India, it is a rolling table-land and the highest portion of the hill mass that comprises most of Meghalaya. The plateau's western, northern, and southern escarpments are called the Garo, Khasi, and Jaintia hills, respectively. The Shillong plateau is an outlier of the plateau of peninsular India and is composed primarily of ancient rocks. It contains coal and iron ore, and limestone is quarried. The highest point is Shillong Peak (1,961 m) located 5 km south of the city of Shillong.

Shiwalik Hills—sub-Himalayan range, also called Siwalik Range, or Outer Himalaya, it extends west-northwest for more than 1,600 km from the Tista River, Sikkim State in India, through Nepal, across northwestern India, and into northern Pakistan. Though only l6-km wide in places, the hills have an average elevation of 900 to 1,200 m. They rise abruptly from the plains of the Indus and Ganga rivers (south) and parallel the main range of the Himalaya (north), from which they are separated by valleys. The Shiwalik are sometimes considered to include the southern foothills of the Assam Himalaya, which extend eastwards for 640 km across southern Bhutan to the bend of the Brahmaputra River. The range proper, to which the name Shiwalik (from Sanskrit, meaning "Belonging to [the God] Shiva") was formerly restricted, is the 320 km of foothills extending from Haridwar, India, on the Ganga River northwestwards to the Beas River. Everywhere in this section the poor scrub forests have long since been removed, and the hills are subject to severe erosion. Periodic floods sweep masses of sand and silt down into ever-changing great stream beds, called *chos*, that are dry except after rains. The Nepal portion of the hills is called the Churia Range.

Siachen Glacier—one of the world's longest mountain glaciers, lying in the Karakoram Range system of Kashmir near the India-Pakistan border, it extends for 70 km from north-northwest to south-southeast. It has a number of fast-flowing surface streams and at least 12 medial moraines. It is the source for the 80 km-long Nubra River, a tributary of the Shyok, which is part of the Indus River system.

Sundarbans—formerly Sunderbunds, this vast tract of forest and saltwater swamp forming the lower part of the Ganga delta, extends about 260 km along the Bay of Bengal from the Hugli (Hooghly) River estuary (India) to the Meghna River estuary in Bangladesh. The whole tract reaches inland for 100-130 km. A network of estuaries, tidal rivers, and creeks intersected by numerous channels, it encloses flat, marshy islands covered with dense forests.

The name Sundarbans is perhaps derived from the term meaning "forest of sundari", a reference to the large mangrove tree that provides valuable fuel. Along the coast the forest passes into a mangrove swamp; the southern region, with numerous wild animals and crocodile-infested estuaries, is virtually uninhabited. It is one of the last preserves of the Bengal tiger and the site of a tiger preservation project. The cultivated northern area yields rice, sugarcane, timber, and betel nut.

T

Tamilnad Plains—eastern coastal lowlands of Tamil Nadu State, in southern India, these are bounded by the Bay of Bengal on the east, the Indian Ocean on the south. the Eastern Ghats on the west, and the Andhra plains on the north. The Tamilnad plains consist of the Cauvery (Kaveri) delta and the deltas of the Vaigai and Palar rivers, which have formed beaches of sand and shingles. Sand dunes (locally known as *theris*) rising 30 m to 65m high and supporting Palmyra palm and thorny scrub are conspicuous features along the relatively straight coast. The flat plains are broken by numerous hills with a distinct north-northeast to south-southwest trend. Natural vegetation consists of littoral forests and plantations of *casuarina* and coconut, together with scattered trees, climbing vines, and grass. The Cauvery, Ponnaiyar, Palar, Vaigai, Tambraparni, Vellar, and Arni rivers flow east into the Bay of Bengal. The soils are red-loamy and sandy-loamy, both rich in iron.

Agriculture is the mainstay of the economy of the region; crops include rice, pulses (legumes), oilseeds, tobacco, and sugarcane. The Cauvery delta has a large irrigation canal system. The early development of industry by the British made the coast of the Tamilnad plains one of the most industrialized areas in India with the manufacture or production of textiles, cement, chemicals, vegetable oils, fertilizers, automobiles, galvanized pipes, calculators, and teleprinters. The railway coach factory at Perambur is one of the largest in Asia. Neyveli town has a large thermal power plant. Railways and roads connect Chennai, Tiruchirappalli, Tirunelveli, Thanjavur, and Chingleput.

Tamilnad Uplands—hilly region in central Tamil Nadu State of southern India, these extend over an area of about 38,000 sq km and are bounded by the Eastern Ghats on the west, the Sahyadris (Western Ghats) on the south, the Tamilnad plains on the east, and the Telangana plateau on the north. The Muslim rule extended from about 1650 to about 1800, when the region came under the domain of the British. The Cauvery (Kaveri), Palar, Vaigai, Tambraparni, and Periyar rivers flow from west to east and drain into the Bay of Bengal. The Cauvery and its tributaries have diversified the terrain, by erosion, into the Tamil Nadu hills, the Coimbatore-Madurai uplands, and the middle Cauvery valley. The Tamilnad uplands have an average elevation of 450 m in the west, decreasing to about 150 m in the east the Cauvery valley is approximately 300 m above sea level.

The soils are mostly loamy and clayey. Forests are almost nonexistent; scattered woodlands and scrub are found in the northern upland region. Agriculture is the principal occupation of most m the population. Crops include rice, millets, oilseeds, pulses (legumes), cotton, and sugarcane. The region is one of the better-developed industrial area in India and produces textiles, machine tools, and chemicals. There are coffee, tea, cinchona, and cardamom plantations. Iron ore, magnesite, beryl, and zinc are mined. Roads and railways link Madurai, Coimbatore, Salem, Vellore, Dindigul, and Erode.

In the Fourth century BC, the region was known as Tamilakam and was ruled successively by the Chera, Chola, and Pandya kingdoms. A number of temples constructed during the Middle Hindu period (AD 800-1300) became the nuclei of towns such as Vellore, Krishnagiri. Dindigul, Coimbatore and Erode.

Tarai—region of northern India and southern Nepal, also spelt Terai, it runs parallel to the lower Himalayan ranges. A strip of undulating former marshland, it stretches from the Yamuna River (west) to the Brahmaputra River (east). At its northern edge are numerous springs forming several streams, including the important Ghaghara River, that intersect the Tarai (meaning "moist land") and are responsible for its marshy character. Interspersed with the Tarai is the *Bhabar*, which is a region of coarse gravel and shingle deposits supporting sal (*Shorea robusta*) forests. Drainage and cultivation of the area, once extremely malarial, have diminished the marshlands. The eastern part of the Tarai is known in West Bengal State and in Bangladesh as the *Duars*.

Thar Desert—a tract of rolling sand hills, also called Great Indian Desert, it is located partly in the Indian State of Rajasthan and partly in Pakistan. It covers 200,000 sq km of territory and is bordered by the irrigated Indus plain to the west, the Aravali Range to the southeast, the Rann of Kachchh to the south, and the Punjab plain to the north and northeast. The desert results from the dryness of the prevailing monsoon winds, which do not bring sufficient rain to keep the region moist. The name Thar is derived from *thul*, the general term for the region's sand ridges.

The desert presents an undulating surface, with high and low sand dunes separated by sandy plains and low, barren hills, or *bhakars*, which rise abruptly from the surrounding plains. The dunes are in continual motion and take on varying shapes and sizes. Older dunes, however, are in a semi-stabilized or stabilized condition, and many rise to a height of almost 150 m. Several *playas* (saline lakes), locally known as *dhands*. are scattered throughout the region.

The desert sands cover early Precambrian gneiss (granitelike metamorphic rocks formed in the oldest geological era, which began 3.8 billion years ago), sedimentary rocks about 2.5 billion to 570 million years old, and more recent material deposited by rivers (alluvium). The surface sand is aeolian (wind-deposited) sand of the Quaternary Period (the most recent geologic period, which began about 1.6 million years ago).

The soils consist of seven main groups —desert soils, red desert soils, sierozems (brownish grey soils), the red and yellow soils of the foothills, the saline soils of the depressions, and the lithosols (shallow, weathered soils) and regosols (soft, loose soils) found in the hills. All these soils are predominantly coarse-textured, well drained, and calcareous (calcium bearing). A thick accumulation of lime often occurs at varying depths. The soils are generally infertile and, because of severe wind erosion, are overblown with sand.

Climate : During January, the coldest month, the mean minimum temperature ranges between 5 °C and 10 °C, and frost is frequent. Dust storms and dust raising winds, often blowing with velocities of 140 km to 150 km per hour, are common in May and June.

The amount of annual rainfall in the desert tract is generally low, ranging from about 100 mm or less in the west to about 500 mm in the east. Precipitation is highly erratic, and there are wide fluctuations in the amount from year to year. About 90 per cent of the total annual rain occurs during the season of the southwest monsoon, from July to September. At other seasons the wind blows from the northeast. May and June are the hottest months of the year with temperatures rising to 50 °C.

Vegetation and Animals : The desert vegetation is mostly herbaceous, or of stunted scrub; trees occasionally dot the landscape. On the hills, gum *Arabic acacia*, and euphorbia may be found. The *khajri* (*Prosopis cineraria*) tree grows throughout the plains.

The thinly populated grasslands support the black buck, the chinkara (gazelle), and some feathered game, notably the francolin and quail. Among the migratory birds, sand grouse, ducks, and geese are common. The desert is also the home of the vanishing great Indian bustard.

There are five major breeds of cattle in the Thar tract; Among these, the Tharparkar breed is the highest milk yielder, while the Kankre breed is good both as a beast of burden and as a milk producer. Sheep are bred for both medium-fine and rough wool. The camel is commonly used for transport, as well as for ploughing the land and other agricultural purposes.

Grasses form the main natural resources of the desert. They provide nutritive and palatable pastures, as well as medicines used locally by the inhabitants. Alkaloids, used for making medicine, and oils for making soap are also extracted. Water is very scarce. Whatever seasonal rain falls is collected in tanks and reservoirs and is used for drinking and domestic purposes. Most groundwater cannot be utilized because it lies deep underground and is often saline. Good aquifers have been detected in the central part of the desert.

Economy : Apart form wells and tanks, canals are the main sources of water throughout the desert. When water is available, crops such as wheat and cotton are grown. The Sukkur (Lloyd) barrage on the Indus River, completed in 1932, irrigates the southern Thar region in Pakistan by means of canals, while the Gang canal brings water from the Sutlej River to part of the northern region. The Rajasthan canal irrigates a vast amount of land in that part of the Thar region in India. The canal begins at the Harike Barrage—at the confluence of the Sutlej and Beas rivers in the Indian Punjab—and continues in a southwesterly direction for 470 km.

The partition of India and Pakistan in 1947 left most of the irrigation canals fed by the rivers of the Indus system in Pakistani territory, while a large desert region remained unirrigated on the Indian side of the border. The Indus Water Treaty of 1960 fixed and delimited the rights and obligations of both countries concerning the use of the waters of the Indus River system. Under the agreement, waters of the Ravi, Beas, and Sutlej rivers are to be made available to the Rajasthan canal to irrigate mainly the desert tract covering parts of western Rajasthan in India.

Most of the inhabitants reside in rural areas and are distributed in varying densities. Customs, rituals, and modes of dress are manifold. Both Islam and Hinduism are practised, and the population is divided into complex economic and social groups. Many nomads are engaged in animal husbandry, crafts, or trade. They do not belong to a specific ethnic group, nor are they associated with a separate area; in general they are symbiotically related to their sedentary population and its economy.

Thermal-power-generating plants, fuelled by coal and oil, are located only in the large towns and supply power only locally. Hydroelectric power is supplied by the Nangal power plant located on the Sutlej River in the Punjab.

Roads and railways are few. One railway line serves the southern part of the region. In the Indian part of the desert, a second line goes from

Merta Road to Suratgarh via Bikaner, while another connects the towns of Jodhpur and Jaisalmer. In the Pakistani part of the desert, a railway line runs between Bahawalpur and Hyderabad.

Tripura Hills—situated in eastern Tripura State of northeastern India, the Tripura Hills, by way of the Mizo Hills of Mizoram State on the east, form a low western extension of the Purvachal, a strategically located highland region fronting the border with Myanmar (Burma). The region belongs to the Assam-Burma geologic province, an unstable seismic zone crisscrossed by several faults and extending into Myanmar.

The hills are a series of parallel north-south folds, decreasing in elevation to the south until they merge into the Eastern plains. Each successive ridge of hills to the east rises higher than the one before; the low Deotamura Range is followed by the Artharamura, Langtarai, and Sakhan Tlang ranges. The Jamrai Tlang Mountains, 74 km in length, have the highest peak, Betling Sib (1,000 m). The Tripura Hills, once heavily forested, now have patches of bare soil where the region's sparse populations have practised *jhum* (slash-and-burn cultivation). The Dhalai, Khowai, Longai, Juri, and Deo rivers originate in the Tripura Hills and flow across the valleys; smaller streams are dry during the winter. Soils are generally coarse-textured sandy loams and are almost devoid of humus. The population consists of the Old Tripuri, Deshi Tripuri, Reang, Jamatia, Bodo, Kuki, and Noatia ethnic groups. Agriculture is the major occupation of the region; crops include rice, jute, cotton, oilseeds, potatoes, sugarcane, and fruit. Industries produce handloomed textiles, cane and bamboo products, metalware, and seasoned timber; carpentry, blacksmithing, and embroidery are also important. Dharmanagar and Kailashahar are the important towns.

Tripura Plains—also called **Agartala plains** lie in southwestern Tripura State of northeastern India and extend over approximately 4,150 sq km. The Tripura plains are located on a section of the greater Ganga-Brahmaputra lowlands (also called the Eastern plains), west of the Tripura Hills. They are dotted with lakes and marshes and there is much forest cover. The soil is thin except in the river valleys, but everywhere the tropical sun and torrential rains have leached minerals from the soils. It is liable to floods causing immense damage to its population. One of the worst floods was in 1984 due to abnormal pre-monsoon rainfall.

Agriculture is the principal occupation; rice, jute, tea, and cotton are the major crops. Industries include cloth weaving; rice and flour milling; fruit canning; utensil making; cane, bamboo, and leather-goods production; and soap manufacture. Tree farming and horticulture as well as fish farming are practised. Agartala is the principal town; also important are Belonia and Khowai.

U

Utkal Plains—coastal plains in eastern Orissa State of eastern India, extend over approximately 41,400 sq km. Fronting the Bay of Bengal on the east, the plains are bounded by the Andhra plain on the south, the lower Gangetic plain on the north, and the Eastern Ghats on the west. The Utkal plains are coastal lowlands consisting chiefly of Mahanadi delta deposits and marine sediments, and they merge with the Eastern Ghats at an elevation of about 76 m. The plains have a nearly straight shoreline.

Comprising recent and tertiary alluvium with, patches of Archaean gneiss and sandstone, the plains are the widest in the deltaic regions. Sand dunes of decomposed granites and zircon, created mainly by the action of wind at low tide, and lagoons are found along the Bay of Bengal. Chilka, the largest lake in the region (in the southwest), is Salty; Samang and Sar (north and northeast of Puri, respectively) are freshwater lakes. Littoral forests are found along the coast of Kendrapara, Jagatsinghpur, Bhadrak, and Baleshwar districts and tropical moist deciduous forests are found inland throughout Puri, Khurda, Cuttack, and Jaipur districts. The Mahanadi, Brahmani, Baitarani, and Subarnarekha rivers are often subject to heavy flooding; it is the combined outflow of these rivers that formed the Mahanadi delta in the east-central part of the plains. The region has fertile red and alluvial soils.

Agriculture is the main occupation, and rice is the principal crop; pulses (legumes) and oilseeds are also grown. Major irrigation projects located in the plains permit double cropping. Industry, centred in urban areas such as Cuttack, Bhubaneshwar, and Puri along the Calcutta-Chennai railway, includes paper mills, refrigerator plants, and the production of ceramics, glass, refractories, textiles, and galvanized pipe. Other industries include sawmilling, coir making, boat repairing, and the manufacture of phosphates, fertilizers, and tyres; there is a railway wagon workshop, stone-cutting and processing mills, and a LPG gas bottling plant. The Cuttack-Choudwar industrial complex in the central part of the Utkal plains near the Mahanadi delta has had a major impact on the industrial development of the State. The plains have a network of roads and railways, and inland waterways in the district of Cuttack, Kendrapara, and Jagatsinghpur, and an airfield at Bhubaneshwar.

Buddhism flourished in the Utkal plains in the third century BC under Emperor Ashoka, and the region is described in the rock edicts of Dhauli (where Ashoka fought the famous Kalinga war), as forming part of the ancient Kalinga territory. Successive ancient dynasties including the Satavahanas, Karas, and Eastern Gangas ruled the region until, in the later half of the sixteenth century, it passed to the Muslims and later to the Marathas, The British assumed control of the plains in 1804.

V

Velikonda Range—range of hills in southeastern Andhra Pradesh State of southeastern India, they trend north to south and form the eastern flank of the Eastern Ghats, which at that point are strongly folded and faulted. The Velikonda are assumed to have been elevated during the Cambrian period (540 to 505 million years ago). They are relics of ancient mountains that were eroded and dissected by numerous streams. Rivers find their way through the hills by narrow gaps, usually marked by rapids. The main railway from Chennai (Madras) to Mumbai (Bombay) runs along the corridor formed by the Penner River between the Velikonda and the Palkonda hills to the south. The Velikonda reach an elevation of 750 m to 900 m but are sparsely wooded and almost devoid of human population except for a few scattered groups of aboriginal Chenchus. The valleys, however, are moderately populated. The narrowness of the corridors through the hills has permitted the streams to be dammed and storage tanks to be built, making a certain amount of cultivation and irrigation possible. Peanuts (groundnuts) and *jowar* (sorghum) are the main crops.

Vindhya Range—A broken range of hills, they form the southern escarpment of the central upland of India, From Gujarat State on the west, it extends about 1,086 km across Madhya Pradesh State to the Ganga River valley near Varanasi (Banares). The mountains form the southern edge of the Malwa plateau and then divide into two branches: the Kaimur Range, running north of the Son River into western Bihar State, and the southern branch, running between the upper reaches of the Son and Narmada rivers to meet the Satpura Range in the Maikala Range (or Amarkantak plateau).

The Vindhya Range, at an elevation of 450 m to 1,100 m, gives rise to the main southern tributaries of the Ganga-Yamuna system, including the Chambal, Betwa, Ken, and Tons rivers. Because of their horizontal sandstone structure, the mountains tend to be flat-topped and plateaulike. The Vindius of the second-century-AD Greek geographer Ptolemy, the range is regarded as marking the border between northern and peninsular India.

W

West Benal Duars—physical region in extreme northeastern West Bengal State of northeastern India, it is bounded by Sikkim State and Bhutan on the north, Assam State on the east, Nepal on the west, and the continuation of West Bengal State on the south.

They constitute a lowland forest belt along the junction between the Himalayan foothills to the north and the north Bengal plain region of the lower Gangetic Plains to the south. The name duars (literally "doors") is derived from the several passes that lead from the region northwards into the lesser Himalaya. Along the northern portion of the West Bengal duars are large banks of boulders, through which flow numerous streams cutting across the slope from the low foothills in the north to the plains in the south. These streams and the Tista River on the western side of the duars occasionally bring devastating floods. The area is covered with dense forests of conifers, including silver fir and oak, magnolia, rhododendron, beech, birch, and sal (*Shorea*). The forests are mainly of four types — riverine, plains, hill, and savannah. There are a number of wildlife sanctuaries in these reserve forests. Much of the forests have been cleared for tea plantations in the Darjeeling foothills in the northeast.

Rice, jute, maize, potatoes, vegetables, and fruits are the other major crops grown. Industries in the area produce foodstuff, beverages, dairy products, leather footwear, and transport equipment; rice, oilseeds, and wheat are milled. Siliguri, Darjeeling, and Jalpaiguri are the region's most important towns and are linked by roads and railways. Siliguri has an airfield at nearby Bagdogra.

Wetlands—terrestrial ecosystem characterized by poor drainage and the consequent presence of sluggishly moving or standing water saturating the soil, wetlands are usually classified, according to soil and plant life, as bogs, marsh, or swamp. Wetlands include a wide spectrum of habitats ranging from peat bogs of the northern temperate regions to mangrove forests of the tropical regions, from seasonal ponds and marshes to floodplains and riparian swamps from shallow lakes and the margins of large reservoirs to salt lakes and brackish lagoons, from estuaries to coastal salt marshes. The oases in deserts, beds of marine algae (kelp), and coral reefs are also wetlands. Paddy fields and fish ponds are man-made and managed wetlands. All these habitats, ranging in area from less than one hectare to thousands of hectares, share two major characteristics: (1) the soils remain waterlogged or are submerged under water for whole or part of the year, and (2) the wetland biota depend upon, and are adapted to, this waterlogging or submergence during at least one part of their life cycle.

Location : Wetlands occur throughout the world in all climatic zones and are estimated to cover about 6 per cent of the earth's surface. These habitats have supported humankind since the beginning of history and have played a crucial role in the emergence of civilization. Indeed, the first human settlements were intimately related to the beginnings of agriculture in the floodplains of the great rivers. Many wetland plants and animals have been a major food resource for humans in all parts of the world. In Indian mythology, culture, and history, wetlands (referred to in Sanskrit as *anupa*), and wetland biota were so important that they often became the objects of reverence. The lotus, swan, turtle, and fish are well-known symbols and icons associated with the various gods and goddesses. The floodplain of the Yamuna River provided the stage for the boyhood activities of Lord Krishna. The serene landscape of reed-fringed shallow lakes, lotuses and water lilies, and flocks of swans inspired many poets and writers. Even today, wetlands continue to provide food staples such as rice and fish for more than half of the world's population.

While in Indian culture, wetlands were regarded with reverence as the abodes of gods, the western world considered them to be the dwellings of ghosts, the reservoirs of diseases, and as obstacles to economic development. Wetlands were hence drained, filled, and reclaimed in the name of progress. The rivers were dammed, regulated, and channelized, resulting in the elimination of floodplains. More than half of the natural wetlands of the world have already been lost to "development" in many countries. Finally, in the 1960s, wetlands were recognized as important habitats for various species of waterfowl (ducks, coots, teals, storks, cranes, and flamingos) of which tens of thousands migrate every year during winter from colder northern regions to warmer wetlands in the south. Scientific studies soon revealed many other benefits and advantages of wetlands which had earlier been either unknown or had been ignored or overlooked. As a re\sult of this new awareness, wetlands became the first, and so far the only, habitat for whose protection an international convention was adopted at Ramsar (Iran) in 1971.

Importance : Wetlands perform several important environmental and ecological functions that make them invaluable resources. They are very rich in their biodiversity, being the habitat of about 15 per cent of all living organisms on earth. Organisms representing all taxonomic groups, ranging from unicellular algae to liverworts, mosses, ferns, and woody angiosperms, from protozoa to mammals, and many kinds of bacteria and fungi, all flourish in wetlands. Common wetland plants include mosses, ferns, cattails, grasses, and sedges; conifers, palms, and other shrubs and trees, besides numerous submerged, free-floating, and rooted, floating-leaved herbaceous plants, and several insectivorous plants occur in different wetlands.

Among animals, arthropods (most of crustacea and insecta) and molluscs are the most dominant species. Oligochaetes are also abundant. Among vertebrates, amphibia, fish, and birds are dominant. Various kinds of avifauna (also called waterfowl) are particularly prominent and are often found in large flocks. The diversity of waterfowl found in a wetland is closely related to the habitat and the floristic diversity. Many mammals such as beavers, otters, and rhinoceros are found exclusively in wetlands. Wetland fauna also includes those animals that utilize this particular kind of habitat for only a part of their life cycle or to meet their particular needs. Many herbivores graze in wetlands seasonally; many insects pass their larval stages in wetlands; a great many terrestrial birds feed on aquatic animals; and the survival of many aquatic animals such as turtles, crocodiles, and many kinds of fish depends on wetlands. Further, large-scale migration of animals, often across entire continents, such as those of waterfowl, turtles, and fish, contributes greatly to the faunal diversity of wetlands.

Many endemic, rare, endangered, or threatened organisms are found in wetlands. Important examples include the one-horned rhinoceros, brow-antlered deer, Siberian crane. West African manatee, marsh deer, leaf monkey, proboscis monkey, and green turtle.

Wetlands are highly productive, often as or even more productive than the adjacent terrestrial and aquatic ecosystems. Wetland plants such as the water hyacinth are among the most productive species. Mangroves are as rich in flora and fauna as tropical rainforests. Many wetland plants are used extensively by humans for food (rice, water chestnut, and lotus-seed, or *makhana*), fibre (jute, cane, reeds, cattails), fodder (grasses), and fuel. Mangroves also yield timber and fuelwood. Fish and prawn are the most important wetland food resource for humans, although frogs, ducks, and other animals are also widely consumed.

Wetlands detain and retain water that would otherwise flood areas lying laterally and/or downstream. Thus, wetlands play a very important role in flood control and aquifer recharge. Wetlands are sometimes the only source of water for both humans and animals. They act as traps for silt because of the detention of water and the reduction in the flow velocity, aided by the vegetation, leading to the settling down of silt and organic debris suspended in flood waters.

The extensive system of below-ground organs (rhizomes, stolons, and roots) of wetland vegetation help in binding the soil and thus protect it against erosion. Mangroves help in dissipating the erosive forces of cyclonic storms, tidal waves, and water currents.

Several physical, chemical, and biological processes occurring in wetlands result in the retention or removal, at least partly, of various nutrients and toxic substances such as heavy metals and pesticides. Thus, wetlands act as a natural filter and help to improve the water quality in adjacent water bodies and downstream regions. Hence, wetlands are sometimes called the “kidneys” of Mother Nature.

Wetlands also significantly influence the global cycles of carbon and nitrogen. Wetlands reduce carbon dioxide levels by converting it to biomass and accumulating peat. Wetlands also produce methane, a greenhouse gas, which may influence the patterns of global climate. Nitrogen fixation by blue-green algae and several wetland plants, as well as denitrification in wetlands influence the global nitrogen budget.

Finally, wetlands also have important non-consumptive social and cultural values as they provide avenues for recreational activities such as swimming, fishing, canoeing, birdwatching, or just relaxing and appreciating nature.

Wetlands also host many organisms such as mosquitoes, molluscs, and other invertebrates which act as vectors of disease-causing organisms, such as malaria, schistosomiasis, filariasis, onchocerciasis, bilharzia, trypanosomiasis, as also a number of arboviral diseases.

Wetlands are created, modified, or destroyed by various natural hydrological processes through sedimentation, accumulation of autochthonous organic matter, shifting river courses, and unusual rainfall events. These processes generally occur on a geological or historical time scale. Natural fires are common in swamps and floodplains throughout the world but frequent and uncontrolled fires are also damaging to wetlands.

Danger to Wetlands : But the most serious threats to wetlands come from human activities, both in the wetlands proper and in their catchment areas and in the adjacent deep water habitats. Wetlands have been lost mostly due to land-reclamation projects which drain and/or fill them. Shallow marshes and floodplains are often the preferred sites for constructing landfills for the disposal of solid urban wastes. Natural wetlands, both saline and freshwater, have also been converted into fish ponds and paddy fields. The overexploitation of biological resources (harvesting plants, fishing, and hunting) has driven many species to near or total extinction. Grazing by domestic and wild animals is common and most wetlands are adapted to it.

Various factors lead to the degradation and reduction of wetlands. These include a wide range of land-use practices such as agriculture, grazing, and mining which increase soil erosion and the inflow of silt and nutrients into the wetlands. Other factors which have an adverse affect on wetlands are the direct regulation of water flows and the disposal of domestic sewage and industrial effluents directly into the wetland itself or in an adjacent water body. Coastal wetlands are also affected by oil spills from ships and motorboats, and offshore oil exploration. Invasive exotic species of plants (water hyacinth, salvinia, alligator weed, and lpomoea) and animals (fish such as tilapia, grass carp, and gambusia) are other major threats to wetlands.

Conservation of Wetlands : Wetlands occur extensively in India. Natural wetlands include swamps and riparian forests along streams and rivers, particularly in the submontane tracts of the Himalaya and at a few places in the Western Ghats; vast flood- plains and marshes, numerous shallow freshwater and saline lakes, and coastal lagoons (including backwaters). Mangroves are widespread along the coasts in the deltas of all the major rivers; the Sundarbans, which lie in the delta of the Ganga and the Brahmaputra rivers, are the single largest mangrove area in the world. Large seasonal and spatial variability in rainfall has necessitated the construction of thousands of large and small reservoirs and irrigation tanks. Whereas vast areas of natural wetlands have been reclaimed or converted to paddy fields and fish ponds, a much larger areas of man-made wetlands has been created in India.

The conservation of wetland habitats began in India long before these regions became the focus of international attention and concern. The Sundarbans of Khulna district (now in Bangladesh) was declared a reserve under the Forest Act of 1879. The area was prohibited by law for human settlement or colonization except for a few fishermen and forest guards. The Keoladeo National Park at Bharatpur, Rajasthan State, was created about 200 years ago out of the floodplains of two seasonal rivers which were dammed to control flooding in the region. The Kaziranga National Park in Assam State, northeast India, is the sole habitat of the one-horned rhinoceros; an alluvial marsh, it was declared a sanctuary many years ago and became a national park in 1974. Many of the national parks and wildlife sanctuaries in India include important saline and freshwater wetland sites. A part of the Indian Sundarbans has been fully protected as a tiger reserve since 1973, and is now designated as a biosphere reserve. Three other marine and saline wetlands (North Andamans, Rann of Kachchh, and Gulf of Mannar) and two freshwater wetlands, Kaziranga (430 sq km) and Manas (391 sq km), have also been named as biosphere reserves.

The *Ramsar Convention on Wetlands* contributed significantly to the cause of wetlands conservation. The countries which signed the convention were required to designate one or more wetlands as "internationally important", and to take necessary action for the protection and sustainable management of all wetlands. The Ramsar Convention came into force in India on February 1, 1982. As a result. Lake Chilka, a coastal lagoon in Orissa State, and the Keoladeo National Park were designated under the convention. Later, Wular (natural lake in Jammu and Kashmir), Harike (reservoir in Punjab), Sambhar (salt lake in Rajasthan), and Loktak (floodplain lake in Manipur) were added to the list of Ramsar sites. Lake Ujni (Maharashtra), Ashtamudi estuary (Kerala), Kolleru (Andhra Pradesh), Upper Lake, Bhopal (Madhya Pradesh), Nal Sarovar (Gujarat), Kabar (Bihar), Pulicat (Andhra Pradesh and Tamil Nadu), Sukhna (Chandigarh), Renuka, Pong Dam and Chandratal (Himachal Pradesh), Kanjli and Ropar (Punjab), Tso Morari (Jammu and Kashmir), Deepar Beel (Assam), and the East Calcutta wetlands (West Bengal) have also been identified as nationally important wetlands.

Although there is an increasing awareness about the value and importance of wetlands, the survival of these regions continues to face threats from anthropogenic activities. It is necessary that the remaining wetlands are protected, managed, and sustained. In this context, the Ramsar Convention promotes the concept of "wise use" which refers to "sustainable utilization for the benefit of mankind in a way compatible with the maintenance of the natural properties of the ecosystem". It is also now widely recognized that wetlands have for long been managed by the local communities, which have been dependent upon them for all their needs. Therefore, while the management objectives of environmental protection have to be clearly identified on the basis of a proper assessment of the functions and values of the wetlands, effective management requires an understanding of the traditional management practices of the indigenous population, and the active participation of all stakeholders and local communities.

Z

Zoji—Situated at an elevation of 3,529 m, the Zoji pass across the Himalaya in Jammu and Kashmir State of northern India carries the only road leading from the Vale of Kashmir eastwards to Leh, in Ladakh district, and on to Tibet. Heavily forested, the pass is the lowest in the western axis of the Himalaya but is extremely precipitous on the south side.

Section : FOUR

STATES AND UNION TERRITORIES

A

Andaman and Nicobar Islands—It is an island group, in the south-eastern part of Bay of Bengal. The Andamans constitute one of the two major groups of islands in the Union Territory. The peaks of a sub-merged mountain range, the islands form an arc 1,000 km long between Myanmar (Burma) and Sumatra (Indonesia) and have a land area of 6,408 sq km.

The Andamans, situated on the ancient trade route between India and Burma (Myanmar), were visited by Lieutenant Archibald Blair of the Bombay Marine (the East India Company's navy) in 1789. Linked administratively by the British in 1872, the two groups became a union territory of the Republic of India in 1956. An attempt was made in 1789 to set up a penal colony here, but it only became possible in 1858, after the first war of independence (the Indian Mutiny, or the Sepoy Mutiny). The first European settlement on the islands was at Port Blair, situated along the eastern coast of South Andaman. The territory is administered by a lieutenant governor, appointed by the President of India. Port Blair, the only major town on the island, is the territorial capital.

The three major islands are North Andaman, Middle Andaman, and South Andaman (closely positioned and collectively known as Great Andaman). Also prominent is Little Andaman, to the south. They all fall in the Andaman district of this territory. Of the original inhabitants, only the Jarawa and Onge, on the islands of South Andaman, Rutland, and Little Andaman, retain a traditional hunting-and-gathering way of life.

The Nicobar group includes the islands of Car Nicobar (north), Camorta (Kamorra) and Nancowrie (central group), and Great Nicobar (south). Car Nicobar is a beautiful spot surrounded by blue water and coral reefs with frequent patches of green vegetative cover. It has 15 villages on the periphery. The original Mongoloid tribes have been caught in a civilization trap. Fishing, hunting, and the collection of coconuts make their livelihood.

Andamans—These islands are the extensions above the sea level of submarine ridges of the Arakan Yoma and Patkoi ranges to the north and the Mentawai group to the south. Recently, a volcano had erupted on Barren Island in the north. The islands are a succession of dome-shaped hill ranges running parallel to each other from north to south. The highest peak is Saddle Peak (732 m) on North Andaman. This is followed by Mount Harriet (365 m). Flat land is scarce and confined to a few valleys, such as the Bitampur and Diglipur. The islands are formed of tertiary sandstone, limestone, and shale and are highly dissected. Their surface is covered with dense forest, and large mangrove swamps occur in the northern part of North Andaman. Perennial rivers are few, and adequate water supply is a continuing problem.

The *terrain* of the Andamans is rough, with hills enclosing narrow longitudinal valleys. Dense tropical forest covers the islands. The coral-fringed coasts of the Andamans are deeply indented, forming safe harbours and tidal creeks, often surrounded by mangrove swamps. Port Blair and Diglipur are important harbours of South Andaman and North Andaman, respectively.

The *climate* is tropical (average temperatures are 29°C but moderated by sea breezes). Up to 3,300 mm of rainfalls annually, mainly during the southwest monsoon (May through September) and the cyclonic storms that follow in October and November. The Andamans provide accurate meteorological data for shipping in the Bay of Bengal (a reporting station was set up at Port Blair as early as 1868).

The Andamanese, the islands' indigenous *population*, are classified among the Negrito peoples. Traditionally, they formed tribes, each comprising small isolated groups with a common language. They used the bow and the dog (introduced c. 1857) for hunting but knew no method of making fire. Turtle, dugong, and fish were caught with nets or harpooned from single outrigger canoes. Their remoteness and the Andamanese practice of killing foreigners prevented major physical or cultural change. Few Andamanese survive today, although traditional ways persist among the indigenous Jarawa and Onge tribes, who live in the interior areas of South Andaman, Rutland Island, and Little Andaman.

Most of the present population of the Andamans are immigrants from the mainland or their descendants.

Agriculture is the principal occupation; crops include cereals, pulses (legumes) coconuts, betel nuts, fruits, cassava, chillies and turmeric. Only South Andaman has roads (blacktop, 955 km; other, 36 km). An interisland steamer service connects Port Blair with North, Middle, South, and Little Andaman. The distance from Port Blair to Nancowrie is 426 km, to South Bay in Greater Nicobar is 556 km, and to Barren Island is 139 km. In these islands, there are 3 hospitals, 24 telephone exchanges, 34 banks, and an installed power capacity of 28,331 KW serving the population.

Over two-thirds of the population is Hindus, followed by Christians and Muslims. There are 259 temples, 156 churches, 51 mosques, and 4 Sikh *gurdwaras*. Further, one-fourth of the population is Bengali-speaking, followed by people speaking Hindi, Nicobari, and Malayalam. Port Blair is the only town and contributes to 26.71 per cent of the territory's population. The rest of the population is in 547 villages, of which 501 are electrified. The average population size of a village is 376. Population (1991) Total 241,453; Rural 166,498; Urban 74,955.

The population of this territory in 1901 was below 25,000. After independence in 1947, the population fell and the 1951 census recorded negative growth. Perhaps this was due to the privilege given to the imprisoned freedom fighters to return to the mainland. But in the following decade, the growth was over 100 per cent owing to the developmental activities there. Several families from erstwhile East Pakistan (now Bangladesh) and Burma (now Myanmar) settled there. In 1964, an Integrated Resource Development Plan was prepared also for the resettlement of incoming population. However, the growth rate has slowly declined to about 49 per cent during 1981-91. There are only 818 females per 1,000 males. The density of population is 36 per sq km. Though there are a limited number of educational institutions (349), this territory has. a recorded literacy rate of 73 per cent.

About 87 per cent of the area is under *forests* (7,171 sq km). The total timber extraction is 126,579 cu m, giving a revenue of Rs 282 million. There are 91 wildlife sanctuaries, and there are national parks at Wandoor, Mount Harriet, Saddle Peak, North Button Island, South Button Island, and Middle Button Island in South Andaman. The annual production of fish comes to 25,477 MT. This territory has a low level of industrialization. There are only five large and small industries and 1,175 small-scale units

The variety of *fauna and flora* is limited. Only 20 species of mammals, including the dugong, are found, although fish and turtles are abundant. Plywood and match-wood industries exist on a small-scale; the Andaman redwood, or padauk (Pterocarpus dalbergioides), the chief timber species, is exported. Crops include rice, coconuts, and betel nuts. Coffee, rubber, and tapioca are also important.

Located on the trade routes from India to East Asia, the Andamans have been known from earliest times. The seventh-century Chinese Buddhist monk I- ching, the Arab travellers of the ninth century, and the Venetian merchant-adventurer Marco Polo are among those who mention the islands. The name Andaman most, likely comes from the Malay Handuman, derived from the monkey god of 'Hindu mythology, Hanuman. The writings of later travellers emphasized the ferocious hostility of the people.

There are four mainland-to-island passenger ships. Passengers, including tourists, come to these islands also by the regular Indian Airlines flights from Calcutta and Chennai. This traffic by sea in 1995-96 was 125,334, while by air from Calcutta it was 26,948 and from Chennai 24,556. However, foreign tourists numbered only 6,036.

Nicobar Islands—The Nicobars are a group of 19 islands (12 inhabited) including Great Nicobar, Car Nicobar, Camorta (Kamona), and Nancowrie (Nankauri) — are situated between the Andaman Islands and the Indonesian island of Sumatra.

Some islands have rat-coral-covered *surfaces*, while the others, such as Great Nicobar, are hilly. Great Nicobar, rising to 642 m and containing numerous fast-flowing streams, is the only island with sufficient fresh surface water. The Nicobars experience temperatures between 18 and 33 °C. The southwest *monsoon* (May through September) bring up to 3,400 mm of rainfall each year. In addition to the ubiquitous areca (betel) and coconut palms, there are many species of *tree ferns*, of the family Cyatheaceae not found in the Andamans. *Animal life* includes snakes, lizards and chameleons, crocodiles, and turtles, and its marine life, such as the Indian crab, is abundant. Many endemic species of flora and fauna have yet to be systematically collected.

The Nicobarese probably descend from both Malay and Myanmar (Mon or Talaing) *peoples*. Their dialects belong to the Mon-Khmer language group; English, Burmese, and Hindustani also are spoken. Most of the population is Hindu, although Christianity has been widely adopted, and there is also a significant Muslim minority. The coconut and betel nut are major crops, and yams and other vegetables are also grown. Fish, turtles, pigs, and fowl are important in the diet.

Area, Population and Headquarters of Districts

S.No.	District	Area (sq km)	Population	Headquarters
1.	Andaman	6,408	3,14,239	Port Blair
2.	Nicobar	1,841	42,026	Car Nicobar

Andhra Pradesh—A state of India, located in the southeastern part of the subcontinent, it is bounded by the States of Tamil Nadu (formerly Madras) to the South, Karnataka (Mysore) to the west, Maharashtra to the northwest and north, and Madhya Pradesh and Orissa to the northeast; the eastern boundary is a 970 km coastline along the Bay of Bengal. The State has an area of 275,045 sq km. The capital is Hyderabad.

The State's name refers to the Andhra people, who have inhabited the area since antiquity and who have developed their own language, Telugu. In its present form, it came into existence in 1956 as a result of the demand of the Andhras for a separate State. Although it is primarily agricultural, there is some mining and a significant amount of industry.

Relief and drainage : The State has three main physiographic regions: the coastal plain to the east, extending from the Bay of Bengal to the mountain ranges; the mountain ranges themselves, the Eastern Ghats, which form the western flank of the coastal plain; and the plateau to the west of the Ghats. The coastal plain runs almost the entire length of the State and is watered by several rivers, flowing from west to east through the hills into the bay. The deltas formed by the most important of these rivers — the Godavari and the Krishna — make up the central part of the plains, an area of fertile alluvial soil. The Eastern Ghats, which do not form a continuous range —being broken by the great river valleys — are part of a larger mountain system extending from central India to the far south and running parallel to the east coast. They have highly porous soils on their flanks.

The plateau to the west of the ranges is composed of gneissic rock (a foliated rock formed within the Earth's interior under conditions of heat and pressure); the plateau has an average elevation of 488 m above sea level. As the result of erosion, this is a region of graded valleys, with red, sandy soil and isolated hills. Black soil is found in certain parts of the region.

Climate : A summer that lasts from March to June, a July-to-September season of tropical rains, and a winter from October to February constitute the three seasons. Throughout much of the State, maximum and minimum temperatures range from 23 to 28 °C and from 10 to 12 °C, respectively. Summers are very warm on the coastal plain, with temperatures reaching as high as 42 °C in some places. On the plateau, summers are cooler and winters colder. Rainfall derives largely from the southwest monsoon winds; some places receive a maximum of 1,400 mm of rain. In coastal areas, rainfall is heavy; in some areas on the plateau, especially in the north and west, it is sparse.

Plant and animal life : Mangrove swamps and palm trees fringe the coastal plain, and the rich deltas support the cultivation of food crops, fruit, and tobacco. The soil on the plateau and the uncertain rainfall restrict farming to dry crops, although the extension of irrigation has permitted the introduction of rice and sugarcane. Thorny-vegetation covers the scattered hills of the plateau. Of the State's total area, about one-quarter is forested. The forests consist of both moist deciduous and dry savanna vegetation; teak, rosewood, bamboo, and wild fruit trees are found. Cashews are grown in the coastal districts. Common trees such as the neem (genus *Azadirachta*, which produces an aromatic oil), banyan, mango, and pipal (*Ficuas religiosa*) also occur, as well as flowering plants — jasmine, rose, and many local varieties. Animal life, apart from common domestic types (dogs, cats, and cattle), includes tigers, leopards, bears, and deer, which abound in the hills and forest areas.

People : The State exhibits a characteristic Indian cultural pattern in the distribution of its languages and religions. Telugu is the official and most widely spoken language in the State; a small minority speaks Urdu. The remaining groups consist of people speaking border-area languages, including Hindi, Tamil, Kannada, Marathi, Oriya, and tribal languages such as Lamani (Banjari). The great majority of the population is Hindu, and there are both Muslim and Christian minorities. The Christians live in urban centres and coastal areas, and the Muslims are concentrated in the Telangana and Rayalaseema areas.

More than one-quarter of the population are urban dwellers, and over a third of these inhabit the industrial and manufacturing areas around the three main cities — Hyderabad, Visakhapatnam, and Vijayawada. With increasing industrial development, these cities are becoming linked with neighbouring urban areas, forming agglomerations. Some important industries and several smaller enterprises, such as sugar factories and service industries, are scattered among medium and smaller urban areas.

The literacy rate is about 50 per cent for men but only about 30 per cent for women. In the Hyderabad, Krishna, and Guntur districts, literacy is higher than elsewhere.

Economy : Canal irrigation in the Telangana and Rayalaseema regions has given rise to agro-industrial complexes rivalling those of coastal Andhra Pradesh. The Nagarjuna Sagar multipurpose project, diverting the waters of the Krishna for irrigation, has substantially increased the production of rice and sugar cane. Rice flour, rice-bran oil, paints and varnishes, soaps and detergents, cardboard and other packaging materials, and cattle feed are all produced from local paddy rice. Other agricultural commodities now grown statewide include chillies, *jowar*, pulses (peas, beans, and lentils), castor beans, peanuts (groundnuts), and cotton — all of which are processed locally as well — and grapes, mangoes, bananas, and oranges. This development in Telangana and Rayalaseema — further stimulated by new agricultural technology, the use of chemical fertilizers and pesticides, and improved transport, marketing, and credit systems — has helped to reduce the political tensions that formerly existed between interior and coastal Andhra Pradesh. Half of the total, investment for development is allotted to agricultural irrigation.

Dominated by the production of foodgrains, *agriculture* is the primary sector of the State's economy. Andhra Pradesh is one of the leading rice-growing States in the country and produces about four-fifths of India's Virginia tobacco. The State's rivers, particularly the Godavari and the Krishna, account for its agricultural importance; for a long time their benefits were restricted to the coastal districts of the Andhra region, which had the best irrigation facilities. Since Independence, great efforts have been made to tap the waters of these and other rivers for the benefit of the dry interior.

The State's forest areas annually yield high-quality timber and forest produce.

Among the State's *mineral resources* are asbestos, mica, manganese, barite, and high-grade coal. Low-grade iron ore is found in the southern parts of the State. Andhra Pradesh produces almost all of the country's barite. It is the only State in southern India that possesses coal reserves. Large deposits of natural gas have been discovered in the deltas of the Godavari and Krishna rivers.

Production at the once world-renowned diamond mines of Golconda, where the Koh-i-noor diamond and other famous stones were found, is being renewed. Quartz, limestone, and graphite also occur. The State has established; mining and metal trading corporation for the exploitation of its mineral resources

Andhra Pradesh, once industrially underdeveloped, has in the latter half of the twentieth century become one of the most highly *industrialized* States in India Industries such as shipbuilding, aeronautics, and the manufacture of electrical equipment, machine tools, and drugs have been established by the central (Union) government in the Visakhapatnam and Hyderabad areas Private enterprises, many of them located in the Vijayawada-Guntur region produce chemicals, textiles, cement, fertilizers, processed foods, petroleum derivatives, and cigarettes. An oil refinery is located in Visakhapatnam, as is the largest shipbuilding yard in the country. Mining and manufacturing industries, however, account for a small percentage of the State's income. The central government has opened a mammoth steel plant at Visakhapatnam where there is easy access to raw materials and port facilities. In recent year the phenomenal increase in power generated by hydroelectric and thermo electric projects augurs well for industrialization and irrigation. With its long coastline and many rivers, the State also has a significant and expanding fishing industry.

Transportation : There are four airports in the State — at Hyderabad, Vijayawada, Tirupati and Visakhapatnam. The rail system serves a major portion of the State and connects it with other parts of India, There is an extensive road system, which includes three national highways connecting Andhra Pradesh with all the major cities of the country. Other roads are maintained by State and local governments. Bus transportation, a large share of which was reprivatized in the late twentieth century, offers facilities for express travel between various cities.

The river canals in coastal areas, especially the saltwater Kommamur (Buckingham) Canal running parallel to the coast from the Krishna River to Chennai, are used for cargo transportation. Visakhapatnam is a major international seaport.

Art and Culture : The Andhras' contribution to India's *cultural heritage* is substantial. Architecture and painting have been highly developed arts in the region since ancient times. The kuchipudi style of dance is unique in the Indian tradition while Carnatic (South Indian) music has derived much from Andhra roots Many of southern India's major classical composers have been Andhras, and Telugu has been the language of most of the compositions. Telugu, one of the four literary languages of the Dravidian family, occupies a prestigious place among Indian languages, being renowned for its antiquity as well as for its mellifluous quality. Andhras also are prominent in the modern Indian literary renaissance, and their writing reflects the impact of the contemporary revolution in literary forms and expression. There are many periodicals in English. Telugu, and Urdu. Muslim culture in the Telangana region further enriches the States cultural diversity.

Before independence, arts and literature thrived mostly under the sponsorship of royal patrons and private organizations, many of which still function. The State has also created autonomous academies to revive, popularize, and promote fine arts, dance, drama, music, and literature.

The conscious pursuit of culture is more an urban than a rural phenomenon, for cultural performances, literary meetings, and religious discussions occur mostly in towns or cities. In rural areas, folk culture predominates. Cultural evolution in different parts of the State, under different historical circumstances, resulted in the occurrence of recognizable variations in dialect, in the caste structure, and in habits, thus diversifying the folk arts. Folk media such as minstrel-ballad performances, puppet shows, and mythological story-telling are indigenous to the area; use of these media in social and political communication is also common. The penetration of the mass media, especially of radio and television, to rural parts has helped to bring an awareness of classical culture to the rural folk and of folk arts to the urban population. Andhra Pradesh is among the few major moviemaking States of India.

During the nineteenth century, which witnessed the *rise of Indian nationalism*, the Andhras came to the forefront of the movement. Leaders such as Kandukuri Veerasalingam pioneered social reform. In the struggle against British rule, Andhra leaders played decisive roles. Pride in their historical and linguistic achievements led them to demand a separate province. Simultaneously, a movement was also organized to unite the Telugu-speaking peoples living under British rule and those under the *nizam's* administration. The Andhras' demand for separate statehood became so insistent that, when the central government refused to comply, a local leader. Potti Sreeramulu, fasted to death in 1953 to dramatize the issue. The government finally acceded to the people's request by creating on October 1, 1953, the Andhra State, which included the Telugu-speaking districts of the former Madras State, thus paving the way for the formation of linguistic States throughout India in 1957. The erstwhile

State of Hyderabad, which had joined independent India in 1949, was split up, and its nine Telugu-speaking districts (constituting Telangana) were joined to the Andhra State on November 1, 1956, to form the new Slate of Andhra Pradesh. In 1960, 573 sq km in the Chingleput and Salem districts of Madras (now Tamil Nadu) were transferred to Andhra Pradesh in exchange for 1062 sq km from Chittoor district.

Area, Population and Headquarters of Districts

S.No.	*District*	*Area in 000'sq km*	*Population 2001*[1]	*Headquarters*
1.	Adilabad	16.1	24,79,347	Adilabad
2.	Ananthapur	19.1	36,39,304	Ananthapur
3.	Chittoor	15.2	37,35,202	Chittoor
4.	Cuddapah	15.4	25,73,481	Cuddapah
5.	East Godavari	10.8	48,72,622	Kakinada
6.	Guntur	11.4	44,05,521	Guntur
7.	Hyderabad	0.2	36,86,460	Hyderabad
8.	Karimnagar	11.8	34,77,079	Karimnagar
9.	Khammam	16.0	25,65,412	Khammam
10.	Krishna	8.7	42,18,416	Machilipatnam
11.	Kumool	17.7	35,12,266	Kumool
12.	Mahaboobnagar	18.4	35,06,876	Mahaboobnagar
13.	Medak	9.7	26,62,296	Sangareddy
14.	Nalgonda	14.2	32,38,449	Nalgonda
15.	Nellore	13.1	26,59,661	Nellore
16.	Prakasam	17.6	30,54,941	Ongole
17.	Nizamabad	8.0	23,42,803	Nizamabad
18.	Ranga Reddy	7.5	35,06,670	Hyderabad
19.	Srikakulam	5.8	25,28,491	Srikakulamt
20.	Visakhapatnam	11.2	37,89,823	Visakhapatnall
21.	Vizianagaram	6.5	22,45,103	Vizianagaram
22.	Warangal	12.9	32,31,174	Warangal
23.	West Godavari	7.7	37,96,144	Eluru

[1] Provisional

Arunachal Pradesh is a state of India, in the extreme northeastern part of the country. It is bordered by the kingdom of Bhutan to the west, the Tibet Autonomous Region to the north, Myanmar to the southeast, the State of Nagaland to the south, and the State of Assam also to the south and southwest. It is a sparsely populated mountainous area. The total area is 83,743 sq km. The capital is Itanagar (Naharlagun).

The name Arunachal Pradesh means "Land of the Rising Sun". It has been mentioned in such ancient literature as the Kalika Purana, Ramayana, and Mahabharata. Formerly the North East Frontier Agency, it became a Union Territory in 1972 and a State in 1987.

History : The northern boundary, about 885 km, in dispute between India and China, is known as the McMahon Line because Sir Henry McMahon was secretary in the Indian foreign department and represented Great Britain at the conference held in Simla (Shimla) (1913-14) to settle frontier and other matters relating to Tibet. The line was regarded by the British as the natural, ethnic, and administrative boundary. Representatives of Britain, China, and Tibet agreed that the frontier between Tibet and northeastern India should follow the crest of the high Himalaya. Two days later the Chinese republican government disavowed its plenipotentiary (diplomatic representative) and refused to sign a convention. Prior to that, the British-Indian government had made agreements with the indigenous tribes and set up the Balipara frontier tract in the west, the Sadiya frontier tract in the east, Abor and Mishmi hills and Tirap frontier tract of Assam State, together constituting the North East Frontier Agency (1912-13) and including undoubted Assamese territory.

After the independence of India in 1947, China made claims to practically the whole area covered by the districts of East and West Kameng, Lower and Upper Subansiri, East and West Siang, and Lohit, arguing that the McMahon Line had never been accepted by China and was the result of British "aggression". In letters to the Indian prime minister, Jawaharlal Nehru, the Chinese prime minister, Zhou Enlai, quoted a map in the 1929 edition of *Encyclopaedia Britannica* showing the disputed territory as Chinese, with the boundary following the alignment of Chinese maps. The Survey of India map (1883) showed the disputed tribal areas as de facto administered by British India. British and Indian maps since 1914 have usually followed the McMahon Line. If the Chinese claims were allowed, the Indian-Chinese border would follow roughly the margin of the Assam plain, a frontier almost impossible to defend. Following this dispute, Chinese troops crossed the

McMahon Line on August 26, 1959, and captured an Indian outpost at Longju, a few miles south of the line. They abandoned this in 1961 but in October 1962 crossed the line, this time in force. After first striking toward the Tanglha ridge and Tawang near the Bhutan border, the Chinese later extended their attack along the whole frontier. Deep inroads were made at a number of points. Later the Chinese agreed to withdraw approximately to the McMahon Line and in 1963 returned the Indian prisoners of war.

Relief: Most of Arunachal Pradesh is mountainous. Its terrain consists of plateaus and ridges that separate deep valleys and rise to the peaks of the Great Himalaya.

Three broad physiographic regions can be identified in the State. Farthest south are a series of foothills, similar in type to the Shiwalik Hills, that emerge from the Assam plains to elevations of 300 to 1,000 m. These hills rise northward to reach the Lesser Himalaya, where ridges and spurs reach elevations as high as 3,048 m. Farther north, along the Tibeian border, lie the main ranges of the Great Himalaya (Kangto, near Tulang Pass, is 7,090 m high).

Drainage : The major rivers of the State are the Brahmaputra and its tributaries (the Dibang, Lohit, Subansiri, Kameng, and Tirap). The Brahmaputra (known as the Tsangpo in Tibet and the Dihang in Arunachal Pradesh) flows eastward from Mansarowar Lake in Tibet before dipping south through the Himalaya into north-central Arunachal Pradesh. The river then winds its way southward across the length of the State, cutting a narrow, steep-sided gorge into the mountainous terrain. The Brahmaputra finally emerges on the Assam plains near the town of Pasighat. It is joined by the Dibang and the Lohit rivers a few miles beyond Pasighat, just south of the Assam-Arunachal Pradesh border. West of the Brahmaputra, the Subansiri is the only tributary to cross the main Himalayan ranges. The Kameng rises on the southern flanks of the mountains. The Tirap River drains southeastern Arunachal Pradesh.

Climate : The Climate of Arunachal Pradesh varies with topography and altitude. The foothill zone is subtropical and has a hot and humid climate; in the lower valleys, maximum summer temperatures reach 35 °C, while winter minimums drop below 14 °C . Annual rainfall in the State averages about 3,000 mm, falling mostly between April and September. In East and West Siang districts (in the centre of the State), however, this figure approaches 4,064 mm. The average temperature decreases as elevations increase in the mountains.

Plant and animal life : Arunachal Pradesh's diverse terrain, climate, and soils are reflected in the richness of its fauna and flora. About two-thirds of the State is forested. A wide belt of swampy rain forests lies along the foothills. In the lower elevations tropical evergreen, subtropical pine, and subtropical mixed broad-leaved forests are found. With increasing elevation these change to temperate forests, both mixed and coniferous. A great variety of medicinal plants are available which the natives use for treatment and cure.

Animal life includes tigers, clouded and snow leopards, elephants; monkeys such as: hoolock gibbon, slow loris, macaque, and capped langur; as well as many species of deer and wild buffalo. The musk deer and takin (a kind of goat) are rare species still found in the State. The other animals found are goats such as serow and goral, and high-altitude animals including bharal, black bear, and red panda. Fish are found in abundance. Also found are many varieties of snakes and more than 500 species of birds.

The people : density of population is only 10 persons per sq km. The total population of 864,558 (1991) resides in 3,649 villages and three towns. These towns are Pasighat (9,139), Along (8,074), and Itanagar (6,406). About one-tenth of the population is urban. More than half of the population belongs to scheduled tribes. There are about 25 tribal groups in the State. These tribes generally follow endogamy (marriage within a specific group), while the clans within the tribes follow exogamy (marriage outside a specific group). Most of the population of Arunachal Pradesh is of Asiatic origin and shows physical affinities with the peoples of Tibet and the Myanmar hill region. There are dozens of tribes and subtribes, each with a specific geographic distribution. In western Arunachal Pradesh the main tribes are the Nissi (Nishi, or Dafla), Sulung, Sherdukpen, Aka, Monpa, Apa Tani, and Hill Miri. The central region is occupied by the Adi, the largest tribal group in the State. The Mishmi occupy the northeastern hills, and the Wancho, Nocte, and Tangsa inhabit the southeastern district of Tirap. The tribes are integrated into independent groups having similar lifestyle and occupation. The rural settlement pattern is scattered. The dispersed villages and isolated farmsteads are a typical feature of this area.

These tribal groups speak about 50 distinct languages and dialects, belonging mostly to the Tibeto-Burmese branch of the Sino-Tibetan language family. They are often mutually unintelligible and, thus, Assamese, Hindi, and English are used as lingua francas (common languages) in the region. As a rule, the tribes do not intermarry, and each follows distinct social, cultural, and religious practices. The most common religious practice is animism, in which deities of nature and various spirits are worshipped. Ritual sacrifice is also common, and the mithun (domesticated gaur, or wild ox) is especially revered as a sacrificial animal. Hindu beliefs and practices have penetrated the region, especially among populations near the Assam lowlands.

Tibetan Buddhism is found among groups near the Tibetan border, and some tribes along the Myanmar border practise the Southeast Asian form of this religion, Hinayana Buddhism.

Economy : The State's rugged terrain makes transport and communications extremely difficult. With few surfaced roads and no railways in Arunachal Pradesh, links with the rest of India are limited. Historically, however, a thriving trade has existed within the region, connecting villages at different elevations and even crossing the Himalayan passes into Tibet. Intraregional air service is provided by Vayudoot. The nearest airport is Lilabari in Assam, 67 km from Itanagar. The nearest railhead is Harmuty again in Assam, 33 km from Itaganar. Further, this town is connected by daily bus service from Guwahati and other towns of Assam. State transport buses and private operators run such services, particularly connecting Guwahati (381 km), Shillong (481 km), Tezpur (216 km), Dibrugarh (375 km), Tinsukia (415 km), Jorhat (245 km). Nowgaon (275 km), and Namsai (495 km). Taxis are also available on some routes.

Over 60 percent of the workers are engaged in agriculture. However, only 4.15 per cent of the land comes under operational holdings. Shifting cultivation (*jhum*) is traditionally practised among the hill people of Arunachal Pradesh; rice, maize, millet, and buckwheat are among the chief crops grown by this method. The commercial crops grown are oilseeds, potato, ginger, sugarcane, and vegetables. Some tribes supplement their diet by hunting, fishing, and gathering forest products. Settled agriculture is practised on less than half of the area that is cultivable. The mithun is widely domesticated, and the yak is important in the higher elevations. The Monpa tribe herds sheep Millet and rice beer are popular drinks, as is tea.

Arunachal Pradesh has great, unutilized, resource potential, including extensive forests, numerous areas for hydroelectric power production, coal, oil, and other mineral deposits. However, there are no major industries in the State. Basketry, weaving, and carpets are the important handicraft industries. Small-scale industries include rice and oil mills, fruit-processing plants, forest-based products, steel fabrication, and sericulture. Different varieties of silk yarns including *eri, dak tasar, muga,* and mulberry, are produced here. Industrial development is actively encouraged by the State government, and industrial estates have been set up at Itanagar, Naharlagun, Pasighat and Deomali.

Cultural life : Tribal peoples in Arunachal Pradesh wear distinctive garments and headdress. The art of weaving is especially important, and textile designs are unique to each group. Dances are an integral part of community life. Bootir Boori, Losar, Nyokum, Mopin, and Solung are the major tribal festivals.

Area, Population and Headquarters of Districts

S.No.	District	Area (sq km)	Population	Headquarters
1.	Tawang	2,172	34,705	Tawang
2.	West Kameng	7,422	74,595	Bomdila
3.	East Kameng	4,134	57,065	Seppa
4.	Papum-Pare	2,875	1,21,750	Yupia
5.	Lower Subansiri	10,135	97,614	Ziro
6.	Upper Subansiri	7,032	54,995	Daporijo
7.	West Siang	8,325	1,03,575	Along
8.	East Siang	4,005	87,430	Pasighat
9.	Upper Siang	6,188	33,146	Yingkiong
10.	Dibang Valley	13,029	57,543	Anini
11.	Lohit	11,402	1,43,478	Tezu
12.	Changlang	4,662	1,24,994	Changlang
13.	Tlrap	2,362	1,00,227	Khonsa
14.	Kurung-Kumey	NA	NA	Laaying-Yangte

Assam—state of India, it is located in the northeastern part of the country and has an area of 78,438 sq km. The name Assam is derived from the ancient Ahom word *asama*, meaning "peerless." The neighbouring State of Arunachal Pradesh, Nagaland, Mizoram, and Meghalaya were once part of Assam. The capital, formerly Shillong (now the capital of Meghalaya), was shifted to Dispur, a suburb of Guwahati, in 1972. It is bounded to the north by the kingdom of Bhutan and the State of Arunachal Pradesh; to the east by the States of Nagaland and Manipur; to the south by the States of Mizoram and Tripura; and to the west by the State of Meghalaya, the State of West Bengal, and Bangladesh

History : In the earliest times Assam was part of Kamarupa, a State that had its capital at Pragjyotisapura (modern Guwahati). Ancient

Kamarupa included roughly the Brahmaputra valley, Bhutan, the Rangpur region (now in Bangladesh), and Koch Bihar, in West Bengal. King Naralkasura and his son Bhagadatta were famous rulers of Kamarupa in the Mahabharata period (at least as early as 1000 BC). A Chinese traveller, Xuanzang, left a vivid account of the country and its people in about AD 640. Although information about the following centuries is meagre, copperplates, clay seals, and stone inscriptions dating from the seventh to the mid-twelfth centuries indicate that the inhabitants of the region attained considerable power and a fair degree of civilization. The copperplates further provide clues as to the locations of important ancient settlements and the routes connecting them.

Assam was ruled by various dynasties — the Palas, Koches, Kacharis, and Chutiyas — and there was constant warfare among these princes until the coming of the Ahoms in the thirteenth century. The Ahoms crossed the Patkai Range from Myanmar (Burma) and conquered the local chieftains of the Upper Assam Plain. In the fifteenth century the Ahoms, who probably gave their name to the region, were the dominant power in Upper Assam. Two centuries later, they defeated the Koches, the Kacharis, and other local rulers to gain control of Lower Assam up to Goalpara. The power and prosperity of the Ahoms reached a zenith during the rule of King Rudra Singh (1696-1714).

Dissension and jealousy among the princes gradually weakened the central administration until 1786, when the ruling prince, Gaurinath Singh, sought aid from the British in Calcutta. A British army officer, sent by the British governor-general in India, restored peace and was recalled in spite of the protests of the Ahom king. Internal strife then caused one crisis after another until, in 1817, Myanmar warriors entered Assam in response to the appeal of Badan Chandra, a rebellious *bar phukan* (governor). They swept over the area three times, bringing destruction and misery.

The British, whose interests elsewhere were threatened by these developments, ultimately drove out the Myanmar invaders, and, after the Treaty of Yandabo was concluded with Myanmar in 1826, Assam became a part of British India. A British agent, representing the governor-general, was appointed to administer Assam, and in 1838 the area was incorporated into British-administered Bengal. By 1842 the whole of the Assam Valley had come under British rule. In 1874 a separate province of Assam was created (administered by a chief commissioner), with its capital at Shillong.

In 1905 Bengal was partitioned and Assam was amalgamated with eastern Bengal; this created such resentment, however, that in 1912 Bengal was reunited, and Assam was once more made a separate province. During World War II, Assam was a major supply route for allied forces operating in Burma. Several battles fought in the area in 1944 (for example, at Bishenpur in Manipur and Kohima in Nagaland) were decisive in halting the Japanese advance into India.

With the partition and independence of India in 1947, the district of Sylhet (excluding the Karimganj subdivision) was ceded to Pakistan. Assam became a constituent State of the Indian Union in 1950. In 1961 and 1962 Chinese armed forces, disputing the McMahon Line as the boundary between India and Tibet, occupied part of the North East Frontier Agency (present Arunachal Pradesh but then part of Assam). In December 1962, however, they voluntarily withdrew to Tibet.

Since the early 1960s Assam has lost much territory to new States emerging from within its borders. In 1963 the Naga Hills district became the sixteenth State of the Indian Union under the name of Nagaland. Part of Tuensang, a former territory of the North East Frontier Agency, was also added to Nagaland. In 1970, in response to the demands of the tribal peoples of the Meghalaya Plateau, the United Khasi and Jaintia Hills and the Garo districts were formed into an autonomous State within Assam; in 1972 it became a separate Slate under the name of Meghalaya. Also in 1972 Arunachal Pradesh (the North East Frontier Agency) and Mizoram (from the Mizo Hills in the south) were separated from Assam as Union Territories; both became States in 1986.

Despite the separation of these ethnicity-based States, communal tensions and violence have remained a problem in Assam. In the early 1980s, resentment among the Assamese against "foreigners", mostly immigrants from Bangladesh, led to widespread violence and considerable loss of life. Subsequently, disaffected Bodo tribesmen (in Assam and Meghalaya) agitated for an autonomous State. The militant United Liberation Front of Assam waged a guerrilla campaign for the outright secession of Assam from India until agreeing to end their rebellion in 1992.

Relief and drainage: Assam, a land of plains and river valleys, has three principal physical regions—the Brahmaputra River valley in the north, the Barak River valley in the south, and the hilly region within the districts of Karbi Anglong and North Cachar Hills, lying between these two valleys.

Geologically the Brahmaputra and Barak valleys lie on alluvial sediments up to 1.6 million years old, which themselves cover a variety of tertiary deposits (from 1.6 to 66.4 million years old). Among these deposits are hard sandstone, soft and loose sand, conglomerates, coal seams, shales, sandy clays, and limestone.

The Brahmaputra River valley is the dominant physical feature of Assam. As per the Hindu mythology, this river — son of Lord Brahma — rises from a sacred pool of Brahmakund in the neighbouring Arunachal Pradesh. The river enters Assam near Sadiya in the extreme northeast and runs westward across the length of Assam for nearly 724 km before turning south to enter the plains of Bangladesh. The river valley — studded with low, isolated hills and ridges that rise abruptly from the plain — is rarely more than 80 km wide and is surrounded on all sides, except on the west, by mountains. Numerous streams and rivulets flow from the neighbouring hills to empty into the Brahmaputra.

The Barak River valley in the southeast forms an extensive lowland area that is important for agriculture and supports a relatively dense population. Only a small portion of this valley, however, is within the State's borders.

The Karbi Anglong and the North Cachar Hills form part of the Meghalaya Plateau, which may have been an extension of Gondwanaland (an ancient landmass in the Southern Hemisphere that once grouped together South America, Africa, Australia, and part of the Indian subcontinent). Isolated from the main plateau by the embankments of the Kepili River, this upland displays a rugged topography. It has, roughly, a northerly slope, with average elevations ranging from about 457 m in the Mikir Hills to about 1,006 m in the central portion of the Karbi Anglong district.

The northern ranges, which extend from Dabaka (east of Dispur) in the southwest to Bokakhat in the northeast, attain an average elevation of 610 m. Major peaks in the north include the Basundhari Hills (774 m), Raisang (738 m), Mehekongthu (639 m), and the Kud Hills (626 m). The Rengma Hills in the south average about 914 m; their most prominent peaks are Chenghehishon (1,359 m) and khunbaman Hills (1,311 m).

Earthquakes are common in Assam. The most severe ones in modern times occurred in 1897, with the Shillong Plateau as the epi-centre; in 1930, with Dhubri as the epicentre; and in 1950, with Zhihou (Rima) in Tibet at the Arunachal Pradesh border as the epicentre. The 1950 earthquake is considered to have been one of the most disastrous earthquakes in history. It created heavy landslides that blocked the courses of many hill streams. The floods that followed the bursting of these artificial dams caused more loss of life and property than the earthquake itself.

Climate : Average temperatures vary between about 29 °C in the hottest month, August, and 16 °C in January. The cool season is marked by fogs and brief showers. Assam escapes the normal Indian hot, dry season. Some rain occurs from March onward, but the real force of the monsoon is felt between June and September, when widespread and destructive flooding often occurs. Rainfall in Assam is not only the highest in the country but also ranks among the highest in the world; its annual average varies from 1,778 mm in the west to more than 3,048 mm in the east.

Plant and animal life : Forests—formerly extending over nearly 39 per cent of the State's area but much reduced by the creation of Meghalaya and Mizoram. The recorded forest area is 30,708 sq km while the actual forest cover is 23,824 sq km, that is, 30.4 per cent of the geographical area. In fact the forest cover has decreased 237 sq km during 1995-97. Among the State's wildlife reserves are the Kaziranga National Park (on the bank of River Brahmaputra) and the Manas Wildlife Sanctuary (bordering Bhutan), which are refuges for the fast-disappearing great Indian one-horned rhinoceros. Both the national parks arc World Heritage Sites. Timber and bamboo, firewood, and lac (the source of shellac) are important forest products. There are about 74 species of trees, of which two-thirds are commercially exploited. The production of commciaal plywood amounts to some 32,956,000 sq m. The forests are inhabited by wild animals such as elephants, tigers, deer, and wild pigs.

The people : This State is inhabited by about 22.4 million persons, out of which 12.82 per cent are scheduled tribes and 7.4 per cent scheduled castes. The density is 286 persons per sq km. About 89 per cent of the population is rural. Recent increases in the State's urban population reflect the growth of industries increased commercial activity, and the desire of the Bangladeshi refugees to live near towns. The annual growth late is 2.17 per cent. Only Guwahati has a fairly large urban population. The sex ratio is 923 females per 1,000 males.

The distribution of population is uneven, reflecting the hilly terrain, the number of rivers, the forests, the small amount of cultivable land, and the lack industrialization. Population growth in the twentieth century has been unusually rapid owing mostly to the immigiarion into Assam of tea-garden labourers, herders from Nepal, Muslims from West Bengal and refugees from what is now Bangladesh.

The Ahoms are considered to be a Thai-Buddhist tribe who arrived in this area during the thirteenth century and established their capital in Sibsagar. Later they adopted Hinduism. The people of the plains of the Brahmaputra and Barak valleys are mainly Indo-Iranian. By the time of their arrival in the Brahmaputra valley, it would appear that the original Aryan people of Assam had become intermixed with Asiatic peoples. Assamese is the official and principal language of the State. An unbroken record of Assamese literary history is traceable from the fourteenth century. The people of the Cachar district in the Barak valley mostly speak Bengali.

The tribes of Assam are classified among the Asiatic peoples. They speak dialects of Tibeto-Burman origin, with the exception of the Khasis, who speak an Austro-Asiatic tongue. Many of the hill tribes have been converted to Christianity by missionaries, but the majority still observe the customs and festivals of their traditional religion, which is based on animism. The Mikirs and Kacharis of the Karbi Anglong and North Cachar Hills are mostly Hindus; although they speak dialects of Tibeto-Burman origin, they have adopted Assamese as their first language.

About two-thirds of the Assamese are Hindus, and about a quarter are Muslim. The Muslims are mostly recent settlers from Bangladesh or converts belonging to the lower strata of Hindu society. The percentage of Hindus varies from 29 per cent in Dhubri district to 94 per cent in Dhemaji district. Over 50 per cent of the Muslim population in the State is in Dhubri, Goalpara, Barpeta, and Hailakandi. There is a considerable concentration of Christian population in Kokrajhar, Goalpara, Karbialang, and the North Cachar Hills. A majority of the Hindus follow Vaishnavism, which venerates the deity Vishnu.

Economy : The workers share 36 pet cent of the population. Agriculture is of basic importance to Assam, engaging about two-thirds of the total working population. Another 10 per cent are employed on tea plantations, in forestry, or in other occupations related to *agriculture.*

Rice accounts for about two-thirds of the sown area. Tea and jute, widely cultivated in the Brahmaputra valley, are important foreign-exchange earners. Assam grows about half of the country's tea. Other crops include oilseeds, pulses (legumes such as peas, beans, or lentils), sugarcane, rape (an oil-yielding plant, the leaves of which are used for fodder), mustard, potatoes, and fruits. The State produces a surplus of cereals, but there is a shortage of oilseeds and pulses. Double-cropping and other improved methods of cultivation are being introduced. Winter rice is grown in 1,739,000 ha of land, followed by autumn rice (619,000 ha), jute (95,000 ha), and maize (20,000 ha). There are about 7,090 sericulture villages. The production of silk of all varieties is 3,220,000 kg.

Minerals exploited commercially in the State include petroleum, coal natural gas, and limestone. Oil is found, in the districts of Dibrugarh and Sibsagar in northeastern (Upper) Assam; Assam produces about 5,111,000 tonnes of petroleum and 963 M Cu M of natural gas. In the last century extensive oil reserves were found, and Digboi became the first oil refinery in Asia. Later such refineries were also established in Guwahati and Noonmati. Coal — used locally by the railways, tea estates, and steamships — is found in Upper Assam and in the district of Karbi Anglong. Limestone is quarried in the Mikir Hills. The production of coal is about one million tonnes, while the production of cement and limestone is 151,900 tonnes and 212,000 MT respectively. The State is served by 1,087 banks.

Assam has few *industries* of significance except for tea and oil. Industrial development is inhibited by its isolation from the rest of India, by a bad transport system, by a small local market, and by the lack of sufficient capital. Several industrial enterprises have nevertheless been started, including a fertilizer plant; jute, paper, silk, and sugar mills; and a cement factory. Sawmills and plywood and match factories make use of timber resources. An oil refinery at Digboi dates from the early wentieth century, and a refinery near Guwahati started production in 1962. A refinery in Bihar State is supplied with crude oil from Assam through a pipeline. There are only 2,623 registered factories and 15,382 units of small-scale industries. The installed capacity of power is 1,086,600,000 KWH.

Poor *transport and communication* systems have hindered economic development in Assam. Geography has limited accessibility and inhibited the growth of efficient transport systems. The Brahmaputra, for example, is a major barrier to integrating the road and rail networks lying north and south of the river. (Assam is linked to India by only one railway line and one major highway.) Inland-water transport, historically of major importance, was curtailed after 1947, when the partition of India placed the lower Brahmaputra in East Pakistan (now Bangladesh). There is considerable air traffic between Assam and Calcutta. Towns with air service include Guwahati, Dibrugarh, Jorhat, Tezpur, and Silchar. The road length is 28,930 km.

Cultural life : The Cultural life of Assam is interwoven with the activities of a number of cultural institutions and religious centres, such as satra (seat of a head, the Stradhikar) and *namghar* (prayer hall). Satras in Assam have been looking after the religious and social well-being of the population for the last 400 years. The Assamese people observe all the pan-Indian religious festivals, but the most important celebrations are the three Bihu festivals. Originally agricultural festivals, these are observed with great enthusiasm irrespective of caste, creeds and religious affinity. The.Bohag Bihu, celebrated in the spring (usually mid-April) to mark the commencement of the new year (first day of the Bohag or Baishakh month), is the most important one. Also known as Rangali Bihu (*rang* means "merrymaking" or "fun"), it is accompanied by much dancing and singing. On this day women present a hand-woven *gamocha* (towel) to each family member. The Magh Bihu, celebrated in mid-January (in the month of Magh), is a harvest festival. Known also as Bhogali Bihu (*bhog* means "enjoyment" and "feasting"), it is a time of community feasts and bonfires. The third Bihu festival, the Kati Bihu (in mid-October), is also called the Kangali Bihu (*kangali* means "poor") because by this time of year the house of a common man is without food-grains, as the stock is usually consumed before the next harvest.

Weaving is another important aspect of the cultural life of the people of Assam, particularly of the women. Every Assamese house, irrespective of caste, creed, and social status, has at least one loom, and each woman is required to be skilled in producing fine silk and cotton cloths.

Area, Population and Headquarters of Districts

S.No.	District	Area in (000') sq km	Population (in lakh)[1]	District Headquarters
1.	Dhubri	2,838	16.35	Dhubri
2.	Kokrajhar	3,129	9.30	Kokrajhar
3.	Bongaigaon	2,510	9.06	Bongaigaon
4.	Goalpara	1,824	8.22	Goalpara
5.	Barpeta	3,245	16.42	Barpeta
6.	Nalbari	2,257	11.38	Nalbari
7.	Kamrup	4,345	25.15	Guwahati
8.	Darrang	3,481	15.04	Mangaldoi
9.	Sonitpur	5,324	16.78	Tezpur
10.	Lakhimpur	2,277	8.89	North Lakhimpur
11.	Dhemaji	3,217	5.89	Dhemaji
12.	Morigaon	1,704	7.76	Morigaon
13.	Nagaon	3,831	23.15	Nagaon

S.No.	District	Area in (000') sq km	Population (in lakh)[1]	District Headquarters
14.	Golaghat	3,502	9.46	Golaghat
15.	Jorhat	2,851	10.09	Jorhat
16.	Sibsagar	2,668	10.53	Sibsagar
17.	Dibrugarh	3,381	11.72	Dibrugarh
18.	Tinsukia	3,790	11.50	Tinsukia
19.	Karbi-Anglong	10,434	8.12	Diphu
20.	North Cachar Hills	4,888	1.86	Haflong
21.	Karimganj	1,809	10.04	Karimganj
22.	Hailakandi	1,327	5.43	Hailakandi
23.	Cachar	3,786	14.42	Silchar

[1] Provisional

B

Bihar—One of the major states of the Indian Union, Bihar is bounded on the north by Nepal, on east by West Bengal, on west by Uttar Pradesh and on south by Jharkhand. Bihar has a number of rivers, the most important of which is the Ganga. The other rivers are the Sone, Poonpoon, Falgu, Karmanasa, Durgawati, Kosi, Gandak, Ghaghara, etc.

History : Bihar finds mention in the *Vedas*, *Puranas*, epics, etc., and was the main scene of activities of Buddha, and 24 Jain Tirthankars. Great rulers of the State before the Christian era were Bimbisar, Udayin, who founded the city of Pataliputra Chandragupta Maurya and Emperor Ashoka and Maurya dynasty, the Sungs and the Kanvas. Then came the Kushan rulers followed by Chandragupta Vikramaditya of the Gupta dynasty. Muslim rulers made in-roads into the territory during medieval period. The first conqueror of Bihar was Mohammed-bin-Bakhtiar Khaiji. The Tughluqs and then the Mughals followed the Khaljis.

Economy: Bihar has a total geographical area of about 93.60 lakh hectare, out of which only 56.03 lakh hectare is the net cultivated area and gross cultivated area being 79.46 lakh hectare About 33.51 lakh hectare net area and 43.86 lakh hectare gross area receive irrigation from different sources. Principal food crops are paddy, wheat, maize and pulses. Main cash crops are Sugarcane, potato, tobacco, oilseeds, onion, chillies, jute and mesta. Bihar has notified forest area of 6,764.14 sq km, which is 7.1 per cent of its geographical area.

Major Industries are: Railway Wagon Plants of Bharat Wagon Limited at Muzaffarpur and Mokamah; Oil Refinery of Indian Oil Corporation at Barauni; Fertilizer Manufacturing Plant of Hindustan Fertilizer Corporation Limited (HPCL) at Barauni and Pyrites Phosphates & Chemicals Limited (PPCL) at Amjhor; Cotton Spinning Mills at Siwan, Pandaul, Bhagalpur, Mokamah and Gaya; 13 sugar mills in private sector and 15 in the public sector located in south and north Bihar with a total crushing capacity of 45,000 TPD. In addition, distilleries at Gopalganj, West Champaran, Bhagalpur and Riga (in Sitamarhi district); Finished Leather Industry in West Champaran, Muzaffarpur and Barauni; Jute Mills at Katihar and Samastipur; Medicine Manufacturing Unit at Hajipur; Food Processing Units as also Vanaspati Manufacturing Units at Aurangabad and Patna; besides Kalyanpur Cement Limited at Banjari, are notable in the industrial map of Bihar.

Bihar has an *irrigation* potential of 93.38 lakh hectare. Out of this, 53.53 lakh hectare is to be created through major and medium irrigation schemes and 44.85 lakh hectare through minor irrigation schemes. Irrigation potential of 53.53 lakh hectare is targeted for creation by the end of the Twelfth Five-Year Plan. *Major power projects* under the state sector are: Barauni Thermal Power Station (320 MW), Muzaffarpur Thermal Power Station (220 MW), Kosi Hydel Power (19.2 MW) under the Bihar State Electricity Board and Tenughat Power Station under Tenughat Vidyut Nigam Limited. Under the Central sector, the major power station is Kahalgaon Super Thermal Power Project (840 MW) under National Thermal Power Corporation. Besides, Bihar receives its shan of power from Farakka Super Thermal Power Station and Talcher Super Thermal Power Project under the National Thermal Power Corporation Durgapur Thermal Power Station under DVC and Chukka Hydel Power Station under National Hydro-electric Power Corporation.

Roads : Up to March 2001, Bihar had 13,412.80 km of *pucca* roads including 2,461.7 km of national highways and 10,951.07 km of state highways and major district roads. In addition to this, the length of rural roads is 15,000 km.

Railways : Bihar has a fairly good 'railway network. Communication in north Bihar is difficult as there is only one railway bridge at Mokamah. A few railway routes connecting important places like Mlizaffarpur-Samastipur-Barauni-Katihar and Muzaffarpur-Chapra-Siwan have been converted into broad gauge. The main rail junctions are at Patna, Gaya, Muzaffarpur, Katihar and Samastipur.

There is an international airport at Patna, besides landing grounds in all major districts of the State.

Tourist Centres : Important places of tourist interest are Rajgir, Nalanda, Vaishali, Pawapuri (where Lord Mahavira breathed his last and attained *Nirvana*), Bodh Gaya, Vikramshila (ruins of Buddhist University of higher learning), Gaya, Patna (ancient city of Patliputra), Sasaram (tomb of Shershah Suri) and Madhubani (known for famous Madhubani Paintings).

Area, Population and Headquarters of Districts

S.No.	District	Area (in sq km)	Population	Headquarters
1.	Araria	2,796.8	21,24.831	Araria
2.	Auranpabad	3,389.2	20,04,960	Aurangabad
3.	Begusarai	1,889.1	23,42,989	Begusarai
4.	Bhagalpur	2,501.9	24,30,331	Bhagalpur
5.	Banka	3,020.2	16,08,778	Banka
6.	Bhojpur	2,337.0	22,33,415	Arrah
7.	Buxar	1,633.6	14,03,462	Buxar
8.	Kaimur (Bhabhua)	1,840.3	12,84,575	Bhabhua
9.	Darbhanga.	2,502.0	32,85,473	Darbhanga
10.	East Champaran	4,154.8	39,33,636	Motihari
11.	Gaya	4,941.0	34,64,983	Gaya
12.	Gopalganj	2;009.2	21,49,343	Gopalganj
13.	Jahanabad	1,569.3	15,11,406	Jahanabad
14.	Jamui	2,996.5	13,97,474	Jamui
15.	Sakarsa	1,195.6	15,06,418	Saharsa
16.	Katihar	3,009.9	23,89,533	Katihar
17.	Khagaria	1,485.8	12,76,677	Khagaria
18.	Kishanganj	1,938.5	12,94,063	Kishanganj
19.	Madhepuia	1,797.4	15,24,596	Madhepura
20.	Madhubani	3,477.8	35,70,651	Madhubani
21.	Mungr	-	11,35,499	Munger
22.	Lakhisarai	3,302.2	8,01,173	Lakhisarai
23.	Sheikhpura	-	5,25,137	Sheikhpura
24.	Muzaffarpur	3,122.7	37,43,836	Muzaffarpur
25.	Nalanda	2,361.7	23,68,327	Biharsharif
26.	Nawada	2,497.5	18,09,425	Nawada
27.	Patna	3,130.1	47,09,851	Patna

S.No.	District	Area (sq km)	Population	Headquarters
28.	Purnea	3,202.3	25,40,778	Purnea
29.	Rohtas	3,838.2	24,48,762	Sasaram
30.	Samastipur	2,578.7	34,13,413	Samastipur
31.	Saran	2,624.1	32,51,474	Chapra
32.	Sitamarhi	2,627.7	26,69,887	Sitamarhi
33.	Sheohar	-	5,14,288	Sheohar
34.	Siwan	2,213	27,08,840	Siwan
35.	Supaul	2,984.9	17,45,069	Supaul
36.	Vaishali	1,995.3	27,12,389	Hazipur
37.	West Champaran	4,249.9	30,43,044	Bettiah

C

Chandigarh is a city and Union Territory of India. About 265 km north of New Delhi, Chandigarh Union Territory is bounded by the State of Haryana on the east and by the State of Punjab on all other sides. The chief executive of the Union Territory is the governor of Punjab, designated as the "administrator" for this purpose. He is assisted by a senior officer, appointed by the government of India as "adviser to the administrator". The city of Chandigarh is the capital of the Union Territory of the same name. It is also the capital of both the States of Punjab and Haryana.

The Union Territory of Chandigarh was constituted on November 1, 1966. It included the city of Chandigarh, three towns, and a number of adjoining villages, which together cover 114 sq km. Chandigarh derives its name from Chandi Mandir ("Temple of the Goddess Chandi"), located near Mani Majra town.

Chandigarh lies on the Indo-Gangetic Plain, just south of the Shiwalik Hills, and between two seasonal hill torrents, the Sukhna Cho and the Patiali Rao. The land is a flat and fertile tract of alluvial soils. Its rural farmland produces wheat, maize, and rice. The city of Chandigarh covers more than half the area of the union territory. Planned from scratch, beginning in the late 1940s, the city has a modern infrastructure and a relatively low density of population. It consists, of more than 50 rectangular sectors, which are designed to be self-contained in civic amenities; the sectors are separated from each other by broad roads carrying the city's fast-moving arterial traffic. Modern facilities available in the city are in marked contrast with not only the villages around, but also most other cities in India.

About three-fourths of the Union Territory's *population* consists of Hindus, and one-fifth of Sikhs. Muslims, Christians, and Jains constitute a small proportion of the population. One out of every six persons in the territory belongs to the Scheduled Caste. Hindi and Punjabi are the most widely spoken languages.

The Union Territory of Chandigarh came into existence in 1966, with the linguistic reorganization of the earlier Punjab into two new States: the Punjabi-speaking Punjab and the Hindi-speaking Haryana. The city, bounded entirely by between Punjab and Haryana, was made the joint capital of the two States, in addition to being the capital of the Union Territory itself. Under the terms of the 1986 Punjab Accord, the entire union territory was to become part of Punjab, while some Hindi-speaking villages of Fazilka and Abohar development blocks were to be transferred from Punjab to Haryana; for various reasons, however, this plan has not been carried out. Population (1991) Union Territory Total 642,015; Rural 66,186; Urban 575,829.

Chhattisgarh—Chhattisgarh is bounded by southern Jharkhand and Orissa in the east, Madhya Pradesh and Maharashtra in the west, Uttar Pradesh and western Jharkhand in the north and Andhra Pradesh in the south. Chhattisgarh carved out of Madhya Pradesh came into being on 1 November 2000 as the 26th State of the Union. It fulfills the long-cherished demand of the tribal people. In ancient times the region was known as Dakshin-Kausal. This finds mention in *Ramayana* and *Mahabharata* also. Between the sixth and twelfth centuries Sarabhpurias, Panduavanshi, Somvanshi, Kalchuri, and Nagvanshi rulers dominated this region. Kalchuris ruled in Chhattisgarh from 980 to 1791 AD. With the advent of Britishers in 1854 Raipur gained prominence instead of capital Ratanpur. In 1904 Sambalpur was transferred to Orissa and estates of Sarguja were transferred from Bengal to Chhattisgarh.

Economy : More than 80 per cent population depends on agriculture. The area under cultivation is 43 per cent. Main crops are paddy, wheat, maize, groundnut, pulses and oilseeds. Forests occupy 45 per cent of the area.

Apart from Bhilai Steel Plant with 40 lakh tonnes capacity, eight sponge iron plants in the private sector, 13 ferro-alloy plants, 125 steel rolling mills and one H.R. strip plant have also been established. Chhattisgarh has nine major cement plants. Besides iron casting units, engineering and fabrication units, agro-based food processing, chemical and plastic industries have been established

Chhattisgarh is rich in *mineral resources*. Twenty per cent of the country's steel and cement is produced in the State. Iron-ore, limestone, dolomite, coal, bauxite are found in abundance. It is the only tin-ore producing state in the country. Other minerals such as korandum, garnet, quartz, marble, diamond are also found in Chhattisgarh. Compared to 1998-99, the production of coal, iron ore and limestone registered an increase of 29.49 lakh tonnes, 13.40 lakh tonnes and 30.13 lakh tonnes respectively in 1999-2000. The revenue receipt from minerals in 2001-02 is likely to increase to Rs. 455 crore from Rs. 394.50 crore during the preceding year.

The *irrigation* potential of 13.39 lakh hectares was created during 1999-2000. An additional irrigation potential of 0.18 lakh hectares was created during 2000-01. Ravishankar Sagar Mahanadi project, Hasdeo-Bango, Kodar, Jonk, Pairi and Arpa are some of the important irrigation projects.

The total capacity of State Electricity Board is 1,360 MW out of this the *thermal power* share is 1,240 MW. Korba based National Thermal Power Corporation's capacity is 2,000 MW and a new unit of the plant is being established at Bilaspur. A hydel project in district Sarguja is in the advance stage of commissioning. Around 90 per cent of 19,720 inhabited villages of Chhattisgarh have been electrified.

Transport : The total length of the *roads* in the State is 35,388.54 km. The length of the national highways is 1,827.30 km, state roads 2,073.78 km, district roads 3,094.86 km and of rural roads 28,392.60 km.

Raipur, Bilaspur, Durg, Rajnandgaon and Raigarh are important railway stations. Total *railways* route length is 1,000 km.

Raipur is connected with New Delhi and Nagpur by daily flights and with Mumbai and Bhubaneshwar by tri-weekly flights. Bilaspur, Bhilai, Raigarh, Ambikapur, Korba, Jashpurnagar and Rajnandgaon are having temporary airstrips/helipads.

Cultural Life : Chhattisgarh is famous for its festivals. *Pola, Nawakhai, Dussehara, Deepawali, Holi, Govardhan Pooja* are celebrated with gaiety and festivity.

The Sabari temple of Kharod Janjgir Champa, Nar Narayan temple of Sivarinarayan, Vishnu temple of Janjgir are important religious places.

The Keshkal valley, Chitrakoot and Teerathgarh fountain, Kangerghat National park, Kailash caves and Kutumbsar caves are rich in natural beauty. In Bilaspur, Mahamaya temple at Ratanpur, Khutalghat waterfall, Dindneswari Devi temple of Mallahar and the Achanakmar sanctuary, Udanti sanctuary near Raipur, Pali and Kendai waterfall of Korba district are important places of tourist interest.

Area, Population and Headquarters of Districts

S.No.	District	Area (in sq km)	Population	Headquarters
1.	Bastar	17,016	13,02,253	Jagdalpur
2.	Bilaspur	8,569	19,93,042	Bilaspur
3.,	Durg	8,702	28,01,757	Durg
4.	Raigarh	6,528	12,65,084	Raigarh
5.	Raipur	13,445	30,09,042	Raipur
6.	Rajnandgaon	8,023	12,81,811	Rajnandgaon
7.	Sarguja	16,034	19,70,661	Ambikapur
8.	Koria	5,978	5,85,455	Baikunthpur
9.	Jashpur	6,457	7,39,780	Jashpur
10.	Janjgir-Champa	4,467	13,16,140	Janjgir
11.	Korba	5,769	10,12,121	Korba
12.	Kanker	6,434	6,51,333	Kanker
13.	Dantewara	15,610	7,19,065	Dantewara
14.	Mahasamund	4,963	8,60,176	Mahasamund
15.	Dhamatari	4,081	7,03,569	Dhamtari
16.	Kawardha	3,958	5,84,667	Kawardha

D

Dadra and Nagar Haveli : union territory of India, it is located on the western part of India between the States of Gujarat and Maharashtra, 24 km from the Arabian Sea, 129 km north of Mumbai. It consists of two sectors: Dadra with 3 villages, and Nagar Haveli with 69 villages. The total area is 491 sq km. The capital is Silvassa.

History : The history of Dadra and Nagar Haveli before the mediaeval period remains obscure. In AD 1262, a Rajput invader defeated the local Koli chieftains of the area and became the ruler of Ramnagar, a small State that included Nagar Haveli in its territory. The region remained under Rajput rule until the mid-18th century, when the Marathas acquired Nagar Haveli.

Dadra and Nagar Haveli came under Portuguese rule in the late eighteenth century. The Marathas ceded Nagar Haveli in 1783 as compensation for a Portuguese vessel that their navy had destroyed.

Two years later the Portuguese acquired Dadra, which became a kind of fief. After India achieved independence in 1947, Goan nationalists sought to break away from Portugal; and their first successes were the seizure of Dadra on the night of July 21, 1954, and their capture of Nagar Haveli two weeks later. A pro-Indian administration was formed in these enclaves, and, on June 1, 1961, it requested accession to the Indian Union. The Indian government had already acknowledged their incorporation into the union from the day of liberation but made it official on August 11, 1961. Population (1991) Union Territory Total 138,480; Rural 126,752; Urban 11,725.

Physical and human geography : The *terrain* to Dadra and Nagar Haveli is undulating and hilly, reaching elevations of 305 m in the northeast and east near the Western Ghats. The lowland areas are limited to the central plains, which are crossed by the Damanganga River and its tributaries. The only navigable river in Dadra and Nagar Haveli, the Damanganga rises in Maharashtra and flows northwest through the territory toward Daman, a port once famous for its docks.

The *climate* is typical of the region: extremely hot in summer (the mean maximum temperature in May approaches 34°C), with annual rainfall averaging about 3,050 mm, most of it falling between June and September. Forests cover some 40 per cent of the territory.

About four-fifths of the *population* consists of Adivasi tribal peoples, the most numerous being the Varli, Dhodia, and Konkan, speaking a variety of tribal dialects. The majority of the tribals live in the rural areas, practising agriculture and animal husbandry. Farming is the chief occupation, much of it done on terraced land. Rice and ragi (finger millet) are the major food crops. Wheat and sugarcane also are grown. Completion of the Damanganga Reservoir Project in neighbouring Gujarat was expected to extend irrigation in the territory significantly. Gujarati and Marathi also are spoken in the region. The population is predominandy Hindu, with small minorities of Christians and Muslims.

Timber production is mainly centred on the valuable native teak. There is very little large-scale *industry*; industrial estates have been set up in Piparia, Massate, Khadoli, and elsewhere for producing such items as engineering goods, plastics, chemicals, and fertilizers. Industrial growth has resulted in an influx of labour rather than benefiting the local population.

Daman and Diu : It is a union territory of western coastal India comprising two widely separated districts. Daman with an area of 72 sq km is an enclave on Gujarat's southern coast, situated about 160 km north of Mumbai. Diu, an island 40 sq km in area, lies off the southern coast of Gujarat's Kathiawar peninsula, 64 km southeast of Veraval.

History : The name Daman probably is derived from the Damanganga River, while Diu is from the Sanskrit word *dvipa*, meaning "island". Since the times of the Mauryas (third century BC), both have been subject to various local and regional powers ruling in western India. In the thirteenth century. Daman formed part of the Ramnagar State, which then became a tributary of the Gujarat sultans. Similarly, numerous dynasties in Kathiawar (Saurashtra) ruled Diu until it fell to the sultan of Gujarat in the early fifteenth century.

The Portuguese acquired both Daman and Diu as part of their grand design to control the trade of the Indian Ocean. In 1535, under a treaty with Bahadur Shah of Gujarat, the Portuguese built a fort at Diu, an important port on the flourishing commercial and pilgrimage routes between India and the Middle East. By the mid-1550s, all Gujarati ships entering and leaving the Gulf of Khambhat (Cambay) ports were required to call at Diu to pay Portuguese duties. Renowned for its docks and ship-building yards. Daman (known in Portuguese as Damao) was conquered by the Portuguese in 1559. Both areas were subject to the governor-general of Goa as part of the Portuguese overseas province Estado da India (State of India). They remained under Portuguese rule for more than four centuries, though the decline of the Portuguese empire in Asia greatly diminished their strategic significance. Daman and Diu survived as outposts of Portuguese overseas territory until 1961, when they became part of India. Diu is known for its magnificent Cathedral of Se Matriz and its idyllic beauty. Population (1991) Union Territory Total 101,586 (Daman 62,101; Dili 39,485).

Physical and human geography : Daman lies on an alluvial coastal plain, although outcrops of basalt create low plateaus and headlands in the area. The Damanganga River flows through the territory with Daman town situated where the river enters the Arabian Sea. Mean daily maximum temperatures range from 29°C in January to 34°C in May. The annual rainfall received between June and September averages 2,057 mm. Diu's territory includes a small area of the mainland that is separated from the Kathiawar peninsula by a narrow swampy creek. Much of the island is covered by salt, silt, and sand. Temperatures are similar to those of Daman, though rainfall is significantly less (584 mm annually). The people of Daman and Diu are predominantly Hindu, with small Muslim and Christian minorities, Gujarati is the main language of both districts. *Agriculture and fisheries* dominate the economy of Daman and Diu. Rice, ragi (finger millet), pulses (legumes), and beans are the main crops of Daman. In Diu, however, only about one-fifth of the land area is cultivated; crops such as *bajra* (pearl millets) and wheat are raised, as they are more suited to Diu's arid climate.

Industries are now growing and being promoted by the Goa Industrial Development Corporation. The towns of Daman and Diu are commercial and service centres; educational institutions are also developing.

Delhi : Delhi, the capital city of India, is also a metropolitan region and a State of India. The city is of great historic significance the metropolitan region an important commercial, transport, and cultural hub, and the State the political nerve centre of India. The city is in fact two "cities". Old and New Delhi. The State consists of these and the surrounding rural territories covering an area of 1,485 sq km at an altitude varying between 213 and 305 m. The city lies in the north-central part of the country astride the Yamuna River, a major tributary of the Ganga. It is bounded on the east by the State of Uttar Pradesh and on the north, west, and south by Haryana. The urban agglomeration of Delhi is the third largest in the country, with a recorded population of 9.47 million (1991). Legend has it that the city acquired its present name from Raja Dhilu who reigned over its territories in the first century BC. In written texts, however, the names Dhilli or Dhillika occur for the first time in the Bijola inscription (AD 1170).

History : Delhi has one of the most interesting archaeological landscapes, with monuments belonging to several millennia silhouetted side by side. Thirteen cities, built on new or on fortified old sites, have left their evidence in a limited area of about 180 sq km of the Delhi-Aravali triangle. There is said to be a prophecy that whoever builds a new city in Delhi will lose it. The earliest settlement, pdraprastha, built about 1400 BC and mentioned in the great epic the Mahabharata written by Ved Vyasa, was said to be the capital of the Pandavas. The second city of Delhi to emerge in the triangle was Anangpur, or Anandpur, established by Anang Pal, a Tomar Rajput, in about AD 1020, as a royal resort. The city was near a bunded (embanked) semicircular masonry tank called the Suraj Kund (Sun Tank). Anang Pal later shifted his city some 10 km west to the citadel he established at Lal Kot.

Lal Kot was occupied for about a century by Tomar kings, perhaps until Vishal Deva, a Chauhan Rajput, conquered it in 1153. His grandson, Prithviraj III, or Rai Pithora, extended Lal Kot in AD 1164 by building massive ramparts around it. This became the third city of Delhi and was popularly known as Qila Rai Pithora. Many historians consider it the first of the seven cities of Delhi. Muhammad Ghuri, a Muslim invader, killed Prithviraj in battle in 1192. Ghuri soon left with his booty, appointing Qutb-ud-Din Aibak, his slave, as his viceroy in India. After Ghuri's death in 1206 Qutb-ud- Din Aibak enthroned himself as the sultan of India and made Lal Kot the seat of his empire. For the next three centuries (1192-1398) the city remained, with minor breaks, the capital of the reigning kings of the Sultan dynasties. Lal Kot was also given another important monument, the Qutab Minar, by Qutb-ud-Din. It was a victory tower and perhaps also a *minar* (tower) to the mosque. However, the tower, as it stands today, was completed by Firuz Shah with an addition of two more storeys with copious marble inlays, raising its height to 74 m. It was, as it were, a statement of the arrival of the Sultans in India, boastful and triumphant.

During the reign of the Khaljis (1290-1320) the region was invaded by Mongol plunderers who ravaged the defenceless suburbs. To ensure that the Mongols did not ravage the suburbs and gardens again, Ala-ud-Din in 1303 built a new circular fortified city, 1.7 sq km in area. It was initially called Lashkar, or Lashkargah (army encampment), in contrast to the Qutb-Lal Kot complex known as the Shahr (city) DihIi-i-Kuhna (Old Delhi). This walled city complementary to Lal Kot was later named Siri and was designated as the Khaiji capital (Darul Khilafa). Its perimeter wall was about 1.5 km, and had many towers and gates. Siri is generally counted as the second city of Delhi but was the first completely new city to be built by the Muslim conquerors in India.

Delhi in the fourteenth century hence consisted of DihIi-i-Kuhna, or Old Delhi, at the Qutb-Lal Kot complex; the Shahr-i-Nau, or new city, at Ghayaspur-Kilokhari; and, the Danil-Khilafa, or capital city, at Siri. Delhi passed into the hands of Tughluqs in 1320 as the last Khaiji king died without leaving a male survivor. Eleven Tughluq kings ruled over Delhi, but only three of them showed an interest in architecture, each of them adding a new capital city to the existing urban conglomeration in the Delhi triangle. These cities demonstrate the militarisric nature of the

Sultanate and the obsession the Tughluqs had for defence. The first of these capitals, raised as a stronghold then as a city, was the fortified citadel of Tughlaqabad (1320-1325) built by Ghiyas-ud-Din.

Muhammad bin Tughluq (reigned 1325-1351) conceived of a capital city that reflected his master plan for his empire, which was to consolidate rather than to expand. Border raids had not subsided, so he decided to build a protective wall to enclose Qutb Delhi, Siri, and Tughlaqabad and form a new city to be named Jahanpanah, This city was disarrayed soon after it had been consolidated. Muhammad Tughluq suddenly decided to shift his capital to Deogiri, which he named Daulatabad, in the Deccan in order to supervise the territories he had recently annexed in that region. The population of Jahanpanah was ordered to proceed to the new capital in 1338. The depopulated Delhi had visibly crumbled, and its decaying buildings became a rich source of bricks for the new city of Firozabad, the third and the last Tughluq city. Set up in 1354 on the banks of the Yamuna, it was about 8 km northeast of Siri. This city, the fifth Delhi, was built by Firuz Shah (1351-1388) and was named after him.

It has been said that, in the Delhi of the fourteenth century what, Tughlaqabad was to the army establishment and Nizamuddin to the mendicants, so was the suburb of Hauz Khas to the savants. Educated refugees from Samarkand and Central Asian university towns had flocked to Delhi after the Mongol conquests. The Hauz Khas *madarsah* was a college whose academic reputation had spread throughout the Sultanate.

The Sayyid (c. 1414-1451) and the Lodhi (1451-1526) dynasties, which followed the Tughluqs, confined themselves within the precincts of Firozabad. They lived through turbulent times and had no time to build cities. Babur, the first Mughal king of India came here in 1526 and made his base at Agra. His son Humayun ascended the throne in 1530, and for 10 turbulent years he ruled from Delhi. In 1533 he celebrated the establishment of his dynasty by building a new city, Dinpanah. The site was carefully selected on the banks of the Yamuna. No trace of the city now remains, as it was completely destroyed by Sher Shah Suri.

The next two Mughal rulers Akbar and Jahangir preferred to rule India from Agra but, realizing the importance of Delhi, paid frequent ceremonial visits to the city. In 1639 Shah Jahan instructed his engineers, architects, and astrologers to choose a location with a mild climate somewhere between Agra and Lahore. The choice was the Hazrat Delhi of the Sultans, on the western bank of the Yamuna, just north of Purana Qila. Shah Jahan started the construction of the new capital, initially focussing on his fort called Urdu-i-Mualla. Popularly called Lal Qila, or the Red Fort it was completed in eight years, and on April 19, 1648, Shah Jahan entered his fort, and his new capital, Shajahanabad, from the riverfront gate.

The fort had a monumental entrance, Lahori Gate, from which emerged the main street of the city, terminating at the Fatehpuri Mosque. This Street, about 36 m wide, formed the main axis of the city. Pale moonlight shining on the central pool gave the street its name, Chandni Chowk ("Moonlight Square"). It was the ceremonial street of Delhi, where Shah Jahan and Aurangzeb marched in all their regality. Nadir Shah and Ahmad Shah Abdali rode defiantly, and the Marathas and the Rohilas walked in triumph. It was on this street that Lord Hardinge was taken in procession when the British came to announce Delhi as the new capital of British India. The Jama Masjid, commenced in 1644, and the city wall, constructed between 1651 and 1658, were the next most important structures to have been completed in the city. The wall was a semicircular, 8 m high, 3.5 m thick, and 6 km long, and enclosed an area about 6.4 sq km. It was punctuated with seven large gates (Kashmiri, Mori, Kabuli, Lahori, Ajmeri, Turkomani, and Akbarabadi), and the wall fronting the river had three gates (Raj Ghat, Qila Ghat, and Nigambodh Ghat). The main streets of the city culminated at these gates. Set on a small hill, Shahjahanabad's Jama Masjid, also known as the *badshahi masjid* ("royal mosque"), was the largest in India. A fire in 1662 killed 60,000 people, and in 1716, 23,000 died when their houses caved in after the rains.

Just 10 years after founding it, Shah Jahan lost Shahjahanabad to his son Aurangzeb who imprisoned him at Agra fort, and crowned himself emperor in July 1658. Aurangzeb inherited a very prosperous and populous city, but life was to gradually ebb out of this metropolis because its new ruler was of a very different disposition than its founder. Shah Jahan nurtured the arts and enjoyed the pleasures of life, Aurangzeb deliberately shunned them. He had neither the inclination nor the opportunity to build or beautify cities. He abandoned Shahjahanabad as a permanent seat of residence. His successors reigned over a dismembered impoverished empire. The final blow to the city came from the heinous attack of Nadir Shah, the Persian marauder.

When the British captured Delhi in 1803 it was still a major commercial and trading centre, though the walled city had become a "grand but crumbling slum". There were about 130,000 inhabitants living inside the wall and about 20,000 in the suburbs. For reasons of space and security, the British commanders and officers in service of the East India Company set up their paraphernalia in areas just adjoining the Red Fort that were not densely populated. In the north were laid the Residency, with its garrisons, stables, timber lines, the magazine and powder store, a customhouse, a bank, two hospitals, a few "bungalows', and a church. Some modifications were made in the fortifications to suit the new military requirements.

The cantonment, occupying an area larger than the walled city, was shifted to the ridge in the northwest in 1828. An alternative "Residency", with classical and Gothic features, was built on a high spot on the ridge, followed by the larger Metcalf House, whose owner, replacing the Resident, later became the Agent of Delhi. By the 1840s a new, almost self-sufficient, and culturally segregated residential suburb had taken shape near the cantonment and was called the civil station. Many of the early British occupants in Delhi, such as William Fraser and Charles Metcalf, were hypnotized by the richness of the city's cultural legacy. The Mughal court was allowed their traditional ceremonies, and coins were minted in the emperor's name. Everything, however, changed after the so-called Indian Mutiny of 1857, including the British attitude in and towards Delhi.

The Mughal emperor Bahadur Shah II was deposed to Rangoon (now Yangon) after the Indian Mutiny, and his family was murdered. The military took over the palace and converted it into a fort. All territory lying within 457 m of the fort and along the wall were zoned for military use, and all buildings between it and the Jama Masjid were levelled to form an esplanade. The cantonment was brought back into the city and established in confiscated properly in the area extending from the Kashmiri Gate to Daryaganj, with the wall in the east and Delhi bank and the esplanade, in the west. The cantonment occupied a third of the area of the walled city. Many Europeans moved out of the city to the civil station, and the natives from Daryaganj to the Chandni Chowk.

Once the crown took over the governance of Delhi, its morphology acquired the characteristics of a classic colonial town with three functional "quarters" — the *native* city, the *cantonment*, and the *civil station*, often called the civil lines. Delhi was also gradually modernized. In 1867 the first regular railway train had entered Delhi from Calcutta By 1910 the city had municipal governance, water distribution and sanitation systems, telephone and telegraph lines, and electricity. Chandni Chowk was bequeathed a Victoria Clock Tower, its canal was filled up, and an electric tram line was built over it. In 1877 the first of a series of great *durbars* (courts) was launched to demonstrate the British dominion over India. The second *durbar* was held in 1903 to celebrate the coronation of Edward VII. The third *durbar* was held in 1911 and proved to be a turning point for Delhi: during the celebrations George V announced that the capital of India was to be shifted back to the city from Calcutta. The decision was justified on both political and administrative grounds.

In January 1912 a three-member committee was formed to "work on the practical details of the political decision". It had as a member the architect Sir Edwin Lutyens, who was ultimately to give shape to the city. The committee set out to choose a site. The Raisina Hill just south of the walled city, neither too far nor too close to it, was chosen.

The committee accepted the general features of Lutyens's plan for Delhi city in December 1912. In the plan the viceroy's House, the Council Chamber, and the Secretariats were brought together, unlike in Calcutta where they were separated, and were to be built on the "acropolis" at Raisina Hill, which become the central motif of the plan.

The *architectural* style in the new capital, Hardinge had declared, was to be a blend of Eastern and Western architecture. From the viceroy's House emerged the dominant central axis, the Kings way, which was 3.2 km long and headed towards the river. The axis was bisected midway by a less majestic north-south axis called the Queensway. The axis was rounded off with a triumphal arch, the India Gate, to commemorate the valiant dead in the First World War. Sir Herbert Baker, Lutyens's collaborator, was asked to design the Assembly building when the political situation made it clear that there has to be a transfer of power from the viceroy to a Legislative Assembly. Baker designed a circular building and placed it north-west of the Red Fort and on the axis towards the old city. Another circular building was the commercial centre of Connaught Place, designed like the one at Bath, England, The new capital was inaugurated in January 1931.

The plan of the *network of roads* in New Delhi was based on the belief in "geometric aestheticism". The total plan was a series of hexagons comprising 96 km of main streets with the mall (Kingsway, now Rajpath) as the grand base. These hexagons were fitted between the three axes, which radiated from the governor's house to the historically significant Jama Masjid, Indraprastha, and tomb of Safdarjang, linking, as it were, the present with the past. The residential structure of the city was planned with the main purpose to "organize" accommodation. Gardens and parks were everywhere and all streets were lined with trees. The new cantonment, occupying some 44 sq km, was built to the west of the city and followed a rigid grid-iron layout.

Baron Charles Hardinge, viceroy of India, had desired a synthesis of Old and New Delhi and had instructed that they should be planned as one and not two cities. Lutyens, however, clung to his narrow aesthetic view of urban design, and in his grind plan Old Delhi was nothing but an incompatible decaying urban mass and should be allowed to remain so. This prejudice proved ruinous for the old city, which had to accommodate the bulk of the near million refugees that were added to the population of Delhi between 1941 and 1951. While New Delhi perfected its living environment at densities ranging between 6 and 8 persons per hectare, Old Delhi collapsed under 336 to 400 persons per hectare.

The anomaly between the two cities of Old and New Delhi has been the bane of planners ever since. The first *master plan* had marked Old Delhi as a slum, and it was only in the 1980s, when the second master plan was being formulated, that it was given some importance as a heritage zone. Lutyens's Delhi has always been treated as sacrosanct territory, and any change suggested in its original plan and density pattern is generally opposed both by public and planners. In the 1970s and 1980s the DDA (Delhi Development Authority) almost monopolized the housing business in Delhi and created huge estates around the existing urban nucleus. There, accommodation was provided in terms of high-income, middle-income, and low-income groups. Those outside these income brackets continued to proliferate the *jhuggi jhopris* (slums), now popularly known as the JJ colonies, or "unauthorized colonies". To make the unauthorized colonies eligible for urban amenities, 567 of them were regularized under political pressure. The overspill in Delhi's population is accommodated across the eastern bank of the Yamuna, where another Delhi is gradually coming into existence. Many up-market housing estates and walled villas of the super-rich have come up on the peripheries in the south, west, and north.

Architecture : A varied history has left behind a rich architectural heritage in Delhi. The earliest buildings in the city belong to the Sultanate period and are not homogenous in construction and ornamentation. The influence of Hindu Rajput craftsmen is visible in the naturalistic motifs, the serpentine tendrils, and the curves of the alphabets of Quranic inscriptions. Some artists, poets, and architects from Central Asia brought with them the Seljuq tradition of architecture, characterized by the lotus-bud fringe on the underside of the arch, ornamental reliefs, as well as bricks laid endwise and lengthwise in alternating courses in the masonry face. The phase of experimentation and improvisations in Islamic architecture was over by the time of the Khaijis, and a specific method and idiom had been established in Islamic architecture called the Pashtun style. This style had some characteristic features, most notably the true arch, which was usually in the shape of a pointed horseshoe, as well as windows fitted with perforated screens, decorations of mouldings, arabesques (intricate, detailed patterning), and inspirational, spiritual texts. The materials used were mostly red sandstone with inlays of white marble.

The Tughluqs changed the tradition and reduced the element of ornamentation in their architecture. They had a preference for plain, austere surfaces of grey stone. Cross vaults, inscribed borders, and encaustic tiles were incorporated in their structures to great effect. The Tughluqs gave their buildings an aura of grandeur by underplaying decoration but emphasizing scale. During the Sayyad and Lodhi periods two complex types of tomb structures came into vogue: the low octagonal with a bigger mass and area at the ground level, and the higher square with a facade broken by a stringcourse (a horizontal band, like a cornice, or moulding used as a decorative element) and series of panels giving it a semblance of two or three storeys. Garden tombs were also built during the Lodhi period. The mosques in this time did not have minarets.

The first important piece of Mughal architecture in Delhi was Humayun's tomb, which also is the first mature garden tomb in India and the precursor of the Taj Mahal. It introduced high arches and double domes to Indian architecture. The most representative pieces of Mughal architecture are found in the Lal Qila (the Red Fort). They include the *naqqar khana* (drum house), *diwan-i-am* (ball of public audience), *diwan-i-khas* (hall of private audience), palaces and entertainment halls, projecting balconies, *hammams* (baths) and indoor canals, well-laid-out geometrical gardens, and an ornate mosque. The Jama Masjid is an example of the true Mughal mosque, as it is the first to have minarets. Marble was the main construction material in most of the buildings, which were also beautifully carved and were decorated with panels inlaid with multicoloured stones.

British architecture in Delhi can be typified as colonial and Mughal. It ranged from the grand — as represented by the Viceroy's House, the Parliament building, and the Secretariat buildings? — to the utilitarian, as represented in the bungalows and institutional buildings.

Architecture in independent India has tried to evolve its own language. It is a synthesis of the Western arid the indigenous, and a revival of vernacular idioms. Classic examples of these attempts are the Supreme Court, the Vigyan Bhavan, offices of the various ministeries, and institutional buildings congregated around Connaught Place. In recent years Delhi has produced a few architects of international fame who have added some impressive buildings to the city's landscape which may be called postmodern. Mentionable amongst these latter are the Institute of Immunology, the headquarters of the Life Insurance Corporation, and the Bahai Temple.

Delhi is situated on the watershed which divides the river systems of the Ganga and the Sind. The most significant topographic feature of Delhi is the ridge, a culminating spur of the ancient Aravali hills of Rajasthan State, which are perhaps the oldest mountain ranges in the world, now completely denuded. Appearing like two sides of a triangular rampart and skirting an area of about 180 sq km on the northwest, west, and south, the ridge adds variety to the plain alluvial landscape and provides Delhi with some exquisite flora and fauna. The third side of this triangular rampart is formed by the Yamuna River. Within this triangle have been born the famous seven cities of Delhi between 1000 BC and the seventeenth century AD.

Climate : Delhi has a subtropical climate which is greatly influenced by its inland location. The summer months of May and June are extremely dry and scorching, and day temperatures sometimes reach 43-45 °C. Monsoons normally break in July and bring down the temperatures, but the weather until the end of September is hot, sultry, and very uncomfortable. The average annual rainfall is only about 660 mm. The period between October and March is quite pleasant, although December and January can be very cold and foggy with occasional wet spells. The mean daily winter minimum temperature is around 7 °C, but some nights can be cold, with the mercury dipping to 1-3 °C. The transition from winter to spring is gradual.

Flora : The changing climate of Delhi results in three vegetation seasons, though the paucity of rain and a depleting groundwater level does not allow any luxuriant growth of natural vegetation. About 1,000 species of flowering plants, most of them indigenous and naturalized, grow in the city and its environs. The vegetation on the ridge and the riverine tract are distinctly different. The permanent vegetation on the ridge consists of acacias, wild date palms, and gregarious undershrub dotted with some flowering species. Grasses, climbers, and twiners constitute the ephemeral vegetation, which emerges only during the rainy season. The vegetation on the sandy and alkaline riverine tract, on the other hand, is rich and varied, especially during the monsoon and winter months.

Fauna : The fauna of Delhi is fairly rich, varied, and oriental and falls under the Cis-ljangetic Zoological type. The Carnivora are its principal indigenous mammals. Hyenas, wolves, foxes, jackals, and leopards once walked its low forests but are now found in the ravine lands or the hilly ridges bordering the city The Ungulata, or hoofed animals, are represented by antelopes and boar These are now rarely found in the wild state. Porcupines, hares, rats, and squirrels constitute the city's rodents, and bats, hedgehogs, and shrews are the insectivores of Delhi. The monkey is the only indigenous primate, found in the city around some temples and historical ruins.

The bird life of Delhi is also very rich and varied. The homing pigeon, the house sparrow, kites, jungle crows, parrots, bush quail, and partridges art found throughout the year. The lakes around Delhi attract many a migratory bird in winter. Sixty-five species of fish are found in the Yamuna River.

Administration and planning : Delhi has seen many changes in its administrative setup. On August 2, 1858, Parliament passed the Government of India Act, transferring British power over India from the East India Company to the British Crown. In 1876 Queen Victoria added the title "Empress of India" to her reagality. Delhi was a British province headed by a chief commissioner until 1947. After the country's independence it became a centrally administered State in 1952, but in 1956 its status was changed to that of a Union Territory under the central government. A unified corporation for both urban and rural areas was established in 1958. The administrative setup was further modified by the Delhi Administrative Act of 1966, which introduced a three-tier system consisting of a lieutenant governor and an executive council, an elected metropolitan council, and the municipal corporation. It was granted a special Statehood and an elected legislative assembly in 1991 under the sixty-ninth Constitutional Amendment. Delhi is headed by a lieutenant governor nominated by the president of India and is administered by a chief minister appointed from the elected party.

Delhi Slate nests in different layers of administrative and planning regions. It covers an area of 1,485 sq km and consists of the Delhi urban agglomeration and 209 villages distributed in the Delhi and *Mehrauli tehsils*. At the macro level it is part of the National Capital Region (NCR), a planning region carved out in 1971 by the Town and Country Planning Organisation (TCPO) to guide future growth around Delhi. The NCR comprises the Delhi State and the bordering districts, or *tehsils*, in Haryana, Uttar Pradesh, and Rajasthan. It extends over a radius of about 100 km around the Delhi metropolis and covers an area of 30,242 sq km. The NCR Board was set up in 1985 for preparing an integrated master plan for future balanced development of the region. At the submacro level is the Delhi Metropolitan Area, which incorporates the State as well as the contiguously urbanized parts in the adjoining States and covers an area of 3,182 sq km. At the micro level is the Delhi urban agglomeration, with an area of 446 sq km, which consists of three statutory towns: New Delhi Municipal Committee (NDMC), Municipal Corporation, Delhi (Urban) [MCD(U)] and Delhi Cantonment, as well as 23 census towns.

The metropolitan governance of Delhi 'is essentially in the hands of the NDMC, the MCD and the Cantonment Board. The MCD is an elected body, the NDMC members are nominated by the government, and the Cantonment Board consists of partially elected and partially nominated ex-officio members. The MCD performs obligatory municipal and discretionary welfare functions. Slum clearance and improvement have been its main functions. It operates through zonal committees comprising local councillors and one alderman or more. The NDMC was created in 1933 and is essentially responsible for New Delhi (as it was configured by architect Edwin Lutyens) and its adjoining areas. The municipal functions in the cantonment are administered by the Ministry of Defence.

The planning of metropolitan Delhi has been in the hands of the Delhi Development Authority (DDA), constituted in 1957 by an Act of Parliament. The first 20 year master plan for the city was prepared by the TCPO and implemented by the DDA in 1962 with the avowed purposes of checking the haphazard growth of Delhi and providing affordable and appropriate housing. An area of about 24,000 ha has been acquired by the government and handed over to the DDA for urban development, making it the largest real estate developer of nationalized land outside the communist world. The delayed second master plan came into force in 1986 and focussed on deindustrialization, decentralization, provision of multinodal mass transport, and low-rise highdensity housing.

People : Metropolitan Delhi, like all capital cities, is a seething cauldron of activity. At the end of the nineteenth century, bereft of its Mughal splendour, it was a small city with half a million people, but gradually it has grown into a giant. The Delhi urban agglomeration would have a population in the vicinity of 12 million by 2001, and Delhi State would reach about 15 million inhabitants. Demographic trends indicate that about 90 per cent of the population of the State will remain urban, 85 per cent of it residing in the three statutory towns.

The census of 1991 reported the sex ratio (females per 1000 males) in urban Delhi as 830 and in its rural component as 807, indicating the high incidence of single male migrants in the city. The literacy rate in the urban areas was 76 per cent and in the rural areas was 67 per cent, much higher than the national averages.

In the demographic history of Delhi, 1947 was a turning point when thousands of refugees from Pakistan converged on the city and changed not only its demographic structure but also its sociocultural texture and its economy. Since then the city has grown through its migrants. The birth rate in the city has declined in recent decades, but the migrant population has swelled. Almost 100,000 people arrive every year and, on an average, constitute more than one-third of its population.

The main religious groups in the city (as per the 1991 Census) are Hindus (about 83 per cent), Sikhs (about 4 per cent), and Muslims (about 9 per cent). Jains, Christians, Buddhists, and others make up the remaining 4 per cent of the population. Most people in Delhi speak Hindi or a modified version called Hindustani. Gurumukhi is spoken by the Sikhs, and Urdu by the Muslims. Migrants from different States speak their own languages but try to acquire a working knowledge of Hindi. English is understood and spoken by the educated.

Economy : Delhi, like any historical capital city, has essentially been an administrative centre with a diversified economy in which administration, services, and manufacturing are mixed in good measure. It has been a centre for a great variety of arts and crafts. In the Mughal period Delhi was famous for its jewellery, damascene work, cloth embroidery, gold braids, silk and brocades, engravings of all kinds, sculpture, and miniature paintings. It was also an important regional trading centre.

Delhi's more recent administrative importance dates back to the time when the East India Company transferred the governance of India to the crown, and the capital of the British Empire in India was shifted from

Calcutta to Delhi. It has subsequently emerged as an important administrative, commercial, and service centre with about three-fourths of its working population engaged in trade, public administration, community, social, and personal services. Modern industries came to the city at the beginning of the twentieth century. The major industries were cotton ginning, spinning, and weaving; flour grinding and packaging; and sugarcane and oil pressing. Minor industries included printing presses, shoemaking and embroidery workshops, bakeries, breweries, and iron and brass works. Industrial growth in Delhi picked up substantially only in the 1980s, when the number of registered industrial units increased from 50,000 in 1981 to 81,000 in 1990. Industrial investment, production, and employment also almost doubled during this period. The 1990s have brought important changes in the economic structure of the city. New Delhi has become an important node in the inter-national corporate and financial network, and Old Delhi has further consolidated its position as an important wholesale centre of North India.

G

Goa—A State of India, with an area of 3,702 sq km, comprises a mainland area, with an offshore island and is located 400 km south of Mumbai. It is bounded by Maharashtra State in the north, by Karnataka State in the east and south, and by the Arabian sea in the west. The capital is Panaji. Formerly a Portuguese possession, it became a part of India in 1962 and attained Statehood in 1987.

History : The ancient Hindu city of Goa, of which hardly a fragment survives, was built at the southernmost point of the island, and it was famous in early Hindu legend and history. In the Puranas and certain inscriptions, its name appears as Gove, Govapuri, and Gomant. The medieval Arabian geographers knew it as Sindabur, or Sandabur, and the Portuguese as Velha Goa. It was ruled by the Kadamba dynasty from the second century AD to 1312 and by Muslim invaders of the Deccan from 1312 to 1367. It was then annexed by the Hindu kingdom of Vijayanagar and later conquered by the Bahmani dynasty, which founded Old Goa in 1440.

With the subdivision of the Bahmani kingdom after 1482, Goa passed into the power of Yusuf Adil Khan, the Muslim king of Bijapur, who was its ruler when the Portuguese first reached India. The city was attacked in March 1510 by the Portuguese under Afonso de Albuquerque. The city surrendered without a struggle, and Albuquerque entered it in triumph.

Three months later Yusuf Adil Khan returned with 60,000 troops, forced the passage of the ford, and blockaded the Portuguese in their ships from May to August, when the cessation of the monsoon enabled them to put to sea. In November, Albuquerque returned with a larger force and, after overcoming a desperate resistance, recaptured the city, massacred all the Muslims, and appointed a Hindu, Timoja, as the governor of Goa.

Goa was the first territorial possession of the Portuguese in Asia. Albuquerque and his successors left almost untouched the customs and constitutions of the 30 village communities on the island, abolishing only the rite of *suttee* (*sati*, the immolation of widows on the funeral pyres of their husbands).

Goa became the capital of the whole Portuguese empire in the east. It was granted the same civic privileges as Lisbon, reaching the climax of its prosperity between 1575 and 1600. The appearance of the Dutch in Indian waters precipitated the decline of Goa. In 1603 and 1639 the city was blockaded by Dutch fleets, though never captured, and in 1635 it was ravaged by an epidemic. In 1683 a Mughal army saved it from capture by Maratha raiders, and in 1739 the whole territory was attacked by the same enemies and saved only by the unexpected arrival of a new viceroy with a fleet.

The seat of the government was moved to Mormugao (now Marmagao) and in 1759 to Punjim (now Panaji). Cholera epidemics were one of the chief reasons for the migration of the inhabitants from Old Goa to New Goa. Between 1695 and 1775 the population of Old Goa dwindled from 20,000 to 1,600, and in 1835 the city was inhabited by only a few priests, monks, and nuns.

During the nineteenth century, events of importance affecting the settlement included its temporary occupation by the British in 1809 as a result of Napoleon's invasion of Portugal; the governorship (1855-1864) of the conde de Torres Novas, who inaugurated a great number of improvements; and the military revolts of the second half of the century. The most notable of these was the revolt of September 3, 1895, which necessitated the dispatch of an expeditionary force from Portugal. The infante Affonso Henriques, duque de Oporto, accompanied this expedition and exercised governor's powers from March to May 1896.

After Indian claims on Goa in 1948 and 1949, Portugal came under increasing pressure to cede Goa, with its other possessions on the subcontinent, to India. In mid-1954, Goan nationalists seized the Portuguese enclaves of Dadra and Nagar Haveli and established a pro-Indian administration. Another crisis occurred in 1955 when *satyagrahis* (nonviolent resisters) from India attempted to penetrate the territory of Goa. At first the *satyagrahis* were deported; but later, when large numbers attempted to cross the borders, the Portuguese authorities resorted to force, and casualties were inflicted. This led to the severance of diplomatic relations between Ptortugal and India on August 18, 1955. Tension between India and Portugal came to a head when on December 18, 1961, Indian troops supported by naval and air forces invaded and occupied Goa, Daman, and Diu. Portuguese India was, by constitutional amendment, incorporated into the Indian Union in 1962.

Physical and human geography : Goa, with a coast of 105 km, has sandy beaches, estuaries, and head-lands. In the interior, there are low plateaus and a portion of the Western Ghats (Sahyadris), rising to nearly 1,220 m. Between the mouths of Goa's two major rivers, the Mandovi and the Zuari, lies the island of Goa (Ilhas). The Cape (Cabo) apex of this triangular island is a rocky headland that provides two anchorages. There are three cities; Marmagao, or Marmugoa (including Vasco da Gama), Madgaon, and Panaji (Navagoa). Old Goa is, for the most part, a city in ruins but has been well-cared for since Goa's joining the rest of India, Panaji, originally a suburb of old Goa, is also situated on the left bank of the Mandovi: it is a well-planned city, having splendid churches, the Archbishop's palace, the Secretariat, markets, and a large bus terminal, adjoining which is the railway station lying on the Konkan railway. The Basilica of Bom Jesus (built sixteenth century), a World Heritage monument that enshrines the remains of St. Francis Xavier, is located at Old Goa. There is also the Se Cathedral (sixteenth century).

Educational and training institutes range from schools to technical and collegiate institutions. The University of Goa is situated near Panaji. Wharves and jetties teem with activity, and beyond the Miramar beach lies the Institute of Oceanography, which is famous for its research and expeditions to Antarctica. The Cabo headland has the imposing Government House. Asia's largest oceanorium is being planned here. Urban growth now extends, across the Mandovi, to cover Porvorim.

Marmagao, sheltered by a promontory and outfitted with a modern breakwater and quay, is the best port between Mumbai and Kozhikode (formerly Calicut, Kerala). It specializes in the export of iron ore and manganese. A railway line via Vasco da Gama urban area and Madgaon connects it with the main southern railway line via Londa in Karnataika. The new Konkan railway running from north to south promises further economic development of Goa.

Goa's climate is equable, with rains received from the southwest monsoon between June and September.

Goa's agricultural production consists of rice, pulses, (legumes), coconut, cashews, and mango. These crops are important in Goa's life and living. Forests cover low plateaus and the slopes of the Western Ghats. Teak, bamboo, and cashew are important economic products. Though efforts are being made to regenerate them, open-cast mines of iron ore and manganese constitute a great threat to the environment.

Fisheries are important; government policy and concessions have promoted Goa's rapid industrialization, through its industrial estates. Fertilizer, chemicals, pharmaceuticals, iron, and sugar are the leading large-scale industries. There are also medium and small-scale industries including traditional handicrafts. Industrial products find a good market in India and abroad.

The People : Hindus and Christians are the main components of the Goan population. Portuguese was the language of administration and the elite. Portuguese rule and economic conditions caused emigration of Goans not only to the former Portuguese-African colonies, but also to the rest of India. The impact of Portuguese culture is seen in their personal names and surnames, and the style of churches and villas. The cultural landscape of Goa shows interesting contrasts: the western coastland and estuaries are dotted with wayside crosses, churches, and marked by a predominant Roman Catholic Christian style of living; and the hummocky and hilly east with Hindu temples and shrines, and a population that is mainly Hindu, with some tribals. Yet, unmistakably, there is a cultural blend that is "Goan", and which expresses itself in the resurgent and effulgent Konkani language.

Tourism : Tourism in Goa is a flourishing enterprise; long sandy beaches, fringed with coastal vegetation and coconut palms, heritage hotels, and the Dabolim airport attract foreigners in large numbers, and now, Indian tourists also. This growth, however, threatens Goa's natural environment.

Area, Population and Headquarters of Districts

S.No.	District	Area (sq km)	Population (1991 Census)	Headquarters
1.	North Goa	1,736	6,64,804	Panaji
2.	South Goa	1,966	5,04,989	Margao

Gujarat—This State of India is located on the country's western coast. It is bounded by the Arabian Sea to the west and south-west, Pakistan to the northwest, and the States of Rajasthan to the north, Madhya Pradesh to the east, and Maharashtra to the southeast. Its coastline is 1,596 km long, and no part is more than 161 km from the sea. Its area is 196,024 sq km. The capital is Gandhinagar, on the northern outskins of Ahmedabad, the former capital, largest city in the State, and one of the greatest cotton textile centres in India. It was there that Mahatma Gandhi built his Sabarmati ashram (retreat, or hermitage) as a headquarters for his campaigns.

Gujarat derived its name from the Gurjara (supposedly a subtribe of the Huns), who ruled the area during the eighth and ninth centuries AD. The State assumed its present form in 1960, when the former Bombay State was divided between Maharashtra and Guiarat on the basis of language.

History : Human settlements have been traced back to the Stone Age period in the valleys of the Sabarmati and Mahi rivers in the eastern part of the State. The historic period is linked with the spread of the Harappan (Indus Valley) civilization, which flourished in the third and second millennia BC. Centres of this civilization have been found at Lothal, Rangpur, Amri, Lakhabaval, and Rozdi (mostly in the Kathiawar Peninsula).

The known history of Gujarat began with the extension over the area of the rule of the Maurya dynasty, as is evidenced by the edicts of the emperor Ashoka (c. 250 BC), carved on a rock in the Girnar Hills of the Kathiawar Peninsula. After the fall of the Maurya Empire, Gujarat came under the rule of the Shakas (Scythians), or western Kshatrapas (AD 130-390). The greatest of these, Mahaksatrapa Rudrādaman, established his sway over Malwa, Saurashtra, Kachchh, and Rajasthan.

During the fourth and fifth centuries, Gujarat formed a part of the Gupta Empire, until the Guptas were succeeded by the Maitraka dynasty of the kingdom of Valabhi, which ruled over Gujaral and Malwa for three centuries. The capital, Valabhipura (near the eastern coast of the

Kathiawar Peninsula), was a great centre of Buddhist, Vedic, and Jain learning. The Maitraka dynasty was succeeded by the Gurjara-Prariharas (the imperial Gurjaras of Kannauj), who ruled during the eighth and ninth centuries; they, in turn, were followed shortly afterward by the Solanki dynasty. The boundaries of Gujarat reached their farthest limits in the time of this dynasty, when remarkable progress was made in the economic and cultural fields. Siddharaja Jayasimha and Kumarapala were the best-known Solanki kings; the famous writer Hemacandra flourished during this period (twelfth century). Karnadeva Vaghela, of the following Vaghela dynasty, was defeated in about 1299 by Ala-ud-Din Khaiji, sultan of Delhi; Gujarat then came under Muslim rule. It was Ahmad Shah, the first independent sultan of Gujarat, who founded Ahmedabad (1411). The end of the sixteenth century saw Gujarat under Mughal rule; this lasted until the mid-eighteenth century, when the Marathas overran the State.

Gujarat came under the administration of the British East India Company in 1818. After the Indian mutiny and rebellion of 1857-1858, the area became a province of the British crown and was divided into Gujarat province, with an area of 25,900 sq km, and numerous native States. With Indian independence in 1947, all of Gujarat except the States of Kachchh and Saurashtra was included in Bombay State; the province was enlarged in 1956 to include the two States. On May 1, 1960, Bombay State was split into present-day Gujarat and Maharashtra States.

In April 1965, fighting broke out between India and Pakistan in the Rann of Kachchh, an area that had long been in dispute between them. A ceasefire came into force on July I, and the dispute was submitted to arbitration by an international tribunal. The tribunal's award, published in 1968, gave nine-tenths of the territory to India and one-tenth to Pakistan. Gujarat was again gripped by violence in 1985. Touched off by proposed changes in the concessions reserved for the scheduled castes, the disturbances soon escalated to Muslim-Hindu riots and continued for five months.

Physical Geography : Gujarat is a land of great contrasts; it stretches from the wet, fertile, rice-growing plains of the west coast, north of Mumbai (formerly Bombay) city, to the almost rainless salt deserts of Kachchh in the northwest. Kachchh, comprising a single district, is bounded on the south by the Gulf of Kachchh and on the north and east is separated from Pakistan and the mainland of India by the Rann of Kachchh, best described as a vast salt marsh covering about 20,720 sq km. The Rann floods during the rainy season, slight though the rains may be, and Kachchh is converted into an island; in the dry season it is a sandy, salty plain plagued by dust storms. To the south of Kachchh is the large peninsula of Kathiawar (Saurashtra), lying between the Gulf of Kachchh and the Gulf of Khambhat (Cambay). It also is arid and rises from the coasts to a low, rolling area of hill land in the centre, covered with scrub or sparse woodland. The chief towns are found in the more fertile spots and were formerly the capitals of small States. Soils are mostly poor, having been derived from a variety of old crystalline rocks, but among the State's valuable products are the fine building stones of Porbandar. Rivers, except for seasonal streams, are absent. On the southern shores of the peninsula is the former Portuguese territory of Diu. Northeastern Gujarat is mainly a region of small plains and low hills. The highest point in the State is at Girnar Hills (1,117 m). Rainfall is low; January temperatures may drop almost to the freezing point, while a temperature 48 °C has been recorded in the hot season. Crops include millet and some cotton.

Southward in central Gujarat the rainfall increases; temperature ranges are less extreme; and soils arc more fertile, being derived partly from the basalts of the Deccan region. The focus of this area is the city of Vadodara (Baroda), formerly the capital of a rich and powerful State. South of what is now the Vadodara district, the important river, the Narmada, empties into the Gulf of Khambhat, and it is the silt deposited by this river and the Tapi (Tapti) that is responsible for the shallowness of the Gulf of Khambhat and the decline of its former ports.

Southern Gujarat, the districts of Bharuch (Broach) and Surat, are famed for their rich soils and fine crops of cotton. The great Tapi River, flowing in a deep trench from the east, cuts through Surat; and in the eastern parts of south Gujarat the country is mountainous. This is, indeed, the northern extension of the Western Ghats, which attract a heavy rainfall from the rain-bearing summer monsoon winds. Farther south, the mountains are forested. The small district of the Dangs is in this area. Along the coastal plains conditions begin to approach an equable climate, with rainfall nearing 2,000 mm.

Forests cover only 10 per cent of Gujarat, reflecting human activity as well as meagre rainfall. Scrub forest occurs in the drier areas, the main species being the babul acacia, the caper, the Indian jujube, and the toothbrush bush (*Salvadora persica*). Where annual rainfall approaches 1,016 mm — the Kathiawar tablelands and northeastern mainland — such deciduous species as teak, catechu (cutch), bakligum, axlewood, and Bengal kino (butea gum) are found. Deciduous forests are concentrated in the wetter southern and eastern hills. They produce valuable timbers: woolly tomentosa, Vengai padauk (resembling mahogany), Malabar simal, and the heartleaf adina. The west coast of Kathiawar is known for its algae, and the east coast produces the papyrus, or paper plant (*Cyperus papyrus*).

The Gir National Park in Kathiawar contains the last Indian lions, the only remaining members of the Asiatic species; in a sanctuary near the Little Rann of Kachchh, the only surviving Indian wild asses are found. The Nal Sarovar Bird Sanctuary, near Ahmedabad, attracts about 140 species of birds migrating from the Siberian plains and elsewhere in winter. These include the sarus crane, Brahmini duck, bustard, pelican, cormorant, ibis, stork, heron and egret. The Rann of Kachchh is the only nesting ground of the greater flamingo in India. There is excellent offshore and inland fishing in Gujarat Fish catches include pomfret, salmon, hilsa (a type of shad), jewfish (scianid fish), prawn, Bombay duck (a food fish), and tuna.

The people : The diverse *ethnic groups* represented in the Gujarati population may be broadly categorized as Indic (i.e., northern-derived) or Dravidian (southern derived). The former include the Nagar Brahman, Bhatia, Bhadela, Rabari, and Mina castes (the Parsis, originally from Persia, represent a much later northern influx); among the peoples of southern origin are the Bhangi, Koli, Dubla, Naikda, and Macchi-Kharwa tribes. The rest of the population, including the aboriginal Bhil tribe, exhibit mixed characteristics. Members of the scheduled castes (formerly "untouchables") and aboriginal tribes form nearly one-fifth of the State's population. There is one entirely tribal district of Dangs. Ahmedabad district has the highest proportion of scheduled castes.

The main *concentration of population* in Gujarat is seen in the plain area in the districts of Ahmedabad, Kheda, Baroda, Surat, and Vulsar. This area is agriculturally productive and highly industrialized. Another concentration of population is seen in the southern coastal area of Saurashtra from Mongrol to Mahuva and pockets around Rajkot and Jamnagar. The distribution of population gradually decreases towards the north (Kachchh) and the eastern hilly region. The mean density of population per sq km is 211; it is lowest in Kachchh (27 persons per sq km in 1991) and highest in Vulsar (614 persons per sq km in 1991), and the decennial growth rate was 21.19 per cent in 1991.

Gujarati and Hindi are the State's *official languages*. Gujarati, the most widely spoken of the two, is an Indo-European language derived from Sanskrit through Prakrit, ancient India languages other than Sanskrit, and Apabhramsha, a language spoken in northern and western India from the tenth to the fourteenth century. Gujarat's contact by sea with foreign countries has also led to the introduction of Persian, Arabic, Turkish, Portuguese, and English words. The prodigious writings in Gujarati of Mahatma Gandhi are noted for their vigour and simplicity and have had a strong influence on modern Gujarati prose.

Hinduism is the *religion* of most of the population, with a minority of adherents to Islam, Jainism, and Zoroastrianism. The policy of the State has always been marked by the religious tolerance of its people. In the late twentieth century, however, increasing communal tensions led to outbreaks of violence.

In Gujarat the process of *urbanization* is taking shape differently in different parts of the State. The most urbanized part of the State is the Ahmedabad-Vadodara (Baroda) industrial belt. An emerging megalopolis (a continuous urban area of many large cities) is coming up along the National Highway number 8 in the industrial plains region from Unjha in the north to Vapi in the south. A hierarchical settlement system is visible in the Saurashtra agricultural region, while scattered small settlements are seen in the peripheral areas of the north and east, which are dry, hilly, or forested. The tribal population is concentrated in these marginal, unproductive areas.

Economy : Unlavourable climatic conditions, salinity of soil and water, and rocky terrain are some of the physical problems, which have hampered Gujarats agricultural activities. The State mostly depends on irrigation. Surface water harvesting is needed, as groundwater is becoming depleted. It is important that the Narmada canal system gets operational for the purpose of irrigation. The main food crops are *jawar* (sorghum), *bajra* (millet), rice, and wheat. The production of cash crops is important in Gujarat. These include cotton, peanuts (groundnuts), tobacco, oilseeds, spices, fruits, and sugar.

Although most of the people are engaged in *agriculture*, there is a cohesive and comparatively prosperous merchant community that thrives on trade and commerce. Gujarati business castes have spread across India and even overseas. Gujarat occupies a leading place in the industrial economy of India, The State is rich in *minerals* such as limestone, manganese, gypsum, calcite, and bauxite; there are also deposits of lignite, quartz sand, agate, and feldspar. Gujarat is India's major petroleum-producing State along with Assam. Output of soda ash and salt amounts to most of the national production; the cement, vegetable oil, chemical, and cotton textile *industries* are important. The pharmaceutical industry, concentrated at Vadodara, Ahmedabad, and Atul (Valsad), manufactures much of India's output. The oil refinery at Koyali has created a nearby fast-growing petrochemical industry. Cooperative commercial dairying also is important. The "white revolution" in milk production took place in the State, which accounts for four-fifths of the infant milk-food production in India. The steady growth of small industries has been significant. The Gandhian approach to labour problems — strict reliance on the truth, nonviolence, settlement by arbitration, minimal demands, and the use of the strike only as a last resort — has had a great impact in the field of industrial relations in Gujarat, which has remained relatively free from labour unrest.

A thermal power station is located at Dhuvaran. The State also receives power from the Tarapur nuclear facility in Maharashtra State. The long-delayed Sardar Sarovar dam on the Narmada River was projected to become the State's largest producer of hydroelectric power and to provide water for extensive irrigation.

Road and rail connections are good, and coastal shipping routes link Gujarat's many ports. Kandia is a major international shipping terminal. There is air service both within the State and to major Indian cities outside Gujarat.

Cultural life : Much of the folklore and folk culture of Gujarat reflects the mythology surrounding the Hindu deity Krishna (an incarnation of the god Vishnu), as transmitted in the Puranas, a class or Hindu sacred literature. The *rasnritya* and *raslila* dances in honour of Krishna have survived in the form of the popular folk dance, the garba. This dance is performed at the Navaratra festival, which honours the goddess Durga; the dancere move in a circle, singing and keeping time by clapping their hands or clashing together sticks called *danda*. A folk drama, the *bhavai*, also has survived.

Shaivism (the cult of the god Shiva), has long flourished in Gujarat; so, too, has Vaishnavism (the worship of the god Vishnu), from which has emerged the cult of *bhakti* (devotion). Notable Vaishnava saints, poets, and musicians include Narasimha, who composed *padas* (verses) in the fifteenth century; Mira Bai, a sixteenth-century Rajput princess who renounced her royal home and composed *bhajans* (devotional songs); Premanand, an eighteenth-century poet and writer; and Dayaram, an eighteenth-century composer of songs who popularized the *bhakti* cult.

Jainism, with its nonviolence and vegetarianism, gained a stronger hold in Gujarat than in any other part of India. The Parsis, Zoroastrians who fled Persia some time after the seventh century, settled initially on the coast of Gujarat. The great majority of the community later relocated to Bombay.

The *architectural style* of Gujarat, known for its luxuriousness and perfection, is preserved in monuments and temples such as those at Somnath, Dwarka, Modhera, Than, Ghumli, Girnar, and Palitana. A distinctive Indo-Islamic style evolved under Muslim rule. Gujarat is famous, too, for its art and craft products. These include the *jari* (gold and silver embroidery) of Surat; the *bandhani* work (a tie-and-dye technique) of Jamnagar; the *patola*, a fine silk fabric of Patan; the toys of Idar, the perfumes of Palanpur, the hand-loomed products of Konodar, and the decorative wood-work of miniature temples and mythological figures at Ahmedabad and Surat.

Among the most durable and effective of the State's *cultural institutions* are the trade and craft guilds known as the *mahajans*. Often coterminous with castes and largely autonomous, the guilds have in the past solved disputes, acted as channels of philanthropy, and encouraged arts and culture.

Area, Population and Headquarters of Districts

S.No.	*District*	*Area (sq km)*	*Population*	*Headquarters*
1.	Ahmedabad	8,707	58,08,378	Ahmedabad
2.	Amreli	6,760	13,93,295	Amreli
3.	Anand	—	18,56,712	Anand
4.	Banaskantha	12,703	25,02,843	Palanpur
5	Bharuch	9,038	13,70,104	Bharuch
6.	Bhavnagar	11,155	24,69,264	Bhavnagar
7.	Dahod	—	16,35,374	Dahod
8.	Dang	649	1,86,712	Ahwa
9.	Gandhinagar	1,764	13,34,731	Gandhinagar
10.	Jamnagar	14,125	18,16,029	Jamnagar
11.	Junagadh	10,607	24,48,427	Junagadh
12.	Kheda	7,194	20,23,354	Nadiad
13.	Kuchchh	45,652	15,26,331	Bhuj
14.	Mehsana	9,027	18,37,696	Mehsana
15.	Narmada	—	5,14,083	Rajpipla
16.	Navsari	—	12,29,250	Navsari
17.	Panchmahal	8,866	20,24,883	Godhara

S.No.	District	Area (sq km)	Population	Headquarters
18.	Patan	—	11,81,941	Patan
19.	Porbandar	—	5,36,854	Porbandar
20.	Rajkot	11,203	25,71,931	Rajkot
21.	Sabarkantha	7,390	20,83,416	Himatnagar
22.	Surat	7,657	49,96,391	Surat
23.	Surendranagar	10,489	15,15,147	Surendranagar
24.	Vadodara	7,794	36,39,775	Vadodara
25.	Valsad	5,244	14,10,680	Valsad

H

Harayana—a state in northwestern India, it is bounded on the northwest by the State of Punjab and the Union Territory of Chandigarh, on the north by Himachal Pradesh, on the east by Uttar Pradesh and the Union Territory of Delhi, and on the south and southwest by the State of Rajasthan. Its area is 44,212 sq tan. The city of Chandigarh, which lies within the Chandigarh Union Territory, is the capital of not only that territory but also of the States of Punjab and Haryana.

Haryana came into existence on November 1, 1966, as a result of the linguistic reorganization of the former State of Punjab into two States— Punjabi-speaking areas as Punjab, and Hindi-speaking areas as Haryana. This reorganization followed an agitation by the Sikh Akali Party for a Punjabi-speaking State. Simultaneously with Punjab, it resulted in the formation of Haryana, meeting the aspirations of the people of the Hindi-speaking zone. Haryana means "The Abode of God", from Hari (the Hindu god Vishnu) and *ayana* (home).

History : The region now known as Haryana — the *madhyama desh* (middle region) of the later Vedic Period (c. 800-500 BC) — is said to be the birthplace of the Hindu religion. It was in this area that the first hymns of the Aryans were sung and the most ancient manuscripts written.

Lying across the routes of overland invasions from the northwest and central Asian areas, Haryana underwent attacks from successive waves of armies from the time of Alexander the Great (326 BC), and was the scene of many decisive battles in Indian history. These include: the battles of Panipat in 1526 (when the Mughal leader Babur defeated lbrahim Lodi and established Mughal rule in India), 1556 (when the Afghan forces were defeated by the army of the Mughal emperor Akbar), and 1761 (when Ahmad Shah Abdali decisively defeated the Marathas, paving the way for British control in India), and the battle of Karnal in 1739 (when Nadir Shah of Persia dealt a blow to the crumbling Mughal Empire).

The area included in the present State of Haryana was ceded to the British East India Company in 1803. In 1832 it was transferred to the then North-Western Provinces, and in 1858 this area became a part of Punjab. It remained as such after the partition of India in 1947. The demand for a Haryana State, however, is thought to have been raised even before India's independence in 1947. Lala Lajpat Rai and Asaf Ali, prominent figures in the national movement, advocated a separate State of Haryana. Even while a part of Punjab before and after independence, it was considered a distinct cultural and linguistic unit. In socio-economic terms, however, it was backward. Sri Ram Sharma, a veteran freedom fighter, headed a Haryana Development Committee to focus attention on the concept of an autonomous State. The demand for unilingual States by the Sikhs of the Punjabi-speaking northern Punjab, and the Hindus of the Hindi-speaking Haryana zone in the south, gained momentum in the early 1960s. But it was the persistent demand of the Sikhs for a Punjabi-speaking State that really forced the issue. In 1966, with the passage of the Punjab Reorganization Act, Haryana became a separate State of India, simultaneously with Punjab. Given dynamic and able leadership, the formation of small States has proved a successful experiment from the point of view of social and economic development, as illustrated by these two States.

Physical Structure, Climate and Soils : Haryana has two major *physiographic* regions: the flat alluvial plain covering most of the State, and, in the northeast, a narrow strip of highly dissected Shiwalik Hills and the narrow foothill zone. The plain, between 210 m and 270 m in elevation, is drained by only one perennial river, the Yamuna, flowing along the State's eastern margin. Several seasonal streams flowing from the Shiwalik Hills pass through the plain. The most notable of these is the Ghaggar (near the State's northern boundary), which is thought to have once flowed far enough to join the Indus River, now in Pakistan. Evidence of pre-Aryan settlements has been uncovered along the lower course of this river. In addition, some south-north-trending remnants of the Aravali mountain system which extends up to Delhi, are found in parts of Mahendragarh, Rewari, and Gurgaon districts in southern Haryana.

Much of Haryana suffers from arid to semi-arid conditions. Only in the northeast do sub-humid conditions prevail. Although the State has a system of canal irrigation and widespread tubewells, there still remain some chronic drought-prone areas, particularly in the southern and southwestern parts. There are, however, occasional floods from the Yamuna and tributaries of the Ghaggar. The summers are very hot and the winters are markedly cold. The maximum temperature in summer (May-June) goes up to 46 °C. The minimum temperature occasionally falls to the freezing point in January. The city of Hissar has the hottest temperature in the State.

The *soils* are deep and fertile, except in the badly eroded northeast foothill zone and the hills, and are sandy in the southwest bordering the Rajasthan Desert. Of the net area sown, which is nearly four-fifths of the total area, about three-fourths is irrigated. While the northern, eastern and south-eastern parts receive irrigation from tubewells, canal irrigation is mostly dominant in the southwest. There is hardly any forest cover in the State. Eucalyptus trees are planted along the highways and in wastelands. *Shisham* (*Dalbergia sissoo*) trees are commonly found along the roads and canals in the northern half of the State, while *kikar* (Acacia arabica) and scrub are common in the southern and southwestern Haryana.

People : Of Haryana's population of 16,463,648 in 1991, Hindus constituted 89.2 per cent (with one-fifth belonging to the scheduled caste, formerly "untouchables"), Sikhs 5.8 per cent, Muslims 4.6 per cent, and others 0.4 per cent. The Sikhs are mostly concentrated in the northeast and northwest, and the Muslims in the southeastern districts around Delhi. Hindu jats (a peasant caste) form the backbone of Haryana's agricultural economy and, like the Sikhs of Punjab, are prominent in India's armed forces. Although 75 per cent of the State's population is rural, cities have been growing rapidly as industrial, commercial, and agricultural market-centres. Cities with 100,000 or more population include the Faridabad complex, Yamunanagar, Rohtak, Panipat, Hissar, Karnal, Sonepat, Ambala (city and cantonment), Gurgaon, Bhiwani, and Sirsa.

Economy : Haryana is an *agriculturally* prosperous State, contributing a large amount of wheat and rice to the Central Pool (a national repository system of surplus foodgrain). Cotton, rapeseed, mustard, *bajra* (pearl millet), gram, sugarcane, *jowar* (sorghum), maize, and potatoes are other major crops. The State's agricultural prominence is attributed to the Green Revolution, which has involved large-scale investment in irrigation, fertilizers, and high-quality seeds. About 58 per cent of Haryana's total workforce is engaged in agriculture.

Haryana has made substantial progress in agro-based and manufacturing *industries*. Important among these are cotton and sugar processing, farm machinery, chemicals, and a great variety of consumer goods, notably bicycles. Major highways and railway lines passing through Haryana and converging on Delhi, have become corridors of industrial and commercial development, especially in areas adjoining the Union Territory of Delhi. Notably, some of the State's industrial investment has come from Punjabi entrepreneurs who thought it safer and more profitable (because of the proximity to the Delhi market) to do it in Haryana rather than in Punjab.

Cultural life : Haryana's cultural life reflects both the seasonal rhythm of its agricultural economy and a treasure of traditions and legends originating in ancient India. Haryana has a distinctive dialect and its own native idioms. Its folklore and dances depict the cultural life of the region in their own charming way. They are full of vigour and linked to various facets of local culture. The boisterous spring festival of Holi is celebrated by the people showering coloured powder (or coloured powder mixed with water) on each other, irrespective of age or social status. Janmashtami, the birthday of Krishna (an incarnation of god Vishnu), is of special religious importance in Haryana because it was on the battlefield at Kurukshetra that Krishna is said to have delivered to the warrior Arjuna the teachings contained in Bhagavadgita (a part of the epic Mahabharata).

The solar eclipse bathing festival at Kurukshetra attracts hundreds of thousands of pilgrims from across the country. Among numerous ancient pilgrimage centres in the State are Agroha (near Hisar) and Pehowa. Agroha is known to be the birthplace of Agarsen who is considered to be the ancestral head or the originator of the Agarwal community and its various subcastes. Agroha, accordingly, is the *janambhumi* ("birthplace") of the entire Agarwal community now spread all over the country. They are among India's leading trading classes. To honour Agarsen's birthplace, the community established a medical college at Agroha some years back, Pehowa, situated on the bank of the sacred Sarasvati River (identified in the Vedas with Sarasvati, the Hindu goddess of learning and the arts), is considered an important sacred place for performing propitiatory rites (*shraddh pinda*) for ancestors. Religious rites for people who die unnatural deaths or die in bed are also performed at Pehowa for the salvation of their souls. Fairs in honour of various deities and saints are an important element of Haryana's culture. Cattle fairs are also held at several locations. The region is known for its fine breed of milch cattle, particularly buffaloes, and also sturdy bullocks for ploughing the land and as draft animals.

Haryana's *havelis* ("traditional family homes") are known for their *architectural* beauty, especially the structures of their gates. Not only are there variations in the layout, design, and workmanship on the gates of the *havelis* but an amazing array of subjects is also touched upon. *Havelis* impart a medieval character and an aesthetically pleasing look to Haryana's alleys. These buildings have podiums used for residential, defence, religious, and court functions. These indicate the social status of the owner of the building. The figurative art on the podiums is a reminder of the region's rich cultural heritage.

Area, Population and Headquarters of Districts

S.No.	District	Area (sq km)	Population	Headquarters
1.	Ambala	1,574	10,13,660	Ambala
2.	Bhiwani	4,778	14,24,554	Bhiwani
3.	Faridabad	2,151	21,93,276	Faridabad
4.	Fatehabad	2,520	8,06,158	Fatehabad
5.	Gurgaon	2,766	16,57,669	Gurgaon
6.	Hissar	3,983	15,36,417	Hissar
7.	Jhajjar	1,834	8,87,392	Jhajjar
8.	Jind	2,702	11,89,725	Jind
9.	Kaithal	2,317	9,45,631	Kaithal
10.	Karnal	2,538	12,74,843	Kamal
11.	Kurukshetra	1,530	8,28,120	Kurukshetra
12.	Mahendergarh	1,859	8,12,022	Narnaul
13.	Panchkula	898	4,69,210	Panchkula
14.	Panipat	1,268	9,67,338	Panipat
15.	Rewari	1,582	7,64,727	Rewari
16.	Rohtak	1,745	9,40,036	Rohtak
17.	Sirsa	4,277	11,11,012	Sirsa
18.	Sonipat	2,122	12,78,830	Sonipat
19.	Yamuna Nagar	1,768	9,82,369	Yamuna Nagar

Himachal Pradesh—A state in northern India it derives its name from the snow-covered slopes (Sanskrit: *hima*, "snow"; *achal*, "slopes"). It is located in the Himalaya. It is bounded by the State of Jammu and Kashmir in the north, by the Tibet Autonomous Region of China in the east, by the State of Uttar Pradesh in the southeast, by the State of Haryana in the south, and by the State of Punjab in the west. The State displays an attractive scenery of towering, snow-clad mountains, deep gorges, steep, thickly-forested valleys, large lakes, and cascading rivers. Flights of terraced, green fields climbing up the slopes add to the charm of the scenery. The State is spread over an area of 55,673 sq km. Shimla, the capital of the State, is located at an elevation of 2,164 m. It is a large and popular hill resort of India. Beginning as a Union Territory in 1948, Himachal Pradesh became a full-fledged State on January 25, 1971. It comprises 12 districts.

History : The history of this mountainous State is complex, tentative, and fragmented. It is believed that a number of the Aryan groups drifted into the more productive valleys during the Vedic period (c. 1500-1200 BC) and mixed with the pre-Aryan population and assimilated their culture. Later, successive Indian empires, such as the Maurya (c. 321-185 BC), the Gupta (c. AD 320-540), and the Mughal (1526-1761), all emerging in the Indo-Gangetic plain, sought to exercise varying degrees of control over trade and pilgrimage routes into this area and between India and Tibet across the Himalaya.

The remote, predominantly Buddhist area of Lahaul and Spiti was controlled by Ladakh from the decline of the Mughal Empire (about the mideighteenth century) until the early 1840s when it came briefly under the Sikh rule. Also, during this period, warring semi-autonomous, petty rulers controlled the trade routes as well as the better-yielding agricultural and pastoral land, in other areas of what is now Himachal Pradesh. The British domination of this region followed the Anglo-Sikh Wars of the 1840s and continued, directly or indirectly, for the next 100 years.

In 1948 Himachal Pradesh was constituted as an administrative unit comprising 30 Princely States, governed by a chief commissioner as the representative of the Government of India. This event, however, was preceded by a movement for the end of feudal rule, and one of the Princely States, Suket, virtually surrendered to peaceful demonstrators, hastening the process of change.

Between 1948 and 1971 (when it became a State), Himachal Pradesh went through various changes in size and administrative form. Initially, a Union Territory headed by a lieutenant governor, it acquired the status of a full-fledged State when the entire district of Kangra, Una tehsil of Hoshiarpur district, Shimla district, Dalhousie, Dagshai, and Kasauli merged into Himachal Pradesh. In 1971 the Nalagarh tehsil of Ambala district was also transferred to the Solan district of Himachal Pradesh. Y.S. Parmar, who had, since the 1940s, led the hill people of Himachal Pradesh in the quest for self-government, became the State's first chief minister.

Land : Himachal Pradesh has an impressive diversity of terrain. Wide river valleys gorges, river terraces, cascading rivers with rapids, and high mountains with snow-clad peaks form the landscape. Four parallel physiographic regions corresponding to the northwest-southeast trending ranges have been identified. Adjacent to the Punjab and Haryana plains are the Outer Himalaya formed of two Shiwalik hill ranges separated by long, narrow valleys. In this tract the elevations range from about 488 m in the south to about 900 m to 1,500 m in the north. To the north of the Outer Himalaya stretch the Lesser or Lower Himalaya which rise almost to 4,700 m. In this region are the high, spectacular, snow-capped Dhaolo Dhar and Pir Panjal ranges. Beyond the Lesser Himalaya Stretch up north the Greater Himalaya, mainly the Zaskar ranges, which attain the towering heights of more than 6,700 m. Many high, active valley glaciers originate in these mountains. Of the four principal rivers of the State, Sutlej, Beas, Ravi, and Chenab, the first rises in Tibet while the others rise in the Greater Himalaya. Beyond the Zaskar spread the large, barren, and cold Trans-Himalaya.

A wide range of *climates*, *soils*, and *vegetation* types are observed in Himachal Pradesh. The Outer Himalaya have cool and dry winters and hot summers with moderate southwestern monsoon rainfall. With an increase in elevation towards the north, the climate becomes wet and cool and in the Greater Himalaya it is bitterly cold with snowy, long winters.

People : The *population* of Himachal Pradesh consists of several distinctive ethno-linguistic tribes and castes, including Gaddis, Lahaulis, Kinnaras, Gujars, and Pangwalis. A large number of Punjabi immigrants have settled in the towns and large villages of the State after 1947. Hindus comprise 95 per cent of the population and are the dominant religious and social group. Buddhists are the dominant group in the Trans-Himalayan districts of Lahaul and Spiti, and Kinnaur. The State also has some Sikhs, Muslims, and Christians. Western Pahari Hindi is the State language. Every former Princely State has its own dialect named after it. A Sino-Tibetan language is spoken in the Lahaul and Spiti, and Kinnaur districts.

Himachal Pradesh is the *least urbanized* State in India. Its urban population of 449,196 forms only 10 per cent of its total population of 5,170,877 (1991). There are about 55 towns, of which only the State capital Shimla, has a population exceeding 80,000. The capitals of the former Princely States are now district headquarters and towns. These include Nahan, Bilaspur, Mandi, Chamba, and Kullu. Dalhousie, Kasauli, and Sabathu are hill-resorts of British origin. Kangra, Palampur, Solan, and Dharmshala are some of the other towns of this State.

Economy : For their livelihood, most people in Himachal Pradesh depend on *agriculture, pastoralism*, *transhumance, horticulture*, and *forestry*. The industries of the State include making of agricultural implements, turpentine oil, and resin at Nahan; television sets, fertilizers, beer, liquor, and bulbs at Solan; cement at Rajban; processed fruits, tractor parts, and electronic goods at Parwanoo; electrical goods near Shimla; and paper and hardboard at Baddi and Barotiwala. The State has initiated its development, based on its abundant hydropower, minerals, and forest resources. It is also developing its road network and tourism resources. Himachal Pradesh produces about 20 per cent of the nation's hydroelectric power. The existing hydroelectric stations are Jogindranagar Hydropower House located on Uhl River, the high and massive Bhakra dam on Sutlej River, the Pong dam across Beas River, and the Giri dam on Giri River. Himachal Pradesh, along with the Central Government, has launched new hydroelectric projects such as the Nathpa-Jhakri in Shimla district. It has launched a programme of widespread reforestation in order to combat the serious soil erosion problem in the outer Himalaya and to protect the fragile ecosystem of the Himalaya. It has also initiated a strict enforcement of the existing environmental laws. Besides its road network, it has two narrow-gauge railways, from Kalka to Shimla and from Pathankot to Jogindarnagar. Roads criss-cross through the ranges and valleys and serve as lifelines of the State. More than 140 State-owned bus routes operate within Himachal Pradesh.

Cultural life : The fairs and festivals of the hill people are occasions of joyful song and dance. Exquisitely designed shawls of Kinnaur, the distinctive woollen caps of Kullu, and the embroidered handkerchiefs of Chamba accent their colourful, festive clothing. Himachal Pradesh is also known for its Kangra Valley school of painting.

The Shimla hills, the Kullu valley (including the town of Manali), and Dalhousie are great tourist attractions. Skiing, golfing, fishing, trekking, and mountaineering are activities for which Himachal Pradesh is ideally suited. Pilgrims from neighbouring States and from within the State itself converge in large numbers to worship at shrines of legendary antiquity.

The Kullu valley is known as the valley of gods; its pine and deodar forests, lush green and flower-spangled meadows, and fruit orchards provide the setting to the colourful Dussehra festival held each autumn.

The temple gods are taken in caparisoned palanquins accompanied by bands of singers and dancers. Dharamshala has become sacred for Buddhists (especially Tibetans) ever since it became the home of the Dalai Lama after he fled from Tibet in 1959 in the wake of China's occupation of Lhasa. In early 2000, the 14-year-old seventeenth Karmapa also fled from Tibet to Dharamshala and sought asylum.

Area, Population and Headquarters of Districts

S.No.	District	Area (sq km)	Population (1991 Census)	Headquarters
1.	Bilaspur	1,167	2,95,387	Bilaspur
2.	Chamba	6,528	3,93,286	Chamba
3.	Hamirpur	1,118	3,69,128	Hamirpur
4.	Kangra	5,739	11,74,072	Dharamshala
5.	Kinnaur	6,401	71,270	Reckong Peo
6.	Kullu	5,503	3,02,432	Kullu
7.	Lahaul and Spiti	13,835	31,294	Keylong
8.	Mandi	3,950	7,76,372	Mandi
9.	Shimla	5,131	6,17,404	Shimla
10.	Sirmaur	2,825	3,79,695	Nahan
11.	Solan	1,936	3,82,268	Solan
12.	Una	1,540	3,78,269	Una

J

Jammu and Kashmir—This state of India is located in the northern part of the Indian subcontinent in the vicinity of the Karakoram and western mountain ranges. Formerly one of the largest Princely States of India, it is bounded on the northeast by the Uighur Autonomous Region of Sinkiang and the Tibet Autonomous Region, (both parts of China), on the south by the States of Himachal Pradesh and Punjab, and on the west by Pakistan.

History : According to legend, an ascetic named Kashyapa reclaimed the land of Kashmir from a vast lake, and the reclaimed land came to be known as Kashyapamar and, later, Kashmir, Buddhism was introduced by the Maurya emperor Ashoka in the third century BC, and later from the ninth to the twelfth century AD, the region gained prominence as a centre of Hindu culture. A succession of Hindu dynasties ruled over

Kashmir until the mid-fourteenth century, when it came under Muslim rule; it was annexed to the Sikh kingdom of the Punjab in 1819 and to the Dogra kingdom of Jammu in 1846.

The Kashmir region in its contemporary form, dates from 1846, when, by the treaties of Lahore and Amritsar at the conclusion of the First Sikh War, Raja Gulab Singh, the Dogra ruler of Jammu, was created *maharaja* (ruling prince) of an extensive but somewhat ill-defined Himalayan kingdom "to the eastward of the River Indus and westward of the River Ravi", For the British the creation of this Princely, protected State helped to safeguard their northern flank in their advance to the Indus and beyond during the latter part of the nineteenth century. The State thus formed part of a complex political buffer zone interposed by the British between their Indian empire and the empires of Russia and China to the north. For Gulab Singh, confirmation of title to these mountain territories marked the culmination of almost a quarter of a century of campaigning and diplomatic negotiations with the petty hill kingdoms along the northern borderlands of the Sikh empire of the Punjab.

Some attempts were made in the nineteenth century to define the boundaries of the territory, but precise definition was, in many cases, defeated by the nature of the country and by the existence of huge tracts lacking permanent human settlement. In the far north, for example, the maharaja's authority extended to the Karakoram Range, but beyond that lay a debatable zone on the borders of theTurkistan and Sinkiang regions of Central Asia, where the boundary was never demarcated. There were similar doubts about the alignment of the frontier where this northern zone skirted the region known as Aksai Chin (Akesaiqin), to the east, and joined the better known and more precisely delineated boundary with Tibet, which had served for centuries as the eastern border of the Ladakh region. The pattern of boundaries in the northwest became clearer in the last decade of the nineteenth century, when Britain delimited boundaries in the Pamir region in negotiations with Afghanistan and Russia. At this time Gilgit, always understood to be part of Kashmir, for strategic reasons was constituted as a special agency in 1889 under a British agent.

Physiography : More than 90 per cent of the State is mountainous. The physiography of the territory as a whole is divided into seven zones that are closely associated with the structural components of the western Himalaya. From southwest to northeast these zones consist of the plains, the foothills, the Pir Panjal Range, the Vale of Kashmir, the Great Himalaya zone, the upper Indus Valley, and the Karakoram Range.

The narrow zone of *plains* country in the Jammu region is characterized by interlocking sandy alluvial fans that have been deposited by streams discharging from the foothills and by a much-dissected pediment (eroded bedrock surface) covered by loams and loess (wind-deposited silt) of the Pleistocene age (about 10,000 to 1,600,000 years old). Precipitation is low, amounting to about 380 to 500 mm a year, and it occurs mainly in the form of heavy but infrequent rain showers in the summer (June to September), when the monsoon winds blow. The countryside has been almost entirely denuded of trees, and thorn scrub and coarse grass are the dominant forms of vegetation.

The *foothills* of the Himalaya, rising from 610 to 2,134 m, form outer and inner zones. The outer zone consists of sandstones, clays, silts, and conglomerates, influenced by Himalayan folding movements and eroded to form long ridges and valleys (*duns*). The inner zone consists of more massive sedimentary rock, including red sandstones of the Miocene age (about 5.3 to 23.7 million years old), that has been folded, fractured, and eroded to form steep spurs and plateau remnants. River valleys are deeply incised and terraced, and faulting has produced a number of alluvium-filled basins, such as those of Udhampur and Poonch. Rainfall increases with elevation, and the lower scrubland gives way to pine forests at higher altitudes.

The Pir Panjal Range constitutes the first mountain rampart associated with the Himalaya comprising the westernmost of the Lesser Himalaya. It has an average crest line of 3,810 m, with individual peaks rising to about 4,600 m. Consisting of an ancient rock core of granites, gneisses, quartz rocks, and slates, it has been subject to considerable uplift and fracturing and was heavily glaciated during the Pleistocene epoch. The range receives considerable precipitation in the forms of winter snowfall and summer rain and has extensive areas of pasture above the tree line.

The *Vale of Kashmir* is a deep, asymmetrical basin lying between the Pir Panjal and the western end of the Great Himalayan ranges at an average elevation of 1,600 m. During the Pleistocene epoch it was occupied at times by a lake, known as Lake Karewa; it is now filled by lacustrine sediments and alluvium deposited by the upper Jhelum River. Soil and water conditions vary considerably. The climate is characterized by an annual rainfall of about 750 mm, some of which is derived from the summer monsoon winds and some from winds associated with winter low-pressure systems. Snowfall is often accompanied by rain and sleet.

Temperatures are considerably modified by altitude; at Srinagar an average minimum temperature of about -2 °C occurs in January and an average maximum temperature of 31 °C in July.

Up to 2,100 m, woodlands of deodar cedar, blue pine, walnut, willow, elm, and poplars occur; from 2,100 to 3,200 m coniferous forests with fir, pine, and spruce are found; from 3,200 m to about 3,600 m, birch is dominant; and above 3,600 m there are meadows with rhododendrons, dwarf willows, and honeysuckle.

Geologically complex and topographically immense, the *Great Himalaya* contain ranges reaching more than 6,100 m in altitude and deeply entrenched, remote valleys. The region was heavily glaciated in the Pleistocene epoch, and remnant glaciers and snowfields are still present. The zone receives some rain from the southwest monsoon winds in the summer months — and the lower slopes are forested — but the mountains constitute a climatic divide, representing a transition from the monsoon climate of the Indian subcontinent to the dry, continental climate of Central Asia.

The *valley of the upper Indus River* is a well-defined feature that follows the geological strike (structural trend) westwards from the Tibetan border to the point in the Pakistani sector where it rounds the great mountainous mass of Nanga Parbat to run southwards in deep gorges cut across the strike. In its upper reaches the river is flanked by gravel terraces; each tributary builds an alluvial fan out into the main valley. The town of Leh in the Indian State stands on such a fan, 3,500 m above sea level, with a climate characterized by almost total lack of precipitation, intense insolation (exposure to the sun's rays), and great diurnal and annual ranges of temperature. Life depends on meltwater from the surrounding mountains, and vegetation is Alpine (above the limit of tree growth), growing on thin soils.

The great granite-gneiss massifs of the *Karakoram* contain some of the world's highest peaks, including K2, with an altitude of 8,611 m; at least 30 other peaks exceed 7,300 m. The range, which is still heavily glaciated, rises starkly from dry, desolate plateaus characterized by extremes of temperature and shattered rock debris. The Karakoram region is aptly named the "roof of the world".

Settlement patterns and the People : The State's physiographic diversity is matched by the considerable variety of *human occupation*. In the plains and foothills, colonization movements from the Punjab region over a long period of time have produced numerous agricultural settlements; both the people and their culture are similar to those of adjacent parts of the Punjab and other lowlands to the west. In parts of the *duns* and lower valleys where alluvial soils and the availability of water for irrigation make agriculture possible, the population is sustained by crops of wheat and barley, which are gathered in the spring (*rabi*) harvest, and of rice and maize gathered in the late summer (*kharif*) harvest. Livestock are also kept. The upper sections of the valleys support a sparser population that depends on a mixed economy of maize, cattle, and forestry. Seasonal migration by herders to higher pastures in the spring is necessary for the production of milk and clarified butter, or *ghee*, for southern lowland markets. In winter the hill-dwellers return to lower areas to work in government-owned forests and timber mills. Agricultural hamlets and nucleated villages predominate, and towns such as Jammu and Udhampur function essentially as market centres and administrative headquarters for the rural populations and estates in the vicinity.

Among the wild animals found in the State are the Siberian ibex, the Ladakh urial (a species of wild sheep with a reddish coat), the rare *hangul* (Kashmir stag) found in Dachigam National Park, black and brown bears, and many game birds, including vast numbers of migratory ducks.

Jammu, the winter capital of the *maharajas* and second-largest city of the State, was traditionally the seat of Dogra power. Of the total population of Jammu, more than two-thirds are classed as Hindus; of these the greater part live in the southeastern portion of the region. Culturally, ethnically, and linguistically, they are closely related to the Punjabi-speaking peoples in Punjab State, many speak the Dogri language. The majority of the State's sikhs also live in the Jammu region. To the northwest, however, the proportion of Muslims increases, with Muslims constituting a dominant majority in the area around the western town of Poonch.

The *Vale of Kashmir* with its surrounding highlands (Kashmir proper) has always retained something of its own individuality. The vast majority of the people are Muslims who speak either Kashmiri or Urdu. Culturally and ethnically, the closest links are with peoples in the northwestern highlands of the Gilgit district in the Pakistani sector. The Kashmiri language is influenced by Sanskrit and belongs to the Dardic branch of Indo-Aryan languages also spoken by the various hill tribes of Gilgit. It has a rich folklore and literary traditions. The great majority of the population resides in the lower reaches of the Vale. Srinagar, Jammu and Kashmir's largest city, is located on the Jhelum River.

The Great Himalaya are an ethnic and cultural, as well as a physical, divide. *Ladakh* (sometimes called "Little Tibet"), to the northeast, is thinly populated. To the east, around Leh, the inhabitants are predominantly Buddhists of Tibetan ancestry and language (Ladakhi). In the region around Kargil to the west, however, the population is predominantly Muslim, most belonging to the Shia branch of Islam.

Resources and agriculture : The State has limited mineral and fossil fuel resources, much of it being concentrated in the Jammu region. Small reserves of natural gas are found near Jammu, and bauxite and gypsum deposits occur in the Udhampur district. Other minerals include limestone, coal, zinc, and copper. The pressure of population on land is apparent everywhere, and all available resources are utilized. The lakes and rivers provide fish, water-chestnuts, hydroelectric power, and transport, and are a tourist attraction. The mountains supply many kinds of timber as well as pasture for livestock. Gujar and Gaddi nomads practise transhumance in the mountains, keeping sheep, goats, yaks, and ponies,

The majority of people are engaged in subsistence agriculture of diverse kinds on terraced slopes, each crop adapted to local conditions. Rice, the staple crop, is planted in May and harvested in late September. Maize, millet, pulses (legumes such as peas, beans, and lentils), cotton, and tobacco are — with rice — the main summer crops, while wheat and barley are the chief spring crops. Many temperate fruits and vegetables are grown in areas adjacent to urban markets or in well-watered areas with rich organic soils. Sericulture is also widespread. Large orchards in the Vale of Kashmir produce apples, pears, peaches, walnuts, almonds, and cherries. In addition the Vale is the sole producer of saffron in the Indian subcontinent. Lake margins are particularly favoured, intensive cultivation of vegetables and flowers is practised in reclaimed marshland or on artificial floating gardens.

Cultivation in Ladakh is restricted to such main valleys as those of the Indus, Shyok, and Suru rivers, where it consists of small irrigated plots of barley, buckwheat, turnips, and mustard. Plants introduced in the 1970s by agricultural scientists have given rise to orchards and vegetable fields. Pastoralism — notably yak herding — has long been a vital feature of the Ladakh economy; sheep and goat farming, as well as cattle breeding, have been encouraged. The Kashmir goat, which is raised in the region, provides cashmere (also called pashmina) for the production of fine textiles.

Trade and industry : All the principal towns, including Leh, and a majority of the villages are electrified, and hydroelectric and thermal generating plants have been constructed to provide power for industrial development based on local raw materials. Major power stations are located at Chineni and Salal and on the upper Sind and lower Jhelum rivers. Phase I of Uri hydroelectric project was commenced towards the end of the twentieth century. Land reforms have been undertaken, grain production increased, and the quantity of major exports — timber, fruits and dry nuts, and handicraft products — vastly expanded since 1947. Metalware, precision instruments, sport goods, furniture, embroidery, matches, resin, and turpentine are the major industrial products of the State.

Srinagar possesses many specialized agricultural markets, retail shopping centres, and associated industries. The industries have developed from rural crafts and include handloom weaving of local silk, cotton, and wool, carpet weaving, wood carving, and leatherwork. Such industries, together with silverwork, and copperwork, and jewellery, were stimulated in the past by the presence of the royal court and later by the tourist trade and also owe something to the important position achieved by Srinagar in west Himalayan trade. In the past the city acted as an entrepot for the products of the Punjab region on the one hand and of the high plateau region east of the Karakoram, Pamir, and Ladakh ranges on the other. Routes still run northwestwards into Gilgit via the Raj Diangan pass and northeastwards via the Zoji pass to Leh and beyond. Handicraft manufacture is also important in Ladakh, particularly the production of cashmere shawls, carpets, and blankets.

Transportation and tourism : Transportation within Jammu and Kashmir remains a vital problem. The Indian Union (central) government has made a huge investment in developing highways and communications in the State. As a result of the partition, the route through the Jhelum valley from Srinagar to Rawalpindi, Pakistan, was blocked. This made it necessary to transform a longer and more difficult cart road through Banihal Pass into an all-weather highway in order to link Jammu with the Vale; included was the construction of the Jawahar Tunnel, which at the time of its completion in 1959, was one of the longest in Asia. This road, however, is often made impassable by extreme weather, which causes shortages of essential commodities in the Vale. A road also connects Srinagar with Kargil and Leh. Jammu is the terminus of the Northern Railway of India. Srinagar and Jammu are connected by air to

New Delhi and other Indian cities, and there are flights between Srinagar and Leh, Leh-Jammu, and Leh-Delhi.

Facilities have also been improved considerably for tourists, although the potential has remained largely untapped. *Tourism* has had a significant socio-economic impact on Ladakh, which was largely isolated from outsiders until the 1970s. In addition to historical and religious sites, visitor destinations include the snow-sports centres at Gulmarg, south of Baramula in the Pir Panjal Range, at Pahalgam, located by the banks of the river Lidder, the hot sulphur mineral springs at Chumathang near Leh, and Panamic (Nobra) and Puga of Changthang, which are famous for early curing of joints and rheumatic disease.

Area, Population and Headquarters of Districts

S.No.	*District*	*Area (sq km) (Estimated)*	*Population*	*Headquarters*
1.	Anantnag	3,984	11,70,013	Anantnag
2.	Badgarn	1,371	6,32,338	Badgam
3.	Baramulla	4,588	11,66,772	Baramulla
4.	Doda	11,691	6,90,474	Doda
5.	Jammu	3,097	15,71,911	Jammu
6.	Kargil	14,036	1,15,227	Kargil
7.	Kathua	2,651	5,44,206	Kathua
8.	Kupwara	2,379	6,40,013	Kupwara
9.	Leh	82,665[1]	1,17,637	Leh
10.	Pulwama	1,398	6,48,762	Pulwama
11.	Poonch	1,674	3,71,561	Poonch
12.	Rajouri	2,630	4,78,595	Rajouri
13.	Srinagar	2,228	11,83,493	Srinagar
14.	Udhampur	4,550	7,38,965	Udhampur

[1] Includes 37,555 sq km under illegal occupation of China.

Jharkhand—Jharkhand State is bounded by West Bengal in the east, Uttar Pradesh and Chhattisgarh in west, Bihar in the north and Orissa in the south.

History : Jharkhand, which came into being on 15 November 2000 as the 28th State of the Union, is the homeland of the tribals for which they had been dreaming for centuries. According to legend, Raja Jai Singh Deo of Orissa had declared himself the ruler of Jharkhand in the 13th century. It largely comprises forest tracks of Chhotanagpur plateau and Santhal Pargana and has distinct cultural traditions. In post-independence era, the Jharkhand Mukti Morcha started a regular agitation which impelled the government to establish the Jharkhand Area Autonomous Council in 1995 and finally a full-fledged State.

Economy : Principal foodgrain crops are paddy, wheat, maize and pulses.

Industry and Minerals : Jharkhand has the country's two biggest steel plants at Bokaro in the public sector and Tata Iron and Steel Company (TISCO) in Jamshedpur in the private sector. Other important industries are Tata Engineering and Locomotive Company, Sriram Bearings, Usha Martin, Indian Tube Company, etc. The State is abundantly rich in minerals—copper, coal, iron, manganese, mica, chromite, bauxite, etc., and has the potential of becoming one of the most prosperous states of India.

Power : The installed capacity of power in Jharkhand is 2,590 MW. This includes 420 MW (Tenughat Thermal Power Station), 840 MW (Patratu Thermal Power Station), 130 MW (Sikkidri Hydel) and 1,200 MW (DVC, Thermal/Hydel). The prospects of capacity addition in both the thermal and hydel sectors of various power stations is 4,736 MW. This includes 686 MW hydel generation.

To provide electricity to all villages and rural areas, the State government has made a provision of Rs 30 crore during 2001-02.

Transport : Roads : The total length of roads in the State is 4,311 km. This includes 1,600 km national highways and 2,711 km state highways.

Railways : The state has a well-developed railway system. Ranchi, Bokaro, Dhanbad, Jamshedpur are some of the major railway stations.

Aviation : Ranchi is connected with Delhi, Patna and Mumbai. Jamshedpur, Bokaro, Giridih, Deoghar, Hazaribagh, Daltonganj and Noamundi have air strips.

Tourist Centres : There are many scenic attractions, waterfalls, temples, hillocks scattered around Ranchi. Hundru, Hironi, Dosna and Dasam are the waterfalls. Other places are Chaibasa, Deoghar, Dumka (centres of pilgrimage), Belta (Palamu National Park), Hazaribagh (Wildlife reserve), Dalma Wildlife Sanctuary, etc.

Name of the districts: Ranchi, Gumla, Lohardaga, Palamau, Garhwa, Dhanbad, Bokaro, Hazaribagh, Chatra, Giridih, Kodarma, East Singhbhum, West Smghbhum, Dumka, Deoghar, Godda, Pakur and Sahebganj.

K

Karnataka—This State of India measures 676 km north to south and 483 km east to west. Karnataka is bound by Tamil Nadu on the east, Andhra Pradesh in the northeast, Maharashtra in the north, the Arabian Sea in the west, and Kerala in the southeast. Bangalore, near the southeast border, is the capital of the State. The erstwhile Princely State of Mysore was renamed as Karnataka in the year 1973. The areas with Kannada-speaking people in the neighbouring districts were added to form the new State of Karnataka. The State had an area of 191,791 sq km to which additional areas were added, and now the State borders the Arabian Sea and has a coastline of about 322 km.

Mysore State was landlocked endowed with resources such as gold, iron ore of high-grade, and abundant water. Sivasamudram in Karnataka was the first place to generate hydroelectricity in Asia. The monsoon forests in the southern part of the State have two wildlife sanctuaries and a bird sanctuary on the Cauvery (Kaveri) River.

History : The name Mysore (from the Sanskrit word for "buffalo town") derives from the legend of the destruction of the buffalo-demon Mahishaṣura by the goddess Chamunda (Chamundi). The prehistory of Mysore is lost in legends that concern the struggle that took place in southern India between the Aryan peoples and the original inhabitants; in legendary form this struggle is represented as a conflict between devils and demons on the one hand and gods and goddesses on the other. The subsequent history of the region deals mainly with the Princely State of Mysore as it was before 1953, for no dynasty succeeded in ruling the whole region occupied by the Kannada-speaking people.

After the reign of Ashoka, the Maurya emperor of the mid-third century BC, the principal dynasties in the area of Mysore were the Kadambas of Banavasi, the western Gangas (who were in power from the third to the eleventh century AD), the Banas, and other feudatories of the Pallava dynasty, who ruled from about the fourth to the ninth century. The rich lands of the upper Tungabhadra region and the land between the Tungabhadra and the Krishna rivers were taken from the Kadambas in the sixth century by a central Karnataka dynasty, the Chalukyas. Their efforts and those of their competitors, the Rashtrakuta dynasty, to unite the plateau and exploit the softer lands of the coastal plains, enriched Mysore but led to reprisals from the Tamils to the east and south. By the twelfth century the Hoysala dynasty absorbed Gangavai (as the State of Mysore was then called). But after the Hoysalas were obliged to submit to the sultan of Delhi, Mysore gradually came under the sway of the State of Vijayanagar, whose capital of the same name stood on the site now partly occupied by the village of Hampi on the Tungabhadra River, in contemporary Karnataka. In the latter part of the sixteenth century the Vijayanagar emperor faded, giving place to Mughal power north of the Tungabhadra River and to the rajas of Mysore in the South. In the seventeenth century the Wodeyars or Wadiyars, ("rulers") of Mysore profited from the conflict between the Mughal Empire and the Marathas in western India, to expand their rule. In 1610 the Wodeyar of Mysore seized Seringapatam; later, Bangalore was also acquired and Wodeyar power consolidated. Maladministration at home and interference in wars of succession in the plains allowed the military adventurer Hyder Ali to usurp power in 1761. His invasions of Malabar and the Karnataka plains extended Mysore's dominion but eventually led, after the resulting Mysore Wars, to the death of his colourful and energetic son Tipu Sultan in 1799 and to the conquest of Mysore by the British, who sponsored the restoration of Wodeyar rule. Mysore was governed by a British commissioner from 1831 to 1881, when administration was once again restored to the Wodeyars. The last of the Wodeyars became governor of the State after the territorial reorganizations of 1953 and 1956.

The land : Pysiographically, Karnataka is divided into four distinct regions — the coastal plain, the hill ranges (the Western Ghats), the Karnataka plateau to the east, and the black cotton-growing soil tract to the northwest. The coastal plain represents a continuation of the Malabar Coast and experiences heavy rainfall from the southwest monsoon from June to September. Coastal sand dunes give way towards the inland to small alluvial plains with coconut-fringed lagoons. The coast is difficult to access except by sea. To the east, the land rises sharply to the slopes of the Western Ghats, which have an average height of 760 to 915 m above sea level. The forested upland terrain of the Ghats is known as Malnad; the region is also a watershed, and from its crest numerous swift streams flow to the plains, including the Sharavati River which is associated with the Jog (Gersoppa) falls, 253 m in height. Other streams flow over the undulating Karnataka plateau, which slopes gently eastwards. The plateau region has an average height of about 457 m above sea level; its soils are generally porous and infertile. The basins of its rivers, which include the Cauvery (Kaveri) to the south and the

Tungabhadra, a tributary of the Krishna River, to the north, are, however, loamy and of some fertility. From early times, the smaller streams have been dammed to form irrigation reservoirs; in recent times much hydroelectric-power development has taken place. In the northwestern part of the State underlying volcanic rock produces a soil known as *regur*, the humus-rich, black cotton-growing soil of India.

Passing from west to east, the Malnad gives way on the plateau to more open plain country, known as the Maidan, where rainfall is less and where monsoon forests are replaced by scrub forests and scrub land. The monsoon forests are rich in wildlife, which include tigers, elephants, bisons (gaurs), and deer. Wild boars, bears, and leopards inhabit the Maidan. One of the common birds is the peacock. The State has a wildlife sanctuary located at Dandeli and national parks at Bandipur and Nagarhole.

People : Ethnologically, the population of Karnataka is predominantly Dravidian. The Dravidians were the original inhabitants of India and are related to the peoples of the Malay peninsula, Sumatra, and Madagascar. Over the centuries, however, much intermixture with other races has occurred. In the north of the State, Indic traits mixed with Dravidian occur. Some Anglo-Indians, representing a mixture of European and Dravidian are occasionally encountered, particularly in Bangalore.

Kannada, spoken by more than 70 per cent of the population, is the official State language. Hindustani (a mixture of Hindi and Urdu) is often used in trade and business. Towards the borders of the State, other languages, such as Tamil, Telugu, Marathi, and Konkani are also spoken. Konkani is associated particularly with the city of Mangalore. The major religion is Hinduism, but Jainism and Buddhism, once widespread, still survive. Small percentages of the population follow Islam and Christianity.

Although about three-quarters of the population is rural, the trend towards urbanization is becoming more marked as industrialization increases. The major cities are Bangalore, the capital, and Mysore. Major towns are Hubli-Dharwad, Mangalore, Belgaum, Gulbarga, Bellary, Devangere, Bijapur, Shimoga, and Bhadravari.

Economy : Agriculture is the occupation of 70 per cent of the population. The coastal plain is intensively cultivated with rice grown as a food crop and sugarcane as a cash crop. Other major food crops are *jowar* (sorghum) and *ragi* (millet). Other cash crops are cashew, cardamom, betel nut, and grape. Coffee and tea plantations occupy the cool slopes of the Western Ghats. In the eastern region irrigation makes possible the cultivation of sugarcane and a little rubber, and of fruits such as bananas and oranges. The black soil of the northwest supports cotton, oilseeds, and peanuts (groundnuts) too.

The *forests* of the Malnad region in the west produce teak, sandalwood, bamboo, and other products such as tanning dyes, gums, and lac (a resinous substance used in the manufacture of varnishes). Other trees include eucalyptus and rosewood. Sandalwood oil is processed at Mysore city and is a leading State export. In places, the Precambrian rocks of Karnataka, which are at least 570 million years old, are highly mineralized. Karnataka is the largest producer of chromite in India; it is also one of the only two States in India (the other being Tamil Nadu) producing magnesite. High-grade iron ore reserves are largely located in Chikmagalur and Chitradurga districts; mica, copper ore, bauxite, and garnet are obtained in small quantities. India's gold is derived from the region of the Kolar Gold Fields. The principal gold mines, now nationalized, are up to 2,743 m deep.

The *mineral resources* of the State provide the basis for the iron and steel industry at Bhadravati and heavy engineering works at Bangalore. Other *industries* in the State include cotton milling, sugar processing, and the manufacture of textiles, food products, electrical machinery, fertilizers, cement, and paper. Both Mysore city and Bangalore have old, established, silk industries producing most of India's mulberry silk. Sharavati project near Jog Falls is the largest of several hydroelectric plants that provide power to Karnataka's industries.

The obstacle formed by the Western Ghats had previously prevented the building of *railroads* linking the ports to the plateau in the interior. But now Bangalore is linked with Mangalore via Hassan. Bangalore, in the southeast, is the main focus of rail transportation. The port of Mangalore, in the south-west, is connected with Mumbai (formerly Bombay) by the Konkan Railway via Goa.

The *import and export trade* relies primarily on road transport, but many roads in the western part of the State become impassable during the rainy season. National highways run from Bangalore towards east to Chennai (formerly Madras), then north to Hyderabad, northwest to Mumbai and west through Hassan to the coast of Mangalore. Airports are located at Bangalore, Belgaum, and Mangalore.

Cultural life : Karnataka possesses a rich cultural heritage by the contributions of successive dynasties, which have fostered various religions and philosophies; these have influenced literature, architecture, folklore, music, painting, and minor arts.

The town of Shravana Belgola, 90 km from Mysore, contains notable examples of Maurya architecture and sculpture such as a giant stone figure, believed to be a thousand years old, of Bahubali (Gommateshvara), a Jain saint. Huge monolithic Jain statues are peculiar to the Kannada culture. The influence of the Chalukya and the Pallava dynasties is still apparent in temple architecture dating from the seventh century AD.

The advent of the Western powers introduced western architecture and lifestyles among the elite of the urban areas. Similarly the Muslim rulers not only introduced Islam but also influenced the architecture. The west coast of Karnataka was influenced by Christianity to a great extent.

Area, Population and Headquarters of Districts

S.No.	*District*	*Area (sq km)*	*Population*	*Headquarters*
1.	Bagalkot	6,594	13,94,542	Bagalkot
2.	Bangalore	2,190	48,39,162	Bangalore
3.	Bangalore Rural	5,815	16,73,194	Bangalore
4.	Belgaum	13,415	35,83,606	Belgaum
5.	Bellary	8,419	16,56,000	Bellary
6.	Bidar	5,448	12,55,798	Bidar
7.	Bijapur	10,475	15,33,448	Bijapur
8.	Chamarajanagar	5,685	8,83,365	Chamarajanagar
9.	Chikmagalur	7,201	10,17,283	Chikmagalur
10.	Chitradurga	8,388	13,12,717	Chitradurga
11.	Dakshina Kallnada	4,843	16,33,392	Mangalore
12.	Davanagere	6,018	15,59,222	Davanagere
13.	Dharwad	4,230	13,74,895	Dharwad
14.	Gadag	4,657	8,59,042	Gadag
15.	Gulbarga	16,224	25,82,169	Gulbarga
16.	Hassan	6,814	15,69,684	Hassan
17.	Haveri	4,851	12,69,213	Haveri
18.	Kodagu	4,102	4,88,455	Madikere
19.	Kolar	8,223	22,16,889	Kolar
20.	Koppal	8,458	9,58,078	Koppal
21.	Mandya	4,961	16,44,374	Mandya
22.	Mysore	6,269	22,81,653	Mysore
23.	Raichur	5,559	13,51,809	Raichur
24.	Shimoga	8,465	14,52,259	Shimoga
25.	Tumkur	10,598	23,05,819	Tumkur
26.	Udupi	3,598	10,60,872	Udupi
27.	Uttara Kannada	10,291	12,20,260	Karwar

Kerala—A state of India, it has an area of 38,863 sq km, only about I per cent of the total area of the country. The State stretches for 580 km along the Malabar Coast on the southwestern side of the Indian peninsula; its width varies from 32 to 121 km. It is bordered by the States of Kamataka (formerly Mysore) to the north and Tamil Nadu to the east and by the Arabian Sea to the west. Its capital is Thiruvananthapuram (formerly Trivandrum).

Isolated from the Indian interior by the mountainous belt of the Western Ghats, but possessing a long coastline that opens it to foreign influences, Kerala has evolved a unique culture. It is a highly politicized region, but it has a long tradition of religious amity. It is an educationally advanced State with its own language, Malayalam, and it has the highest rate of literacy among Indian States. Owing to the former matrilineal system, women in Kerala enjoy a high social status. Some of India's most isolated tribes exist in Kerala's wilderness areas.

History : Kerala was first mentioned (as Keralaputra) in a third-century-BC rock inscription left by the Maurya emperor Ashoka. In the last centuries BC this region became famous among the Greeks and Romans for its spices (especially pepper). During the first five centuries AD, the region was a part of Tamilakam and thus was sometimes partially controlled by the eastern Pandya and Chola dynasties, as well as by the Cheras. Jewish immigrants arrived in the first century AD, and Syrian Orthodox Christians believe that St. Thomas the Apostle visited Kerala in the same century. Much of Kerala's history from the sixth to eighth century AD is obscure, but Arab traders introduced Islam later in the period. Under the Kulashekhara dynasty (c. 800-1102) Malayalam emerged as a distinct language, and Hinduism became prominent. The Cholas often controlled Kerala during the eleventh and twelfth centuries. By the beginning of the fourteenth century, Ravi Varma Kulashekhara of Venad established a shortlived supremacy over southern India. After his death, Kerala became a conglomeration of warring chieftaincies,, among whom the most important were Calicut in the north and Venad in the south. The era of foreign intervention began in 1498, when Vasco da Gama landed near Calicut. In the sixteenth century the Portuguese superseded the Arab traders and dominated the commerce of Malabar. Their attempt to establish sovereignty was thwarted by the *zamorin* (hereditary ruler) of Calicut. The Dutch ousted the Portuguese in the seventeenth century. Marthanda Varma ascended the Venad throne in 1729 and crushed Dutch expansionist designs at the battle of Kolachel 12 years later. Marthanda Varma then adopted an European mode of martial discipline and expanded the new southern State of Travancore. His alliance in 1757 with the raja of the central State of Cochin, against the *zamorin*, enabled Cochin to survive. By 1806, however, Cochin and Travancore, as well as Malabar in the north, had become subject States under the British Madras Presidency. Two years after India's independence was achieved in 1947, Cochin and Travancore were united as the Travancore-Cochin State. The present State of Kerala was constituted on a linguistic basis in 1956 when Malabar and the Kasargod *taluka* of South Kanara were added to Travancore-Cochin. The southern portion of the former Travancore-Cochin State was attached to Tamil Nadu.

Relief : Kerala is a region of great natural beauty. Anai Peak 2,695 m, the highest peak of peninsular India, crowns the Western Ghats. Between the coastal plain and the rocky highlands is a sequence of plantation crops: rubber in the foothills and above that coffee and then tea. A linked chain of lagoons and backwaters along the coast, interspersed with vast coconut palm groves, form the so-called "Venice of India". Among the rivers that flow to the Arabian Sea, the more important are the Bharatapuzha, Chalakudi, Periyar, and Pamba.

Climate : The climate is equable and varies little from season to season. The temperature normally ranges from 27 to 32 °C on the plains but drops to about 21 °C in the highlands. Kerala is directly exposed to the southwest monsoon but also receives rain from the reverse (northeast) monsoon. Rainfall averages about 3,000 mm annually Statewide, with some slopes receiving more than 5,080 mm.

Plant and animal life : The state's riverine and montane rainforests, tropical deciduous forests, and upland temperate grasslands are inhabited by an extraordinary variety of wildlife, including the sambar deer, gaur (wild bison), Nilgiri tahr (wild goat), elephant, leopard, tiger, bonnet monkey, the rare liontailed macaque, the Hanuman and Nilgiri langurs, spectacled and king cobras, peafowl, and hornbill. The Periyai Tiger Reserve is the largest wildlife sanctuary, and there are two national parks (Eravikulam and Silent Valley) and several other wildlife sanctuaries.

The people : Kerala is me *most densely populated* State in India. While only about one-fifth of the population is urban, this low proportion is deceptive because of the close proximity of scattered rural houses, especially in the coastal plain. Thus, in parts of the State there are tropical-rural equivalents of megalopolises. The major urban and industrial complexes are Kannur (formerly Cannanore), Kozhikode

Kozhikode (formerly Calicut), Alwaye, Kochi (formerly Cochin)-Ernakulam, Alappuzha (formerly Alleppey), and Kollam (formerly Quilon). Most Malayalis, the Malayalam-speaking people of Kerala, are of Dravidian ancestry, with some Indo-European admixture representing the ancient so-called Aryan influx. The latter element remains strongest among the Nambudiri caste of orthodox Hindus. A few tribal people in the mountains may exhibit affinities with the Negrito local race of Southeast Asia.

Kerala has a unique record in India of harmonious coexistence of *diverse religions*. Majority of the Malayalis are Hindus. There is no conflict between the Dravidian *naga* (serpent-god) worship and that of Kali (the mother goddess) on the one hand and the Hindu pantheon on the other, nor between the rival sects of Shaivism (worship of the god Shiva) and Vaishnavism (worship of the god Vishnu). The small population of Jains live mainly in the far north. The Jewish community remains a small, exclusive sect; there is an ancient synagogue at Kochi. The Christians, who form more than a third of the population, belong broadly to the Orthodox Syrian, Roman Catholic, and Protestant churches, though each has many sects. While Muslims reside throughout the State, the Mapillas of the Malabar Coast constitute Keralas largest Islamic community.

Economy : Geographic and geologic factors seriously circumscribe Kerala's economy. The amount of arable land is insufficient for the needs of the crowded population. The State lacks major deposits of fossil fuels and minerals, except for ilmenite (the principal ore of titanium), rutile (titanium dioxide), and monazite (a mineral consisting of cerium and thorium phosphates), which are found in beach sands Kerala has great hydroelectric potential. and the ldukki complex is the largest power-generating facility.

The educational system, a developed banking system, and execllent transportion facilities provide optimum conditions for further economic development. *Agriculture* is the State's main economic activity. *Commercial plantings* on less than half of the total land under cultivation earn a sizable amount of foreign exchange but have also necessitated the importation of food for local consumption. Kerala's principal cash yielders are perennial areca nut, cardamom, cashew nut, coconut, coffee, ginger, pepper, rubber, and tea; the major annual food crops are rice, pulses, lentils, sorghum, and tapioca. Commercial poultry farming is well developed. The forests yield valuable timbers such as ebony, rosewood, and teak, as well as industrial raw materials such as bamboo (used in the paper and rayon industries), wood pulp, charcoal, gums, and resins. Foreigners regularly attend the tea and timber auctions held in Kochi. Kerala ranks first among Indian States in fish production.

Most of the population is unaffected by *industrialization.* Unemployment is acute, and a high level of education among the jobless accentuates the problem. Traditional low-wage cottage industries, such as the processing of coconut fibre and cashews or weaving, employ most workers. More than one-fourth of Kerala's workers provide services. Food processing is the largest industrial employer. Other products include fertilizers, chemicals, electrical equipment, titanium, aluminum, plywood, ceramics, and synthetic fabrics. Kerala has well-developed road and railway systems. It is connected with the States of Tamil Nadu and Karnataka by national highways. A railway coming from the east through the Palghat Gap meets with a railway running from north to south through the State and on to Kanniyakumari, the southernmost town of India. There are three major ports — Kozhikode, Kochi-Ernakulam, and Alappuzha — that handle both coastal and foreign traffic. Kochi-Emakulam also has major shipyard and oil refining facilities and serves as the headquarters for Indian coast guard and navy commands. More than 1,770 km of inland waterways form main arteries for carrying bulk freight to and from the ports. Thiruvananthapuram has an international airport, and Kozhikode and Kochi have airports for domestic flights.

Cultural life : Kerala's cultural heritage contains elements of ancient Hindu culture that have been enriched by centuries of contact with both East and West. The State's impressive array of Hindu temples with copper-clad roofs, later Islamic mosques with "Malabar gables" (triangular projections at the rooftops), and Portuguese colonial baroque churches attests to this interweaving. Traditional art forms include intricate paintings on wood, thematic murals, and an amazing variety of indoor and outdoor lamps (which has earned Kerala the sobriquet "Land of Lamps").

Literature and learning, in both Tamil and Sanskrit, flourished from the second century AD. The Malayalam language, though an offshoot of Tamil, has absorbed the best in Sanskrit and has a prolific literature. Notable names in Malayalam poetry are Thunchath Ezhuthachan and Kunjan Nambiar among classical poets, and Kumayn Asan and Vallathol in the present century.

Area, Population and Headquarters of Districts

S.No.	District	Area (sq km)	Population (1991 Census)	Headquarters
1.	Alappuzha	1,414	20,01,217	Alappuzha
2.	Emakulam	2,407	28,17,236	Emakulam
3.	Idukki	5,019	10,78,006	Painavu
4.	Kannur	2,996	22,51,727	Kannur
5.	Kasaragode	4,992	10,71,508	Kasaragode
6.	Kollam	2,491	24,07,566	Kollam
7.	Kottayam	2,203	18,28,271	Kottayam
8.	Kozhikode	2,345	26,19,941	Kozhikode
9.	Malappuram	3,550	30,96,330	Malappuram
10.	Palakkad	4,480	23,82,235	Palakkad
11.	Pathanamthitta	2,642	11,88,352	Pathanamthitta
12.	Thimvananthapuram	2,192	29,46,650	Thimvnanthapuram
13.	Thrissur	3,032	27,37,311	Thrissur
14.	Wayanad	2,132	6,72,128	Kalpetta

L

Lakshadweep–This union territory of India was formerly (1956-1973) Laccadive, Minicoy, and Amindivi Islands. The Lakshadweep archipelago consists of 12 atolls, 3 reefs, 5 submerged banks, and islands. It is a group of some three dozen islands with a total land area of 32 sq km scattered over 77,700 sq km of the Arabian Sea. The total associated lagoon area is about 4,200 sq km while territorial water extends to 20,000 sq km and economic zone to 400,000 sq km. Minicoy and Amandivi are the principal islands separated by the Nine Degree Channel. The easternmost island lies about 300 km off the western coast of the State of Kerala. Ten of the islands are inhabited. The administrative centre is Kavaratri. The name Lakshadweep means "Hundred Thousand Islands" in Malayalan and Sanskrit. The whole Union Territory has only one district. It is considered to be the *coral paradise* of India.

History : These islands have been mentioned by a first century Greek sailor as a source of tortoise-shell which were then obtained by the Tamils. Missionary activity in the seventh century AD and continued contact with

Arab traders eventually led to the conversion of all the islanders to Islam. The dynasties of the southern Indian were always trying to extend their sovereignty over these islands. Sometime before 1100 a small Hindu kingdom on the Malabar coast annexed the islands, and after the fall of the Kulashekhara dynasty of Kerala in 1102 they passed to the Kolathiris, another small Hindu dynasty. Later in the twelfth century, after a Kolathiri princess married a Muslim convert, a separate kingdom (including the islands that eventually formed Lakshadweep) was set up in the Cannanore area in order to protect the Kerala tradition of matrilineal descent. It is claimed that Marco Polo visited the Minicoy Island in the thireenth century and named it a "Female Island", possibly because of the preponderance of women. In Winterbotham's account of this island in 1876, there were 1,179 females against 351 males. Apparently, all able-bodied men were on ships and boats, mostly engaged in the fishing. Portuguese found these islands in 1498, perhaps during the days of Vasco da Gama and built a fort for control and trade, particularly in coir. However, there was an uprising in 1545 by the local islanders.

Successive *bibis* (female rulers) and their husbands ruled the islands, until control of the Amindivis passed to Tipu Sultan in the 1780s. After the Treaty of Srirangapatanam in 1792 the southern group of islands was permitted to be administered by the local chiefs. When Tipu was killed in battle with the British in 1799, the Amindivis came under British control. Ameri, Chetlat, Kadmath, Kiltan and the inhabited island, Bitra, were attached to the South Kanara district collectorate; while Agathi, Kavaratti, Andrott, Kalpeni, Minicoy, and the inhabited Suheli were attached to the Malabar. The *bibi* and her husband were permitted to retain the other islands and receive income from them in exchange for an annual payment. These payments were repeatedly in arrears, and in 1908 the *bibi* ceded direct administration of these islands to the British. The British appointed Amins belonging to the Karanava, or Koya, sect, subordinate to the Malabar collectorate to govern each inhabited island. Assessors from the same community assisted the Amins. In the case of the Amini group of islands, resident managers were appointed who in turn were assisted by accountants known as Karanis. Sovereignty was transferred to India upon Indian independence in 1947, and the islands were constituted a Union Territory in 1956.

Relief : The Amindivis are the northernmost islands of the group and Minicoy Island the southernmost. All but one of the inhabited islands are coral atolls. These islands are of coral origin developed around volcanic peaks. A large variety of corals grow in the crystal-clear water of the lagoons. The higher eastern sides of the islands are the most ideally suited for human habitation, while the low-lying lagoons on the western sides protect the inhabitants from the southwest monsoon. The islands are small, none exceeding 2 km in breadth. The sandy soil, derived from the coral, supports a rich growth of coconut palms and perennial garden plants. Cyclones moving up the Arabian Sea rarely cross the islands, but the winds and waves associated with them can considerably alter the land features. The weather observatory was established in Minicoy towards the end of the nineteenth century. This was upgraded to a class I observatory in 1963. Before it became a Union Territory, the properties were assessed in terms of coconut palms. Cadastral survey (showing the extent, value, and ownership of land) was carried out in the middle of the twentieth century.

Apart from coconut, the other important *flora species* are breadfruit, banyan, casurina, tamarind, *poovarasu* (*Thespesia populnea*), *punna* (*calophyllum*), wild almond (*Terminalia catappa*), *parathimaram*, screw pine, *tamara*, papaya, drumstick, areca nut, betel vine, and colocasia. The important marine fauna are sharks (*sura*), bonitos, skip jack (tuna), snapper (*chempalli*), flying fish (*parava*), deer fish (*aya kura*), sail fish (*olumin*), devil ray (*kottaru*), gastropods, chanka and cowry shells, sea slangs, octopus (edible), crabs, turtles, and sea birds like herons, teals, sea gulls, water herons, and terns (migratory group).

People : Most of the islanders are Muslim Mapillas who speak Malayalam, Mahi, or Mahl, which is akin to old Sinhalese, is spoken in Minicoy. Some people also understand Hindi. Out of 36 islands, 10 are inhabited. The well-populated islands are Andrott (9,122), Kavaratti (8,677), Minicoy (8,320), and Amini (6,447). The density of population in these islands is very high, over 1,900 persons per sq km. The total population in 1991 was 51,707 with 48.52 per cent females or 943 females per 1,000 males, and 93.15 per cent scheduled tribes. The matrilineal kinship and a rigid caste system are characteristics of the Hindu system of Kerala. There is a college affiliated with the University of Calicut in Kerala. There are 56 educational institutions and two hospitals. The jurisdiction of the Kerala High Court extends over Lakshadweep.

Economy : About 44 per cent of the area is the net sown area. The soils and climatic conditions are ideal for coconut cultivation. Coconut palms are the *agricultural mainstay*. Annual production is about 26.3

million. In some places the underlying coral has been excised and the tracts fertilized with organic matter; these support the cultivation of bananas, vegetables, edible root crops, and millet. Coir (coconut husk fibre), a State monopoly, is traded for rice from the mainland. Copra is also produced and exported to the mainland.

The chief *industry* is fishing, and it is supported by boat-building facilities and by a cannery on Minicoy that processes tuna. Annual landed fish is about 9,400 tonnes. The traditional process of drying bonito (a small tuna fish with dark stripes) is also practised on Minicoy. The government operates several coir mills, but the manufacture of the fibre — which largely employs women — remains a major cottage industry. Sailors continue their ancient tradition of skilled navigation, and some still sail between the islands and the mainland in distinctive crafts called *odams*.

Kozhikode (formerly Calicut) is the nearest *seaport* in the mainland, There are three mainland-island passenger ships and two passenger-cum-cargo ships. Mainland and inier-island helicopter services are also in operation. Road length is only 9 km. Recendy a Society for Promotion of Recreation Tourism and Sports (SPORTS) has initiated tour programmes for Indian tourists from Kochi (formerly Cochin) and Beypore. The islands, which are open for tourism, are Bangaram, Kavaratti, Minicoy, and Andrott. Foreign tourists are only allowed on two islands. Less than 2,500 foreign and domestic tourists visit these islands every year. These islands are served by one post office, nine telegraph offices, and eight banks. The installed power capacity is only 5,014 KW. There are 14 factories and 263 small-scale industries. These include coir production-cum-demonstration centres, defibering plants, a hosiery factory (at Kalpeni), a weaving centre (at Chetlat), as well as a tuna canning factory and two boat-building yards.

M

Madhya Pradesh—The State of Madhya Pradesh is bounded by Chhattisgarh in the east, Rajasthan and Gujarat in the west, Uttar Pradesh in the north and Maharashtra in the south.

History : The undivided Madhya Pradesh was founded on 1st November 1956. Madhya Pradesh, is its present form, came into existence on 1st November 2000 following its bifurcation to create a new state of Chhattisgarh.

Because of its central location in India, Madhya Pradesh has remained a crucible of historical currents from north, south, east and west. King Ashok first of all ruled over Ujjain. A sizeable portion of Central India was part of the Gupta empire (300-500 AD). The Muslims came into Central India in the beginning of 11th century. First of all Mahmud of Ghazni came over here and then Mohammad Gouri who incorporated some parts of Central India into his ruling territory of Delhi. Central India was also part of the Mughal empire. During the period between the beginning of the influence of Marathas and the death of Madhoji Scindia in 1794, Marathas were on the ascendant in Central India but later on the small states started coming into existence These small states became the cause of perpetuation of British power in the country. Queen Ahilyabai Holkar of Indore, the Gond Maharani Kamla Devi and Queen Durgawati, etc., were some women rulers whose names have left an indelible imprint on Indian History for their outstanding rule.

Economy : Agriculture : Agriculture is the mainstay of State's economy as 74.73 per cent of the total population lives in rural areas. About 49 per cent area of the state is cultivable. The principal crops are wheat, rice, *jowar*, cotton, oilseeds, pulses, soyabean gram and linseed. Total foodgrain production has been 15.48 million metric tonne (MMT), wheat production 8.37 MMT, soyabean production 4.43 MMT rice production 1.68 MMT and of pulses 3.29 MMT. Oilseed production was 5.46 MMT, cotton 4.6 lakh bales and production of jaggery sugar (*gur*) from sugarcane was 20 lakh tonnes in the state.

Industry and Minerals : Madhya Pradesh has entered the era of high-tech industries such as petrochemicals, electronics, telecommunications, automobiles, etc. Madhya Pradesh is producing optical fibre for telecommunication needs. A large number of automobile industries have been established at Pithampur near Indore. Prominent industries in the public sector in the State are Bharat Heavy Electricals Limited at Bhopal, Security Paper Mill at Hoshangabad, Bank Note Press at Dewas, Newsprint Factory at Nepanagar and Alkaloid Factory at Neemuch. During 1999-2000, 81.13 million metre cloth was manufactured in the handloom sector and 131.59 million metre cloth by the powerlooms. Total production of saleable steel in 1998-99 was 3.35 million tonne while that of aluminium was 91.8 thousand tonne. Production of cement touched 11.24 million metric tonne mark. The state produced about 58.4 thousand tonne newsprint. An Air Cargo Complex, Indo-German Tool Room and an Inland Container Depot are being established at Pithampura.

Madhya Pradesh is one of the leading States in the country in *mineral production.* Coal, bauxite, iron-ore, manganese-ore, rock phosphate, dolomite, copper-ore, limestone are being mined on a large scale. During 1999-2000, over 43 million tonnes of coal and 92 thousand tonnes of iron ore were produced. Production of diamond was 46,668 carats and that of bauxite 248 thousand tonnes. Production of lime-stone was 22.31 million tonnes and that of copper ore 74 thousand, tonnes during 1999-2000. The State is famous for its traditional handicrafts and handloom cloths manufactured at Chanderi and Maheswar.

Irrigation and Power : The net area under irrigation was 5.66 million hectare in the year 1999-2000. Of this 0.24 m.ha. was under paddy, 3.40 m.ha. under wheat, 1.08 m.ha. under pulses and 0.32 m.ha. under oilseeds.

Total installed power generation capacity in 2000-01 was 2,900 MW. There are eight hydro-electric power stations with 747.5 MW installed capacity. A total of 50.271 out of 51,806 villages had been electrified by 2000-01. Power generation is 14,023.7 m.kwh.

The State Government has formed a joint.venture (Narmada Hydro Electric Development Corporation) with National Hydro-Electric Power Corporation for execution of 1,000 MW Indira Sagar Hydro Electric Project and 520 MW Omkareshwar Hydro-Electric Power Project.

Transport : Roads : Total length of roads in the state is 67,600 km. The length of national highways in the state is 3,700 km while State highways extend to 7,300 km.

Railways : The main rail route linking northern India with southern India passes through Madhya Pradesh. Main junctions in the State are Bhopal, Bina, Gwalior, Indore, Itarsi, Jabalpur, Katni, Ratlam and Ujjain. The divisional railways headquarters are at Bhopal, Ratlam and Jabalpur.

Aviation : There are airports at Bhopal, Gwalior, Indore and Khajuraho.

Cultural life : Festivals : A number of festivals are celebrated in Madhya Pradesh. An important tribal festival is Bhagoriya marked by traditional gaiety and enthusiasm. Shivratri is celebrated in Khajuraho, Bhojpur, Pachmarhi and Ujjain and has its own local flavour while Ramnavami festival at Chitrakoot and Orchha has a unique sense of devotion imbued with tradition. Festivals of Orchha, Malwa, Pachmarhi bring to the fore, repertoire of culture and art of the people. Tansen Music

Festival. Gwalior, Ustad Allauddin Khan Music Festival of Maihar, Kalidas Samaroh, Ujjain and Festival of Dances at Khajurahc are some of the well known art festivals of Madhya Pradesh.

Perfectly preserved *medieval cities*, refreshing and enchanting *wildlife sanctuaries* and some of the holiest and most revered *pilgrim centres* offer to the tourist the most fulfilling experience. Tranquil beauty of Pachmarhi, glittering splendour of Marble Rocks and roaring sound of Dhuandhar Fall at Bhedaghat, Kanha National Park, with its unique Barasingha and Bandhavgarh National Park with its prehistoric caves and wildlife are some of the major attractions of the state. Gwalior, Mandu, Datia, Chanderi, Jabalpur, Orchha, Raisen, Sanchi, Vidisha, Udaygiri, Bhimbetika, Indore and Bhopal are the places well-known for their historical monuments. Maheshwar, Omkareshwar, Ujjain, Chitrakoot and Amarkantak are major centres of pilgrimages. Unique temples of Khajuraho are famous all over the world. The temples of Orchha, Bhojpur and Udaypur attract large number of tourists as well as pilgrims. Archaeological treasures are preserved in the museums at Satna, Sanchi, Vidisha, Gwalior, Indore, Mandsaur, Ujjain, Rajgarh, Bhopal, Jabalpur, Rewa and many other places.

Area, Population and Headquarters of Districts

S.No.	*District*	*Area (sq km)*	*Population (1991 Census)*	*Headquarters*
1.	Badwani	-	8,32,422	Badwani
2.	Balaghat	9,229	13,62,731	Balaghat
3.	Betul	10,043	11,80,527	Betul
4.	Bhind	4,459	12,14,480	Bhind
5.	Bhopal	2,772	13,50,302	Bhopal
6.	Chhatarpur	8,687	11,58,853	Chhatarpur
7.	Chhindwara	11,815	15,63,332	Chhindwara
8.	Damoh	7,306	8,97,544	Damoh
9.	Datia	2,038	3,97,743	Datia
10.	Dewas	7,020	10,32,522	Dewas
11.	Dhar	8,153	13,66,626	Dhar
12.	Dindori	-	5,83,019	Dindori
13.	Guna	11,065	13,09,451	Guna
14.	Gwalior	5,214	14,14,948	Gwalior
15.	Harda	-	3,80,762	Harda

S.No.	District	Area (sq km)	Population (1991 Census)	Headquarters
16.	Hoshangabad	10,037	13,65,970	Hoshangabad
17.	Indore	3,898	18,30,870	Indore
18.	Jabalpur	10,160	26,45,232	Jabalpur
19.	Jhabua	6,782	11,29,356	Jhabua
20.	Katni	-	8,81,925	Katni
21.	Khandwa (East Nimar)	10,779	14,32,855	Khandwa
22.	Khargone (West Nimar)	13,450	20,26,317	Khargone
23.	Mandla	13,269	12,91,313	Mandla
24.	Mandsaur	9,791	15,55,481	Mandsaur
25.	Morena	11,594	17,07,619	Morena
26	Narsinghpur	5,133	7,84,523	Narsinghpur
27	Neemuch	-	5,98,339	Neemuch
28.	Panna	7,135	6,84,721	Panna
29.	Raisen	8,446	8,77,369	Raisen
30.	Rajgarh	6,154	9,92,315	Rajgarh
31.	Ratlam	4,861	9,71,309	Ratlam
32.	Rewa	6,314	15,50,140	Rewa
33.	Sagar	10,252	16,46,198	Sagar
34.	Satna	7,502	14,62,412	Satna
35.	Sehore	6,578	8,40,427	Sehore
36.	Seoni	8,758	9,99,762	Seoni
37.	Shahdol	14,028	17,43,068	Shahdol
38.	Shajapur	6,196	10,32,520	Shajapur
39.	Shayopur	-	4,31,480	Shayopur
40.	Shivpuri	10,278	11,31,933	Shivpuri
41.	Sidhi	10,256	13,71,935	Sidhi
42.	TIkamgarh	5,048	9,40,609	TIkamgarh
43.	Ujjain	6,091	13,86,465	Ujjain
44.	Umaria	-	4,20,815	Umaria
45.	Vidisha	2,742	9,71,097	Vidisha

Maharashtra–This state of India, located in the western part of peninsular India, is bounded by the States of Gujarat, Madhya Pradesh, Andhra Pradesh, Karnataka, and Goa and, on the west by the Arabian Sea. Resembling roughly a triangle in shape, its broader part flanks the Arabian Sea over a length of 725 km tapering eastwards over a distance of about 805 km. The linguistic State of Maharashtra was formed in 1956 through the merging of Vidharba of the Central Provinces and Marathwada of the former Nizam's Dominion with a part of the earlier British Indian Territory of Bombay Presidency, Its ancient culture, obscured to some extent by the British rule, survives and gets strengthened, largely through a strong literary heritage. A common literature in Marathi, the predominant language, has in fact, played an important role in nurturing a sense of unity among the Maharashtrians. The State's capital Mumbai (earlier known as Bombay) dominates the economic, social, and political life of Maharashtra and exerts influence all over India, Maharashtra is a leader among (he Indian States in industrial production, diversity of crops, trade, transport, and education.

History : The name Maharashtra, denoting the western upland of the Deccan, first appeared in a seventh-century inscription and in the account of a contemporary Chinese traveller, Hsuan-tsang (Xuanzang). According to one view, the name derives from the word maharathi (great chariot driver), which refers to a skilful northern fighting force that migrated southwards into the area. The group's language, intermingled with the speech of the earlier Naga settlers, became Maharastri, and this by the eighth century developed into Marathi. There was also a continuous influx of people from remote Greece and Central Asia.

During this early period the territory constituting the modern State of Maharashtra was divided among several Hindu kingdoms: Satavahana, Vakataka, Kalachuri, Rashtrakuta, Chalukya, and Yadava. After 1307 there was a succession of Muslim dynasties. Persian, the court language of the Muslims, had a far-reaching effect on Marathi. By the middle of the sixteenth century Maharashtra was again fragmented among several independent Muslim rulers, who fought each other endlessly. It was in the midst of this chaos that a great leader, Shivaji Bhonsle, was born in 1627. Shivaji showed astonishing prowess by founding a large Maratha empire that shook the Delhi-based Mughal rule to its foundations.

During the eighteenth century almost all of western and central India, as well as large segments of the north and east, were brought under Maratha suzerainty. This empire began to succumb to the British from the early nineteenth century onwards. When India became independent in 1947 the province, long known as the Bombay Presidency, became Bombay State. A number of former Princely States (notably Baroda) were merged into the new State, and, on November 1, 1956, a major linguistic and political reorganization of the States of peninsular India resulted in the addition of large parts of Madhya Pradesh and the erstwhile Hyderabad to Bombay State. The outcome of this reorganization was a State in which most of the Gujarati-speaking peoples lived in the north, while most of the Marathi-speaking peoples lived in the south. Because of the demands of the two language groups, the State was divided into two parts on May I, I960, thus creating Gujarat in the north and Maharashtra in the south.

Landforms and rivers : Maharashtra presents an interesting range of landforms. The Narmada River, flowing into the Arabian Sea through a rift valley, marks a part of the northern boundary of the State. The other rift valley, of the Tapti River, also flowing into the Arabian Sea, marks the other part of the northern boundary. These two river valleys are separated by a horst known as the Satpura Range. South of the Tapti valley, stretches the Konkan coastland along the Arabian Sea flanked in the east by an escarpment known as the Sahyadri mountains or the Western Ghats. The foothills of the Sahyadri mountains reach within 6.4 km of the Arabian Sea in the Konkan. The Konkan coastland is narrow, interspersed with hilly spurs from the Sahyadri mountains and is drained by many small swift, west-flowing rivers: of these, the Ulhas in the north is the biggest.

The Sahyadri mountains run like a wall with a north-south trend, almost continuously for 640 km. But several passes through it provide important road and rail links between the coastlands and the interior. The eastern slopes of the Sahyadris descend gently to the Deccan Plateau sculptured by the east sloping valleys of the Godavari, Bhima, and Krishna rivers. The inter-fluves of these rivers form the Mahadeo, Ajanta, Balaghat, and other hill ranges. These hill ranges and valleys within Maharashtra are formed of trap lava with thickness reaching close to 3,050 m in places. Differential erosion of the lava results in characteristic step-like flanks with tabletop appearance in many hills. In the east, beyond Nagpur, the trap country ends, yielding to landforms made of ancient crystalline rocks. From the Mahadeo hills and the Maikala range further east, many important tributaries of the Godavari River flow towards the southeast, of which the Wardha, Wainganga, and the Penganga are the most important. This region abounds in lakes. Further east, the country is rugged with many hills covered with forests and is relatively inhospitable.

Soils : A major part of Maharashtra has black cotton soil, which is a derivative of the decomposed lava. Drift along slopes has changed this soil into medium brown and light soils. In the Wardha-Wainganga valley light-reddish-coloured sandy soils have formed as derivatives of granite rocks. Saline soils in some valleys are the results of impeded soil drainage followed by intense evaporation.

Climate : Southwest monsoon rains break on the Mumbai coast in the first week of June and last until September, during which period they account for 80 per cent of the annual rainfall. Four seasons are normal: March-May (hot and dry), June-September (hot and wet), October-November (warm and dry), and December-February (cool and dry). The Sahyadris and the northern ranges act as orographic barriers, confining very wet conditions on its windward side to the Konkan coast. On the leeward side, the interior plateaus remain relatively dry. Rainfall in the Konkan averages 2,540 mm, and some of the wettest spots including the Sahyadris record 6,350 mm. East of the Western Ghats, rainfall diminishes to one-fifth of the Konkan rainfall. Rainfall again increases in the eastern areas, recording 1,016 to 2,032 mm as conditioned by hills.

The coastal regions enjoy equable temperatures, ranging, as at Mumbai, between a few degrees below or above 27 °C. Pune on the plateau benefits from cooler temperatures almost throughout the year. In the central part of Maharashtra and in its eastern regions, summer temperatures average to 43 °C with winter temperatures around 21 °C. Rainfall in Maharashtra is variable between years, which has been significantly mitigated through the development of irrigation in the latter half of the twentieth century to combat crop failures.

Plant and animal life : Forests cover less than one-fifth of the area of the State. These are mainly confined to the Sahyadries together with their promontory ranges as also on the Satpuras, the Melghat, and the eastern Vidarbha hills. There are typically deciduous species with teak, dhavada, shisham, tendu, palas, khair, and other species. Thorny, savanna-like vegetation occurs in the hilly areas with less rainfall. *Subtropical vegetation* is found in higher areas like Mahabaleshwar, having heavy rainfall and milder temperatures. Mangrove vegetation occurs in marshes and estuaries along the coast, whereas the interior low plateaus of the Konkan support some patches of the wet deciduous type. Teak, bamboo, myrobalan, berries and herbs are important products from the forests.

Wild animals include tigers, leopards, bison, deer, hyenas, wild hogs, sloth bears, and varieties of monkeys and snakes. Besides the national parks of Tadoba, Chikhaldhara, and Borivali, there are several other protected parks. The Forest Department looks after the forest wealth for conservation, promotion, and careful utilization.

The people : Maharashtrians are racially heterogeneous. In the Sahyadris and in other mountain ranges, live Katkari, Warii, Gond, Korku, Govari, and other tribal communities. Amongst the non-tribal components of population, the Marathas and the Kunbis are the leading communities. Jewish and Parsi communities, retaining their identity, have mainly settled in urban areas. So have the Sindhis, after the partition of 1947. Marathi is the official language and is spoken by more than 80 per cent of the population. The other important languages are Gujarati, Telugu, Kannada, Urdu, Bengali, Sindhi, Malayalam, and English. Muslims speak Urdu, though not exclusively. Literacy has risen during the recent decades.

About one-third of the population lives in cities and towns. Mumbai's immense population (almost 10 million) reflects its overwhelming dominance in the commercial and industrial economy of the State as well as in India. It is a centre of business, finance, manufacturing, education, research, and administration. As India's best-equipped port with a natural harbour, its share in India's foreign trade is the highest. It has an international airport. Refineries based on the "Bombay High", referring to the submarine deposits of natural gas and oil off the Mumbai coast, have enhanced Mumbai's national importance.

Pune, Nagpur and Sholapur are the lesser cities and towns of Maharashtra and are the inheritance of the British Administration, though Satara, Kolhapur, Ahamadnagar, and Aurangabad have their historical importance. The *taluka* towns provide links between urban and rural Maharashtra. Rural Maharashtra: consisting of some 40,000 villages, has regional variety in form lifestyle, and economic activities, influenced by their specific geographical settings. Amongs these, economic development has been remarkable in Pravaranagar, Warananagar, and Akluj area.

Economy : Two-thirds of Maharashtra's inhabitants are farmers. Measures to ensure adequate crop production include electrification, use of hybrid seeds, intensive cultivation, and incentives offered to farmers. To counteract the constraints of insufficient and variable rainfall, several irrigation projects have been constructed and some more are underway. Millets, *jowar* (sorghum), and pulses (legumes) dominate the cropped area; rice is grown in areas where rainfall exceeds 1,016 mm; wheat is a winter crop in fields that retain moisture. Cotton, tobacco, and peanuts (groundnuts) are major crops in areas having 610 to 990 mm rainfall. An accent on *horticulture* is a current trend. Fruit crops especially grape, mango, banana, and cashewnut are popular. Irrigation has made Maharashtra the largest sugarcane and sugar-producing region of India. Sugar has promoted thriving agro-industrial areas. Considerable success has been achieved in problems related to soil erosion, and storage, transport, and marketing of agricultural products. In marine *fisheries,* Maharashtra ranks behind Kerala in production.

Maharashtra's *mineral resources* include manganese, coal, limestone, iron ore, copper, bauxite, and silica sand. Most of these are found in the districts of Bhandara, Nagpur, and Chandrapur with some deposits in the south, Konkan. Bauxite also occurs in many parts of the Sahyadri region. Production of hydrocarbon is increasing in the "Bombay High".

Maharashtra has become a well-developed and prosperous State of India through *private and public enterprise. Power production* has been one of the most important contributory factors in this respect. Maharashtra produces hydroelectricity by utilizing the waterfalls in the Western Ghats. Thermal power production dominates in the eastern regions. Super-thermal plants are located at Nagpur and Chandrapur. India's first nuclear power station is located 113 km north of Mumbai. To meet increasing demands for power, new power plants are coming up, including such projects as the power plant at Dabhol, co-promoted by the American energy company Enron, which, on completion, would be one of the largest private projects in the world.

The oldest units of *manufacturing industries* are the cotton textile mills. While some are relegated sick units, most of these form the largest modern industries in Mumbai and Nagpur.

The Mumbai-Pune complex boasts of the State's greatest concentration of *heavy industry and high technology.*

Ichalkaranji and Malegaon are well known for the production of powerloom textiles. Diversified industrial production in Mumbai, Nagpur, Akola, Amravati, and Sholapur is developing fast. Centres of traditional agro-industries include Jalgaon, Dhule, Kolhapur, Sangli, and Miraj. Fruit canning is economically important in Nagpur, Bhusawal, Mahabaleshwar, Ratnagiri, and Mumbai. Forest products include timber, bamboo, sandalwood, and tendu leaves (used to roll *bidis* or Indian cigarettes). Small-scale agro-processing units for foodgrains and other crops are virtually ubiquitous. Bakeries are gaining importance.

Transport : Foremost amongst the transport systems is the rail network centred in Mumbai. The new Konkan Railway, connecting Mumbai with the settlements in the coastal plain flanking the Arabian Sea, now strengthens it. Wardha and Nagpur are important junctions on the rail routes. Public sector investments have brought every village within 8 km of a major road. Missing links between State highways were completed and the district roads developed in inaccessible areas. Five national highways connect the State with Delhi, Allahabad, Calcutta, Hyderabad, and Bangalore. Truck transport has increased heavily on these highways and other roads. So has the passenger traffic through the State transport buses and special buses operated by private enterprise. Daily air services connect Mumbai with Pune, Aurangabad, Nagpur, and Nasik within Maharashtra and with all metropolitan cities of India. Mumbai's international airport connects the city with major cities of North America, Europe, Southeast and East Asia, Singapore, and Australia. Inland water transport plays a minor role. The Konkan seaports are receiving increasing attention.

Cultural life : Cultural life in the State is a blend of ancient Indian culture and civilization, and the influences of historical events. The evolution of Marathi language and literature expresses the cultural identity of Maharashtra. Devotion to local and regional deities, teachings of saint-poets like Jnaneshwar and Tukaram, and respect for Chhatrapati Shivaji and other political and social leaders, are characteristic of Maharashtra culture. Holy places like Kolhapur, Tuljapur, Pandharpur, Nashik, Akola, Phaltan, Ambejogai, Chiplun, and others draw devotees from far and wide. No less important are the fairs and festivals. Local and regional fairs (*Yatra*) and festivals like Ganesh-Chaturthi, Ramnavmi and others are important in the cultural life of Maharashtra. They generate local and regional circulation of people and promote social solidarity. Festivals of other religions, too, are attended in large numbers, and represent the cosmopolitan nature of cultural life. The Mahanubhava sect and Buddhism revived by Dr. Ambedkar have given new facets to the cultural life. The stage has received special attention during the 1990s in Maharashtra; leading playwrights like V. Khadilkar and Vijay Tendulkar and actors like Balgandharva raised the status of Marathi drama as an art form. The film industry in India owes its beginnings to pioneers like Dadasaheb Phalke and Baburao Painter; the Prabhat Film Company in Pune became famous for its productions like *Sant Tukaram* and *Dhyaneshwar*. Maharashtrian artistes like Nana Patekar and Madhuri Dixit have been very successful in the competitive field of Hindi cinema.

Music in Maharashtra like Marathi literature, has an ancient tradition. It became allied with Hindustani music in about the fourteenth century. In recent times, Pandit Paluskar and Pandit Bhatkhande gave a new orientation to Indian classical music. No less important was the contribution of instrumentalists like Vilayat Hussain, Allah Rakha, and others. Today, vocalists like Pandit Bhimsen Joshi and Lata Mangeshkar represent the shining role of music in the cultural life of Maharashtra.

Art in Maharashtra has an ancient tradition, as can be seen in the Ajanta and Ellora caves and in the designs in textiles, gold and silver ornaments, wooden toys, leather goods and pottery. The Sir J.J. School of Art established in 1833, was the first modern institute of art education. Now most of the cities and larger towns in Maharashtra have art institutions. Classical dance forms have attracted talent, and schools for instructions in these are flourishing in the larger cities like Pune. Folk arts like *lavani* (romantic song), *powada* (heroic ballad) and *tamasha* containing music, drama, and dance have seen a revival. The Directorate of Arts and Films and the State Board of Literature and Culture evince the keen interest of the State government. Maharashtrian cultural influence extends beyond Maharashtra, in the capitals of the former Maratha Empire like Baroda (now Vadodara) and Gwalior and in many other cities where Maharashtra mandals take an active part.

Area, Population and Headquarters of Districts

S.No.	*District*	*Area (sq km)*	*Population (1991 Census)*	*Headquarters*
1.	Ahmednagar	17,048	33,72,935	Ahmednagar
2.	Akola	5,429	13,51,959	Akola
3.	Amravati	12,210	22,00,057	Amravati
4.	Aurangabad	10,107	22,13,779	Aurangabad
5.	Bhandara	3,895	10,04,662	Bhandara
6.	Beed	10,693	18,22,072	Beed
7.	Mumbai City	69	31,74,889	Mumbai City
8.	Mumbai (Sub.)	534	67,51,002	Mumbai (Sub.)
9.	Buldhana	9,661	18,86,299	Buldhana
10.	Chandrapur	11,443	17,71,994	Chandrapur
11.	Dhule	8,063	14,73,170	Dhule
12.	Gadchiroli	14,412	7,87,010	Gadchiroli
13.	Jalgaon	11,765	31,87,634	Jalgaon
14.	Jalna	7,718	13,64,425	Jalna

S.No.	District	Area (sq km)	Population (1991 Census)	Headquarters
15.	Kolhapur	7,685	29,89,507	Kolhapur
16.	Latur	7,157	16,76,641	Latur
17.	Nagpur	9,892	32,87,139	Nagpur
18.	Nanded	10,528	23,30,374	Nanded
19.	Nashik	15,530	38,51,352	Nashik
20.	Osmanabad	7,569	12,76,327	Osmanabad
21.	Parbhani	6,517	13,05,492	Parbhani
22.	Pune	15,643	55,32,532	Pune
23.	Raigad	7,152	18,24,816	Alibag
24.	Ratnagiri	8,208	15,44,057	Ratnagiri
25.	Sangli	8,572	22,09,488	Sangli
26.	Satara	10,480	24,51,372	Satara
27.	Sindhudurg	5,207	8,32,152	Oras
28.	Solapur	14,895	32,31,057	Solapur
29.	Thane	9,558	52,49,176	Thane
30.	Wardha	6,309	10,67,357	Wardha
31.	Yavatmal	9,892	32,87,139	Yavatmal
32.	Nandurbar	5,034	10,62,545	Nandurbar
33.	Washim	5,134	8,62,312	Washim
34.	Gondia	5,425	11,02,967	Gondia
35.	Hingoli	4,524	8,09,278	Hingoli

Manipur—This state of India is located in the north-eastern part of the country. It has an area of 22,327 sq km, making it one of the smaller States of India. It is bordered by the States of Nagaland to the north, Assam to the west, and Mizoram to the southwest, and by Myanmar (Burma) to the south and east. The capital is Imphal. The name Manipur means "Land of Gems". Like other northeastern States, it is largely isolated from the rest of India. Its economy centres on agriculture and forestry, and there is lively activity in trade and cottage industries.

History : Due to its geography, Manipur has been relatively independent of its neighbouring areas. Although ancient hoes of ground stone reportedly have been found in the region, the earliest recorded history goes back only to AD 900. The beginning of Manipur's more recent history dates from 1762, when Raja Jai Singh concluded a treaty with the British to repel an invasion from Myanmar. Further communication was minimal until 1824, when the British were again requested to expel the intruders from Myanmar. Disputed successions were a continual source of political turmoil until Chura Chand, a five-year-old member of the ruling family, was nominated raja in 1891. For the next eight years the administration was conducted under British supervision; slavery and forced labour were abolished, and roads were constructed.

This territory was associated with India through the Treaty of Yandaloo at the end of Indo-Burmese War in 1826. The British sovereignty was recognized in 1891. In 1907 the government was assumed by the *raja* and the *durbar*, or council, whose vice-president was a member of the Indian Civil Service. Subsequently, the administration was transferred to the raja, and the vice-president of the *durbar* became its president. After an uprising of the Kuki hill tribes in 1917, a new system of government was adopted; the region was divided into three subdivisions, each headed by an officer from the neighbouring government of Assam.

With the accession of Manipur to India in 1947, the political agency exercised by Assam was abolished. Two years later, Manipur became a Union Territory governed by a chief commissioner and an elected territorial council. In 1969 the office of chief commissioner was replaced by that of lieutenant governor, whose status was changed to governor when Manipur became a constituent State of the Indian Union on July 21, 1972. Population (1991) State Total 1,837,149; Rural 1,331,504; Urban 505,645.

Physiography : The State has *two major physiographic regions,* the Manipur River valley and a large surrounding tract of mountainous country. The valley, some 1,787 sq km, runs north-south and lies at an elevation of 792 m. Its main physical feature is the Logtak Lake, covering about 104 sq km, which is the source of the Manipur River. It is also the largest freshwater lake in northeastern India. The river flows southwards through the valley into Myanmar, where it joins the Myittha River, a tributary of the Chindwin.

The *hill ranges*, connected by spurs and ridges, run generally north-south. These ranges include the Naga Hills to the north, the East Manipur hills along the eastern Myanmar border, the Mizo and Chin hills to the south, and the West Manipur hills to the west. Average elevations vary between 1,524 and 1829 m, although the hills in the north rise to more than 2,896 m. The ridges are separated by deep valleys forming curves and coils. The slope varies from 15 to 30 per cent. Further, nearly 1,800 sq km hill areas have slopes more than 30 per cent.

In the west the Surma River, known as the Barak River in Manipur, has cut a narrow, steep-sided valley through the West Manipur hills as it flows to join the Meghna River in Bangladesh. This river rises from the northeastern peaks (2,700 m) of Manipur, about 5 km east of village Ujeme. Further down, this river forms the interstate boundary with Nagaland. Its drainage basin forms a narrow strip stretching northeast to southwest covering an area of 3,865 sq km of Manipur State.

The climate is temperate in the valley and cold in the hills. Rainfall is abundant, with about 1,650 mm of precipitation occurring annually. The hills are densely covered with mixed forests containing stands of bamboo and teak. Other trees include oak, magnolia, and chinquapin. The Luzon pine grows in the Naga hills. Among the State's notable plants are rhododendrons, primroses, and blue poppies. Animal life includes the Asiatic elephant, tiger, leopard, and wild buffalo. The rhinoceros is hunted for its horn, which, when ground, is valued as an aphrodisiac. The brow-antlered deer is in danger of extinction. Gaur are the largest wild bison in the world; the mithan (or gayal), the domesticated form, is widely distributed in the State.

The people : About two-thirds of the people are the Meithei, who occupy the Manipur valley and are largely Hindus. Meithei women conduct most of the trade in the valley and enjoy high social status. Hindus constitute about 60 per cent of the population followed by Christians (29.68) and Muslims (6.99). The majority of Hindus are Vaishnavites belonging to the Meithei tribe.

Nearly 34 per cent of the population belongs to scheduled tribes. Indigenous hill tribes, such as the Naga in the north and the Kuki in the south, make up the rest of the population. Divided into numerous clans and sections, the people of these tribes speak languages of the Tibeto-Burman family and practise traditional animist religions. Some of the Naga have been converted to Christianity. More than 60 per cent of the population speaks Manipuri, which, along with English, is the official language of the State.

The economy : Agriculture and forestry are the main sources of income. Rice (grown in 72 per cent of the area) is the major crop, and the rich soil also supports maize (1.79 per cent), sugarcane, mustard, tobacco, fruit orchards, vegetables (potato: 1.7 per cent), and pulses (such as peas and beans). Terracing is common in the hills, where the tribes plough the ground with hand hoes. Among some of the hill tribes, domestic animals are kept only for meat and are not milked or used for hauling. Irrigation is provided by canals. The Naga are known .to use intoxicants to catch fish. Annual fish catch is about 7,500 tonnes valued at Rs. 500,000. The recorded forest area is 15,154 sq km while the actual cover is 17,418 sq km, which is 78 per cent of the area. Teak and bamboo are major forest products.

Manufacturing is limited to several well-established cottage industries. The designed cloth produced on handlooms is in demand throughout India and abroad. Other industries include sericulture, manufacture of bamboo and cane articles, soap making, carpentry, and tanning. An industrial complex, including an electronics plant, has been established at Imphal. Manipur remains somewhat isolated from the rest of India, and communications within the State are poor. The total road length is 5,344 km while the inter-village road length is 2,398 km. A national highway passes through the State from Tamu on the Myanmar border in the south via Imphal to Dimapur (in Nagaland) in the north; this highway also connects Imphal with the Northeast Frontier Railway near Dimapur, There are air links from Imphal to Guwahati and Silchar in Assam and to Calcutta in West Bengal. There are 623 post offices, two telegraph offices, and 41 banks.

The People: The population of the State is 1.84 million and overall density is 82 persons per sq km. The density varies considerably ranging from 579 and 572 in Imphal and Thoubal to about 20 in Tamenglong and Chandel. The growth rate of population is 2.57 per cent per year while decadal growth (1981-1991) is 29.3 per cent. Workers constitute 42.81 per cent of the population. There are 2,182 villages and 31 towns contributing to 27.52 per cent, of the urban population. About 60 per cent of the population is literate; the State has a university at Imphal and more than 30 colleges and 3,761 schools. There are 89 hospitals and primary health centres. Major health problems include tuberculosis, leprosy, venereal disease, and filariasis. The State continues to have an inadequate number of health facilities.

Cultural life : Polo and hockey are popular sports. Manipur has given birth to an indigenous form of classical dance known as manipuri. Unlike in other Indian dance forms, hand movements are used decoratively rather than as pantomime, bells are not accentuated, and both men and women perform communally. The dance dramas, interpreted by a narrator, are a part of religious life. Themes are generally taken from the life of Krishna, the pastoral god of Hinduism. Long an isolated art form, Manipuri was introduced to the rest of India by the poet Rabindranath Tagore in 1917.

Rasa, Sankirtana dance, and Thang-ta (drum beating) are other important parts of their cultural life. Further, Manipuris are great warriors and practise their skills of wrestling, sword fighting, and martial arts. They also play polo.

There are several places of *tourist interest* in the State. Khonghampat Orchidarium, located at 7 km from Imphal on the National Highway 39 has over 110 species of orchids. Mao, at 1,757 m height and 106 km away from the State capital is a hill station with enchanting scenic beauty. It is mid-way between Imphal and Dimapur. Moreh is located 110 km from Imphal and close to the Myanmar border. It is a commercial town. Bishnupur is only 27 km from Imphal and has an ancient Vishnu temple. Further, Moirang is the place where Netaji Subhas Chandra Bose hoisted the Indian tricolour flag for the first time on Indian soil. It is about 45 km south of Imphal and has an Indian National Army memorial hall and war museum. It is also famous for early Manipuri folk culture. Nearby, Loktak Lake has a superb view and has a deer park in its vicinity. Tourists also visit Tamenglong which is 165 km away for a variety of attractions including waterfalls and exotic orchids.

Kaina (29 km) is a Hindu pilgrimage centre. The Keibul Lamjao National Park is the only floating sanctuary of its kind in the country. Other places of interest include the Old Palace, Shri Govindji temple and Vaishnavite centre, war cemeteries, State museum near polo ground, Langthaband palace, and Khwairamband bazar (Nupi Keithel or Ima Market) — women's market in Imphal. The tourist flow is around 91,000 per year.

Area, Population and Headquarters of Districts

S.No.	District	Area (sq km)	Population	Headquarters
1.	Bishnupur	496	2,05,907	Bishnupur
2.	Chandel	3,313	1,22,714	Chandel
3.	Churachandpur	4,570	2,28,707	Churachandpur
4.	Imphal West	1,228[1]	4,39,532	Lamphel
5.	Senapati	3,271	3,79,780	Senapati
6.	Imphal East	—	3,93,214	Porompat
7.	Tamenglong	4,391	1,11,493	Tamenglong
8.	Thoubal	514	3,66,341	Thoubal
9.	Ukhrul	4,544	1,40,946	Ukhrul

[1] Area of Imphal-East and Imphal-West.

Meghalaya—A State of India, it is located in the north-eastern part of the country. It is bounded on the south and southwest by Bangladesh and on all other sides by the State of Assam. The State occupies an area of 22,429 sq km. The capital is the hill town of Shillong. Meghalaya — literally "Abode (*alaya*) of the Clouds (*megha*)" — occupies a mountainous plateau of great scenic beauty. This name was coined by the great Indian geographer, S.P. Chatierjee. It became a State in 1972.

History : Apart from accounts of the more important Khasi kingdoms in the chronicles; of the neighbouring Ahom and Kachari, little is known of Meghalaya prior to the British period. In the early nineteenth century, however, the British desire to build a road through the region in order to link Bengal and Assam led to a treaty (1827) with the ruler (*syiem*) of the Khasi principality of Nonkhlaw. Opponents of the treaty persuaded the *syiem* to repudiate it in 1829, and a subsequent attack on the British led inevitably to British military operations against the Khasi. By the mid-1830s, most of the local rulers had submitted to the British. For the next century, the British exercised political control over the area, then known as the Garrows and Cossiya (Khasi) States, but the tribes, left to themselves, were able to preserve their traditional way of life in seclusion.

In 1947 the rulers of the region acceded to the newly independent country of India. India's first prime minister, Jawaharlal Nehru, evolved a policy to preserve and protect the way of life of the tribal peoples. Along with other tribal areas, the region was given special protection in the Indian Constitution, and, though included within the State of Assam, it retained a great deal of autonomy.

Even this did not prove enough, however, and when Assamese became the State's official language in 1960, agitation for autonomy and self-rule gathered strength. Unlike in many other hill regions in northeastern India, this movement was largely peaceful and constitutional. Meghalaya was created as an autonomous State within Assam in 1970 and achieved full Statehood on January 21, 1972.

Physiography : Meghalaya is an uplannd area formed by a block detached from the Deccan Plateau by Rajmahal Gap. The rocks and geological structure resemble the Chota Nagpur region of Bihar and Bengal. The rocks consists of Pre-cambrian archaean gneisses and granite, proterozdic Shillong group, lower Gondwana, Sylhet traps and crustaceous-tertiary sedimentary deposits. Its summits vary in elevation from 1,220 to 1,830 m. The Garo Hills in the west rise abruptly from the Brahmaputra valley to about 305 m and then merge with the Khasi

Hills and Jaintia Hills, adjacent highland systems that form a single massif of tablelands separated by a series of eastward-trending ridges. The southern face of the plateau, overlooking the Bangladesh lowlands, is particularly steep. Many rivers and streams flow out of the plateau, creating deep, narrow, steep-sided valleys; the most important is the Umiam-Barapani, which is the major source of hydroelectric power for Assam and Meghalaya.

Climate : One of the world's wettest regions is found in the State — Cherrapunji, with an average of 11,430 mm of annual rainfall over a 74-year period, has the highest-ever rainfall recorded in Asia and the second highest in the world, (Rainfall at Cherrapunji may be exceeded, however, by that at Mawsynram, also in Meghalaya, where an average of 17,780 mm has been claimed.) The climate of Meghalaya is generally mild. In August the mean temperature at Shillong (in the Khasi hills) is 21 °C; it falls to 9.5 °C in January. Annual rainfall in Shillong, only 80 km from Cherrapunji, is about 2,337 mm.

Natural Vegetation : The State is rich in forests (42 per cent of geographical area), and pines, sal, and bamboo are plentiful. Other species include oak, birch, beech, and magnolia. The State abounds in elephants, tigers, leopards, deer, wild pigs, gaur (wild bison), mithan or gayal (the domesticated form of the gaur), wolves, anteaters, monkeys, apes, squirrels, snakes, hares, and sambar deer. Birds in Meghalaya include peacocks, partridges, pigeons, hornbills, jungle fowls, mynahs, and parrots.

People : The plateau region has hilly and rugged topography. The physical and location factors have resulted in the isolation of the tribal communities. Earlier these communities had a very limited interaction with the population in the nearby Brahmaputra and Surma plains. Nearly 86 per cent of the population consists of scheduled tribes. Most of the inhabitants of Meghalaya are Tibeto-Burman (Garo) or Mon-Khmer (Khasi) in origin, and their languages and dialects belong to these groups. The Khasi are the only people in India speaking a Mon-Khmer language, more commonly found in Southeast Asia. Khasi and Garo are the main languages, and, along with Jaintia and English, are the State's official languages; others include Pnar-Synteng, Nepali, and Haijong, as well as the plains' languages of Bengali, Assamese, and Hindi.

Changes in the religious community were brought about by the spread of Christianity and due to the migration of Hindus and Muslims to this State. Christianity, Hinduism, and animistic forms of Hinduism are the major religions in the area. There is also a small minority of Muslims and even smaller groups of Buddhists and Sikhs.

The population is predominantly rural, and few towns exist in the State. Shillong is the largest town; other urban centres, listed in descending order of population, include Tura, Mawlai, Nongthymmai, and Jowai. About 43.4 per cent villages are electrified. The decadal (1981-91) growth rate is 32.86 per cent.

Economy : It is evident that the transition from a nomadic to a settled way of life was due to an increase in the productivity of labour. Abundant land, its communal ownership, and the unilineal system of inheritance contributed to preserving the tribal nature of the economy. Meghalaya has abundant untapped natural resources, including coal, limestone, kaolin, feldspar, quartz, mica, gypsum, bauxite, and other minerals. Its sillimanite deposits (a source of high-grade ceramic clay) are reputedly the best in the world and account for almost all of India's sillimanite output. Meghalaya has no heavy industries; small-scale industries include the manufacture of cement and plywood, and beverage factories, in addition to a newly established electronics plant. In total, there are only 56 registered factories and 1,941 small-scale industrial units. In 1993, the State produced 2,543,000 tonnes of coal and 209,000 tonnes of limestone. The installed capacity of power projects is only about 194 MW. An indication of de-industrialization is also becoming evident.

Agriculture is the dominant economic activity though the net sown area is less than 9 per cent. Land is owned in common, but *jhum* cultivation (burning of trees and planting the cleared areas in a cyclical operation) has left the people extremely poor and has eroded the soil. The main crops are rice, millet, maize, potatoes, pepper, chillies, cotton, ginger, mesta, jute, betel nuts, tapioca, fruits (including pineapple, banana, oranges, and mangoes), and vegetables.

Internal communications are poor, and many areas remain isolated. The road length in the State is only 6,022 km. There are no railways in Meghalaya. A national highway runs through the State from Guwahati (Assam) in the north to Karimganj (Assam) in the south. Shillong is served by Vayudoot (the domestic airline handling short-haul, low-capacity routes). There are only 36 telephone exchanges.

Social life : The State is one of the most underdeveloped in India. Only about half (49.1 per cent) of the people are literate. Literacy in urban areas is about 82 per cent. There are 5,517 educational institutions in the State. North-Eastern Hill University, at Shillong, is the State's only university. The partition of India in 1947 disrupted the tribal populations; some tribes found themselves divided by the new international frontier, resulting in tribal migrations from East Pakistan (now Bangladesh) to India.

Cultural life : The area is rich in tribal culture and folklore. Drinking and dancing to the accompaniment of music from buffalo-horn *singas*, bamboo flutes, and drums are integral parts of religious ceremonies and social functions. Marriages are exogamous. The advent of Christianity in the mid-nineteenth century, along with its strict morality, has disrupted many of the tribal and communal institutions. A curious custom among the Garo is that, after marriage, the youngest son-in-law comes to live in his wife's parents' house and becomes his father-in-laws *nokrom*, or clan representative in the mother-in-law's family. If the father-in-law dies, the *nokrom* marries (and the marriage has to be consummated) the widowed mother-in-law, thus becoming the husband of both mother and daughter. The custom is now dying out. The Khasi formerly practised human sacrifice.

There are several caves, peaks, parks, lake resorts, panoramic views, hot springs, and water falls in the State. The tourist spots are Shillong, Umiam Cherrapunji, Mawsynram, Jakream, Mairang, Jowai, Narriang, Thadlashein Tura, Siju, and Balpakram National Park. In 1993, about 157,000 tourists visited the State.

Area, Population and Headquarters of Districts

S.No.	District	Area (sq km)	Population	Headquarters
1.	East Garo Hills	2,603	2,47,555	Williamnagar
2.	East Khasi Hills	2,748	6,60,994	Shillong
3.	Jaintia Hills	3,819	2,95,692	Jowai
4.	West Garo Hills	3,714	5,15,813	Tura
5.	West Khasi Hills	5,247	2,94,115	Nongstoin
6.	Ri-Bhoi	2,448	1,92,795	Nongpoh
7.	South Garo Hills	1,850	99,105	Baghmara

Mizoram—This State of India is located in the northeastern part of the country and has an area of 21,081 sq. km. It is bounded by Myanmar (Burma) to the east and south and Bangladesh to the west and by the States of Tripura to the northwest, Assam to the north, and Manipur to the northeast. The capital is Aizawl. Mizoram ("Land of the Mizos") became a State in 1987. Formerly the Lushai Hills district of Assam, it was renamed the Mizo Hills district in 1954. Between 1972 and 1987 it was a centrally administered Union Territory under the name of Mizoram. By the 53rd amendment of the Constitution it became a State.

History : Little is known of Mizoram's early history. Between 1750 and 1850 the Mizo (formerly called Lushai) tribes migrated from the nearby Chin Hills and subjugated the indigenous population; these similar tribes were assimilated into their own society. The Mizo developed an autocratic political system based on some 300 hereditary chieftainships.

The tribes of Mizoram remained unaffected by foreign political influence until the British annexed Assam in 1826 under the Treaty of Yandabo. During the following decades, Mizo raids into British territory led to occasional punitive expeditions by the British. Although not formally annexed until the early 1890s, the region had come under British control two decades earlier.

Initially administered as the North Lushai Hills (in the province of Assam) and South Lushai Hills (within the Bengal Presidency), the region was united as the Lushai Hills district of Assam in 1898. The district had come under the government's Inner Line Regulations in 1873, which prohibited the movement of people from the plains into the hills. In 1935 the Lushai Hills was declared an "excluded area" — the provincial legislature was stripped of its jurisdiction over the area, and responsibility for the district's administration was placed directly in the hands of the governor of Assam.

Following India's independence in 1947, the district continued as part of Assam. Increasing discontent among the Mizo, however, led to a declaration of independence by the Mizo National Front in 1966. The ensuing armed rebellion compelled India's Union (central) government to assume Mizoram's administration and to make it a Union Territory in 1972. The insurgency continued until the signing of the Mizoram Peace Accord in 1986. As a result of this accord, Mizoram was granted Statehood in 1987, but other terms of the agreement were not implemented, resulting in renewed unrest among the Mizo. Population (1991) State Total 689,756; Rural 371,810; Urban 317,946.

Land and climate : Geologically the Mizo Hills form a part of the Arakan arc, a series of compact parallel ridges with a north-south axis formed of tertiary sandstone, limestone, and shales (rocks between 1.6 and 66.4 million years old). The ridges, separated by narrow river valleys, rise to 2,157 m. In the south, the Kaladan River and its tributaries flow southwards into Myanmar, while the Dhaleswari (Tiawng) and Sonai (Tuirail) rivers flow north into Assam. Aizawl is at 1,132 m above the mean sea level.

The *climate* in Mizoram is moderate. The annual average temperature at Aizawl is 20 °C. Rainfall occurs mainly during the southwest monsoon (May to September), and the total annual rainfall in some areas is as high as 2,500 mm.

The hills are covered with thick *evergreen forest* containing valuable timber trees, such as *champak*, ironwood, and *gurjun*. The actual forest cover is 18,775 sq km, which is about 89 per cent of the geographical area. The forest provides habitat for many animals, including elephant, tiger, bear, deer, and wild buffalo.

People : Mizoram's population is composed of numerous groups, loosely called Mizo, a local term meaning "highlanders". Tribes in the area, many of whom formerly practised headhunting, include the Kuki, Pawi, Lakher, and Chakma. They are classified among the Tibeto-Burman peoples and speak a number of Tibeto-Burman dialects; some tribes are so isolated that their dialects are unintelligible to groups living in neighbouring valleys. The density of population is 33 per sq km. The density decreases from north to south that is due to a southward increase in the humidity and temperature resulting in general unsuitable conditions for habitation. The density also reduces from west to east. There are 22 towns and 699 inhabited villages out of which 663 are electrified. About 95 per cent of the population belongs to scheduled tribes. Mizo and English are the principal and official languages; having no script of its own, Mizo uses the Roman script. Literacy is among the highest in India (82.27 per cent). As a result of conversions beginning as early as the 1890s (though most occurring in the 1920s and 1930s), about 85.57 per cent of the population is now Christian; the great majority are Protestants. Small minorities of Hindus (5 per cent) and Buddhists (7.83 per cent) also are found in the State. Decadal growth rate during 1981-1991 was 39.70 per cent, which has recorded a reduction from the last decade (48.55 during 1971-1981). The sex ratio is 921 females per 1,000 males.

Economy : *Agriculture* is the dominant economic activity. Both terraced cultivation and *jhum* tillage (in which tracts are cleared by burning and sown with mixed crops) are practised. Rice, maize, oilseeds, cotton, and vegetables are the main crops. People are also engaged in sericulture and produce mulberry, *eri*, muga, and tussar silks. The greater number of people farming has reduced the traditional eight-year *jhum* cycle, and there has been an accompanying decline in yields.

There are no major *industries* in the State. Small-scale industries indude sericulture, handloom and handicrafts industries, sawmills and furniture workshops, oil refining, grain milling, and ginger processing. Out of 3,087 small-scale industries in the State, 287 are in Aizawl district.

The State's poor *transport and communications* are a major obstacle to economic growth. Although a road system is being developed, a single road links the towns of Aizawl and Lunglei in Mizoram to Silchar in Assam and Shillong in Meghalaya. The stretch of roads north-south is 277 km and east-west is 121 km. There are no railways. Vayudoot, India's low-capacity and short-haul domestic airline, provides service from Aizawl to Silchar and to Calcutta in West Bengal.

Cultural life : Music and dance are important elements in Mizo cultural life. Celebrations include the Christian holidays, as well as local agricultural festivals, such as Pawlkut and Mimkut. Aizawl has a campus of North-Eastern Hill University.

Area, Population and Headquarters of Districts

S.No.	District	Area (sq km)	Population	Headquarters
1.	Aizawl	3,576.31	3,39,812	Aizawl
2.	Lunglei	4,538.00	1,37,155	Lunglei
3.	Chhimtuipui	1,399.90	60,823	Saiha
4.	Lawngtlai	2,557.10	73,050	Lawngtlai
5.	Champhai	3,185.85	1,01,389	Champhai
6.	Kolasib	1282.51	60,977	Kolasib
7.	Mamit	3,025.75	62,313	Mamit
8.	Serchhip	1,421.60	55,539	Serchhip

N

Nagaland—The State of India lies in the hills and mountains of the northeastern part of the country. One of the smallest States of India, it has a total area of just 16,579 sq km. It is bordered by the States of Manipur on the south, Assam on the west and northwest, and Arunachal Pradesh on the northeast. Myanmar (Burma) lies to the east. The capital is Kohima.

History : Nagaland has no early written history, although mediaeval chronicles of the neighbouring Ahom kingdom of Assam tell of the Naga tribes, their economy, and their customs. The 1816 Myanmar invasion of Assam led to oppressive Myanmar rule from 1819 until the establishment of British rule over Assam in 1826. The advent of British administration, which by 1892 encompassed the whole of Naga territory (except the rugged Tuensang area in the northeast), ended the practices of headhunting and intervillage raids and brought relative peace to the region.

After India became independent in 1947, the Naga territory initially remained a part of Assam. A strong nationalist movement, however, began seeking a political union of the Naga tribes, and extremists demanded outright secession from the Indian Union. This movement led to a number of violent incidents, and in 1955 the Indian army was called in to restore order. In 1957, after an agreement was reached between Naga leaders and the Indian government, the Naga Hills district of Assam and the Tuensang frontier division to the northeast were brought together under a single unit directly administered by the Indian government. Despite the agreement, unrest continued in the form of noncooperation with the Indian government, nonpayment of taxes, sabotage, and attacks on the army. A further accord reached at the Naga People's Convention of July 1960 resolved that Nagaland should become a constituent State of the Indian Union. Nagaland achieved Statehood in 1963, and a democratically-elected government took office in 1964.

Rebel activity continued, however, increasingly assuming the form of banditry and often motivated more by tribal rivalry and personal vendetta than by political aspiration. Ceasefires and negotiations did little to stop the insurgency, and in March 1975 direct presidential rule was imposed on the State. Although leaders of the underground agreed in November 1975 to lay down their arms and accept the Indian Constitution, a small group of hardcore extremists continued to agitate for Naga independence.

Land and Climate : Nearly all of Nagaland is *mountainous*. In the north, the Naga Hills rise abruptly from the Brahmaputra valley to about 610 m and then increase in elevation towards the southeast to more than 1,800 m. The mountains merge with the Patkai Range along the Myanmar border, reaching a maximum height of 3,826 m at Mount Saramati. The region is deeply dissected by rivers the Doyang and Dikhu in the north, the Barak in the southwest, and the tributaries of the Chindwin River (in Myanmar) in the southeast.

Nagaland has a monsoon *climate*. Annual rainfall averages between 1,800 and 2,500 mm and is concentrated in the months of the south-west monsoon (May to September). Average temperatures decrease with greater elevation; in summer, temperatures range from 21°C to 40 °C, while in winter, they rarely drop below 4 °C, but frost is common over higher elevations. Humidity is generally high.

Pland and Animal Life : The recorded forest area is 8,629 sq km while the actual forest cover is 14,221 sq km which is 85.8 per cent of the geographical area. Below 1,219 m are tropical and subtropical evergreen forests, containing palms, rattan, and bamboo, as well as valuable timber species such as mahogany. Coniferous forests are found at higher elevations. Where clearing for *jhum* (slash-and-burn cultivation) has taken place, secondary growth of high grass, reeds, and scrub jungle has sprung up. Wildlife sanctuaries cover an area of 222 sq km.

Rhinoceros, elephants, tigers, leopards, bears, several kinds of monkey, sambar deer, buffalo, and wild oxen live in the lower hills. Porcupines, pangolins (scaly anteaters), wild dogs, foxes, civet cats, and mongooses are also fouhd in the State. The long tail feathers of the great Indian hornbill are treasured for use in traditional ceremonial dress.

People : The Naga, classified among the Indo-Asiaric peoples, form more than 20 tribes, as well as numerous subtribes, each having a specific geographic distribution. Though sharing many cultural traits, these tribes have maintained a high degree of isolation and lack cohesion as a single people. The Konyak are the largest tribe, followed by the Ao, Tangkhul, Sema, and Angami. Other tribes include the Lotha, Sangtam, Phom, Chang, Khiemnungam, Yimchungre, Zeliangs, Chakhesang (Chokri), and Rengma.

The Naga tribes lack a common language; there are about 60 spoken dialects, all belonging to the Sino-Tibetan language family. In some areas dialects vary even from village to village. Inter-tribal conversation generally is carried on through broken Assamese, and many Naga speak Hindi and English. English is the official language of the State.

The traditional Naga religion is animistic, though conceptions of a Supreme Creator and an afterlife exist. Nature is seen to be alive with invisible forces, minor deities, and spirits with which priests and medicine men mediate. In the nineteenth century, with the advent of British rule, Christianity was introduced and Baptist missionaries became especially active in the region. As a result the population now is predominantly Christian. In 1991, nearly 80 per cent of the people were Christian, followed by Hindus and Muslims. There are remains of the Hindu kingdom of the Cacharis (now in south Assam) at Dimapur that was destroyed by the Ahom in the sixteenth century. About, 87.7 per cent of the population belong to scheduled tribes.

In 1991 the population of the State was over I million out of which nearly 17 per cent live in urban areas. The rest of the population resides in mostly small and isolated villages. Nagaland is basically a rural State. Built on the most prominent points along the ridges of the hills, these villages were once stockaded, with massive wooden gates approached by narrow, sunken paths. The villages are usually divided into *khels*, or quarters, each with its own headmen and administration. The annual rate of growth of population is 4.45 per cent while the decadal growth is high (56 per cent). The sex ratio is 886 females per 1,000 males. About 42 per cent of the population are workers. Dimapur, Kohima, Mokokchung, and Tuensang are the only urban centres with more than 20,000 people. The density is 73 persons per sq km.

Economy : Agriculture employs about 90 per cent of the population. Rice (autumn rice: 70,100 ha; winter rice: 58,900 ha), maize (24,900 ha), small millets (14,000 ha), pulses (legumes such as peas and beans), oilseeds (11,850 ha), fibres, sugar cane, potato, and tobacco arc the principal crops. Nagaland, however, still has to depend on imports of food from neighbouring States. The total area under crops is 330,450 ha while 54,400 ha is irrigated. The widespread practice of *jhum* has led to soil erosion and loss of soil fertility. Only the Angami and Chakhesang of the southern district of Kohima use terracing and irrigation techniques. Traditional implements include the light hoe, the *dao* (a multipurpose heavy knife), and the sickle; except in the plains, the plough is not used. Forestry is also a primary source of income and employment.

Chromium, nickel, cobalt, iron ore, and limestone are found in Nagaland, but only low-grade coal deposits are mined at present. Boreholes drilled in the western district of Wokha have yielded oil, and seepages in the Dikhu valley, near Assam, suggest the presence of exploitable oil reserves.

Until the early 1970s, only cottage *industries* such as weaving, woodwork, basketry, and pottery existed in the State. Lack of raw materials, financial resources, and power, as well as poor transport and communications, have hindered industrial growth. Dimapur, the State's leading industrial centre, now has a sugar mill and distillery, a brick factory, and a television assembly plant. Other industries in the State include a *khandsari* (molasses) mill, rice mills, fruit-canning plants, a paper and pulp factory, a plywood factory, and cabinet and furniture factories. At present there are only three industrial estates. There are 23 sericulture farms as well.

Power generation depends mainly on diesel plants, though hydroelectric output has increased. More than 50 per cent of Nagaland's power is generated in Assam. Nagaland depends mostly on roads for transportation. A national highway runs from Dimapur to Kohima and then on to Imphal in Manipur. Another main road links Mokokchung with Amguri in Assam. A short stretch of the Northeast Frontier Railway passing through Dimapur from Assam is the only rail link with the rest of India. Air service is available from Dimapur to Guwahati in Assam and to Calcutta in West Bengal. There is 2,356 km of surfaced road while other roads cover a length of 5,591 km. The places of tourist interest include the World War II cemetery. State museum, and the zoo at Kohima and Dimapur, the old capital of Cacharis. The annual flow of tourists is about 16,000.

Cultural life : Tribal organization varies from the autocratic *angs* (chiefs) of the Konyak and hereditary chieftainships of the Sema and Chang to the democratic structures of the Angami, Ao, Lotha, and Rengma. A prominent village institution is the *morung* (a communal house or dormitory for young, unmarried men), where skulls and other trophies of war were formerly hung. The pillars are still carved with striking representations of tigers, hornbills, and human and other figures. Women hold a relatively high and honourable position in Naga society. They work in the fields on equal terms with men and have considerable influence in the tribal councils. A central feature of Naga life is the Feast of Merit, a series of ceremonies culminating with the sacrifice of a *mithan* (gayal, *Bos* frontalis). Each tribe has its *gennas*, or festivals, and Naga dance, music, song, and folklore all express an exuberant concern for life.

Area, Population and Headquarters of Districts

S.No.	*District*	*Area (sq km)*	*Population (1991 Census)*	*Headquarters*
1.	Kohima	4,041	3,87,581	Kohima
2.	Mokokchung	1,615	1,58,374	Mokokchung
3.	Mon	1,786	1,49,699	Mon
4.	Phek	2,026	1,02,156	Phek
5.	Tuensang	4,228	2,32,906	Tuensang
6.	Wokha	1,628	82,612	Wokha
7.	Zunheboto	1,255	97,218	Zunheboto
8.	Dimapur	-	-	Dimapur

Orissa–This state of India is located in the northeastern part of the country. It is bounded by the Bay of Bengal in the east and by the States of West Bengal in the northeast, Bihar in the north, Madhya Pradesh in the west, and Andhra Pradesh in the south. Its area is 155,707 sq km. Before India became independent in 1947, Cuttack was Orissa's capital.

The present capital, Bhubaneshwar, was built subsequently in the vicinity of its historic temples.

History : In ancient and mediaeval times, the land \corresponding roughly with modern Orissa passed under the names of Utkala, Kalinga, and Odra Desa, although its boundaries were sometimes much larger. These names were originally associated with peoples. The Okkala or Utkala, the Kalinga, and the Odra or Oddaka were mentioned in literature as tribes. Ancient Greeks knew the latter two as Kalingai and Oretes, Eventually the names became identified with territories. For centuries before and after the birth of Christ, Kalinga was a formidable political power, extending from the Ganga River to the Godavari. Approximately between the eleventh and sixteenth centuries the name fell into disuse; instead, the name Odra Desa was gradually transformed into Uddisa, Udisa, or Odisa, which in English became Orissa. The language of Odisa came to be known as Oriya or Oria.

At the dawn of Indian history, Kalinga was already famous. Buddhist sources refer to the rule of King Brahmadatta in Kalinga at the time of the Buddha's death. In the fourth century BC the first Indian empire builder, Mahapadma Nanda, conquered Kalinga, but the Nanda rule was short-lived. In 260 BC the Maurya emperor Ashoka invaded Kalinga and fought one of the greatest wars of ancient history. He then renounced war, became a Buddhist, and preached peace and nonviolence in and outside India. In the first century BC the Kalinga emperor Kharavela conquered vast territories that collectively came to be called the Kalinga Empire.

Kalinga became a maritime power beginning in the first century AD, and its overseas activities culminated in the eighth century with the establishment of the Sailendra empire in Java. Orissa was ruled during the eighth, ninth, and tenth centuries by the powerful Bhauma-Kara dynasty and in the tenth and eleventh centuries by the Soma dynasty. The temple of Lingaraja at Bhubaneshwar, the greatest Shaiva monument of India, was begun by the Soma King Yayati.

Mediaeval Orissa enjoyed a golden age under the Ganga dynasty. Its founder, Anantavarma Chodagangadeva (1078-1147), ruled from the Ganga to the Godavari with Cuttack as his capital.

He began the construction of the temple of Jagannatha at Puri. Narasimha 1 (1238-1264) built the Sun temple (Surya Deula) of Konarak, one of the finest specimens of Hindu architecture. In the thirteenth and fourteenth centuries, when much of India was overrun by the Muslims, independent Orissa remained a citadel of Hindu religion, philosophy, art, and architecture.

The Gangas were succeeded by the Surya dynasty. Its first king, Kapilendra (1435-1466), won territories from his Muslim neighbours and greatly expanded the Orissan kingdom. His successor, Purusottama, maintained these gains with difficulty. The next and the last Surya king, Prataparudra, became a disciple of Chaitanya, the great medieval saint, and became a pacifist. After his death (1540) Orissa's power declined, and in 1568, when King Mukunda was killed by his own countrymen, Orissa lost its independence to the Afghan rulers of Bengal.

The Mughal emperor Akbar conquered Orissa from the Afghans in 1590-1592. When the Mughal Empire fell in 1761, part of Orissa remained under the Bengal *nawabs*, but the greater part passed to the Marathas. The Bengal sector came under British rule in 1757 after the Battle of Plassey; the Maratha sector was conquered by the British in 1803. Although after 1803 the British controlled the entire Oriya-speaking area, it continued to be administered as two units. It was not until April 1, 1936, that the British heeded calls for unification on a linguistic basis and constituted Orissa as a separate province; 26 Oriya Princely States, however, remained outside the provincial administration. After the independence of India in 1947, all these Princely States except Saraikela and Kharsawan (which merged with Bihar) became part of Orissa.

Relief and drainage: Orissa's geologic formations vary considerably in both age and character. In the interior regions, extending across the stable landmass of the Indian peninsula (a fragment of the ancient continent Gondwanaland), are found some of the oldest rocks of the Earth's crust while along the seaboard are deltaic alluvium or littoral deposits and ridges of windblown sand.

The State can be broadly divided into four natural divisions: (1) the northern plateau, (2) the Eastern Ghats, (3) the central tract, and (4) the coastal plains. The northern plateau (in the northern part of the State) is an extension of the forest-covered, lightly settled, and mineral-rich

Chota Nagpur plateau centred in Jharkhand. The Eastern Ghats, extending roughly parallel to the coast, are remnants of a very ancient line of hills in eastern peninsular India; rising to a height of 1,100 m, the Eastern Ghats are forest-covered, provide a home to a variety of wildlife, and are populated by several tribal groups. The central tract comprises a series of plateaus and basins occupying the inland area west and north of the Eastern Ghats; the plateau areas provide scant resources, but several of the basins — notably the Kalahandi, Balangir, Hirakud, and Jharsuguda — have the soil and the irrigation facilities to support local agriculture. The coastal plains are formed of alluvial soils deposited by the many rivers flowing to the Bay of Bengal; locally the area is known as the Baleshwar coastal plain to the northeast, the Mahanadi delta in the centre, and the Chilka plain to the southwest. The coastal plains are heavily populated, have extensive irrigation, and are devoted almost entirely to the growing of rice during the rainy season.

The main rivers are the Subarnarekha, Burabalang, Baitarani, Brahmani, Mahanadi, Rushikulya, and Vamsadhara. Notable mountain ranges are the Mahendra Hill (Giri; rising to 1,501 m), the Malaya Hill (1,187 m), and the Megasini (1,165 m). Orissas Chilka Lake is the biggest saltwater lagoon in India.

Climate : Orissa is located in a climatic region known as tropical wet-dry (or tropical savanna).

Temperatures average about 26 °C at Cuttack; January is the coldest month, averaging 20 °C, but in May, the warmest month, the mean temperature rises to about 33 °C. The higher elevations of the hills provide some relief from the summer heat, which becomes particularly oppressive in the basins of the Central Tract. Rainfall is concentrated in the months of the southwest monsoon (June to October). Average annual rainfall in the State is about 1,800 m, with even heavier precipitation in the Eastern Ghats; the coastal area south of Chilka Lake is the driest location, averaging 939 mm.

Plant and animal life : Orissa's forests cover more than one-third of the State. They are commonly classified into two categories: tropical moist deciduous and tropical dry deciduous. The first type occupies the hills, plateaus, and more isolated areas within the northeastern part of the State, while the second is found in the south-west. In both forests there are bamboo, teak, rosewood, and padauk. The dense forests northeast gradually become less so towards the southwest, Within the State six wildlife sanctuaries have been set aside to provide a natural habitat for tigers, buffalo, antelope, monkeys, and birds.

Orissa has the same animal life as the rest of peninsular India, Monkeys are common. Carnivores include different types of tigers. The elephant, the wild buffalo, the blackbuck, and the four-horned antelope are found in some areas. The peafowl is a distinctive feature of the Orissa forests. Chilka Lake is a breeding ground for many fish and waterfowl of the Bay of Bengal.

The people : The population of Orissa includes tribal and nontribal peoples. The tribes are divided into three linguistic groups: the Munda-speaking (the Santhal, Savara, and Juang), the Dravidian-speaking (the Khond, Gond, and Oraon), and the Oriya-speaking (the Bhuina). Most tribal people live in the hill areas, but they are also found in the plains. The nontribal population is mainly Oriya-speaking and Hindu.

The tribes for a long time have been undergoing the process of Hinduization. Tribal chieftains have claimed Kshatriya (warrior) status, while many of the Khond, who constitute the largest tribe, have abandoned their Kui language (Dravidian) and speak Oriya, the State's official language. Many tribes are bilingual. Some have become almost indistinguishable from the Hindus and have lost their original language.

The Oriya language does not vary in its written form, but there are some regional variations in the spoken form. The purest Oriya is spoken in the coastal districts of Cuttack and Puri. About 85 per cent of the population use Oriya as their principal language; this proportion is higher in the Mahanadi delta but lower in the hills and in the coastal lowlands of the northeast, where Bengali is widely spoken.

Hindus make up about 95 per cent of the population of Orissa. Muslims are the largest religious minority in all areas of the State except the districts of Sundargarh, Ganjam, Koraput, and Phulabani, where there are greater numbers of Christians. In none of the State's 13 districts, however, does a single minority religion claim more than a tiny fraction of the population.

The caste structure is similar to that in other States of eastern India. Next to the Brahmins are the Karanas (the writer class), who claim Kshatriya status (with the pen as their weapon-rather than the sword). The Khandayats (literally, "Swordsmen") are mostly cultivators but call themselves "Khandayat-Kshatriyas". All castes look to Jagannatha (one of the incarnations of the Hindu god Vishnu) as the centre of their religious faith. For centuries the town of Puri, known as the abode of Jagannatha, has been the only place in India where all castes, including the so-called "untouchables" (the scheduled castes), eat together.

Orissa has a predominantly rural population. The only major cities are Cuttack, Rourkela, Bhubaneshwar, Sambalpur, and Brahmapur.

Economy : About 80 per cent of the population is engaged in *agriculture*, even though much of the land is either unproductive or unsuitable for more than a single annual crop. There are about four million farms in Orissa, averaging about 1.5 ha, but the farmed area per person is less than 0.2 ha. Farms occupy about 45 per cent of the total area of the State. About 80 per cent of the sown area is in rice. Other important crops are oilseeds, pulses, jute, sugarcane, and coconut. Low sunlight availability, modest soil quality, minimal use of fertilizer, and variable volume and timing of the monsoon rains combine to give Orissan farmers low yields and to place them among the poorest in the nation.

A number of agricultural families also engage in nonagricultural pursuits, as most rural people do not get continuous employment the year around. The amount of agricultural land available per person has been declining because of population growth. Attempts at placing ceilings on large landholdings have largely not succeeded. Some marginal lands acquired by the State, however, have been voluntarily turned over to former tenants.

The industrial resources of Orissa are considerable. Orissa leads all States of India in the production of chromite, manganese ore, and dolomite. It is also one of the leading producers of high-quality iron ore. Coal from the important Talcher field in the interior district of Dhenkanal provides the energy base for the States smelting and fertilizer production. The Steel, nonferrous smelting, and fertilizer industries are concentrated in the inland portions of the State, while most of the foundries, rail shops, glass works, and paper mills are located around Cuttack near the Mahanadi delta. Tying the two industrial regions together is the great Mahanadi River system, which has been harnessed by one of the most ambitious multiple purpose projects on the sub-continent: the Hirakud dam and the Machkund hydroelectric project, together with several smaller units, provide flood control, irrigation, and power to the entire lower basin.

Large-scale *industries*, mostly based on minerals, include a steel plant and fertilizer plant at Rourkela, ferromanganese plants at Joda and Rayagarha, refractor-producing factories at Raj Gangpur and Belpahar, a refrigerator manufacturing plant at Choudwar, and a cement factory at Raj Gangpur. There are some large-scale sugar and paper mills at Rayagarha and Choudwar; other industries include textiles, glass, aluminium ingots and cables, and heavy machine tools.

Transportation : Communication facilities were undeveloped before 1947, but the merger of a number of feudatory States with Orissa and the discovery of mineral resources required the construction of a network of good roads. Bold construction programmes — such as the building of bridges over most of the major rivers — were undertaken by the government of Orissa. The State, however, Still lacks adequate railway communications.

An all-weather, sheltered, deep-draft port has been constructed at Paradip at the mouth of Mahanadi River. This port has become an important departing point for the State's exports, especially coal.

The number of hospitals and dispensaries has increased, and the three medical colleges — at Cuttack, Brahmapur (Berhampur), and Burla (Sambalpur) — have expanded considerably.

Cultural life : Orissa has a rich *artistic heritage* and has produced some of the best examples of Indian art and architecture. Artistic traditions are maintained through mural paintings, stone carving, wood carving, icon paintings (known as *patta* paintings), and paintings on palm leaves. Handicraft workers are famous for their exquisite silver filigree ornamentation and decorative work.

In tribal areas, Orissa has a wide variety of *folk dances*. The music of the madal and flute is common in the countryside. The classical dance of Orissa, known as odissi, has survived for more than 700 years. Originally it was a temple dance performed for the gods. The modes, movements, gestures, and poses of the dance are depicted on the walls of the great temples, especially at Konarka (Konarak), in the form of sculpture and in relief carvings. Modern exponents of the dance have made it popular outside the State. The chhau (a dance performed by groups of masked dancers) of Mayurbhanj and Saraikela regions is another feature of Oriya culture. The Kala Vikash Kendra centre was founded at Cuttack in 1952 with a six-year teaching course for the promotion of dancing and music. The National Music Association serves a similar purpose. Other notable dance and music centres in Cuttack are the Utkal Sangit Samaj, the Utkal Smruti Kala Mandapa, and the Mukti Kala Mandir.

There are many traditional *festivals.* A festival unique to Orissa is the ceremony of Boita-Bandana (worshipping of boats) in October or November (the date is set to the Hindu calendar). For five consecutive days before the full moon, people gather near riverbanks or the seashore and float miniature boats as a symbolic gesture that they will leave for the faraway lands (Malaysia and Indonesia) to which their ancestors once sailed.

The town of Puri is the site of the Jagannatha temple ("Lord of the Universe"), perhaps the most famous Hindu shrine in India, and of the temples annual Chariot Festival, which attracts hundreds of thousands of people; the English word juggernaut, derived from the temples name, was inspired by the massive, nearly unstoppable wagons used in the festival. A few miles away, in Konarak, is a temple in the form of a chariot of the sun god, Surya, one of the finest examples of mediaeval Orissan culture.

Area, Population and Headquarters of Districts

S.No.	*District*	*Area (sq km)*	*Population*	*Headquarters*
1.	Angul	6,347	1,39,341	Angul
2.	Balasore	3,706	20,23,056	Balasore
3.	Bolangir	6,552	1,35,760	Bolangir
4.	Boudh	4,289	3,73,038	Boudh
5.	Bhadrak	2,788	13,32,249	Bhadrak
6.	Bargarh	5,832	13,45,601	Bargarh
7.	Cuttack	3,915	23,40,686	Cuttack
8.	Deogarh	2,781	2,74,095	peogarh
9.	Ganjam	8,033	31,36,937	Chatrapur
10.	Dhenkanal	4,597	10,65,983	Dhenkanal
11.	Gajapati	3,056	5,18,448	Palakhemundi
12.	Jagat Singhpur	1,759	10,56,556	Jagatsinghpur
13.	Jajpur	2,885	16,22,868	Panikoili
14.	Jharsugudit	2,202	5,09,056	Jharsuguda
15.	Keonjhar	8,336	15,61,521	Keonjhar
16.	Kalahandi	8,197	13,34,372	Kalahandi
17.	*Koraput*	8,534	11,77,954	*Koraput*
18.	Kendrapara	2,546	13,01,856	Kendrapara
19.	Khurda	2,888	18,74,405	Khurda
20.	Mayurbhanj	10,410	22,21,782	Baripada
21.	Malkangiri	6,115	4,80,232	Malkangirl
22.	Nawarangpur	5,135	*10,18,171*	Nawarangpur
23.	Nayagarh	3,954	8,63,934	Nayagarh
24.	Nawapara	3,408	5,30,524	Nawapara
25.	Purl	3,055	14,98,604	Purl
26.	Kandhamal	6,004	6,47,912	Phulbani
27.	Rayagadao	7,585	8,23,019	Rayagada
28.	Sambalpur	6,702	9,28,889	Sambalpur
29.	Sundargarh	9,942	18,29,412	Sundargarh
30.	Sonepur	2,284	5,40,659	Sonepur

P

Pondicherry–A union territory of India, it was formed in 1962 out of the four former colonies of French India — Pondicherry, Karaikal, and Yanam, scattered along the Coromandel Coast, or eastern seaboard, and Mahe, lying on the western Malabar Coast. The total area of the territory is 492 sq km. The capital is the city of Pondicherry.

History : The French East India Company (formed by Jean-Baptiste Colbert in 1666) established a settlement in 1668 at Surat and another in 1674 at Pondicherry (French: Pondichery; originally Putucceri, from Tamil: *putu*, "new", and *ceri*, "village"). The company's director, Francois Martin, made Pondicherry the capital of the French posts. Mahe was founded in 1725, Yanam in 1731, and Karaikal in 1739. French concerns multiplied in Bengal, with Chandernagore as centre, especially after 1730 under the direction of Joseph-Francois Dupleix who, in 1742 was appointed general director.

From 1763 the French establishments in India, which were under the authority of the king after the abolition of the company in 1769, comprised — apart from a few small posts (loges) — no more than five settlements of moderate size: Chandernagore in Bengal; Yanam, Pondicherry, and Karaikal on the Coromandel Coast; and Mahe on the Malabar Coast. The English conquest of India lessened the commercial activity of the French settlements. They were occupied by the English in 1778 and then again in 1793, but in 1816 they were returned to France. The Second Republic of France granted them local government and representation in the French parliament. Under the Second Empire, commercial liberalism and Anglo-French understanding gave these settlements a fleeling moment of prosperity.

In 1947 the (ports) loges were given back to independent India. Chandernagore was finally transferred in 1951. De facto transfer of the four remaining French possessions to the Union of India took place on November 1, 1954, and de jure transfer on May 28, 1956. Instruments of ratification were signed on August 16, 1962, from which date Pondicherry, consisting of the four enclaves, became a Union Territory.

Land and People : All four areas of the territory are seaside tourist resorts. The city of Pondicherry is divided into two parts by a canal, and all the main streets, running parallel to one another, lead to the open roadstead offshore. The port of Pondicherry does not have a harbour, and ships are forced to lie a mile or two offshore; but its roadstead was once considered the best on the Coromandel Coast. There is a promenade and landing place for cargo, and a new pier was constructed in the 1960s. In and around the town are artesian wells that supply a large quantity of water for irrigation, the chief local crops being paddy, sugarcane, cotton, and peanuts (groundnuts). The main industries are food processing, electrical appliances, textiles, paper, and lumber. The Pondicherry area has about 300 villages and hamlets,

The commune of Karaikal is in the fertile Thanjavur delta, in one of the most important rice-producing areas of India. The exceptional fertility of the region is to some extent reflected in the unusually high density of its rural population. The town is on a branch line, the Mayavaram-Peralam route, of the southern railway.

The Mahe sector consists of two parts: the quaint, picturesque town of Mahe, with all its buildings situated on the left bank of the Mahe River close to its mouth; and the isolated tract known as Naluthrara, on the right bank, comprising the four villages of Chambara, Chalakara, Palour, and Pandaquel. Rice is the chief crop.

Yanam is a small town on the bank of a branch of the Godavari River, about 650 km north of the city of Chennai (formerly Madras), near Kakinada. The major languages spoken in the areas are Tamil, Malayalam, and Telugu. Tamil is predominant in the southern settlements of Pondicherry and Karaikal; Malayalam is predominant in Mahe, and Telugu in Yanam. Other significant languages include Urdu, French, Kannada, Hindi, Gujarati, English, and Marathi. Hindus form the majority in all the four regions; Muslims are an important minority in Karaikal, Mahe, and Yanam; and there are a number of Christians in Pondicherry. There are also a few Sikhs, Buddhists, and Jains. There are no heavy industries or mining in the Union Territory; it purchases its entire power requirement from nearby States.

Pondicherry contains the Hindu *ashram* (religious retreat) of the philosopher Sri Aurobindo Ghose (1872-1950), as well as Auroville, the international township and study centre that was named after him. The Remain Rolland Public Library houses some rare French volumes. A medical college, a law college, and several other colleges for general education are affiliated with the University of Madras.

Area, Population and Headquarters of Districts

S.No.	*District*	*Area (sq km)*	*Population*	*Headquarters*
1.	Pondicherry	290	7,35,004	Pondicherry
2.	Karaikal	161	1,70,640	Karaikal
3.	Mahe	9	36,823	Mahe
4.	Yanam	20	31,362	Yanam

Punjab—A State, located in the northwestern part of India, it is bounded on the north by the State of Jammu and Kashmir, on the east by the State of Himachal Pradesh, on the south by the States of Haryana and Rajasthan, and on the west by Pakistan.

The Punjab in its present form came into existence on November 1, 1966, consequent to the linguistic reorganization of the older unit. Out of the old State, the Punjabi-speaking areas constitute the Punjab, while the Hindi speaking areas form the new Stale of Haryana. The Punjab covers an area of 50,362 sq km. Chandigarh city, within the Chandigarh Union Territory, is the joint capital of the Punjab and Haryana. The word Punjab is a compound of two Persian words, *panj* ("five") and *ab* ("water"), meaning the land of five waters, that is, rivers. These are the Sutlej, Beas, Ravi, Chenab, and Jhelum. The origin can perhaps be traced to *pancha nada*, Sanskrit for "five rivers" and the name of the region mentioned in the ancient epic the Mahabharala. The present Indian State of Punjab, however, is no longer the "Land of Five Rivers". Since the partition of India only the Sutlej and the Beas lie within its territory while the Ravi flows along part of its western border.

History : The foundations of the present Punjab (historical Punjab) were laid by Banda Singh Bahadur, a hermit who became a military leader and, with his fighting band of Sikhs, temporarily liberated the eastern part of the province from Mughal rule in 1709-1710. Banda Singh's defeat and execution in 1716 were followed by a prolonged struggle between the Sikhs on the one hand, and the Mughals and Afghans on the other. By 1764-1765 the Sikhs had established their dominance in the region. Maharaja Ranjit Singh (1780-1839) built up the Punjab into a powerful kingdom and attached to it the adjacent provinces of Multan, Kashmir, and Peshawar.

In 1849 the Punjab fell to the troops of the British East India Company and subsequently became a province under British rule. By the late nineteenth century, however, the Indian nationalist movement took hold in this province. One of the movement's most significant events — the some 400 deaths and 1,200 injuries of the Jallianwalla Bagh massacre, ordered by British general Reginald E.H. Dyer — took place at Amritsar in 1919. When India gained independence in 1947, the British province of the Punjab was divided between the new sovereign States of India and Pakistan, and the smaller, eastern portion became part of India,

Since independence, the history of the Indian side of the Punjab was largely dominated by Sikh agitation for a Punjabi-speaking State, led first by Master Tara Singh and later by his political successor, Sant Fateh Singh. Among other things, the demand was sought to be justified on the basis of an Indian National Congress resolution of 1939 proposing the division of India into linguistic States after achieving independence. In November 1956 the Indian State of Punjab was enlarged by merging PEPSU (Patiala and East Punjab States Union) with it. PEPSU was an amalgamation of the pre-independence Princely States of Patiala, Jind, Nabha, Faridkot, Kapurthala, Kalsia, Malerkotla, and Nalagarh. Sardar Partap Singh Kairon was elected as the leader of the Congress Legislative group (which was in majority) in the Assembly and thus became chief minister of the enlarged State of Punjab, which position he retained from 1956 to 1964. The demand for a Punjabi-speaking State within the Indian Union was eventually agreed to by the government of India. On November 1, 1966 the then Punjab was reorganized on a linguistic basis: the predominantly Punjabi-speaking areas constituting the new, present State of Punjab, while the Hindi-speaking areas generally south and southeast of the Ghaggar River formed the State of Haryana. The northernmost hilly districts of Kangra, Lahul-Spiti, and Shimla were transferred to Himachal Pradesh. The city of Chandigarh, originally built as the capital of the Punjab, along with the immediate surrounding area, became a separate Union Territory. Though not a part of either State, the city of Chandigarh was made the joint administrative headquarters, or the capital, of both the Punjab and Haryana, which arrangement is continuing.

Although the Sikhs had got the Punjabi-speaking State, as demanded earlier, and Punjabi language was getting its rightful place, certain elements, not only extremists from among the Sikhs and the All India Sikh Students Federation but also some foreign-based Sikhs, started demanding the establishment of an autonomous Sikh homeland, or Khalistan, by the 1980s. There has been some confusion about the precise nature of this demand: some interpreted it as one for a separate Sikh State, while others took it in terms of additional autonomy for the Punjab within the Indian Union. In any case, in order to achieve their goal, the militant groups comprising generally rural, unemployed youth from the small peasantry and other sections of Sikh society started resorting to terrorism, including indiscriminate killing of Punjabi Hindus and those Sikhs who opposed the creation of Khalistan. In the process, Sant Jarnail Singh Bhindranwale, who was originally patronized as a religious leader, became a strong force along with a large number of his armed followers. They made the Akal Takht and the premises of the Golden Temple (the

Sikhs' holiest shrine) as their fort. In June 1984, in an effort to dislodge Bhindranwale and his followers from their fortification in the Golden Temple premises, the Indian Army carried out "Operation Bluestar" and stormed the Golden Temple in a bid to root out the terrorists. In this attack, Bhindranwale, and most of his armed followers were killed, as were also some 100 soldiers of the Indian army. In retaliation. Prime Minister Indira Gandhi was assassinated at her Delhi official residence by two of her Sikh bodyguards on October 31, 1984. This, in turn, led to violence against the Sikhs in Delhi and many other places, mostly in northern India, resulting in the killing of several thousands of Sikhs. Despite attempts at a negotiated settlement, a climate of violence, distrust and disorder continued in the Punjab throughout the 1980s, creating conditions of insecurity and political uncertainty.

However, peace has returned to the Punjab since the early 1990s, and ever since the State has been functioning smoothly and normally practically in all spheres of activity. A forward-looking attitude, so characteristic of the Punjabis, is again replacing the pessimism that may have developed earlier.

Land : Most of the Punjab is a flat plain, sloping gently from about 275 m above sea level in the northeast to about 168 m in the southwest. Physiographically, the State can be divided into three parts. The Shiwalik Hills in the northeast, at an elevation between 274 m and 914 m, cover a small fraction of the State's area. To the south of the Shiwalik Hills extends a narrow and undulating foothill zone, which is dissected by closely spaced seasonal torrents, locally known as *chos*, several of which terminate in the plain without joining any stream. The third zone is a broad flat tract with fertile alluvial soils. The low-lying flood plains (*bet*) along the rivers and the slightly elevated flat terraces between them are distinguishable within the plain. The southwestern part of the elevated terraces, formerly strewn with sand dunes, has mostly been levelled off with widespread extension of irrigation, transforming the whole landscape.

With an inland subtropical location, the Punjab's climate varies from semi-arid to sub-humid. Summers are very hot; the mean temperature during June is 34 °C rising above 45 °C on exceptionally hot days. Winters are fairly cold, with the average January temperature at 13 °C and night temperatures occasionally touch freezing point. Annual rainfall is the highest (about 1,245 mm) in the Shiwalik Hills in the northeast, decreasing gradually to about 356 mm in the southwest. About three-fourths of the annual rainfall occurs during July to September, the months of the southwest monsoon. Winter rains from the western disturbances, occurring from December to March, account for less than one-fourth of the total rainfall.

With the growth of human settlement over the centuries, the Punjab plain has been largely cleared of its forest cover. Over large parts of the Shiwalik Hills, bush and scrub vegetation has succeeded trees as a result of extensive deforestation. Efforts are on to raise forests on the hillslopes. Along major roads and on infertile land, including the wasteland, eucalyptus and poplar trees have been planted.

Natural habitat for wildlife has been severely limited with agriculture extending to more than three-fourths of the total area. Even so, many species of birds, rodents, and snakes, as also some animals, have adapted to the farming environment.

People : The people of the Punjab are mainly descendants of perhaps the Aryan tribes that entered India from the northwest during the second millennium BC, as well as the pre-Aryan population, probably Dravidians, who had a highly developed civilization. Relics of this civilization have been unearthed at Ropar and Sanghol. Successive waves of invaders — Greeks, Parthians, Kushans, and Huns — added to the ethnic diversity and left an imprint on the region's culture. Later invaders under the banner of Islam forced the people to convert to Muslim faith, although many conversions were voluntary under the influence of Sufi saints.

Punjabi, the principal spoken language of the present-day Punjab, is also the official State language, written in Gurmukhi script. Nearly two-thirds of the Punjab's population adheres to the Sikh religion, which originated from the teachings of Nanak, the first Sikh Guru. About one-third of the population is Hindu. Muslims, Christians, and commercially prominent Jains are small but significant minorities in some areas. Muslims are concentrated in and around Malerkotla, a former Princely State ruled by a Muslim *nawab*. Scheduled castes constitute 28.3 per cent of the Punjab's population — the highest proportion in India.

Nearly one-third of the Punjab's population lives in towns. Ten of the urban places are cities, each having 100,000 or more population. Ludhiana, Arnritsar, Jalandhar, and Patiala are the four largest cities. Though the cities are fast-growing centres of industry, trade and services, over half of the Punjab's workers are still engaged in agriculture.

After Kerala and Maharashtra, the Punjab has the lowest death rate among the main States of the Indian Union. It also has the lowest birth rate among the northern, central, and several western States of India. Accordingly, the rate of natural increase of its population is among the lowest, though it still has a long way to go to reach the final stage of demographic transition.

Economy : The economy of the Punjab is characterized by a productive, predominantly *commercial agriculture*, and diverse small- and *medium-scale industries*. The Punjab has the highest per capita income among the main States of India. With just about 1.6 per cent of India's total area. The Punjab produces nearly 12 per cent of India's foodgrain. It contributes about two-fifths of the rice stock and around three-fifths of wheat held by the central pool (national repository system of surplus foodgrain).

The Punjab's phenomenal agricultural progress is largely the result of the Green Revolution, which brought modern agricultural technology to the State. With the introduction of high-yielding varieties of wheat and rice seed, there was manifold increase in the yield of these crops. Wheat and rice together account for nearly three-fourth of the total cropped area. Other commercial crops include cotton, sugarcane, potatoes, and oilseeds. Maize, groundnuts (peanuts), gram (chickpea), *bajra* (pearl millet), and some of the pulses (legumes, the main source of proteins) have suffered decline in recent years. The productivity of wheat and rice, though still high, has reached a plateau. Rice requiring heavy watering has led to the washing down of soil nutrients year after year, leading to impoverishment of soils. As a result, more fertilizers have to be used to maintain the achieved yields. For regaining soil fertility with farming as a profitable enterprise, diversification of agriculture has been attempted. Horticulture, floriculture, poultry, and dairy are coming up gradually.

With almost the entire cultivated area receiving irrigation, the Punjab is India's most irrigated State. Government-owned canals and bore-wells are the main sources of irrigation. The Bhakra Dam Project in Himachal Pradesh provides much of the supply of irrigation water for the State. Canal irrigation is largely characteristic of the southern and southwestern Punjab, while borewells (more than three-fourths of them electrically operated) are ubiquitous in the north and the northeast, with a sprinkling in the southwest also. Consolidation of landholdings, completed by about 1970, has been instrumental in the rapid development of private bore-well irrigation, as also in increasing the efficiency of farming including mechanization. In general, farmers with larger landholdings have benefited more from the Green Revolution, resulting in a greater income disparity within the State's rural areas.

The *industries* with the largest number of workers include cotton, woollen, and silk textiles; food products; metal products; transport equipment and parts; and metal and alloy industry. Other important industries are hosiery, bicycles, sewing machines, sports goods, electrical machines, appliances and spare parts. For lack of fossil fuels, the Punjab suffers from insufficient energy for its industries. Nearly three-fourths of the households in the State use electricity. Although new hydroelectric stations and thermal units have been operational, the demand far exceeds supply.

The Punjab has developed a dense network of over 48,000 km of *roads*, four-fifths of which are surfaced. Importantly, nearly all of the villages are linked with roads. A fairly dense and efficient network of the Northern Railway zone, a part of the national railway system, exists in the Punjab. Regular air passenger service from Delhi to Chandigarh and to the cities of Amritsar, Ludhiana, and Bathinda is available. Like the railways, the post and telegraph services and radio and television broadcasting are under the control of the central government.

Cultural life : Folklore, ballads of love and war, fairs and festivals, dancing, music, and literature are characteristic expressions of the States cultural life. The origins of Punjabi literature can be traced to the mystical and religious verse of the thirteenth century Muslim Sufi (mystic) Shaikh Farid, and to the fifteenth-sixteenth century Guru Nanak, founder of the Sikh faith, who were the first to use Punjabi extensively as a medium of poetic expression. The Contribution of Waris Shah to the enrichment of Punjabi literature in the second half of the eighteenth century is immeasurable, Punjabi literature entered its modern phase at the beginning of the twentieth century with the writings of the poet and author Bhai Vir Singh, and the poets Puran Singh and Dhani Ram Chatrik. Contributions of recent writers, poets and novelists depicting various facets of Punjab's culture carry their own significance. Of the poets, Mohan Singh "Mahir" and Shiv Kumar Batalvi were among the most renowned; among the novelists Jaswant Singh Kanwal, Gurdial Singh, and Sohan Singh Shital are most noteworthy; and Kulwant Singh Virk is a well-known writer. One of the most outstanding novels depicting rural life in the Punjab is that of Giani Gurdit Singh, *Mera Pind* ("My village"), almost a classic in Punjabi literature.

The Punjab holds numerous religious and seasonal festivals, such as Dussehra, Diwali, and Baisakhi, as well as anniversary celebrations in honour of gurus and saints. Bhangra, jhumar, and sammi are the popular dance forms. The giddha, a native Punjabi form, is a humorous song-dance performed by women. In addition to Sikh religious music, semi-classical Mughal forms, such as the *khayal*, *thumri*, *ghazal*, and *qawwali*, continue to be popular.

The State's outstanding architectural monument is the Golden Temple (Harimandir) at Amritsar, an exquisite building that conforms well to late Mughal styles. Its chief motifs, such as the dome and the geometric design, are repeated in most Sikh places of worship. The Golden Temple is rich in gold filigree work, panels with floral designs, and marble facings inlaid with coloured stones. Other important buildings include the Martyrs' Memorial at Jallianwalla Bagh in Amritsar, the Hindu Temple of Durgiana (also at Amritsar), a Moorish-style mosque at Kapurthala, and old forts at Bathinda and Bahadurgarh.

Area, Population and Headquarters of Districts

S.No.	*District*	*Area (sq km)*	*Population*	*Headquarters*
1.	Amritsar	5,075	30,74,210	Amritsar
2.	Bathinda	3,377	11,81,236	Bathinda
3.	Faridkot	1,472	5,52,466	Faridkot
4.	Fatehgarh Sahib	1,180	5,39,751	Fatehgarh Sahib
5.	Firozepur	5,865	17,44,753	Firozepur
6.	Gurdaspur	3,570	20,96,889	Gurdaspur
7.	Hoshiarpur	3,310	14,78,045	Hoshiarpur
8.	Jalandhar	2,658	19,53,508	Jalandhar
9.	Kapurthala	1,646	7,52,287	Kapurthala
10.	Ludhiana	3,744	30,30,352	Ludhiana
11.	Mansa	2,174	6,88,630	Mansa
12.	Moga	1,672	8,86,313	Moga
13.	Muktsar	2,596	7,76,702	Muktsar
14.	Nawan Shehar	1,258	5,86,637	Nawan Shehar
15.	Patiala	3,627	18,39,056	Patiala
16.	Roop Nagar	2,117	11,10,000	Roop Nagar
17.	Sangrur	5,021	19,98,464	Sangrur

R

Rajasthan–This State of India is located in the northwestern part of the subcontinent. It is bounded on the west and northwest by Pakistan, on the north and northeast by the States of Punjab, Haryana, and Uttar Pradesh, on the east and southeast by the States of Uttar Pradesh and Madhya Pradesh, and on the south-west by the State of Gujarat. The Tropic of Cancer passes through its southern tip in the Banswara district. The State has an area of 342,239 sq km. The capital city is Jaipur.

Rajasthan, meaning "The Abode of the *rajas*', was formerly called Rajputana, "The Country of the Rajputs" (sons of *rajas*). Before 1947, when India achieved independence from British rule, it comprised 18 Princely States, two chiefships, the small British-administered province of Ajmer-Merwara, and a few pockets of territory outside the main boundaries. After 1947 the Princely States and chiefships were integrated into India in stages, and the State took the name of Rajasthan. It assumed its present form on November 1, 1956, when the States Reorganization Act came into force.

History : Archaeological evidence indicates that early humans lived along the banks of the Banas and its tributaries some 100,000 years ago. Harappan (Indus) and post-Harappan culture (third-second millennium BC) is traceable at Kalibangan, Ahar, and Gilund. Pottery fragments at Kalibangan are carbondated to 2700 BC. The discovery near Bairat of two rock inscriptions (c. 250 BC) of the emperor Ashoka seems to show that his rule extended westwards to this part of the State. Later rulers of the whole or parts of the State were the Bactrian Greeks (second century BC), the Scythians (Shakas; second to fourth centuries AD), the Guptas (fourth to sixth centuries), the Huns (sixth century), and Harshavardhana, a Rajput ruler (early seventh century).

Arising between the seventh and eleventh centuries were several Rajput dynasties, including that of the Gurjara-Pratiharas, who kept the Arab invaders of Sind at bay. Under Bhoja 1 (836-885), the territory of the Gurjara-Pratiharas stretched from the foothills of the Himalaya to the Narmada River and from the lower Ganga Valley to Sind. With the disintegration of this empire by the late tenth century, several rival Rajput clans rose to power in Rajasthan. The Guhilas, feudatories of the Pratiharas, asserted their independence in AD 940 and established control of the region around Mewar (modern Udaipur). By the eleventh century the Chauhans (Chahamana), with their capital at Ajmer and later Delhi, had emerged as the major power in eastern areas of the State. In the following centuries other clans, such as the Kachwahas, Bhattis, and Rathors, succeeded in establishing independent kingdoms in the region.

The second battle of Tarain, fought near Delhi in 1192, initiated a new period in Rajasthan's history. Muhammad Ghuri's victory over a Rajput army under Prithviraja III not only led to the destruction of Rajput power in the Gangetic Plain but also firmly established the Muslim presence in northern India. As Muslim forces pushed south and then west along the traditional routes to Gujarat, the Rajput kingdoms of Rajasthan were encircled. The next four centuries saw repeated, though unsuccessful, attempts by the central power based in Delhi to subdue the Rajput States of the region. The Rajputs, however, despite common historical and cultural traditions, were never able to unite to inflict a decisive defeat on their opponents.

Rajput strength reached its zenith at the beginning of the sixteenth century under Rana Sangram Singh (Sanga) of Mewar, but he was defeated in a fierce battle by the Mughal invader Babur, and the brief splendour of a united Rajput polity waned rapidly. It is largely from this period of Rajasthan's history that the romantic view of the Rajput as a valiant warrior — defending family, honour, and religion against the invading Muslims — is derived.

Towards the end of the sixteenth century the Mughal emperor Akbar was able to achieve, through diplomacy and military action, what his predecessors had been unable to accomplish by force alone. Military campaigns were still undertaken by imperial Mughal forces, and Rajput strongholds, such as Ranthambhor and Chittaurgarh, were besieged and destroyed (1567-1568), but Akbar also entered into a series of alliances with numerous Rajput ruling houses in Rajasthan, arranging marriages with Rajput princesses for himself and for his heirs. Mughal-Rajput marriages continued until the early eighteenth century, and it is noteworthy that the emperors Jahangir and Shah Jahan were both born of Rajput mothers. Thus, many Rajput States of Rajasthan (along with their not insubstantial military resources) were brought into the imperial fold without costly military subjugation. Furthermore, some Rajput rulers, such as Man Singh of Amber (Jaipur) and Jaswant Singh of Marwar (Jodhpur), served with loyalty and distinction in the imperial Mughal forces. Under Akbar the Rajput States of the region were grouped together under the *subah* of Ajmer, an administrative unit of the Mughal Empire.

After the death (1707) of the emperor Aurangzeb, the Rajput State of Bharatpur was developed by a Jat conqueror, but by 1803 most of the rest of Rajasthan paid tribute to the Maratha dynasties of west-central India. Later in the nineteenth century, the British subdued the Marathas and, having established paramountcy in the region, organized the Rajput States into Rajputana province. The government of India was represented in Rajputana by a political officer, with the title of agent to the governor-general, who was also chief commissioner of the small British province of Ajmer-Merwara. Under him were residents and political agents who were accredited to various States.

During this period the idea of Indian nationalism was born. Dayananda Sarasvati wrote his *Satyaratha Prakash* at Udaipur, intended to restore Hinduism to its pristine purity, which created a ferment in Rajputana. Important movements of thought also occurred among the Jain *munis* ("holy men") and scholars. Ajmer was the centre of political activity, and nationalist leaders included Arjun Lal Sethi, Manik Lal Varma, Gopal Singh, and Jai Narain Vyas.

After India became independent in 1947, the Princely States and chiefships of Rajputana were integrated by stages into a single entity. They were first grouped into small unions, such as the Matsya Union and the Rajasthan Union, which were merged with the remaining States to create Greater Rajasthan in 1949. When the new Constitution of India came into force in 1950, Rajasthan became an integral part of India. The Rajput princes — though retaining a recognition of their original title, some special privileges, and a privy purse — surrendered their political powers to the central government. The privileged status given to rulers of the former Princely States was discontinued in 1970.

Physiography : The Aravali Range forms a line across the State running roughly from Guru Peak (Mount Abu), which is 1,722 m high, in the south-west to Khetri in the northeast. About three-fifths of the State lies northwest of this line, leaving two-fifths in the southeast. These are the two natural divisions of Rajasthan. The northwest tract is sandy and unproductive with little water but improves gradually from desert land in the far west and northwest to comparatively fertile and habitable land towards the east. The area includes the Great Indian (Thar) Desert.

The southeastern area, higher in elevation (100 to 350 m above sea level) and more fertile, has a very diversified topography. In the south lies the hilly tract of Mewar. In the southeast a large area of the districts of Kota and Bundi forms a tableland, and to the northeast of these districts is a rugged region (badlands) following the line of the Chambal River. Farther north the country levels out; the flat plains of the northeastern Bharatpur district are part of the alluvial basin of the Yamuna River.

The Aravali forms Rajasthans most important watershed. The drainage to the east of this range flows northeast, as does the Chambal, which is the only large and perennial river in the State. Its principal tributary, the Banas, rises in the Aravali near Kumbhalgarh and collects all the drainage of the Mewar plateau. Farther north, the Banganga, after rising near Jaipur, flows east towards the Yamuna before disappearing. The Luni is the only significant river west of the Aravali. It rises in the Pushkar valley of Ajmer and flows 320 km west-southwest into the Rann of Kachchh. Northeast of the Luni basin, in the Shekhawati tract, is an area of internal drainage characterized by salt lakes, the largest of which is Sambhar Salt Lake. Farther to the west lies the true Marusthali ("Land of the Dead"), the barren wastelands and areas of sand dunes that form the heart of the Great Indian Desert.

In the vast sandy northwestern plain extending over the districts of Jaisalmer, Barmer, Jalor, Sirohi, Jodhpur, Bikaner, Ganganagar, Jhunjhunun, Sikar, Pali, and Nagaur, soils are predominantly saline or alkaline. Water is scarce but is found at a depth of 30 to 61 m. The soil and sand are calcareous (chalky). Nitrates in the soil increase its fertility, and, as has been shown in the area of the Indira Gandhi (formerly Rajasthan) Canal, cultivation is often possible where adequate water supplies are made available. The soils in the Ajmer district in central Rajasthan are sandy; clay content varies between 3 and 9 per cent. In the Jaipur and Alwar districts in the east, soils vary from sandy loam to loamy sand. In the Kota, Bundi, and Jhalawar tract, they are in general black and deep and are well drained. In Udaipur, Chittaurgarh, Dungarpur, Banswara, and Bhilwara districts, eastern areas have mixed red and black and western areas red to yellow soils.

Climate : There is a wide range of *climate* varying from extremely arid to humid, the humid zone comprising the districts in the southeast and east. Except in the hills, the heat during the summer is great everywhere, with a mean maximum of 42 °C. Hot winds and dust storms occur, especially in the desert tract. Winter temperatures vary from 20 °C to 24.5 °C. The western desert has little rain (annual average, 100 mm), but in the southeast rainfall is higher. Southeastern Rajasthan benefits from both the Arabian Sea and Bay of Bengal branches of the southwest (summer) monsoon winds, which bring 90 per cent of the rainfall.

Fauna and Flora : The main floral feature is scrub jungle. Towards the west there are plants characteristic of the arid zone, such as tamarisk and false tamarisk. Trees are scarce, found only sparingly in the Aravali and in eastern Rajasthan.

Tigers are found in the Aravali and in several districts. Leopards, sloth bears, Indian sambar (dark brown Indian deer), and chital (a kind of deer) occur in the hills and forests, where nilgai (blue bulls) are also found in parts; black buck and ravine deer are numerous in the plains. Snipe, quail, partridge, and wild duck occur everywhere except in the desert. The Bikaner region is well known for several species of sand grouse.

Numerous game sanctuaries and wildlife parks have been established in the State. Among the most important are the Sariska Wildlife Sanctuary near Alwar and the Desert National Park near Jaisalmer.

People : Aboriginal people in the Alwar, Jaipur, Bharatpur, and Dholpur areas include the Mina (Mewati); the Meo; the Banjara, who are travelling tradesmen and artisans; and the Gadia Lohar, another itinerant tribe, who make and repair agricultural and household implements. The Bhil, one of the oldest peoples in India, inhabit the districts of Bhilwara, Chittaurgarh, Dungarpur, Banswara, Udaipur, and Sirohi and are famous for their skill in archery. The Grasia and nomadic Kathodi live in the Mewar region. The Sahariya are found in the Kota district, and the Rabari of the Marwar region are cattle breeders.

The Rajput, though representing only a small percentage of the population, are the most important section of the population in Rajasthan. They are proud of their warlike reputation and of their ancestry. The Brahmin class is subdivided into many *gotras*, while the Mahajan (the trading class) is subdivided into a bewildering number of groups. Some of these groups are Jain, while others are Hindu. In the north and west the Jat and Gujar are among the largest agricultural communities.

The principal language of the State is Rajasthani, comprising a group of Indo-Aryan dialects derived from Dingal, a tongue in which bards once sang of the glories of their masters. The four main dialects are Marwari (in western Rajasthan), Jaipuri or Dhundhari (in the east and southeast), Malvi (Maiwi; in the southeast), and, in Alwar, Mewati, which shades off into Braj Bhasha in Bharatpur district. The use of Rajasthani is declining with the spread of modern education, and its place is being taken by Hindi (the official State language of Rajasthan). Hinduism, the religion of most of the population, is generally practised through the worship of Brahma, Shiva, Shakti, Vishnu, and other gods and goddesses. Nathdwara is an important religious centre for the Vallabhacharya sect of Krishna followers. There are also followers of the Arya Samaj, a reforming sect of modem Hinduism, as well as other forms of that religion. Jainism is also important; it has not been the religion of the rulers of Rajasthan but has followers among the trading class and the wealthy section of society. Mahavirji, Ranakpur, Dhulev, and Karera are the chief centres of Jain pilgrimage. Another important religious sect is formed by the Dadupanthi, the followers of Dadu (d. 1603), who preached the equality of all men, strict vegetarianism, total abstinence from intoxicating liquor, and lifelong celibacy.

Islam, the religion of the State's second largest religious community, expanded in Rajasthan with the conquest of Ajmer by Muslim invaders in the late twelfth century. Khwajah Muin-ud-Din Chishti, the Muslim missionary, had his headquarters at Ajmer, and Muslim traders, craftsmen, and soldiers settled there. The State's population of Christians and Sikhs is small. Rajasthan is one of the least densely populated States in India. Most villages and towns lie east of the Aravali. The urban population has been growing faster than the rural, but even so there are only a few large towns, including Jaipur, Ajmer, Jodhpur, Udaipur, Kota, Bikaner, and Alwar. There are industrial complexes at Jaipur, Kota, Udaipur, and Bhilwara.

Rural houses are huts with mud walls and roofs thatched with straw. They have a single door, but no windows or ventilators. The houses of well-to-do farmers and artisans in larger villâges have more than one room. They are roofed with tiles and have a verandah and large courtyard, whose main door can admit a loaded bull cart. The earthen floors are coated with mud and dung.

Economy : Rajasthan is predominantly agricultural and pastoral State and exports food grains and vegetables. Despite a low and erratic rainfall, nearly all types of crops are grown; in the desert area, *bajra* (millet); in Kota, (sorghum); and in Udaipur, mainly maize. Wheat and barley are fairly well distributed (except in the desert area), as are pulses (the edible seeds of legumes, such as peas, beans, and lentils), sugarcane, and oilseeds. Improved varieties of rice have been introduced, and acreage of this crop has expanded in the areas of the Chambal valley and Indira Gandhi canal projects. Cotton and tobacco are important cash crops.

Although most of its area is arid or semi-arid, Rajasthan has a large live-stock population and is the largest wool-producing State. It has a monopoly in camels and in draught animals of various breeds.

Having much arid land, Rajasthan needs extensive irrigation. It receives water from the Punjab rivers and also from the Western Yamuna

(Haryana) and Agra canals (Uttar Pradesh) and from the Sabarmati and Narmada Sagar projects to the south. There are thousands of tanks (village ponds or lakes), but they suffer from drought and silt. Rajasthan shares the Bhakra Nangal project with the Punjab and the Chambal valley project with Madhya Pradesh; both are used to supply water for irrigation and for drinking purposes. The Rajasthan Canal, renamed the Indira Gandhi Canal in the mid-1980s for the late prime minister, carries water from the Beas and Sutlej rivers in Punjab some 644 km to irrigate desert land in northwestern and western Rajasthan.

Rajasthan produces India's entire output of lead and zinc concentrates, emeralds, and garnets. More than 90 per cent of the country's gypsum and silver ore are also produced in Rajasthan. The main industries are based on textiles, vegetable oil, wool, minerals, and chemicals, while handicrafts, such as leather goods, marble work, jewellery, pottery, and embossed brass have earned much foreign exchange. Various industrial concerns received substantial loans and subsidies from the government and from the Rajasthan Finance Corporation, a semi-governmental agency. Kota, which is the industrial capital of the State, has a nylon factory and a precision instruments factory, as well as plants for the manufacture of calcium carbide, caustic soda, and rayon tyre cord. There is a zinc smelter plant near Udaipur.

Electricity supplies are obtained from neighbouring States and from the Chambal valley project. There is a nuclear energy plant at Rawatbhata, near Kota.

Cultural life : Hardly a month passes in Rajasthan without a religious festival. The most remarkable and typical is the festival called Gangor, when clay images of Mahadevi and Parvati (representing the benevolent aspects of the Hindu mother goddess) are worshipped by women of all castes for 15 days and are then taken out to be immersed in water. Their procession is joined by priests and officers and is led to the water by trumpeters and drummers. Hindus and Muslims join in each others' festivals; general enthusiasm and gaiety prevail on these occasions.

Another important festival is held at Pushkar near Ajmer, taking the form of a mixed religious festival and livestock fair. It is visited by farmers (who bring their camels and cattle) from throughout the State and by pilgrims seeking salvation. The tomb of the Sufi mystic Khwajah Muin-ud-Din Chishti at Ajmer is one of the most sacred Muslim shrines in India. As many as 300,000 pilgrims, many from foreign countries, visit the shrine on the occasion of the saints *urs* (death anniversary).

The typical folk dance of Rajasthan is the ghoomar, which is performed on festive occasions only by women. The geer dance (performed by men and women), the panihari (a graceful dance for women), and the kacchi ghori (in which male dancers ride dummy horses) are also popular. The most famous song is "kurja", which tells the story of a woman who wishes to send a message to her absent husband by the kurja (a type of bird), which is promised a priceless reward for its service. Rajasthan has made its contribution to Indian art, and there is a rich literary tradition, especially of bardic poetry. Chand Bardais poem *Prithviraj Rasau* or *Chand Raisa*, the earliest manuscript of which dates to the twelfth century, is particularly notable. A popular source of entertainment is the khyal, a dance-drama composed in verse with festive, historical, or romantic themes. Rajasthan abounds in objects of antiquarian interest, including early Buddhist rock inscriptions, Jain temples, forts, splendid Princely palaces, and Muslim mosques and tombs.

Area, Population and Headquarters of Districts

S.No.	*District*	*Area (sq km)*	*Population*	*Headquarters*
1.	Ajmer,	8,481	21,80,526	Ajrner
2.	Alwar	8,380	29,90,862	Alwar
3.	Banswara	5,037	15,00,420	Banswara
4.	Barmer	28,387	1,96,758	Barmer
5.	Bharatpur	5,066	20,98,323	Bharatpur
6.	Bhilwara	10,455	20,09,516	Bhilwara
7.	Bikaner	27,244	16,73,562	Bikaner
8.	Bundi	5,550	9,61,269	Bundi
9.	Chittorgarh	10,856	18,02,656	Chittorgarh
10.	Chum	16,830	19,22,908	Churu
11.	Dholpur	3,034	9,82,815	Dholpur
12.	Dungarpur	3,770	11,07,037	Dungarpur
13.	Ganganagar	7,944	17,88,487	Ganganagar
14.	Jaipur	11,588	52,52,388	Jaipur
15.	Jaisalmer	38,401	5,07,999	Jaisalmer
16.	Jalore	10,640	14,48,486	Jalore
17.	Jhalawar	6,219	11,80,342	Jhalawar
18.	Jhunjhunu	5,928	1,91,399	Jhunjhunu
19.	Jodhpur	22,850	28,80,777	Jodhpur
20.	Kota	5,481	15,68,580	Kota
21.	Nagaur	17,718	27,73,894	Nagaur

S.No.	District	Area (sq km)	Population	Headquarters
22.	Pali	12,387	18,19,201	Pall
23.	Sawai Madhopur	5,043	11,16,031	S. Madhopur
24.	Sikar	7,732	22,87,229	Sikar
25.	Sirohi	5,136	8,50,756	Sirohi
26.	Tonk	7,194	12,11,343	Tonk
27.	Udaipur	12,511	26,32,210	Udaipur
28.	Dausa	2.950	13,16,790'	Dausa
29.	Baran	6,955	10,22,568	Baran
30.	Rajsamand	4,768	9,86,269	Rajsamand
31.	Hanumangarn	12,690	15,17,390	Hanumangarh
32.	Karoli	5,014	12,05,631	Karoli

S

Sikkim–A state of India, it is located in the northeastern part of the country. It is the second smallest State in India, covering an area of 7,096 sq km in the eastern Himalaya. It is bordered by the independent mountain kingdoms of Nepal to the west and Bhutan to the east; by the Tibet Autonomous Region of China to the north and northeast, and State of West Bengal to the south. Gangtok is the capital. Long a sovereign State, Sikkim became a protectorate of India in 1950 and a State in 1975. Because of its location, it has a political and strategic importance out of proportion to its size.

History : Little is known of Sikkim's history prior to the seventeenth century. The State's name is derived from the Limbu words *su him*, meaning "new house". The Lepcha were the early inhabitants of the region, apparently assimilating the Naong, Chang, Mon, and other tribes. The Bhutia began entering the area from Tibet in the fourteenth century. When the kingdom of Sikkim was established in 1642, Phuntsog Namgyal, the first *chogyal* (temporal and spiritual king), came from this community. The Namgyal dynasty ruled Sikkim until 1975.

Sikkim fought a series of territorial wars with both Bhutan and Nepal beginning in the mid-eighteenth century, and Nepal subsequently came to occupy parts of western Sikkim and the submontane Tarai. It was during this period that the largest migration of Nepalese to Sikkim began. In 1816 these territories were restored to Sikkim by the British in return for its support during the Anglo-Nepalese War (1814-1816), but by 1817 Sikkim had become a de facto protectorate of Britain.

The British East India Company obtained Darjeeling from Sikkim in 1835. Incidents between the British and Sikkim led to the annexation, in 1849, of the submontane regions and the subsequent military defeat of Sikkim, culminating in the Anglo-Sikkimese Treaty of 1861. The treaty established Sikkim as a Princely State under British paramountcy (though leaving the issue of sovereignty undefined), and the British were given the rights of free trade and of road-making through Sikkim to Tibet. In 1890 an agreement was concluded between the British and the Tibetans that defined the border between Sikkim and Tibet. Tibet also acknowledged the special relationship of British India with the kingdom of Sikkim. A British political officer was subsequently appointed to assist the *chogyal* in the administration of Sikkim's domestic and foreign affairs and, in effect, became the virtual ruler of the State.

In 1950, three years after India attained independence, a treaty was signed between Sikkim and India that made Sikkim an Indian protectorate. India assumed responsibility for the external relations, defence, and strategic communications of Sikkim.

After 1947 political parties began to be formed in Sikkim for the first time. Among their aims were the abolition of feudalism, the establishment of a popularly elected government, and the accession of Sikkim to India — all demands resisted by the *chogyal* and his supporters. The terms of the 1950 Indo-Sikkimese treaty, however, included increased popular participation in the government, and five general elections based on adult suffrage were held between 1952 and 1974. In the last of these elections, two rival parties merged to form the Sikkim Congress, which swept the polls. The party launched a campaign to obtain greater political liberties and rights which the *chogyal* attempted to suppress. With the situation getting out of control, the *chogyal* asked the government of India to take over the administration. India prepared a constitution for Sikkim that was approved by its national assembly in 1974. In a 1975 special referendum, more than 97 per cent of the electorate voted for the merger of Sikkim with India. Sikkim became the twenty-second State of the Indian Union on May 15, 1975.

Relief: Sikkim is a basin surrounded on three sides by precipitous mountain walls. There is little lowland, and the variation in relief is extreme. Within 80 km the land rises from an elevation of 229 m in the Tista River valley to 8,598 m at Kanchenjunga, India's highest peak and the world's third highest mountain. The Singalila Range separates Sikkim from Nepal in the west, while the Dongkya Range forms the border with China to the east. Several passes across this range afford easy access to the Chumbi valley in Tibet and beyond to Lhasa, imparting considerable strategic and political value to the region.

About two-thirds of Sikkim consists of perpetually snow-covered mountains, dominated by the Kanchenjunga massif. The Sikkimese have traditionally viewed the mountain as both a god and the abode of gods. The legendary abominable snowman, or yeti, called Nee-gued in Sikkim, is believed to roam its slopes. Other major peaks — all above 7,010 m — include Tent, Kabru, and Pauhunri.

Drainage : The Sikkim basin is drained by the Tista River and its tributaries, such as the Rangit, Rongni Chu, Talung, and Lachung, which have cut deep valleys into the mountains. Originating in a glacier near the Tibetan border, the Tista River descends steeply, dropping about 4,785 m to Rongphu (Rangpo), where it has cut a gorge through the Darjiling Ridge (2,134-2,438 m) before emerging onto the Gangetic Plain. Hydroelectric projects on Sikkim's rivers provide power to Gangtok, Rongphu, Singtam, and Mangan.

Climate : Sikkim exhibits a variety of climatic types, from almost tropical conditions in the south to the severe mountain climates in the north. Depending on altitude and exposure, annual precipitation varies from 1,270 to 5,080 mm, most occurring during the months of the southwest monsoon (May through October). The heavy rains and snows often trigger destructive landslides and avalanches.

Plant and animal life : About one-third of Sikkim is forested. Sal, pandanus, palms, bamboos, ferns, and orchids are common in the subtropical forests found below about 1,524 m. In the temperate forests, found at altitudes between 1,524 and 3,962 m, oak, laurel, maple, chestnut, magnolia, alder, birch, rhododendron, fir, hemlock, and spruce predominate. Alpine tundra replaces forest at the higher elevations. A variety of over 4,000 species of plants — magnolias, rhododendrons, junipers, blue poppies, gentians, and primulas — are found here.

Sikkim has a rich and varied animal life, including the black bear, brown bear, panda, numerous species of deer, wild goat, sheep, goral, and the Tibetan antelope; the tiger, leopard, and lesser cats are also found. Birdlife includes pheasants, partridges, quail, eagles, barbets, Himalayan cuckoos, Tibetan black crows, and minivets.

People : The Lepcha peoples are considered to be the original inhabitants of Sikkim. Invasions from Tibet brought the Bhutia to this State from the fourteenth century onwards. Nepali migrants were encouraged by the British administrators. In fact there was a five-fold increase in the number of Nepalis between 1891 and 1931. Three-quarters of Sikkim's population is Nepalese in origin, speaking Nepali (Gorkhali) dialects and mostly Hindu in religion and culture. The Bhutia, Lepcha, and Limbu are significant minorities; they speak Tibeto-Burman dialects and practise Mahayana Buddhism and the pre-Buddhist Bon religion. Migrants from mainland India since 1985 have added to the Hindu population, and there are also a small number of Christians and Muslims.

The decadal growth of population is 28.47 per cent. In 1991-1993, the birth rate was 22.7 per cent and death rate 6.6 per cent. Nearly 53 per cent of the population is male. The overall density is only 57 persons per sq km, while the populated East district has 187 persons to a sq km. The population is mostly rural, living in scattered hamlets and villages. Gangtok, with fewer than 30,000 people, is Sikkim's largest settlement; other towns, in descending order of population, include Singtam, Rongphu, Jorthang, Nayabazar, Mangan, Gyalshing, and Namchi.

Economy : Copper, lead, zinc, coal, graphite, and limestone are among the *minerals* found in the State, though not all are commercially exploited. Forest resources and hydroelectric potential are considerable. Sikkim, however, is predominantly agricultural. The net sown area is 63,254 ha; a sizeable area is not available for cultivation. Maize, rice, buckwheat, wheat, and barley are produced in terraced fields along the flanks of the valley. Beans, ginger, potatoes, vegetables, fruits, and tea also are grown. Sikkim is one of the world's main producers of cardamom.

Livestock includes cattle, pigs, sheep, goats, and poultry. Catde and buffalo are limited mainly to the subtropical humid belt, while yak and sheep are herded in the higher elevations in the north. Fish production in 1995-1996 was 150 tonnes.

Until the early 1970s, Sikkim had only cottage *industries* — producing handwoven textiles, carpets, and blankets — as well as traditional handicrafts such as embroidery, scroll paintings, and wood carving. There are now a number of small-scale industries, including a flour mill, a tannery, a watch-assembly unit, a distillery, a fruit preservation plant, and a tea processing factory. The installed power capacity is 30.9 MW.

Roads, though not extensive, are the primary mode of travel. Ropeways have also been provided at many points. The capital, Gangtok, is nearly 121 km from the nearest airport at Bagdogra and 113 km from the railhead at Siliguri, both in West Bengal. The road to Siliguri is considered to be the lifeline for this Himalayan State; the road is frequently disrupted by landslides. State buses connect different parts of the State and neighbouring West Bengal. Furthermore, there are telephone exchanges, hospitals, two degree colleges, and one law college in the State. Helicopter services are also available from the Bagdogra airport.

Sikkim has become a new destination for domestic and foreign *tourists*. It is a cool and peaceful place, providing a variety of options. Though foreign tourist flow remains almost constant, the number of domestic tourists is on the increase. Inner line permits are required for foreigners to enter this State. Places of tourist interest are Rumtek monastery (24 km from Gangtok, at an altitude of 1,550 m), Changu lake in East district (36 km from Gangtok, at an altitude of 3,774 m), Gezing (112 km from Gangtok), Pemayangtse monastery (120 km from Gangtok at an altitude of 2,085 m). Pelling monastery, Khechopari lake (26 km from Gangtok), Phodong monastery (35 km from Gangtok), Yumthang hot spring (135 km from Gangtok, at an altitude of 3,700 m), and Kanchendzonga National Park. There are trekking agents available in Darjeeling and Gangtok who conduct tours to different parts of the State. North Sikkim district has a special attraction for nature lovers. The 140-km route to Yumthang (3,658 m from Gangtok) has a fascinating blend of breathtaking views, hot springs, and an alpine environment. River-rafting is popular in Tista and Rangeet rivers. Other sports enjoyed by tourists include yak safaris, mountain biking, and hang-gliding. The use of plastic bags and packets is banned in Sikkim as they obstruct the natural flow of water which has recently caused floods and damaged houses in the capital.

Cultural life : Sikkim's cultural life, despite a strong Tibetan influence, retains a character derived from the various tribes of Sikkim and their pre-Buddhist customs. The most important festival of the year is the two-day Phanglhapsol festival in August or September, in which masked dancers perform in honour of Kanchenjunga, the presiding deity. The Namgyal Institute of Tibetology has one of the largest collections of Tibetan books in the world. Many monasteries are repositories of artistic treasures, including wall paintings, *thang-kas* (religious paintings mounted on brocade), and bronze images.

Area, Population and Headquarters of Districts

S.No.	District	Area (sq km)	Population (1991 Census)	Headquarters
1.	East	954	1,78,452	Gangtok
2.	North	4,226	31,240	Mangan
3.	South	750	98,604	Namchi
4.	West	1,166	98,161	Gyallhing

T

Tamil Nadu—A state of India, it is located in the extreme south of the subcontinent. The State has an area of 130,057 sq km. It is bounded by the Indian Ocean to the east and south and by the States of Kerala to the west, Karnataka (formerly Mysore) to the northwest, and Andhra Pradesh to the north. The capital is Chennai (formerly Madras).

Tamil Nadu represents the Tamil-speaking area of what was formerly the Madras Presidency. The Tamils are proud of their Dravidian language and culture, and they have resisted attempts by the Union (Central) government to make Hindi the national language. While it has an industrial core in Chennai, the State is essentially agricultural.

History : The history of Tamil Nadu begins with the establishment of a trinity of Taml powers in the region — namely, the Chera, Chola, and Pandya kingdoms. By about AD 200 the influence of northern Aryan powers had progressed, and the Aryan sage Agastya had established himself as a cultural hero. The use of Roman gold and lamps and the consumption of Italian wine testify to the extensive foreign trade of the period.

From the mid-sixth century until the ninth century, the Chalukyas of Badami, the Pallavas of Kanchi, and the Pandyas of Madurai fought a long series of wars in the region. The period, nonetheless, was marked by a revival of Hinduism and the advancement of fine arts. From about AD 850, Tamil Nadu was dominated by the Cholas, of whom Rajendra I (reigned 1014-1044) was the most distinguished ruler. In the mid-fourteenth century the Hindu kingdom of Vijayanagar, which included all of Tamil Nadu, came into prominence. During the 300 years of Vijayanagar rule, Telugu-speaking governors and officials were introduced in the administration.

In 1640 the English East India Company opened a trading post at the fishing village of Madraspatnam (now Chennai) with the permission of the local ruler. The history of Tamil Nadu from the mid-seventeenth century to 1946 is the story of the Madras Presidency in relationship to the rise and fall of British power in India. After 1946 the Madras Presidency was able to make steady progress, as it had a stable government. In 1953 the Telugu-speaking State of Andhra Pradesh was formed, and in 1956 the Presidency was further divided into the States of Kerala, Mysore (now Karnataka), and Tamil Nadu.

Relief: The state is divided naturally between the flat country along the eastern coast and the hilly regions in the north and west. The broadest part of the eastern plains is the fertile Cauvery (Kaveri) delta; farther south are the arid plains of Ramanathapuram and Madurai. The high Western Ghats range runs all along the States western border. The lower hills of the Eastern Ghats and its outliers — locally called the Javadi, Kalrayan, and Shevaroy — run through the centre of the region.

The important *rivers* include the Cauvery, the Ponnaiyar, the Palar, the Vaigai, and the Tambraparni, all of which flow eastwards from the inland hills. The Cauvery and its tributaries are Tamil Nadu's most important sources of water and power.

Apart from the rich alluvial soil of the river deltas, the predominant *soils* are clays, loams, sands, and red laterites (soils with a high content of iron oxides and aluminium hydroxide). The black cotton-growing soil known as regur is found in parts of Salem and Coimbatore in the west, Ramanathapuram and Tirunelveli in the south, and Tiruchirappalli in the central region of Tamil Nadu.

Climate : The climate is essentially tropical. The temperature in summer seldom exceeds 43 °C and in winter seldom falls below 18 °C. The lowest temperatures are recorded during December and January, and the highest between April and June. The average annual rainfall, falling mainly between October and December, depends on the southwest and northeast monsoons and ranges between 635 mm and 1,905 mm a year. The most precipitation falls in the Nilgiri and other hill areas, the least in the Ramanathapuram and Tirunelveli districts.

Vegetation : Forests cover about 15 per cent of the State. At the highest altitudes of the Western Ghats — the Nilgiri, Anaimalai, and Palni Hills — the mountains support subalpine vegetation. Along the eastern side of the Western Ghats and in the hills of the northern and central districts, the plant life is a mixture of evergreen and deciduous plants, some of which are markedly adapted to arid conditions. Timber products extracted from the forests include sandalwood, pulpwood, and bamboo. Rubber is also an important forest product. The aquatic birds in the State are represented in the bird sanctuary at Vedantangal; other forms of wildlife may be seen in the game sanctuary at Mudumalai.

People : The *population* of the area has changed little over the centuries, largely representing the ancient Dravidian ancestry indigenous to southern India. Most of the hill tribes exhibit affinities with certain Southeast Asian peoples. In Tamil Nadu, as in the rest of the country, the caste system is still strong, even though discrimination has been banned by the Constitution of India.

Tamil, the official State *language*, is spoken by most of the people. For a considerable percentage of the population that has long resided in the State, Tamil has almost become a mother tongue. Telugu is spoken by almost 10 per cent of the population; Kannada, Urdu, and Malayalam are spoken by much smaller percentages. In the Nilgiri district in the west, Kannada (and its dialect Badga) and Malayalam are stronger. English is spoken as a subsidiary language.

The main *religions* in the State are Hinduism, Christianity, Islam, and Jainism. Followers of the first three religions are found in all districts, but Jains are confined to North and South Arcot and Chennai.

Hindus constitute the overwhelming majority of the population. The largest concentration of Christians is in the Tirunelveli and Kanniyakumari districts. The growth of atheism is a recent development, possibly as a protest against Brahmin ritualism.

Although Tamil Nadu is one of the most urbanized States of India, it is still largely *rural*. Most of the people live in more than 64,000 nucleated villages. The poorest low-caste villagers live in segregated areas called *ceri*. The Chennai metropolitan conurbation (extended urban area), covering the industrial areas, townships, and villages surrounding Chennai, has the largest population, but there are other conurbations, of which those around Madurai, Coimbatore, and Tiruchirappalli are the most important,

Economy : Agriculture is the mainstay of life for about three-quarters of the rural population. From very early times, Tamil farmers have skilfully conserved scarce rainwater in small and large irrigation reservoirs, or "tanks". Government canals, tube wells, and ordinary wells also form part of the irrigation system. Because several of the river valley projects depend for water on the erratic northeast monsoon, the government is trying to tap subsoil water sources.

Agricultural practices have undergone radical improvement since 1950. Multiple cropping, the use of new and better strains of rice, cotton, sugar, and millet, and the use of chemical fertilizers have been widely adopted. By 1967 the State was self-sufficient in the production of food-grains. Rice, peanuts (groundnuts), cotton, chillies, banana, coffee, tea, rubber, and sugarcane are important cash crops.

Improved port facilities and the effective use of electric power resources have helped *industrial development.* The State is one of the most industrialized in India. The important minerals are limestone, bauxite, gypsum, lignite, magnesite, and iron ore. Cotton ginning, spinning, and weaving continue to be the major industries, followed by the production of automobiles, motorcycles transformers, sugar, agricultural implements, fertilizers, cement, paper, chemicals, and electric motors. The railway coach factory at Perambur is one of the largest in Asia; the heavy vehicles factory, producing tanks, is at Avadi, near Chennai. There is an oil refinery at Chennai and a larger thermal power project at Neyveli; both are public sector ventures. The State ranks second only the Kerala in the production of fish.

Tamil Nadu is rich in handicrafts; notable among them are handloom silk, metal icons, leather work, *qalamkari* (hand-painted fabric, using natural dyes) brass, bronze, and copper ware, and carved wood, palm leaf, and cane anicies,

Transportation : The transport system of the southern Indian States converges in Chennai. Many railways run through Tamil Nadu. The artificial harbour of Chennai handles seaborne traffic. Apart from the international airport a Meenambakkam near Chennai, there are three other airports at Tiruchirappalli, Madurai, and Coimbatore. There is a network of motorable roads. Passenger bus transport is being nationalized; express buses take passengers to all important towns and places of interest.

Cultural Life : Despite attempts to break the religious and political power of the priestly Brahmin caste, *Hinduism* remains at the core of the culture. The more than 9,300 larger temples come under the administrative control of the Hindu religious and charitable endowments department. In most towns — and particularly in Chidambaram, Kanchipuram, Thanjavur (Tanjore), and Madurai — the gopurarms or gateway towers, of the temples are dominant.

The cycle of *temple festivals* attracts large congregations of devotees. Noteworthy are the car festivals, during which large chariots decorated with icons are taken in procession around the temple. Hindu families owe allegiance to a number of sectarian monastic institutions, or *maths*, of which the most important is the Shankara Math at Kumbakonam.

Bharatanatyam, one of India's major *classical dance* forms, and *Carnatic music* are both widely practised. Painting and sculpture, however, are less developed, although there are schools that teach the art of sculpture in stone and bronze. Tamil literature rapidly adapted to the Western literary forms of the novel and the short story. The poet Subrahmanya C. Bharati (1882-1921) was one of the first to modify traditional Tamil poetry. Since the 1940s, the motion picture has become the most popular form of mass entertainment. There are both touring and permanent cinema theatres; and sentimental and spectacular films, often featuring light music and dancing, are produced by the film studios situated largely around Chennai.

Hundreds of periodicals are published jn Tamil, most of them, daily newspapers. *Dina Thanthi* is the leading- paper. Among English newspapers. *The Hindu* from Chennai maintains excellent journalistic standards.

Area, Population and Headquarters of Districts

S.No.	*District*	*Area (sq km)*	*Population*	*Headquarters*
1.	Chennai	174	42,16,268	Chennai
2.	Kancheepuram	4,433	28,69,920	Kancheepuram
3.	Thiruvallur	3,424	27,38,866	Thiruvallur
4.	Vellore	6,077	34,82,970	Vellore
5.	Tiruvannamalai	6,191	21,81,853	Tiruvannamalai
6.	Cuddalore	3,999	22,80,530	Cuddalore
7.	Villupuram	7,217	29,43,917	Villupuram
8.	Salem	5,220	29,92,754	Salem
9.	Namakkal	3,429	14(95,661	Namakkal
10.	Dharmapuri	9,622	28,33,252	Dharmapuri
11.	Pudukottai	4,651	14,52,269	Pudukottai
12.	Erode	8,209	25,74,067	Erode
13.	The Nilgiris	2,549	7,64,826	Uthagamandalam
14.	Coimbatore	7,469	42,24,107	Coimbatore,
15.	Trichirappalli	5,114	23,88,831	Trichirappalli
16.	Karur	2,896	9,33,791	Karur
17.	Perambalur	3,691	4,86,971	Perambalur
18.	Thanjavur	3,397	22,05,375	Thanjavur
19.	Nagapattinam	2,716	14,87,055	Nagapattinam

S.No.	District	Area (sq km)	Population	Headquarters
20.	Thiruvarur	2,161	11,65,213	'Thiruvarur
21.	Madurai	6,565	25,62,279	Madurai
22.	Theni	2,889	10,94,724	Theni
23.	Dindigul	6,058	19,18,960	Dindigul
24.	Ramanathapuram	4,232	11,83,321	Ramanathapuram
25.	Sivagangai	4,086	11,50,753	Sivagangai
26.	Virudhunagar	4,288	17,51,548	VITUdhunagar
27.	Tirunelveli	6,810	28,01,194	TIrunelveli
28.	Toothukudi	4,621	15,65,743	Toothukudi
29.	Kanniyakumari	1,685	16,69,763	Nagercoil
30.	Ariyalur	—	6,9,4,058	Ariyalur

Area for S.No. 15, 16, 17, 21, 22 and 30 are subject to finalisation.

Tripura—This state of India is located in the northeastern part. It is bordered on the north, west, and south by Bangladesh, on the east by the State of Mizoram, and on the northeast by the State of Assam. Covering an area of only 10,486 sq km , it is India's third smallest State, after Goa and Sikkim, With its isolation from the rest of the country, hilly terrain, and tribal populations, Tripura shares many of the problems of India's northeastern region. Agartala is the capital of Tripura.

History : According to legend, Tripura existed during the time of the Mahabharata. The history of Tripura includes two distinct periods — the traditional, largely legendary period described in the *Rajamala*, a chronicle of the presumed early kings (*maharajas*) of Tripura, and the period since about 1431-1462, the reigning years of the great king Dharma Manikya. The *Rajamala*, written in Bengali verse, was compiled by the Brahmins in the court of Dharma Manikya. During his reign and that of his successor, Dhanya Manikya (reigned c. 1463-1515), Tripura suzerainty was extended over much of Bengal, Assam, and Myanmar in a series of military conquests. It was not until the beginning of the seventeenth century that the Mughal Empire extended its sovereignty over much of Tripura.

When the British East India Company obtained the *diwani*, or financial administration, of Bengal in 1765, the part of Tripura that had been under Mughal rule came under British control. From 1808 each successive ruler had to receive investiture from the British government. In 1905 Tripura was attached to the new province of Eastern Bengal and Assam and was known as Hill Tippera.

The last ruling *maharaja* of Tripura, Bir Bikram Kishore Manikya, ascended the throne in 1923 and, before his death in 1947, settled that Tripura should accede to the newly independent country of India. Tripura officially became part of India on October 15, 1949, and was made a Union Territory on September 1, 1956. It became a constituent State of the Indian Union on January 21, 1972.

In the 1980s there was considerable ethnic violence in this State, largely fuelled by demands for an independent tribal homeland in Tripura. In 1988 tribal dissidents ceased hostilities and dropped demands for autonomy in return for increased participation in State government. Population (1991) State Total 2,757,205; Rural 2,335,484; Urban 421,721.

Land and Climate : Central and northern Tripura is a *hilly region* crossed by four major valleys — from east to west, the Dharmanagar, Kailashahar, Kamalpur, and Khowai — carved out by northward-flowing rivers (the Juri, Manu and Deo, Dhalai, and Khowai, respectively). The lower valleys in the west and south tend to be open and marshy, although in the south the terrain is heavily dissected and densely forested. North-south-trending ranges separate the valleys. East of the Dharmanagar valley, the Jamrai Tlang rises to elevations between 600 m and 900 m. Altitude decreases westwards through the successive ranges — the Sakhan Tlang, Langtarai, and Artharamura — with the westernmost hills, the Deotamura, attaining height of only 243.76 m.

West of the Deotamura Range is the Agartala *plain*, an extension of the Ganga-Brahmaputra lowlands, with an elevation of less than 60.96 m . It is drained by numerous rivers, the largest of which, the Gurnti, emerges from the eastern hills in a steep-sided valley near Radhakishorepur.

More than 2,000 mm of *rainfall* occurs during the monsoon season from June to September. Maximum temperatures in the lowlands average around 35 °C in the summer, though it is cooler in the mountains.

Forests cover about half the State (57.77 per cent); although extensively cleared for cultivation, they still contain valuable trees, including sal (*Shorea robusta*), a tree that yields hardwood, second in value only to teak. Animal life includes tigers, leopards, elephants, jackals, wild dogs, boars, gayal ox, wild buffalo, and gaur.

People : Tripura is predominantly *rural*. The highest densities of population are in the State's most fertile agricultural lands, located in the western plains and the Gurnti, Dharmanagar, and Khowai valleys.

Apart from Bengalis and Manipuris, Tripura has 19 different tribal communities. Scheduled castes and scheduled tribes form 16.36 per cent and 30.95 per cent population of the State respectively. Of the tribes, the important ones are Tripuri or Tippira (16.12 per cent), Reang (4.095 per cent), Jamatia (2.175 per cent), and Chakma (1.69 per cent). More than half the population speaks Bengali. Tripuri and Bengali are the State's official languages. The other important language is Manipuri. Hinduism (86.50 per cent) is the religion of the majority. There are also small minorities of Muslims (7.13 per cent), Buddhists (4.65 per cent), and Christians (1.69 per cent). *Towns* are concentrated on the western plain, where the State capital of Agartala is located. The four towns after which the northern valleys are named all serve as local marketing centres. There are 18 urban centres in the State contributing to 15.30 per cent of the population. The rest of the population resides in 462 villages, 77 per cent of which are electrified.

Economy : Tripura's economic is primarily *agricultural*. The major crop is rice (46.16 per cent of agricultural production), which is grown throughout the State. Cash crops include jute (used in the manufacture of sacking, burlap, and twine), cotton, tea, sugarcane, mesta, and fruit. Livestock plays only a subsidiary role in the State's agriculture. Forestry-based industries produce timber, firewood, and charcoal. In 1994, the production of tea was 3,555,593 kg.

Manufacturing is largely on a small scale and includes many cottage industries, such as weaving, carpentry, basketry, and pottery making. The State government is active in fostering the growth of small-scale industries. Bamboo and cane handicrafts including room dividers, wall panels, furniture, table mats, and floor mats are made locally. Industrial units also produce tea, sugar, canned fruit, agricultural implements, bricks, and footwear; larger establishments include a spinning mill, a jute mill, a steel mill, a plywood factory, and a pharmaceutical plant.

Energy is provided by diesel-powered thermal plants at Agartala, Ambasa, Khowai, Dharmanagar, Kailashahar, Udaipur, and Bagafa and by the Gurnti hydroelectric project (completed in 1976). The total installed capacity is 6,935 MW. Extensive resources of natural gas have recently been discovered in the State.

Tripura's hilly topography renders *communication* difficult. Moreover, with Bangladesh bordering the State on three sides (839 km), Tripura is virtually isolated from the rest of India; land routes consist only of the Agartala-Karimganj (Assam) road (3,666 km) and a metre-gauge railway link (only 45 km) from Dharmanagar to Kalkali Ghat, Assam. Most rivers carry boat traffic, but this is generally for local transport. Agartala is linked by air to Calcutta (in West Bengal) and various towns in Assam. Intrastate air service is also available.

Cultural life : Tribal customs, folklore, and folk songs are important elements in Tripura's *culture*. Two major annual ceremonies are Garia (April) and Kas (June or July), both of which often include animal sacrifice. Each community has its own dance forms, such as hozagiri of Reang; garia, jhum, malmita, masak sumani, and lebang boomani of Tripuris; bizu of Chakma; cheraw and welcome of Lushai; hai-hak of Malsum; wangala of Garo; sangraiaka, chimithang, padisha, and abhangma of Mog; garia of Katai and Jamatia; ganjan, dhamail, sari, and rabindra of Bengali; and basanta rash and pung chalam of Manipuri. The important musical instruments are khamb, bamboo flute, lebang, sarinda, do-tara, and khengrong. The State has produced famous musicians such as Sachin Dev Burman and Rahul Dev Burman.

Some of the important *fairs and festivals* are Ashokastami (April); Garia and Ganjan festivals (April); Rabindra/Nazrul Jayanti (May); Kharachi festival July); Boat race (August); Mansa Mangal (August); Durga Puja (October); Diwali festival (November); Rash festival (November); and Poush Sankranti Mela (January).

Transport : This State is also connected by rail via Guwahati. The nearest railhead is at Kumarghat. It is to be connected with Agartala, which is about 140 km. Agartala can also be approached by about a 24-hour bus ride from Guwahati via Shillong by the National Highway 44. Good private and public luxury coaches are available on this route. The alternative route is to reach Silchar in Assam by air or road, and proceed further to Agartala by road. Foreign tourists can approach Agartala through Bangladesh via Akhaura border check post. The road journey from Dhaka to Agartala is about three hours.

Tourism : Tripura has several places of *tourist interest*. In 1996, nearly 200,000 tourists visited this State subsequent to the withdrawal of the Restricted Area Permit in May 1995 for domestic as well as foreign tourists. However, the State has the potential to attract larger number of tourists. The State capital, Agartala, can be approached by air from Calcutta and Guwahati. Three small airports are at Khowal, Kamalpur, and Kailashahar.

The places of tourist interest include Ujjayanta Palace, Kunjaban Palace/Rabindra Kanan, Malancha Niwas at Agartala; Neermahal/

Rudrasagar Lake, 55 km from Agartala; and Unakoti rock cut and carvings, 178 km from Agartala and 8 km from Kailashahar. Agartala is also venue of Ashokastami mela (fair) which is held in April every year.

Debtamura rock cut images/Chablmura, 75 km fiom Agartala on the bank of Gumti (Gomati) River between Udaipur and Alarpur, is another tourist site. Located on the right bank of Gurnti River at Udaipur is Bhuvaneshwari Temple where Rabindranath Tagore wrote *Bisarjan* and *Rajarshi.* Twenty five kilometres from Agartala is Sepahijala Wild Life Sanctuary. It has about 150 species of birds as well as the famous spectacled monkey.

The Trishna Wild Life Sanctuary is about 100 km from Agartala in South Tripura district. The Kamalasagar Lake is 27 km away and Jampui Hill is about 200 km from Agartala bordering Mizoram and at nearly 914 m above sea level. The highest peak of Tripura, Betalongchhip (1097 m), is located here.

Area, Population and Headquarters of Districts

S.No.	*District*	*Area (sq km)*	*Population*	*Headquarters*
1.	North Tripura	2,820.63	5,90,655	Kailashahar
2.	South Tripura	2,151.77	7,62,565	Udaipur
3.	West Tripura	2,996.82	15,30,531	Agartala
4.	Dhalai	2,552.47	3,07,417	Ambassa

U

Uttaranchal—Located in the foothills of the Himalayas, the State has international boundaries with China (Tibet) in the north and Nepal in the east. On its north-west lies Himachal Pradesh while on the south is Uttar Pradesh.

History : Uttaranchal finds mention in the ancient Hindu scriptures as Kedarkhand, Manaskhand and Himavant. The Kushanas, Kunindas, Kanishka, Samudra Gupta, the Pauravas, Katuris, Palas, the Chandras and Pawaras and the British have ruled it in turns. It is often called the Land of the Gods (*Dev Bhoomi*) because of its various holy places and abundant shrines. The hilly regions of Uttaranchal offer unspoilt landscapes to the tourist-pilgrim.

The present State of Uttaranchal was earlier a part of the United Province of Agra and Awadh which came into existence in 1902. In 1935, the name of the State was shortened to the United Province. In January 1950, the United Province was renamed as Uttar Pradesh and Uttaranchal remained a part of Uttar Pradesh before it came into being on 9 November 2000, the 27th State of India.

Economy : About 90 per cent of the population of Uttaranchal depends on *agriculture*. The net cultivated area in the State is 12,61,915 hectares.

Agricultural land under irrigation is 5,19,806 hectares (year 1994-95) which is 56 per cent of the total agricultural land. The State has excellent potential for hydropower generation. There are a number of hydro-electric projects on the rivers Yamuna, Bhagirathi, Ganga, Ramganga and Sharda, generating electricity. Out of 15,669 villages, 12,315 villages have been electrified.

The State is rich in *mineral deposits* like limestone, rock phosphate, dolomite, magnesite, copper greyphyte, soap stone, gypsum, etc. The number of small-scale industries is 41,216 with an investment of Rs 305.58 crore providing employment to 1,53,229 persons. One-hundred-and-ninety-one heavy industries with an investment of Rs 2,694.66 crore employ 50,802 persons. Most of the industries are forest-based.

The total length of metalled *roads* in Uttaranchal is 16,652 km. The length of PWD roads is 12,706 km. The length of roads built by local bodies is 1,353 km and by other agencies 2,593 km..

The main *railway* stations are Dehradun, Hardwar, Roorkee, Kotdwar, Kashipur, Haldwani and Kathgodam

There are *air strips* at Jolly Grant (Dehradun), Pantnagar (Udham Singh Nagar) and Naini-Seni (Pithoragarh). Air strips at Gauchar (Chamoli) and Chinyalisaur (Uttarkashi) are under construction.

Cultural life : The world-famous *Kumbh Mela/Ardh Kumbh Mela* is held at Hardwar every twelfth/sixth year interval. Other prominent fairs/festivals are: Devidhura Mela (Champawat), Purnagiri Mela (Champawat), Nanda Devi Mela (Almora), Gauchar Mela (Chamoli), Baisakhi (Uttarkashi), Maga Mela (Uttarkashi), Uttaraini Mela (Bageshwar), Vishu Mela (Jaunsar Vavar), Peerane-Kaliyar (Roorkee), and Nanda Devi Raj Jat Yatra held every twelfth year.

Prominent places of *pilgrimage/tourist* interest are Gangotri, Yamunotri. Badrinath, Kedarnath, Hardwar, Rishikesh, Hemkund Sahib,

Nanakmatta, etc. Kailash Mansarovar Yatra can be performed through Kumaon region. The world-famous Valley of Flowers, Pindari Glacier, Roop Kund, Dayara Bugyal, Auli, and hill stations like Mussoorie, Dehradun, Chakrata, Nainital, Ranikhet, Bageshwar, Bhimtal, Kausani are the important places of tourist interest.

Area, Population and Headquarters of Districts

S.No.	*District*	*Area (sq km)*	*Population*	*Headquarters*
1.	Uttarkashi	8,016	2,94,179	Uttarkashi
2.	Chamoli	7,626	3,69,198	Gopeshwar
3.	Rudra Prayag	2,252	2,27,461	Rudra Prayag
4.	Tehri Garhwal	3,796	6,04,608	New Tehri
5.	Dehradun	3,088	12,79,083	Dehradun
6.	Pauri Garhwal	5,397	6,96,851	Pauri
7.	Pithoragarh	7,218	4,62,149	Pithoragarh
8.	Champawat	1,638	2,24,461	Champawat .
9.	Almora	3,074	6,30,446	Almora
10.	Bageshwar	2,311	2,49,453	Bageshar
11.	Nainital	4,767	7,62,912	Nainital
12.	Udhamsingh Nagar	2,027	12,34,548	Udhamsingh Nagar
13.	Hardwar	1,994	14,44,213	Hardwar

Uttar Pradesh—Uttar Pradesh is located in the north-central part of the country. It is bordered by Nepal and the Tibet Autonomous region of China in the north, the State of Himachal Pradesh in the northwest, the States of Haryana, Rajasthan, and Delhi in the west, the State of Madhya Pradesh in the south, and the State of Bihar in the east. On January 26, 1950, when India became a republic the State was given its present name, Uttar Pradesh (literally, "Northern State"). Lucknow is its capital. Uttar Pradesh ranks fourth among the Indian States in area (294,411 sq. km), which is about one-tenth of the total area of the country.

History : The history of Uttar Pradesh can be divided into five periods: (1) prehistory and mythology (upto c. 600 BC), (2) the Buddhist-Hindu (Brahminic) period (c. 600 BC to c. AD 1200), (3) the Muslim period (c. 1200 to c. 1775) (4) the British period (c. 1775 to 1947), and (5) the post-independence period (1947 to the present). Because of its position in the heart of the Indo Gangetic Plain, it has often been the focal point in the history of all of northern India.

Archaeology is beginning to shed new light on the early civilization of Uttar Pradesh. The remains of several human skeletons, found in the southern district of Pratapgarh, have been dated to about 10,000 BC. Knowledge of the area prior to the seventh century BC has largely been gained through Vedic literature and the two great Indian epics, the Ramayana and the Mahabharata, which describe the Gangetic Plain within Uttar Pradesh. The scene of the Mahabharata is the area around Hastinapur in the western part of the State, while the Ramayana is set in eastern Uttar Pradesh in and around Ayodhya, the birthplace of Rama (an incarnation of the god Vishnu and the hero of the story). Two other fountainheads of mythology in the State are the area around Vrindavan and Mathura, where Krishna (another incarnation of Vishnu) was born; and the Himalayan region, known to Hindus as the home of the god Shiva.

A systematic history of India and the area of Uttar Pradesh dates to the end of the seventh century BC, when 16 *mahajanapadas* (great States) in northern India were contending for supremacy. Of these seven fell entirely within the present-day boundaries of Uttar Pradesh. The Buddha preached his first sermon at Sarnath near Varanasi (Banaras) and founded a religion that spread not only across India but also to many distant lands, such as China and Japan. The Buddha is said to have attained *parinirvana* (freedom of spirit brought about by release from the body) at Kushinagara, located in the eastern district of Deoria. From the fifth century BC to the sixth century AD, Uttar Pradesh was mostly under the control of powers centred outside of its present boundaries, first at Magadha in present-day Bihar State and later at Ujjain in present-day Madhya Pradesh State. Among the great kings of this period who ruled over the State were Chandragupta (reigned c. 325 or 321-297 BC) and Ashoka (c. 268 or 265-238), both Maurya emperors, and Samudra Gupta (c. AD 330-380) and Chandra Gupta II (c. 380-415; identified by some scholars as Vikramaditya). Another of its famous rulers was Harsha (reigned 606-647); from his capital at Kanyakubja (near modern Kannauj), he was able to control the whole of Uttar Pradesh, as well as parts of Bihar, Madhya Pradesh, Punjab, and Rajasthan.

During this period Buddhist and Hindu (Brahminic) culture flourished side by side. Sculpture and architecture symbolic of Buddhist art reached their zenith during the reign of Ashoka; Hindu art saw its greatest development during the Gupta period (c. 320-540). After Harsha's death in about 647, there was a gradual downfall of Buddhism accompanied by a revival of Hinduism. The chief architect of this revival, Shankara, born in southern India, visited Varanasi, travelled through the plains of Uttar Pradesh, and established a famous temple at Badrinath in the Himalaya. The Shankara Temple is considered by Hindus as the fourth and last *math* (centre of Hindu culture).

Although Muslim incursions into the area occurred as early as AD 1000-1030, Muslim rule over northern India was not established until the last decade of the twelfth century, when Muhammad Ghuri defeated the Gahavalas (who occupied much of Uttar Pradesh) and other competing dynasties. For nearly 600 years Uttar Pradesh, like much of India, was ruled by one Muslim dynasty or another, each centred in or near Delhi.

In 1526 Babur defeated Sultan Ibrahim Lodi of Delhi and laid the foundation of the most successful of the Muslim dynasties, the Mughals, whose empire dominated the subcontinent for more than 200 years. The greatest extent of the empire came under Akbar (reigned 1556-1605), who constructed a grand new capital, Fatehpur Sikri, near Agra. His grandson, Shah Jahan (reigned 1628-1658), built at Agra one of the world's greatest architectural achievements, the Taj Mahal (a mausoleum constructed in memory of his wife, who died in childbirth); Shah Jahan built several other architecturally important buildings in Agra as well as in Delhi.

The Mughal Empire, centred in Uttar Pradesh, promoted the development of a new composite culture. Akbar, its greatest exponent, employed in his court men pre-eminent in architecture, literature, painting, and music, irrespective of their caste or creed. The conflict between Hinduism and Islam led to the growth of several new sects seeking a common meeting ground between these two religions and between the various castes of India. Ramananda (c. 1400-1470), a Brahmin and founder of the *bhakti* (devotional) sect, which claimed that salvation was not dependent on one's sex or caste, and Kabir (1440-1518), who preached the essential unity of all religions, focussed their fight against religious intolerance in Uttar Pradesh. The downfall of the Mughals in the eighteenth century led to the shifting of the centre of this composite culture from Delhi to Lucknow, the seat of the *nawab* of Awadh (Oudh, now Ayodhya), where art, literature, music, and poetry flourished in an atmosphere of communal harmony.

The area of present-day Uttar Pradesh was gradually acquired by the East India Company (a British trading company) over a period of about 75 years. Territories wrested from a number of northern Indian dynasties — the *nawab* in 1775, 1798, and 1801, the Scindias of Gwalior in 1803, and the Gurkhas in 1816— were first placed within the Bengal Presidency, but in 1833 they were separated to form the North-Western

Provinces (initially called the Agra Presidency). The kingdom of Awadh, annexed by the company in 1856, was united with the North-Western Provinces in 1877 under the name United Provinces of Agra and Awadh (with borders almost identical with present-day Uttar Pradesh); in 1902 the name was changed to the United Provinces.

The great mutiny and revolt against the East India Company in 1857-1859 was largely confined to the North-Western Provinces. Sparked by a mutiny of soldiers at Meerut on May 10, 1857, the revolt spread within months to more than 25 cities. In 1858, with the revolt virtually crushed, administration of the North-Western Provinces and the rest of British India were transferred from the East India Company to the British crown.

With the rise of Indian nationalism beginning in the late 1880s, the United Provinces stood at the forefront of the movement for independence. It gave India many of the important nationalist political leaders, such as Motilal Nehru, Madan Mohan Malaviya, Jawaharlal Nehru, and Purushottamdas Tandon. In 1922 Mahatma Gandhi's Noncooperarion Movement, designed to shake the foundations of the British Empire in India, spread throughout the United Provinces, but mob violence in the village of Chauri Chaura (in the eastern part of the provinces) caused Gandhi to temporarily suspend the movement. The United Provinces was also a centre of Muslim League politics.

During the British period, there was extensive development of railways, canals, and means of communications within the provinces. The British also promoted the growth of modern education, and a number of colleges and universities, such as the University of Lucknow (1921), were established.

In 1947 the United Provinces became one of the administrative units of the newly independent dominion of India. Two years later the autonomous States of Tehri-Garhwal and Rampur, both within its borders, were incorporated into the United Provinces. With the adoption of a new Indian Constitution in 1950, the United Provinces was renamed Uttar Pradesh and became a constituent State of the new Indian Union.

Since independence, the State has maintained a dominant role within India, It has given the country several prime ministers, including Jawaharlal Nehru and his daughter, Indira Gandhi, as well as prominent leaders of national opposition (minority) parties, such as Acharya Narendra Dev, one of the founders of the Praja Socialist Party, and Atal Bihari Vajpayee, of the Bharatiya Jan Sangh and later Bharatiya Janata Party, the present prime minister of India. State politics, however, have tended to be fractious, and seldom has any chief minister completed a five-year term.

Relief : Uttar Pradesh can be divided into three district *physiographic* regions: (1) the Himalayan region, (2) the Gangetic Plain, and (3) the Vindhyan scraplands. The Himalayan region has a highly varied topography, with snow-covered peaks, deep canyons, roaring streams, and gigantic lakes. It includes three distinctive sections of the Himalaya, the Shiwaliks (the outer Himalaya), the Himachal (the lesser Himalaya), and the Himadri (the greater Himalaya). The Shiwaliks rise gently above 300 m, have flat summits and sometimes attain elevations between 900 m and 1,000 m. In the leeward side of the Shiwaliks are structural depressions like Dehradun. On the north is the Himachal, which abruptly rises above 2,000 m. It has two linear ranges, Mussoorie and Nag Tibba, hill resorts such as Mussoorie, Nainital, and Ranikhet, and several beautiful lakes like Nainital, Bhimtal, and Sattal. North of Himachal lies the Himadri (6,096 m) which is studded with lofty peaks like Nanda Devi (7,817 m), Kamet (7,756 m), Badrinath (7,138 m), Kedarnath (6,940 m), and others.

The Gangetic Plain covers nearly three-fourths of the total area of Uttar Pradesh. It is characterized by flat, monotonous plains with imperceptible slopes. It includes the Bhabar region—submontane region consisting mostly of a narrow bed of gravel and alluvium—the Tarai region, and the plains. Along its southern fringes lies the Tarai area, a damp and marshy tract that has lost is forests due to deforestation. The plains are mostly filled with deep alluvial deposits by the Ganga and its tributaries. Most of this area is featureless, varying in elevation from about 305 m in the northwest to 58 m in the extreme east. The plains are very fertile.

South of the Gangetic Plain lies the Vindhyan scrapland and Bundelkhand uplands which are part of Deccan foreland. It is characterized by dissected terrain. The elevation rarely exceeds 305 m.

Drainage : The State is well drained by a number of *rivers* of the Ganga system that partially assimilates both the Himalayan and the peninsular drainage system. The Ganga and its main tributaries — Yamuna, Ramganga, Gomri, Ghaghara, and Gandak — are fed by perpetual snows of the Himalaya. The Chambal, the Betwa, and the Ken, originating from the Vindhya Range drain the southwestern part of the State before joining the Yamuna. The Son, also originating from the Vindhya Range, drains the southeastern part of the State and joins the Ganga beyond the State border.

Soil : About two-thirds of the area of Uttar Pradesh is covered by a deep layer of *alluvium* spread by the rivers of the Ganga system. These extremely fertile alluvial soils vary in texture from sandy to clayey loam, support more than four-fifths of the State's population and accounts for its rich agricultural production. The soils in the southern part of the State are generally mixed red and black or red to yellow. The black soil is fertile and suited for cotton cultivation while the red soil is low in fertility. The Himalayan region has brown hill soil, which is often shallow and gravelly. The Bhabar soils, which are mostly coarse-textured, sandy to gravelly, highly porous, excessively drained, and largely infertile, are found at the foothill of the Himalaya. The Tarai soil found in the Tarai zone varies in texture from rich clayey loams with some proportions of fine sand and humus. It is well-suited for paddy and sugarcane cultivation.

Climate : The climate of Uttar Pradesh varies from moderately temperate in the Himalayan region to tropical monsoon in the central plains and southern upland region. It is characterized by marked seasonal variations in temperature. January is the coldest month — temperature varies between 5 °C and 17.5 °C from north to south. May is the hottest month when temperature varies between 18 °C and 40 °C. July is the month of southwest monsoons. Uttar Pradesh receives four-fifths of its rainfall from the southwest monsoons. Rainfall decreases from east (1,000 mm to 2,000 mm) to west (610 mm to 1,000 mm). With most of the rainfall concentrated during June to September, floods are a recurring problem and cause heavy damage to crops, life, and property, particularly in the eastern part of the State. Periodic failure of monsoons results in drought conditions and crop failure. Little rainfall is received during the winter season. Winter rainfall decreases from west to east with the decreasing impact of the temperate cyclones originating in the Mediterranean Sea. It is a boon for *rabi* (winter) crops. In the Himalayan region annual snowfall averaging 3 m to 5 m is common between December and March.

Plant and animal life : Four major *forest types* are found in Uttar Pradesh: (1) alpine forests, (2) temperate forests, (3) tropical deciduous forests, and (4) thorn forests. Forests are generally concentrated in the Himalayan region, the submontane region, and the southern uplands. Alpine and temperate forests are found in the Himalayan region. Common species of trees include pine, chir, deodar, oak, fir, blue pine, silver fir, and spruce. Tropical deciduous forests of sal (*Shorea*), teak, and shisham (*Dalbergia sissoo*) occur in the submontane tract. Thorn forests of dhak, babul (*Acacia arabica*), and bushes occur in the southern uplands.

The submontane region of the State is rich in *animal life.* In the region are found tigers, leopards, elephants, wild boars, sloth bears, crocodiles, as well as pigeons, doves, wild ducks, patridges, peafowls, blue jays, quails, and woodpeckers. Several species such as lions and rhinoceros have become extinct there. To preserve its wildlife, the State has established national parks and several game sanctuaries, including the Corbett National Park in the Himalayan foothills.

The people : Uttar Pradesh is the *most populous State* (over 139 million persons) in the country. It has an overall population density of 473 persons per sq km. The Gangetic Plain, which supports over four-fifths of the State's population, has the highest population density. In contrast, the density of population in the Himalayan region and in the southern uplands is very low.

The vast majority of the population belongs to the Aryo-Dravidian ethnic group; only a small minority in the Himalayan region displays Asiatic origins. Hindus constitute about four-fifths of the population, Muslims one-fifth and other religious communities — including Sikhs, Buddhists, Christians, and Jains — together less than I per cent. Hindi (the official language of the State) and Urdu are the mothertongues of 82 and 9 per cent of the people, respectively. Hindustani, the spoken language of the people, contains the simple words of both languages and is widely understood in the State. Other languages include Bhojpuri (5 per cent), Garhwali (less than I per cent), Kumauni (less than I per cent), Punjabi, Awadhi, Bengali, Bundelkhandi, and Nepali (together, nearly I per cent).

More than four-fifths of the State's population lives in *rural areas.* The rural settlements are characterized by compact villages in the western part of the State, groups of hamlets in the eastern part, and a combination of the two in the central region, A typical village in Uttar Pradesh is an assorted, shapeless cluster of mud huts with roofs made of thatch (such as straw) or clay tiles. Although such huts have few amenities of modern living, the process of modernization is evident in some villages near the cities. Cement-plastered homes, paved roads, electricity, and consumer goods, including radios and television sets, are transforming traditional village life, More than half of the urban population lives in cities with populations of over 100,000. The five largest cities of Uttar Pradesh are Kanpur, Lucknow, Varanasi (Banaras), Agra, and Allahabad. All these cities, with the exception of Agra, are located in the central portion of the Gangetic Plain. Kanpur is the premier industrial city of Uttar Pradesh. Lucknow is located about 48 km to the northeast of Kanpur. Varanasi, the most sacred city of the Hindus, is one of the world's oldest continuously inhabited cities, Allahabad, another holy city, is located at the confluence of the Ganga, Yamuna and the mythological Sarasvati. Agra, located in the southwestern part of the State is the site of the Taj Mahal, a mausoleum built by the Mughal emperor Shah Jahan (ruled 1628-1658) in memory of his wife. It is one of the most famous tourist attractions in India.

The population of Uttar Pradesh continues *to grow at a high rate.* Because of the high growth rate and a substantial reduction in infant mortality, there has been a significant increase in the proportion of young adults and children. Towards the end of the nineteenth century, dire poverty and the promise of better opportunities forced many in the State to migrate to distant lands such as Natal (now Kwazulu/Natal, South Africa), Mauritius, Fiji, and the West Indies. In more recent years migration from Uttar Pradesh has mainly been to other parts of the country, particularly to the large cities such as Calcutta, Mumbai (Bombay), and Delhi.

Economy: Economically, Uttar Pradesh is one of the most underdeveloped States in the country. It is largely an agrarian State and more than three-fourths of the working population is engaged in agricultural pursuits. The State lacks mineral and energy resources important for industrialization. Silica, limestone, and coal are the only minerals that are found in considerable quantities. There are small reserves of gypsum, magnesite, phosphorite, and bauxite.

Foodgrains (cereals and pulses legumes]) dominate the *agricultural landscape* of the State; about four-fifths of the total cropped area grows foodgrain. Since the 1960s, with the introduction of high-yielding varieties of seeds for wheat and rice, greater availability of fertilizers, and increased use of irrigation, the State has become the largest producer of foodgrain, sugarcane, and oilseeds. However, farmers still suffer from two major constraints — small uneconomic landholdings (average size is 1.18 ha) and insufficient resources to invest in the technology required for improved production. About three-fourths are marginal landholdings (less than I ha). Livestock and dairy farming often provide supplementary source of income although the yield of milk is low.

Forests in Uttar Pradesh provide timber for construction, fuelwood, and raw materials for a number of industrial products including plywood, paper, and matches. Reforestation programmes of the State government have resulted in some increase in forest area, as well as availability of forest products for industrial uses.

Towards the end of the twentieth century, there were over 1,660 medium and large *industrial undertakings* providing employment opportunities for 568,382 persons, and 296,338 small-scale industrial units providing employment opportunities for 1,276,097 persons. Textiles and sugar refining, both long-standing industries of the State, employ nearly one-third of the State's total factory labour. Most of the mills are old and inefficient, other resource-based industries include vegetable oil, jute, and cement. The Union government has established a number of large factories that manufacture heavy equipment, machinery, steel, aircraft, telephones, electronic equipment, and fertilizers. An oil refinery at Mathura and the development of coalfields in the southeastern district of Mirzapur are also major Union government projects.

Industries that contribute most to the exports of the State include handicrafts, carpets, brassware, footwear, and leather and sporting goods. Carpets from Bhadoi and Mirzapur are prized worldwide. Silk and brocades from Varanasi, ornamental brassware from Moradabad, *chikan* (embroidery work) from Lucknow, ebony work from Nagua, glassware from Firozabad, and carved woodwork from Saharanpur are also important.

The State suffers from chronic shortage of power. Installed capacity has greatly increased since 1951 but the gap between supply and demand has continued to widen. Power is generated at the Obra-Rihand complex (in southeastern Uttar Pradesh), one of India's biggest thermal stations; at a number of hydroelectric plants in various parts of the State; and at a nuclear power station in the western district of Bulandshahr.

Uttar Pradesh is richly endowed with *tourist resources*. Its cultural heritage is well preserved in historical monuments, which are noted for their architectural and sculptural beauty. The Uttar Pradesh Himalayan region, with its snow-capped peaks, glaciers, lush green river valleys, waterfalls, lakes, flora and fauna, and wild life sanctuaries, is an important tourist attraction. There are 37 Hindu pilgrimage centres (21 in the Himalaya), including Mathura, Vrindavan, Ayodhya, Allahabad, Haridwar, Rishikesh, Badrinath, and Kedarnath. Other places of interest are Muslim centres like Barabanki, Faichpur Sikri, and Saharanpur; Buddhist centres like Sarnath, Kushinagar, and Sarasvati; historical places such as Agra, Lucknow, and Kannauj; hill resorts such as Nainital and Mussoorie; and sanctuaries and national parks such as Corbett National Park, Dudhwa National Park, and Rajaii National Park.

Transportation : Although most of the State's cities and towns are connected by a vast network of *roads and railways*, the condition of the roads is generally poor and the railway system suffers due to the incompatibility between the two different gauges of track (broad and narrow). Lucknow is the main junction of the northern network. Major cities in UP are connected by air to Delhi and other large cities of India. The transportation system within the State also includes the three inland waterways of the Ganga, Yamuna, and Ghaghara rivers.

Area, Population and Headquarters of Districts

S.No.	*District*	*Area (sq km)*	*Population*	*Headquarters*
1.	Agra	4,027	36,11,301	Agra
2.	Aligarh	3,431	29,90,388	Aligarh
3.	Etah	4,446	27,88,270	Etah
4.	Firozabad	2,361	20,45,737	Firozabad
5.	Mainpuri	2,746	15,92,875	Mainpuri
6.	Mathura	3,329	20,69,578	Mathura
7.	Hathras	.2,060	13,33,372	Hathras
8.	Azamgarh	4,234	39,50,808	Azamgarh
9.	Ballia	2,981	27,52,412	Ballia
10.	Mau	1,713	16,49,294	Mau
11.	Kaushambi	2,015	12,94,937	Kaushambi
12.	Fatehpur	4,152	23,05,847	Fatehpur
13.	Pratapgarh	3,717	27,27,156	Pratapgarh
14.	Allahabad	5,246	49,41,510	Allahabad
15.	Chitrakoot	3,513	8,00,592	Chitrakoot
16.	Budaun	5,168	30,69,245	Budaun
17.	Bareilly	4,120	35,98,701	Bareilly
18.	Pilibhit	3,499	16,43,788	Pilibhit
19.	Shahjahanpur	4,575	25,49,458	Shahjahanpur
20.	Faizabad	2,015	20,87,914	Faizabad
21.	Ambedkarnagar	2,496	20,25,373	Akbarpur
22.	Bahraich	4,692	23,84,239	Bahraich
23.	Barabanki	4,402	26,73,394	Barabanki
24.	Gonda	3,788	27,65,754	Gonda
25.	Sultanpur	4,436	31,90,926	Sultanpur
26.	Gorakhpur	3,321	*37,84,720*	Gorakhpur
27.	Deoria	2,379	27,30,376	Deoria
28.	Kushinagar	2,874	28,91,933	Padarauna
29.	Maharajganj	2,951	21,67,041	Maharajganj
30.	Banda	4,171	15,00,253	Banda
31.	Hamirpur	4,095	10,42,374	Hamirpur
32.	Jalaun	4,565	14,55,859	Orai

S.No.	District	Area (sq km)	Population	Headquarters
33.	Lalitpur	5,039.	9,77,447	Lalitpur
34.	Mahoba	3,071	9,77,447	Mahoba
35.	Jhansi	5,024	17,46,715	Jhansi
36.	Kanpur *(Nagar)*	3,015	41,37,489	Kanpur
37.	Kanpur *(Dehat)*	3,135	15,84,037	Akbarpur
38.	Farrukhabad	2,288	15,77,237	Fatehgarh
39.	Etawah	2,446	27,88,270	Etawah
40.	Lucknow	2,528	36,81,416	Lucknow
41.	Hardoi	5,986	33,97,414	Hardoi
42.	Lakhimpur Kheri	7,680	32,00,137	Kheri
43	Rai Bareli	4,609	28,72,204	Rai Bareli
44.	Sitapur	5,743	36,16,510	Sitapur
45.	Unnao	4,558	27,00,426	Unnao
46.	BuJandshahar	3,458	29,23,290	Bulandshahar
47.	Meerut	2,564	30,01,636	Meerut
48.	Ghaziabad	1,988	32,89,540	Ghaziabad
49.	Gautam Buddha Nagar	1,501	11,91,263	Noida
50.	Moradabad	3,497	37,49,630	Moradabad
51.	Bijnor	4,561	31,30,586	Bijnor
52.	Rampur	2,367	19,22,450	Rampur
53.	Jyotiba Phule Nagar	2,470	14,99,193	Amroha
54.	Saharanpur	3,689	28,48,152	Saharanpur
55.	Muzaffarnagar	4,008	35,41,952	Muzaffamagar
56.	Varanasi	1,550	31,47,927	Varanasi
57.	Jaunpur	4,038	39,11,305	Jaunpur
58.	Chandauli	2,485	16,39,777	Chandauli
59.	Ghazipur	3,377	30,49,377	Ghazipur
60.	St. Ravi Das Nagar	1,057	13,52,056	Bhadohi
61.	Mirzapur	4,522	21,14,852	Mirzapur
62.	Sonbhadra	6,788	14,63,468	Robertsganj
63.	Basti	2,752	20,68,922	Basti
64.	Balrarnpur	3,457	16,84,567	Balrampur
65.	Shravasti	2,186	11,75,428	Shravasti
66.	Siddharth Nagar	2,797	20,38,598	Navgarh
67.	Bagpat	1,345	11,64,388	Bagpat
68.	Kannauj	2,058	13,85,227	Kannauj
69.	Orraiya	2,054	11,79,496	Orraiya
70.	Sant Kabir Nagar	1,679	14,24,500	Khalilabad

W

West Benal—This state of India was created at independence in 1947 by partitioning the original British-Indian province of Bengal, keeping the western portion in India, and by reorganization in 1956 when some Bengali-speaking areas of Bihar were transferred to it. It is located in the northeastern part of the country. It is bounded on the north by Bhutan and the State of Sikkim, on the northeast by the State of Assam, on the east by Bangladesh, on the south by the Bay of Bengal, on the southwest by the State of Orissa, on the west by the State of Bihar, and on the northwest by Nepal. Its area is 88,752 sq km. Although in area West Bengal ranks as one of the smaller States of India, it is one of the largest in population. Its capital is Calcutta, India's second largest city.

West Bengal has a peculiar configuration. Its breadth varies from 320 km at one point to hardly 16 km at another. Being a State bordering Bangladesh with a 2,172 km long international frontier, which is neither natural nor well defined, it has strategic importance.

History : The name of Bengal, or Bangla, is derived from the ancient kingdom of Vanga, or Banga. References to the place occur in early Sanskrit literature, but its early history is obscure until the third century BC, when it formed part of the extensive Maurya Empire inherited by Ashoka. With the decline of Maurya power, there was anarchy once again. In the fourth century AD the region was absorbed into the Gupta Empire of Samudra Gupta. Later it came under Pala rule. From the beginning of the thirteenth century until Robert Clive's conquest of the province in 1757, Bengal was under Muslim rule, at times under governors acknowledging the suzerainty of the Delhi sultans but mainly under independent rulers.

In 1765 Shah Alam, the Mughal emperor, defeated by the British, granted to the East India Company the *diwani* of Bengal, Bihar, and Orissa - that is, the right to collect and administer the revenues of the area. By the Regulating Act of 1773, Warren Hastings, the governor of Bengal, became the first governor-general of Bengal, which was declared to be the supreme government with powers of superintendence over the other two presidencies, Madras and Bombay, as well.

Britain was not, however, the only European presence in Bengal. The town of Hooghly, about 46 sq km north of Calcutta, was the location of a Portuguese factory (trading post) until 1632, the earliest of all European enclaves in India; Hugli-Chinsurah, the next town south, was the Dutch post until 1825 and is today the location of one of India's premier rice research stations; the next town, Shrirampur (Serampore), was the Danish post until 1845; and Chandarnagar (Chandernagore) remained in French hands until 1949.

In 1854 the governor-general was relieved of the direct administration of Bengal, which was placed under a lieutenant-governor. After that the government of India became entirely distinct from that of Bengal. In 1874 Assam was transferred from the charge of the lieutenant-governor and placed under a separate administration, and, in spite of violent Hindu protests, it was partitioned into two provinces: (1) Western Bengal, Bihar, and Orissa and (2) Eastern Bengal, and Assam, each under a lieutenant-governor. In 1912, because of continued opposition to partition, Bengal was placed under a governor, Bihar and Orissa under a lieutenant-governor, and Assam under a chief commissioner. At the same time, Delhi became the capital of India in place of Calcutta. Under the Government of India Act (1935), Bengal was constituted an autonomous province in 1937. This was the situation until the Indian subcontinent was partitioned into the two dominions of Pakistan and India after the British withdrawal in 1947. The eastern sector of Bengal, largely Muslim, became East Pakistan (later Bangladesh); the western sector became India's West Bengal.

The partition of Bengal left West Bengal with ill-defined boundaries and a constant inflow of non-Muslim, mostly Hindu, refugees from East Pakistan (now Bangladesh). More than 7 million refugees entered the already densely populated State after 1947, and their rehabilitation placed an immense burden on the administration.

In 1950 the Princely State of Cooch Behar (now Kochbihar) was integrated with West Bengal. After the linguistic and political reorganization of Indian States in 1956, West Bengal gained about 8,177 sq km from Bihar; the additional land provided a link between the previously separated northern and southern pans of the State.

Relief and drainage : For its small size, the *physical geography* of West Bengal is quite varied. In the north, it has a share of the young folded mountain system of the Himalaya, where the Kanchenjunga, the second highest peak of the world, from adjacent Sikkim dominates the scene. In the west, the district of Puruliya contains a part of the Deccan Plateau system formed of eroded igneous and metamorphic rocks of very ancient age. Material eroded from the Himalaya by rivers like the Tista,

Jaldhaka, Torsa, and their tributaries have built a complex series of alluvial fans, where the drainage is still unstable. Along the east flank of the low plateau of Purulia stretch the rolling plains of highly oxidized older alluvium. The rest of West Bengal has been formed of the sediments brought down by the tributaries and distributaries of the Ganga River and contains the western part of the largest delta of the world with marshes and shallow lakes formed out of dead river courses. On the ocean-front of this delta flourish the largest mangroves of the world.

The Ganga River flows through West Bengal for a short stretch before entering Bangladesh as the Padma River. It has for centuries been moving steadily eastwards; very little of its water now goes to the sea via the western distributaries, of which the principal one is the Bhagirathi, on which is located Calcutta, the capital of the State. A big barrage on the Ganga River at Farakka now diverts a part of its water to the Bhagirathi to sustain navigability for the port of Calcutta. The other important river of economic importance is the Damodar, which contains a number of India's productive coalfields.

Climate : West Bengal has a *tropical wet and dry monsoon climate*, transitional between tropical savanna in the southwestern part to humid subtropical in the north. Throughout West Bengal there is a pronounced seasonal disparity in rainfall. For example, Calcutta averages 1,650 mm of rainfall per year, of which an average of 330 mm falls in August and only 25 mm in December. The Stare also is subject to considerable variation in rainfall from year to year. In the sub-Himalayan region rainfall is considerably greater. Temperatures in Calcutta average 27 °C for the year and range from 19 °C in January to 31 °C in May. The year may broadly be divided into three marked seasons. The hot and dry season with sultry days and frequent violent thunderstorms known as the "Nor-westers" extend from March to early June. It is followed by the hot and wet season from mid-June to September, when rain-bearing monsoon winds blow from the southwest. A relatively cool season extends from October to February, when days are dry and clear and stable atmospheric conditions prevail.

Plant and animal life : Forests occupy about one-eighth of the total land, and the region as a whole has a rich and varied plant life. In the sub-Himalayan plains the principal forest trees include sal (*Shorea robusta*, a timber tree), sissoo (which yields a valuable wood), and sisum (*Dalbergia sissoo*, Indian rosewood); the forests are interspersed with reeds and tall grasses. On the Himalayan heights vegetation varies according to the altitude, with coniferous belts occurring at higher levels.

In the southwest bordering the peninsula, there are dry peninsular forests also dominated by sal. The delta of the Hugli (Hooghly) constitutes the western end of the dense coastal mangrove forest called Sundarbans. A large portion of this unreclaimed and sparsely populated area bordering Bangladesh and the Bay of Bengal has been set aside as a national park. This is the home of the Royal Bengal tiger.

The forests of the northern districts are inhabited by tigers, panthers, elephants, bison, and rhinoceros, as well as by other animals of the Indian plain, large and small. Reptiles and birds comprise the same species as are common throughout the Indian subcontinent.

The people : About three-quarters of the population lives in villages. Of the remaining quarter living in urban areas, more than half resides in Calcutta.

Of the different *religions,* Hinduism, with its substrata of castes and aboriginal tribes, claims the adherence of more than three-fourths of the population, most of the remainder being Muslim. Throughout the State Buddhists, Christians, Jains, and Sikhs constitute small minority communities.

Bengali is the main *language* of the State, spoken by a large percentage of the population. Other languages include Hindi, Santhali (a tribal dialect), Urdu (primarily the language used by the Muslims), and Nepali. Small minorities speak Oraon (a tribal dialect) and English. Bengali, together with English, is the language of administration, and English and Hindi serve as link languages at the national level. Nepali is spoken largely in the Darjeeling district.

The economy : Despite its small size, West Bengal accounts for about one-sixth of India's net domestic product.

Agriculture dominates both the landscape and the economy. Nearly three out of four persons in the State are directly or indirectly involved in agriculture. West Bengal exceeds all other States in its relative incidence of agricultural land to total area (65 per cent). Rice, which requires extensive irrigation, is the leading crop in every district except Darjeeling, where it is surpassed by millet. Despite the small area of the State, West Bengal plants 14 per cent of the nation's rice area and produces 16 per cent of its harvest. This high yield is attributable to both intensive crop tending and relatively heavy application of fertilizer. Jute, the second leading crop, is especially prominent in the districts along the Bangladesh border and south of the Ganga River. Wheat and potatoes are produced as winter crops throughout the southern districts; Darjeeling and Jalpaiguri have long been known for their production of high-quality tea. Darjeeling also produces oranges, apples, pineapples, ginger, and cardamoms. Mango, jackfruit, and bananas are widely produced in the southern and central portions of the State.

At the end of the twentieth century *mineral resources* of West Bengal that sustained nationally significant exploitation were coal and clay for brick-making. Jute and tea have been the State's traditional *industries.* Along the Hugli River, a corridor extending from Calcutta some 48 km in the north to 19 km in the south has historically grown as the most important industrial belt. The key to this extended industrial development is its location, being less than 322 km east of coal, iron ore, and limestone deposits of the Chota Nagpur region of Bihar. The other significant industrial region is along the Damodar River. Besides the alloy steel plant at Durgapur, there are two more steel plants at Durgapur and Burnpur and a locomotive plant at Chittaranjan. Calcutta and its sister port of Haldia further south handle international trade. Haldia, the terminus of the oil pipeline from Assam and site of eastern India's largest oil refinery, has now a petrochemical industry. *Other important industries* are shipbuilding, automobile manufacture, chemical fertilizer, wagon building, electronics and cable, paper, and cotton textile industries. The State has a large number of small scale and cottage industries.

Transportation : The State saw the inauguration of the *railway* system in eastern India in 1854. *River steam navigation* was also first introduced here in the nineteenth century between Calcutta, Allahabad, and Guwahati. The deltaic rivers provided scope for the development of a local river transport system. The partition at independence and deterioration of the channels has totally disrupted the river transport system. At present the State has two local railway headquarters and is linked with the rest of India by national highways. State highways connect the districts. Calcutta possesses an international airport equipped to accommodate modern jet aircraft. There are eight other airfields within the State. Calcutta is the only Indian city with an underground metro railway system.

Culture life : Bengalis have always fostered *literature, art, music*, and *drama.* Bengali literature dates before the twelfth century. The Chaitanya movement, an intensely emotional form of Hinduism inspired by the mediaeval saint, Chaitanya (1485-1533), shaped the subsequent development of Bengali poetry until the early nineteenth century, when contact with the West sparked a vigorous creative synthesis. The modern period has produced, among others, the Nobel laureate poet, Rabindranath

Tagore (1861-1941), whose contributions still dominate the Indian literary scene.

Theatre is popular, and performances — amateur as well as professional — are sophisticated. *Jatras*, traditional open-air performances that are now changing from predominantly mythological and historical subjects to contemporary themes, are popular both in the countryside and in urban areas. The *kavi* is an impromptu duel in musical verse between village poets. The *kathakata*, a religious recital, is another traditional form of rural entertainment, based on folklore.

The *film industry* is a well-established modern form of popular entertainment. Bengali films have earned national and international awards for their delicate handling of Indian themes; the works of directors like Satyajit Ray, Tapan Sinha, Mrinal Sen, and Aparna Sen are of special significance,

Traditional music takes the form of devotional and cultural songs. Rabindra Sangeet, songs written and composed by Tagore, which draw on the pure Indian classical as well as traditional folk music, exert a powerful influence on the cultural life of the Bengalis.

Visual arts have, by tradition, been based mainly on clay modelling, terracotta work, and decorative painting. In Calcutta, the Indian Association for the Cultivation of Science, the Bose Research Institute, and the science laboratories of the University of Calcutta have made notable contributions to science. The Asiatic Society of Bengal, the best-known Indian historical-research body in the nineteenth century, is located in West Bengal. Vishva-Bharat University, founded by Rabindranath Tagore in Shantiniketan, is a world famous centre for the study of Indology and international cultural relations.

Area, Population and Headquarters of Districts

S.No.	*District*	*Area (sq km)*	*Population*	*Headquarters*
1.	Bankura	6,882	31,91,822	Bankura
2.	Bardhaman	7,024	69,19,698	Bardhaman
3.	Birbhum	4,545	30,12,546	Suri
4.	Kolkata	185	45,80,544	Kolkata
5.	Darjeeling	3,149	16,05,900	Darjeeling
6.	Howrah	1,467	42,74,010	Howrah
7.	Hoogly	3,149	50,40,047	Chinsurah
8.	Jalpaiguri	6,227	34,03,204	Jalpaiguri
9.	Coochbehar	3,387	24,78,280	Coochbehar

S.No.	District	Area (sq km)	Population	Headquarters
10.	Malda	3,733	32,90,160	English Bazar
11.	Medinipur	14,081	96,38,473	Medinipur
12.	Murshidabad	5,324	58,63,717	Berhampore
13.	Nadia	3,927	46,03,756	Krishnagar
14.	North 24 Parganas	4,094	89,30,295	Alipore
15.	South 24 Parganas	9,660	69,09,015	Barasat
16.	Purulia	6,259	25,35,233	Purulia
17.	Uttar Dinajpur	3,140	24,41,824	Raigunj
18.	Dakshin Dinajpur	2,219	15,02,647	Baluighat

●●●

Section : FIVE

MISCELLANEOUS INFORMATION

Coastal Community Programme

Shore to Fishing Vessel Communication System—For demonstrating the usefulness of communication system to the fisherfolk who are at sea, shore stations were set up at seven places, viz., Shankarpur and Frasergunj in West Bengal, Paradeep and Chandipur in Orissa, Salegao in North Goa and Periya Veerampattinam in Pondicherry. Out of these, four centres in West Bengal and Orissa were operationalised. Construction of shore stations and erection of towers/mast for fixing antenna in Andaman & Nicobar Islands is in progress.

Island Development—The National Institute of Ocean Technology (NIOT), Chennai has taken up new initiatives towards helping island communities in their needs relating to Ocean Science and Technology as well as marine resource enhancement. The first activity taken up by NIOT is a programme on lobster resource enhancement for islands under the DOD project on Living Marine Resources Enhancement (LMRE). The programme on lobster resource enhancement is already underway by utilising the hatchery facility of Tamil Nadu Fisheries Development Corporation (TNFDC) available at Neelankarai, Chennai. Several experiments have already been carried out in the following areas: (a) Fattening of spiny lobster *Panuliris homarus* using different live feeds (mussels and clams); (b) Biochemical analysis of lobsters and live feeds; (c) Water quality and disease management; (d) Spawning and larval rearing; and (e) Survey of lobster resources in Gulf of Mannar and Andaman Islands.

Coastal Research Vessels—Two Coastal Research vessels, namely, *Sagar Purvi* and *Sagar Paschimi* are used for the coastal oceanographic research programmes of DOD and NIOT (National Institute of Ocean

Technology) including COMAI'S. The vessel times are also made available to public and private sectors on a payment basis depending on the nature of the programme. Both the vessels undertook cruises covering sampling stations for collecting water, sediment, CTD and plankton samples during 2000-2001.

Heavy Water Production—Heavy water is used in the pressurised heavy water reactors as moderator and coolant. To meet the heavy water requirements of the Indian nuclear power and research reactors, eight heavy water plants have been installed at Manuguru (Andhra Pradesh), Kota (Rajasthan), Hazira and Baroda (both in Gujarat), Thal (Maharashtra), Tuticorin (Tamil Nadu), Talcher (Orissa) and Nangal (Punjab). The heavy water plants at Manuguru and Kota arc based on indigenously developed hydrogen sulphide-water exchange process, The other heavy water plants use ammonia-hydrogen exchange process. The plant at Nangal uses electrolysis of water for producing heavy water. Self-sufficiency has been achieved in the production of heavy water. So far 116 tonnes of heavy water has been exported to South Korea.

Height of Some Important Indian Mountain Peaks

	Peak	*Height in meter above Mean Sea Level*	
1.	K2	8,611	in Pak-occupied territory
2.	Kanchenjunga	8,598	
3.	Nanga Parabt	8,126	
4.	Gasher Brum	8,068	in Pak-occupied territory
5.	Broad peak	8,047	in Pak-occupied territory
6.	Disteghil Sar	7,885	in Pak-occupied territory
7.	Masher Brum E	7,821	
8.	Nanda Devi	7,817	
9.	Masher Brum W	7,806	in Pak-occupied territory
10.	Rakaposhi	7,788	in Pak-occupied territory
11.	Kamet	7,756	
12.	Saser Kangri	7,672	
13.	Skyang Kangri	7,544	in Pak-occupied territory
14.	Sia Kangri	7,422	in Pak-occupied territory
15.	Chaukhamba (Badrinath Peak)	7,138	

	Peak	Height in meter above Mean Sea Level
16.	Trishul West	7,138
17.	Nunkun	7,135
18.	Pauhunri	7,128
19.	Kangto	7,090
20.	Dunagiri	7,066

The Human Settlements System

A wide range of human settlements are found In India which vary in size, structure, economy and morphology. There are single dwelling units such as thoroughly scattered homesteads in Kerala, and in parts of Assam and West Bengal as well as very small nucleated settlements In mountainous regions. There are also a variety of villages and towns ranging from small hamlets lo high density metropolitan cities. Broadly, the human settlement system in India comprises three major types, viz., urban, rural and tribal.

Urban Settlements : Urban settlements comprise all those places which have either a municipality, corporation, cantonment board or a notified area committee. According to the Census of India, a place becomes urban when (1) it has a minimum population of 5,000; (II) more than 75. per cent of its working population is engaged in non-agricultural activities and (III) the density of population exceeds 1,000 persons per square kilometre. However, there are come exceptions to these norms.

According to 1991 Census there were 4,689 towns in the country with a total urban population of about 217.6 million persons.

Uttar Pradesh and Uttaranchal have the largest number of towns (704), followed by Tamil Nadu (434), Madhya Pradesh (327) and Maharashtra (307). Tripura, Sikkim and Nagaland have 10, 8 and 7 towns respectively. Andaman and Nicobar island, and Dadra and Nagar Haveli have only one town each.

Urbanisation Trends : The process of urbanisation has been very slow in India. The number of towns and cities has grown at a low rate from 1,916 in 1901 to 4,689 in 1991, a little less than three-fold increase in 90 years. However, the urban population has increased from about 26 million to around 217 million over this period.

The following table shows the growth in urban population of the country since 1901 and the percentage of rural and urban population to the total population of India.

Relative Growth of Rural and Urban Population

Year	*Urban Population (million)*	*Percentage of total population*	
		Rural	*Uban*
1901	25.8	89.0	11.0
1911	25.9	89.6	10.4
1921	28.0	88.7	11.3
1931	33.5	87.8	12.2
1941	44.1	85.9	14.1
1951	62.4	82.4	17.6
1961	78.9	81.7	18.3
1971	108.9	79.8	20.2
1981	162.2	76.3	23.7
1991	217.6	74.3	25.7

Within the urban population, the greatest increase has been in the case of larger towns having a population of 1 lakh and above. The period between 1951 and 1981 saw a rapid growth of large towns (Class 1 towns with a population of 1 lakh and above), their number going up from 74 In 1951 to 296 In 1991 and the population increasing from less than three crores to over 16 crores during these forty years. The bigger cities (those with a population of 10 lakhs and above) recorded a still sharper increase in their population. According to 1961 census there were 12 such cities In India, whereas their number has gone up to 23 in 1991, and the population of these cities has increased from nearly four crores to over seven crores between these ten years.

Rural Settlements : According to the 1991 Census, 629 million people, out of a total population of 846 million persons, lived In rural areas. In 1961, the rural population was 522 million out of the total population of 664 million. The 1981 Census shows that there are 5,57,137 Inhabited and 48,085 uninhabited villages in India. Uttar Pradesh alongwith Uttaranchal, with its 1,12,566 inhabited and 1,680 uninhabited villages has the highest number of villages in the country. Madhya Pradesh together with Chhattisgarh has 71,352 villages while Sikkim has only 440 villages.

Tribal Settlement : Tribal settlements are largely found in the forest areas and the nearby haunts as the tribal groups mainly pursue primitive occupations such as hunting, food gathering and collecting the forest produce. The tribal population of India was estimated at 67.8 million in 1991.

Major Tribes in India

Abors	:	Assam, Arunachal Pradesh
Apatemis	:	Arunachal Pradesh
Badagas	:	Nilgiri (Tamil Nadu)
Baiga	:	Madhya Pradesh, Rajasthan. Gujarat
Bhotias	:	Garhwal and Kumaon regions of Uttaranchal
Birtor	:	Hazaribagh (Jharkhand)
Chenchus	:	Andhra Pradesh, Orissa
Chhutia	:	Assam
Gaddis	:	Himachal Pradesh
Gallong	:	North East Himalayan Region
Garos	:	Meghalaya
Gonds	:	Madhya Pradesh, Chhattisgarh, Bihar, Jharkhand, Orissa, Andhra Pradesh
Jarawas	:	Little Andamans
Khas	:	Jaunsar-Babar area in U.P.
Khasis	:	Assam, Meghalaya
Khonds	:	Orissa
Kol	:	Madhya Pradesh
Kolam	:	Andhra Pradesh
Kotas	:	Nilgiri (Tamil Nadu)
Kuki	:	Manipur
Lepchas	:	Sikkim
Lushals	:	Tripura
Mina	:	Rajasthan
Murias	:	Bastar region in Chhattisgarh)
Mikirs	:	Assam
Monpa	:	Arunachal Pradesh
Mundas	:	Jharkhand
Nagas (Angami, Semi, Ao, Tangakul, Lahore)	:	Nagaland, Assam
Oarons (also called Kunukh)	:	Bihar and Jharkhand, Orissa
Onges	:	Andaman & Nicobar Islands

Santhals	:	Birbhum region in Bengal, Hazaribagh, Ranchi and Palamau in Jharkhand
Sentinelese	:	Andaman and Nicobar
Shompens	:	Andaman and Nicobar
Todas	:	Nilgiri (Tamil Nadu)
Uralis	:	Kerala
Warlis	:	Maharashtra

Integrated Coastal and Marine Area Management

During the Ninth Plan period, the DOD took up for implementation infrastructure development and capacity building activities to facilitate adoption of the concept of Integrated Coastal and Marine Area Management (ICMAM) in the coming years. These activities focus on development of expertise in ICMAM oriented activities, and dissemination of knowledge (gained) to the users like coastal states through organised training programmes. The Department established a ICMAM Project Directorate at Chennai which is implementing various activities as planned in the following main areas from 1998-99 onwards.

Under the project 'Environment Management Capacity Building' coordinated by the Ministry of Environment and Forests, the capacity building activities funded by the World Bank are being carried in the following areas: (i) Development of GIS based information system for 11 critical habitats like coral reefs, mangroves, etc., in Gulf of Khambat, Gulf of Kutch, Malvan, five islands off Karwar, three islands off Cochin, Gulf of Mannar, Pitchavaram, Coringa mangrove, Gahirmata, Sunderbans and Kadamat (Lakshadweep). GIS for habitats Pichavaram mangrove. Gulf of Mannar, Kadamat island, islands off Karwar, Malvan, and Gulf of Kutch have been completed; (ii) Determination of waste load allocation based on waste assimilation characteristics of selected estuaries (fapi estuary and Ennore creek) was carried out. The studies have been concluded (iii) Development of EIA guidelines for major coastal developmental activities and processes like construction of ports, harbours and breakwaters, waste disposal from domestic and industrial wastes, marine transportation and coastal tourism undertaken; (iv) Environmental Impact Assessment (EIA) guidelines for ports and harbours is completed; (v) Under the project on Development of model ICMAM plans for Chennai, Goa and Gulf of Katch, a design for Decision Support System has been completed for Chennai; and (vi) Under Infrastructure, Training, R&D and Survey component, infrastructure facilities are being created to house a long term training programme for utilising the capacity built under the Capacity Building programme. The training will be provided to the coastal states in the development of ICMAM Plans and use of GIS in the management of critical habitats. R&D activities like determination of Use Classification for coastal waters and determination of No Impact Zone in critical habitats such as mangroves, lagoons, etc., as part of the pre-requisites for adoption of ICMAM, are being carried out.

Length of Some Important Indian Rivers

	River	*Length (km)*
1.	Indus	2,900
2.	Brahmaputra	2,900
3.	Ganga	2,510
4.	Godavari	1,450
5.	Narmada	1,290
6.	Krishna	1,290
7.	Mahanandi	890
8.	Kaveri	760

Minerals Exploration and Mining

Surveys, prospecting and exploration of uranium, thorium, rare metals and rare earths, titanium and zirconium mineral resources are done by the Atomic Minerals Directorate for Exploration and Research (AMD).

Mining and processing of uranium ores and mineral sands are carried out by the Uranium Corporation of India Limited (UCIL) and the Indian Rare Earths Limited (IRE) respectively. The exploratory efforts of AMD have led to. the opening of uranium mines at Jaduguda, Bhatin and Narwapahar in Jharkhand. These mines have been meeting the needs of the Indian Nuclear Power Programme. The discovery of Donuasiat uranium deposit in Meghalaya has been one of the major successes in recent years. AMD has also located sizeable uranium deposits at Wahkyn in Meghalaya, Lambapur-Yellapur and Tummalapalle in Andhra Pradesh, Turamdih, Bagjata, Kanyaluka and Mohuldih in Jharkhand, and Bodal and Jajawal in Madhya Pradesh. Favourable uranium mineralization has been identified at Gogi in Kamataka, Koppunuru and Gandi in Andhra Pradesh and Rohil in Rajasthan. AMD has also established a number of beach sand mineral deposits of ilmenite, zircon, monazite, garnet and sillimanite.

UCIL which started operations at Jaduguda, later opened two mines at Bhatin and Narwapahar (all units situated in the Singhbhum (East) district of Jharkhand). The natural uranium from these mines is processed as yellow cake and sent to the Nuclear Fuel Complex (NFC) at Hyderabad for fabrication of fuel for PHWR.

The Indian Rare Earth Limited (IRE) has three mineral sands separation plants at Manavalakurichi (Tamil Nadu), Chavara (Kerala) and OSCOM-Chhatrapur (Orissa). These plants produce industrial minerals, namely ilmenite, rutile, monazite, zircon, sillimanite and garnet. IER exports products to advanced markets of the world. During 1999-2000, the sales turnover of IRE reached Rs 215 crore and foreign exchange earned through exports was Rs 78.25 crore. IRE has bagged an order of US $ 2.33 million from Egypt, for setting up a mini-pilot plant for monazite processing.

National Animal

The magnificent tiger, *Panthera tigris* (Linnaeus), is a striped animal. It has a thick yellow coat of fur with dark stripes. The combination of grace, strength, agility and enormous power has earned the tiger its pride of place as the national animal of India. Out of eight races of the species known, the Indian race, the Royal Bengal Tiger, is found throughout the country except in the north-western region and also in the neighbouring countries, Nepal, Bhutan and Bangladesh. To check the dwindling population of tigers in India 'Project Tiger' was launched in April 1973. So far, 27 tiger reserves have been established in the country under this project, covering an area of 37,761 sq km.

National Bird

The Indian peacock, *Pavo cristatus* (Linnaeus), the national bird of India, is a colourful, swan-sized bird, with a fan-shaped crest of feathers, a white patch under the eye and a long, slender neck. The male of the species is more colourful than the female, with a glistening blue breast and neck and a spectacular bronze-green train of around 200 elongated feathers. The female is brownish, slightly smaller than the male, and lacks the train. The elaborate courtship dance of the male, fanning out the tail and preening its feathers, is a gorgeous sight.

The peacock is widely found in the Indian sub-continent from the south and east of the Indus river, Jammu and Kashmir, east Assam, south Mizoram and the whole of the Indian peninsula. The Peacock enjoys protection from the people as it is never molested for religious and sentimental reasons. It is fully protected under the Indian Wildlife (Protection) Act, 1972.

National Flower

Lotus (*Nelumbo nucifera*) is the National Flower of India. It is a sacred flower and occupies a unique position in the art and mythology of ancient India and has been an auspicious symbol of Indian culture since time immemorial.

National Atlas and Thematic Mapping Organisation

While Survey of India meets the national needs in cartography, some specialised thematic maps required to meet the needs of the specific users are taken care of by the National Atlas and Thematic Mapping Organisation (NATMO), operating under the Department.

Ocean Observations and Information Services

The Ocean Observations and Information Services (OOIS) envisage generation and dissemination of reliable coastal and ocean data products such as waves, winds, temperature, current, salinity, upwelling, potential fishing zone information, coastal maps, etc., to support coastal and off-shore developmental activities and for furthering quality oceanographic research. The OOIS also envisages development of systems for ocean state forecast, on experimental basis by terminal year of the Ninth Plan. The OOIS programme consists of four major components, viz.. Ocean Observing Systems, Ocean Information Services, Ocean Dynamics and Modelling, and Satellite Coastal and Oceanographic Research.

Ocean Observing Systems : The objective of Ocean Observing Systems (OOS) programme is to acquire *in situ* oceanographic and surface meteorological parameters on real-time basis from the seas around India. The parameters being measured under the programme include surface winds, waves, atmospheric pressure, temperature, sea surface temperature, salinity, temperature profiles, dissolved oxygen, hydrocarbons, nutrients, radio-activity, sea-level, etc. The instruments deployed for measurements of these parameters are moored data buoys, drifting buoys, expendable bathythermographs (XBT), current meter arrays and tide gauges. Validation of the satellite sensors would also be undertaken using the sea truth data generated under this programme. The

OOS project consists of three sub-projects, viz.. National Data Buoy Programme, Sea Level observation and Drifting buoy and other Observing systems.

Under the National Data Buoy Programme, being implemented by NIOT, 12 data buoys have been deployed in the Indian seas. The buoys are equipped with state-of-the-art sensors for measurement of winds, waves, currents, atmospheric pressure, atmospheric temperature, sea surface temperature, dissolved oxygen, chlorophyll, radioactivity, hydrocarbon and turbidity. A shore station was commissioned at NIOT for retrieval, processing, analysis and storage of the data from the buoys on a real time basis. The met-ocean data from these buoys are being disseminated to Meteorological Department Coast Guard, Port Trusts on a daily basis.

Under the programme being implemented through NIO, Goa envisages deployment of drifting buoys, expendible bathythermographs (XBTs), and current meter arrays, for augmentation of *in situ* oceanographic data. About 48 drifting buoys, three current meter arrays and 900 XBTs would be deployed under this programme during the Ninth Plan period.

Under the Sea Level Observation project, 10 modem tide gauges stations were established at Mumbai, Porbunder, Goa, Kochi, Chennai, Visakhapatnam, Paradip, Kavaratti, Machlipatnam and Tuticorin for systematic and accurate monitoring the tidal level to derive long term variations in the mean sea levels. The data from these tide gauges are collected regularly and sent to the National Tide Data Centre at Survey of India, Dehradun. Based on the sea level data collected along the Indian coast, a numerical model has been constructed to simulate circulation in the Northern Indian Ocean.

The Land Ocean Interaction in the Coastal Zone (LOICZ) project envisages estimation of fluxes of material in the land and ocean boundary and its variability for understanding the changes in the coastal-zones at regional and global scale particularly with respect to global climate change. Two coastal areas such as Godavari Basin and Eastern Arabian Sea Margin have been considered for undertaking these studies.

Ocean Information Services : The National Centre for Indian National Ocean Information Services (INCOIS) was set up at Hyderabad in February 1999 as an autonomous body of the Department for generation and dissemination of user oriented data products, on operational basis. Near real-time data and data products such as Sea

Surface Temperature (SST) and Potential Fishing Zone (PFZ) advisories, upwelling zones, maps, eddies, chlorophyll, suspended sediment load, etc., consultancy services to the Central Government, States, corporate sector industries, will be available to the user agencies under one roof.

Ocean Dynamics and Modelling : Knowledge of ocean dynamics is a prerequisite for prediction of ocean state based on ocean models. During 1998-99, dynamics of marine ecosystem and air-sea exchange of carbon dioxide were studied, using Modular Ocean Model. Air-sea interaction process of monsoon prediction was studied, using ocean-atmosphere coupled model. A storm surge prediction model for estimating inland inundation in Andhra coast was developed and a seven component Nitrogen-based Ecosystem Model completed.

Satellite Coastal and Oceanographic Research : The project envisages development of algorithms and models for retrieval of met-ocean parameter *i..e.*, sea surface temperature, winds, waves, bathymetry, suspended matter, mixed layer depth, chlorophyll, aerosol, water vapour; clouds, currents and sea level from satellite sensors. The data-assimilation models on wave and ocean circulation would also be developed. During the year development of retrieval algorithms and validation of Sea Surface Temperature and waves from ERS-I was completed which includes customization of the software. Studio on latent heat flux and eddies would be completed from ERS and Altimeter respectively. Development of software for estimation of coastal bathymetry from SAR and Altimeters was completed.

Marine Research and Capacity Building : The Department of Ocean Development lays special emphasis on encouraging basic and applied research in ocean related subjects. The focus is on assisting the Universities and on building up a skilled human resource base in Marine Science. The objective of this programme is to encourage research in newly emerging and front line areas of Coastal Engineering, Marine Chemistry, Marine Biology and Microbiology, Pharmacology, Coastal Zone Management, Exploration and Exploitation of Marine Resources, etc., to create infrastructure facilities in Universities and to inculcate scientific temper among the people on Ocean Science.

For promotion of front-ranking research in Ocean Science & Technology and related human resource development, Ocean Science & Technology Cells (OSTCs) have been set up in the following disciplines at nine centres: (i) Marine Microbiology - Goa University, Goa; (ii) Marine Coastal Ecology (E. Coast) - Berhampur University, Berhampur;

(iii) Marine Coastal Ecology (W. Coast) - Bhavnagar University, Bhavnagar; (iv) Marine Geology and Geophysics - Mangalore University, Mangalore; (v) Coastal Marine Culture Systems - Andhra University, Visakhapatnam; (vi) Beach Placers - Tamil University, Tanjore; (vii) Marine Biology - Annamalai University, Parangipettai; (viii) Marine Benthos - Cochin University of S & T, Kochi; and (ix) Ocean Engineering & Underwater Robotics - IIT, Kharagpur

Survey of India

Survey of India (SOI), the national survey and mapping organisation under the Ministry of Science & Technology was set up in 1767. The primary responsibility of SOI is to maintain topographical map coverage on 1:250 K, 1:50 K and 1:25 K scales. The topographical map coverage on 1:250 K and 1:50 K scales covering the entire country have been completed and the map sheets are being updated at regular intervals to depict latest spatial information. Surveys on 1:25 K scale are being taken up as national requirement keeping in view the priorities indicated by the Central/State governments and other user agencies.

SOI has been called upon extensively to deploy its expertise in the field of geodetic & geophysical surveys, study of seismicity and seismotectonics, glaciology, participation in Indian Scientific Expedition to Antarctica and projects related to digital cartography and digital photogrammetry, etc., to provide basic data to keep pace with Science & Technology Development. SOI has undertaken creation of Digital Cartographic Data Base of Topographical maps on various scales. The digital data is being used by various agencies for planning and GIS applications. It also undertakes large scale surveys for various developmental projects including hydro-electric, irrigation, command area, canal area, cantt. area schemes, etc.

The Department is responsible to fix the external boundary of India, their depiction on maps published in the country and it also offer advice on the demarcation of inter-State boundaries.

Survey of India also provides support to neighbouring countries in the field of survey education, transfer of technology and various other surveying technologies under bilateral arrangements.

In the recent time, a Task Force was set up for the establishment of a National Geospatial Data Infrastrucutre (NGDI). Survey of India with its vast storehouse of Geospatial data, will serve as the engine for the NGDI. The creation of NGDI framework will provide the necessary facilities and structure of relationships among the data producers and users that will facilitate data sharing.

Survey Training Institute, Hyderabad is a premier institution for training in various disciplines of surveying and mapping to the trainees sponsored by the department, other State/Central Government organisations and neighbouring countries.

Wadia Institute of Himalayan Geology, Dehradun offers basic research in areas of biostratigraphy, petrology and geochemistry, sedimentology, tectonics and environmental geology to understand the geodynamics of the Himalayan region.

●●●